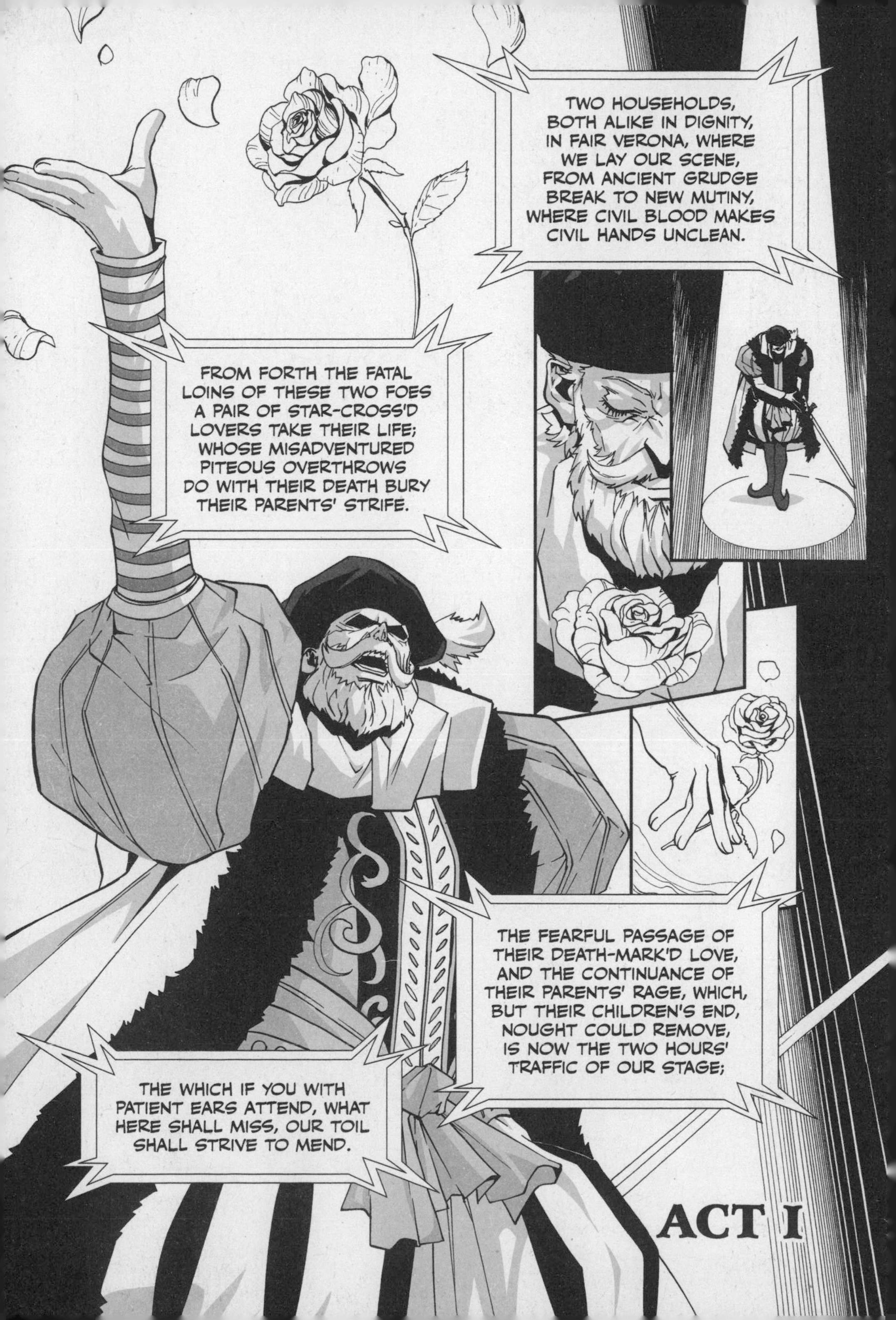
TWO HOUSEHOLDS, BOTH ALIKE IN DIGNITY, IN FAIR VERONA, WHERE WE LAY OUR SCENE, FROM ANCIENT GRUDGE BREAK TO NEW MUTINY, WHERE CIVIL BLOOD MAKES CIVIL HANDS UNCLEAN.
FROM FORTH THE FATAL LOINS OF THESE TWO FOES A PAIR OF STAR-CROSS'D LOVERS TAKE THEIR LIFE; WHOSE MISADVENTURED PITEOUS OVERTHROWS DO WITH THEIR DEATH BURY THEIR PARENTS' STRIFE.
THE FEARFUL PASSAGE OF THEIR DEATH-MARK'D LOVE, AND THE CONTINUANCE OF THEIR PARENTS' RAGE, WHICH, BUT THEIR CHILDREN'S END, NOUGHT COULD REMOVE, IS NOW THE TWO HOURS' TRAFFIC OF OUR STAGE;
THE WHICH IF YOU WITH PATIENT EARS ATTEND, WHAT HERE SHALL MISS, OUR TOIL SHALL STRIVE TO MEND.
ACT I

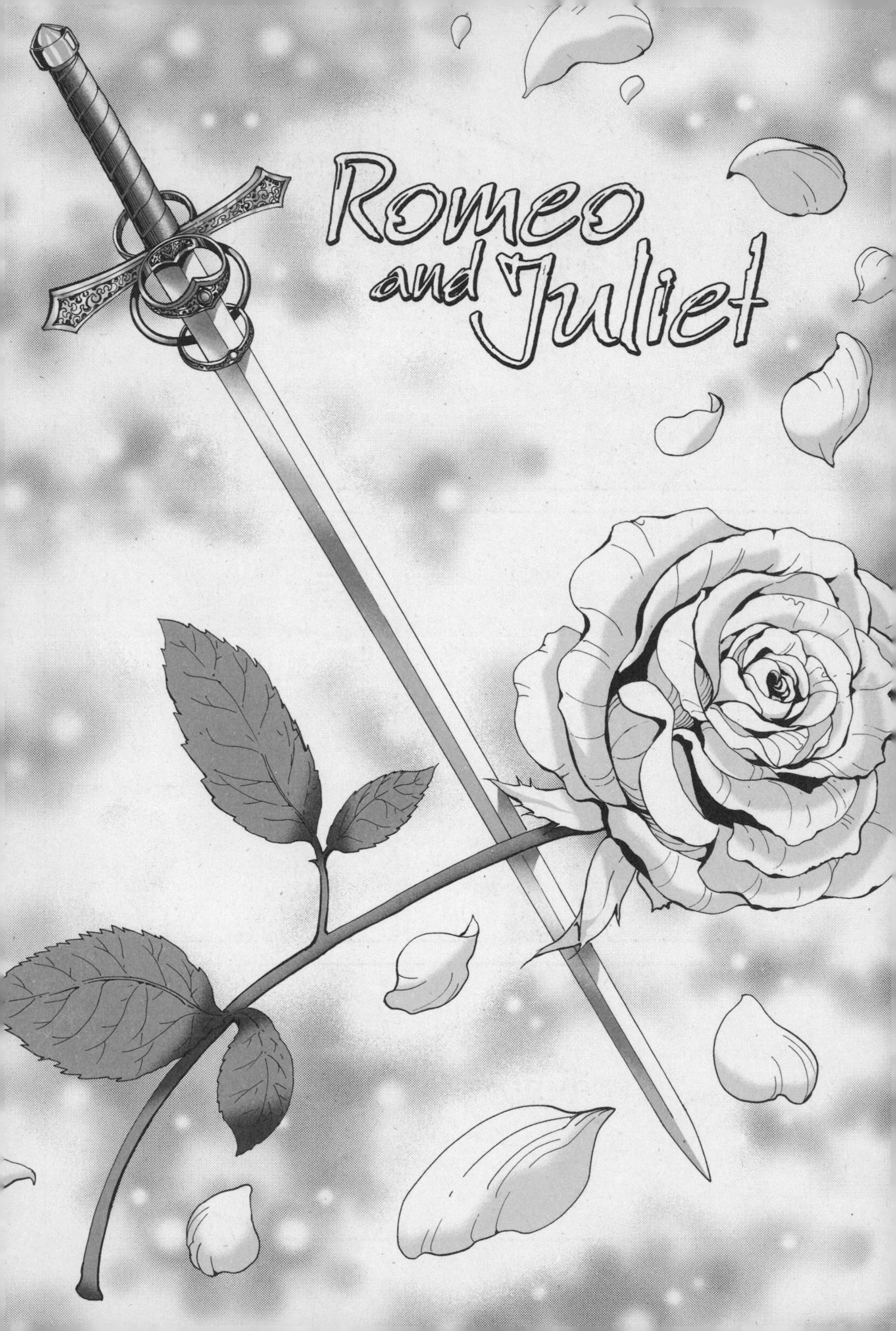
Romeo and Juliet

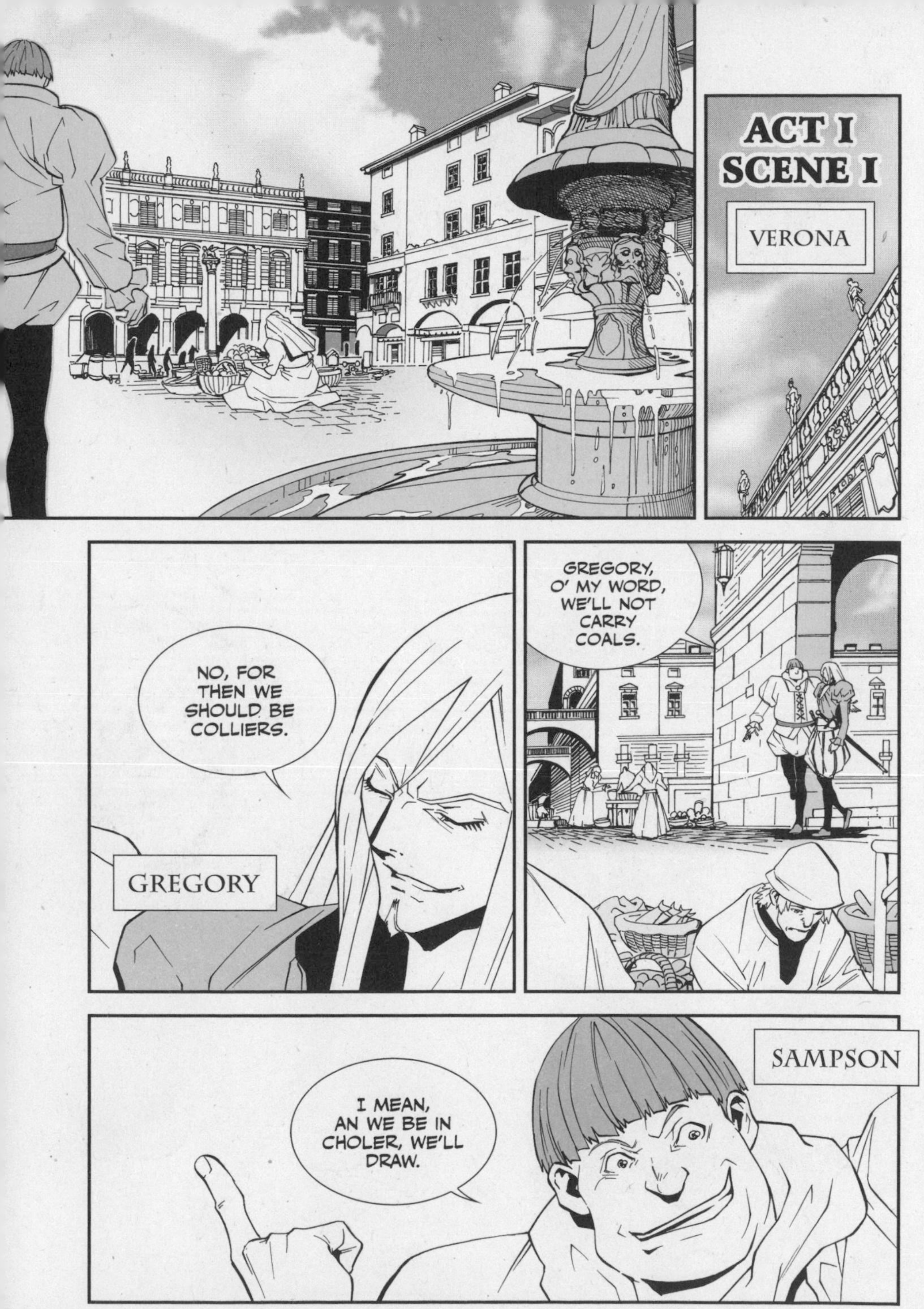

ACT I
SCENE I
VERONA
GREGORY, O' MY WORD, WE'LL NOT CARRY COALS.
NO, FOR THEN WE SHOULD BE COLLIERS.
GREGORY
SAMPSON
I MEAN, AN WE BE IN CHOLER, WE'LL DRAW.

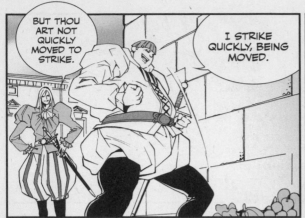

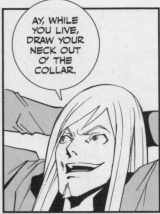

AY, WHILE YOU LIVE, DRAW YOUR NECK OUT O' THE COLLAR.
I STRIKE QUICKLY, BEING MOVED.
BUT THOU ART NOT QUICKLY MOVED TO STRIKE.
A DOG OF THE HOUSE OF MONTAGUE MOVES ME.
TO MOVE IS TO STIR; AND TO BE VALIANT IS TO STAND: THEREFORE, IF THOU ART MOVED, THOU RUNN'ST AWAY.
A DOG OF THAT HOUSE SHALL MOVE ME TO STAND: I WILL TAKE THE WALL OF ANY MAN OR MAID OF MONTAGUE'S.
THAT SHOWS THEE A WEAK SLAVE; FOR THE WEAKEST GOES TO THE WALL.

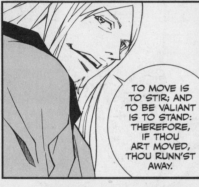

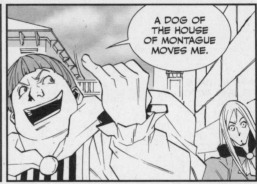

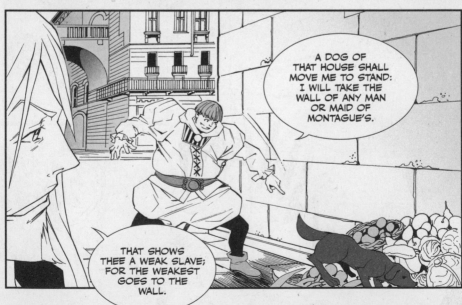

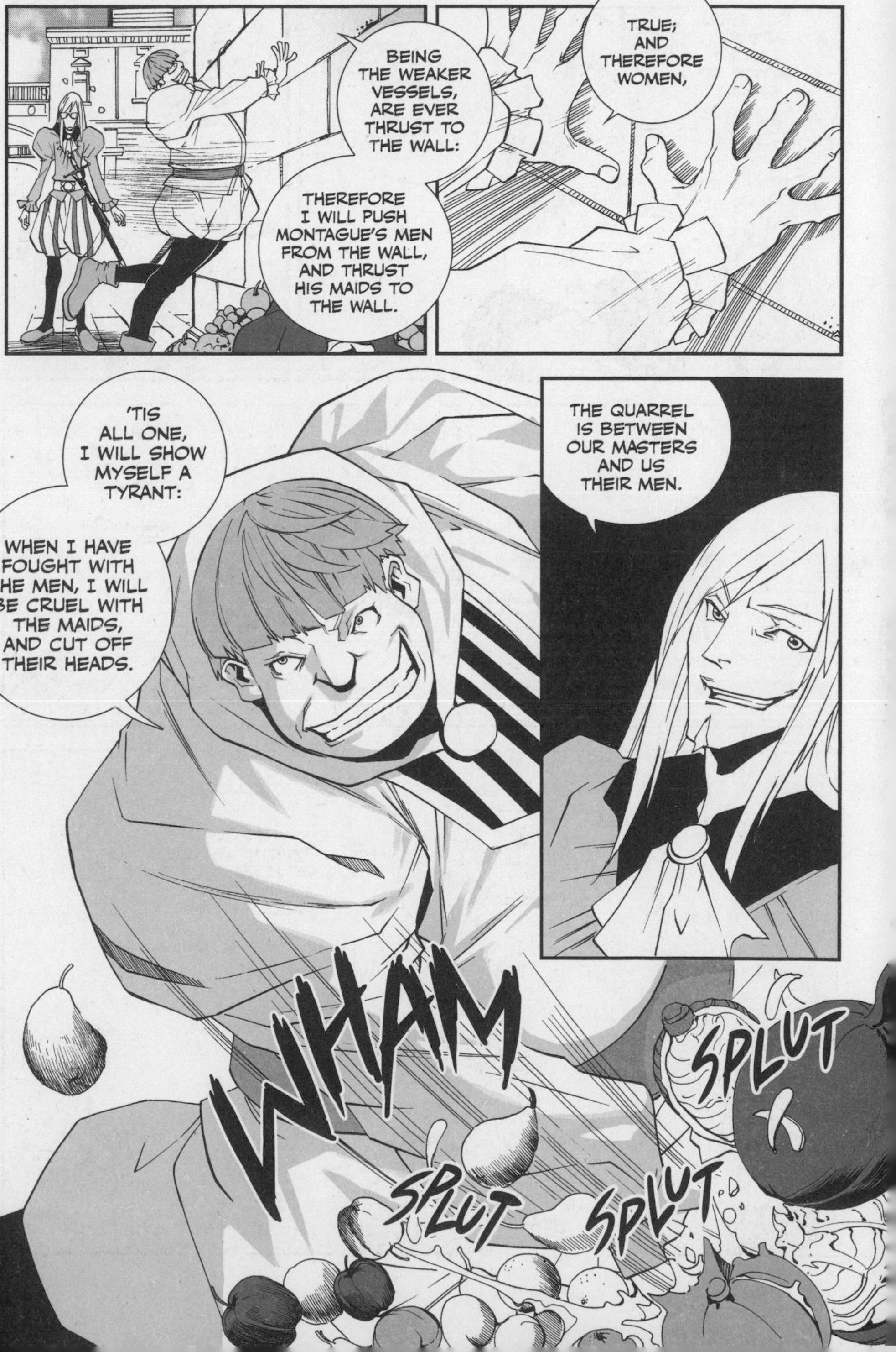
TRUE; AND THEREFORE WOMEN,
BEING THE WEAKER VESSELS, ARE EVER THRUST TO THE WALL:
THEREFORE I WILL PUSH MONTAGUE'S MEN FROM THE WALL, AND THRUST HIS MAIDS TO THE WALL.
THE QUARREL IS BETWEEN OUR MASTERS AND US THEIR MEN.
'TIS ALL ONE, I WILL SHOW MYSELF A TYRANT:
WHEN I HAVE FOUGHT WITH THE MEN, I WILL BE CRUEL WITH THE MAIDS, AND CUT OFF THEIR HEADS.
SPLUT
WHAM
SPLUT
SPLUT

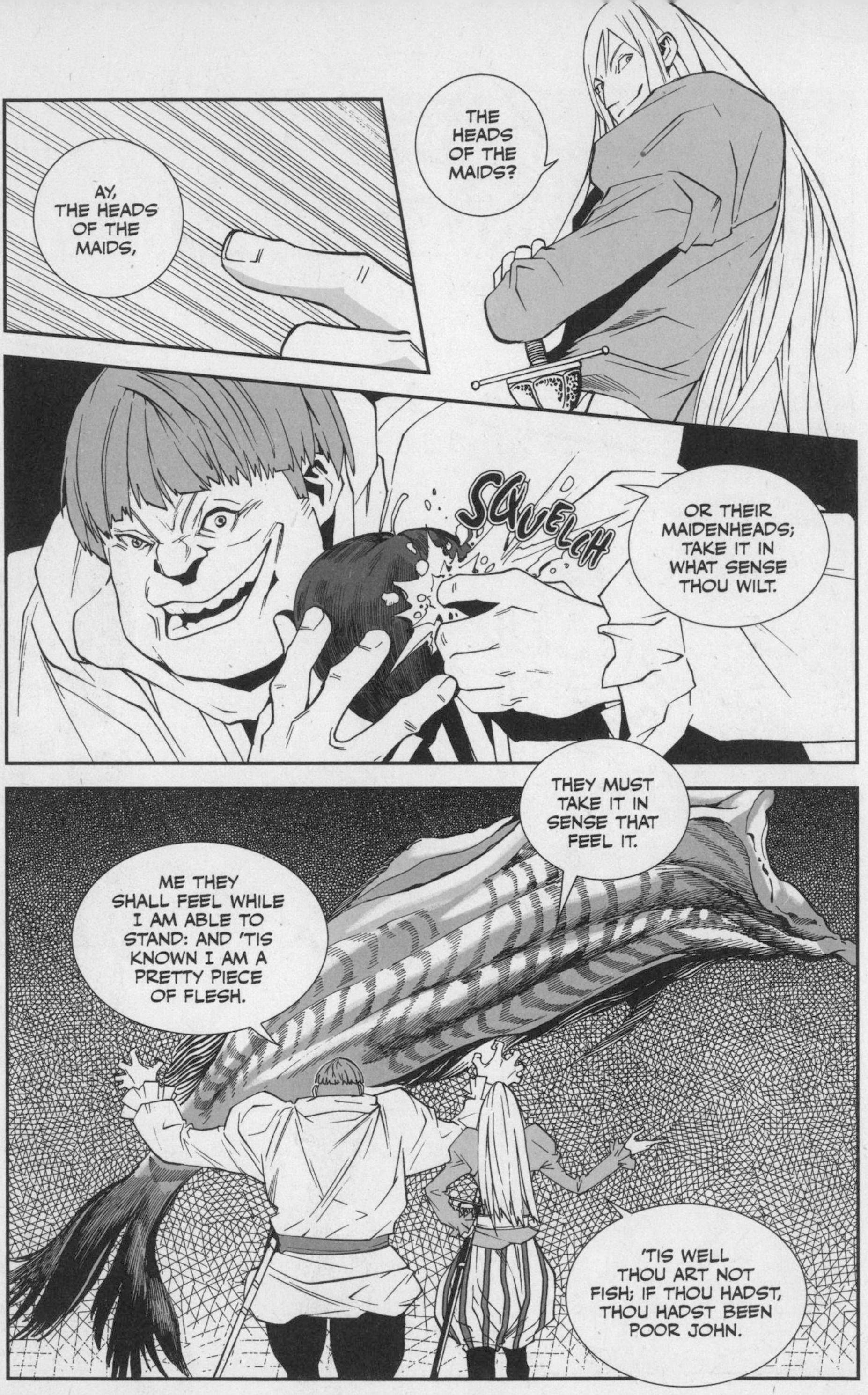
THE HEADS OF THE MAIDS?
AY, THE HEADS OF THE MAIDS,
SQUELCH
OR THEIR MAIDENHEADS; TAKE IT IN WHAT SENSE THOU WILT.
THEY MUST TAKE IT IN SENSE THAT FEEL IT.
ME THEY SHALL FEEL WHILE I AM ABLE TO STAND: AND 'TIS KNOWN I AM A PRETTY PIECE OF FLESH.
'TIS WELL THOU ART NOT FISH; IF THOU HADST, THOU HADST BEEN POOR JOHN.

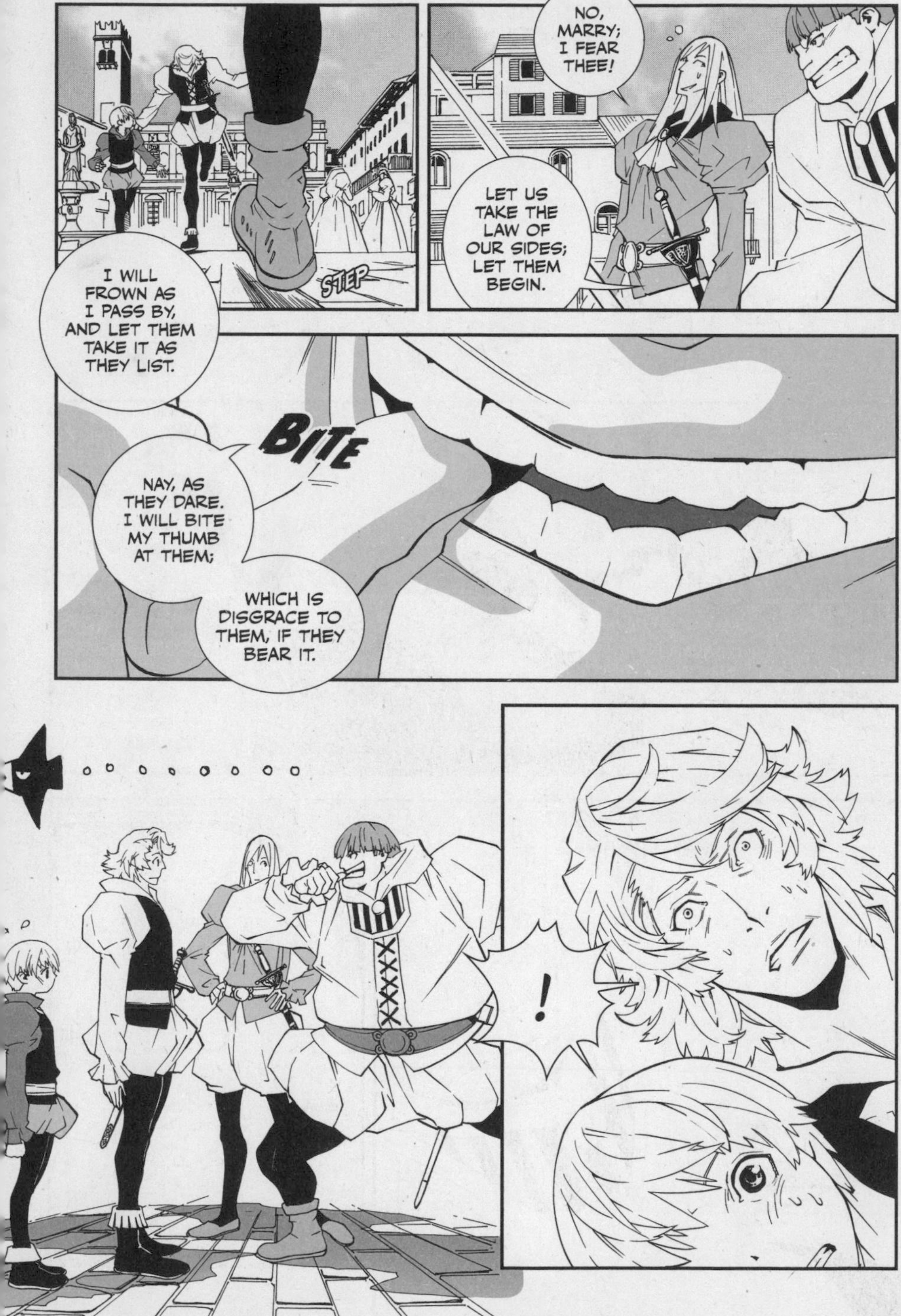
NO, MARRY; I FEAR THEE!
LET US TAKE THE LAW OF OUR SIDES; LET THEM BEGIN.
STEP
I WILL FROWN AS I PASS BY, AND LET THEM TAKE IT AS THEY LIST.
BITE
NAY, AS THEY DARE. I WILL BITE MY THUMB AT THEM;
WHICH IS DISGRACE TO THEM, IF THEY BEAR IT.
!
....

NO, SIR, I DO NOT BITE MY THUMB AT YOU, SIR, BUT I BITE MY THUMB, SIR.

QUARREL, SIR? NO, SIR.

DO YOU QUARREL, SIR?

BUT IF YOU DO, SIR, I AM FOR YOU.

NO BETTER?

I SERVE AS GOOD A MAN AS YOU.

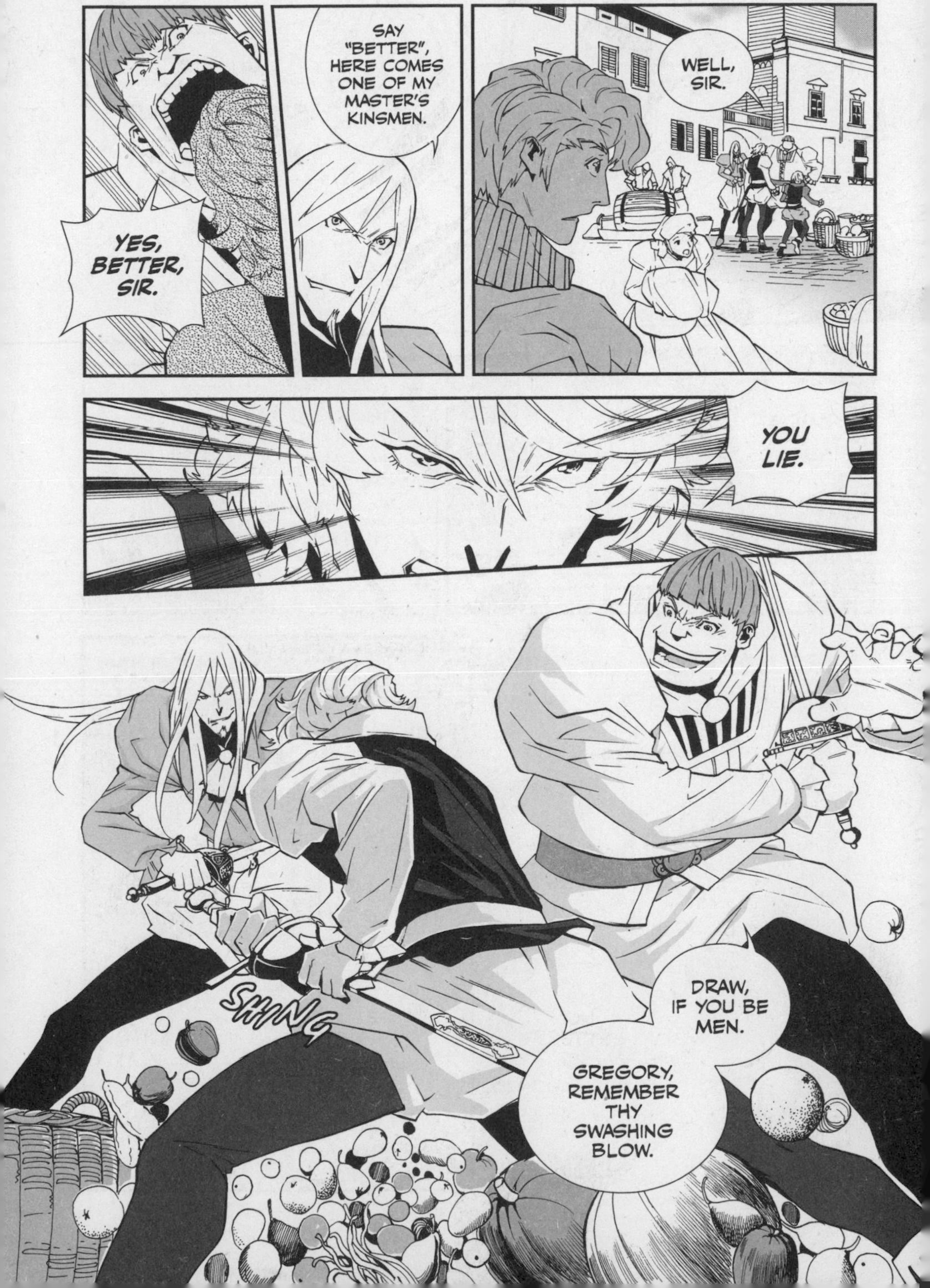
WELL, SIR.
SAY "BETTER", HERE COMES ONE OF MY MASTER'S KINSMEN.
YES, BETTER, SIR.
YOU LIE.
DRAW, IF YOU BE MEN.
GREGORY, REMEMBER THY SWASHING BLOW.
SHING

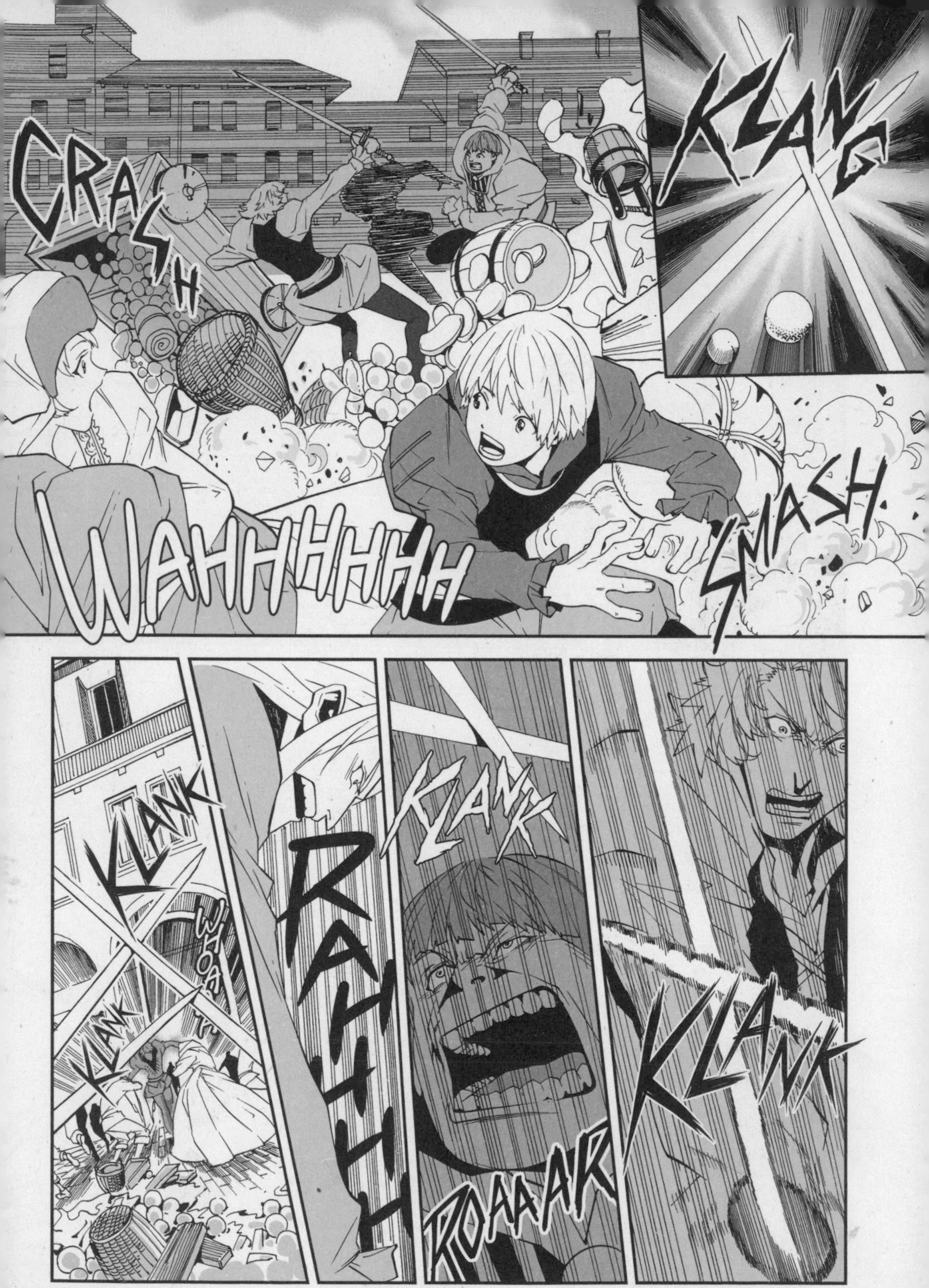
KLANG
SMASH
CRASH
WAHHHHHH
KLANK
KLANK
ROAAAR
KLANK
RAHHHH
KLANK
WHOA
KLANK

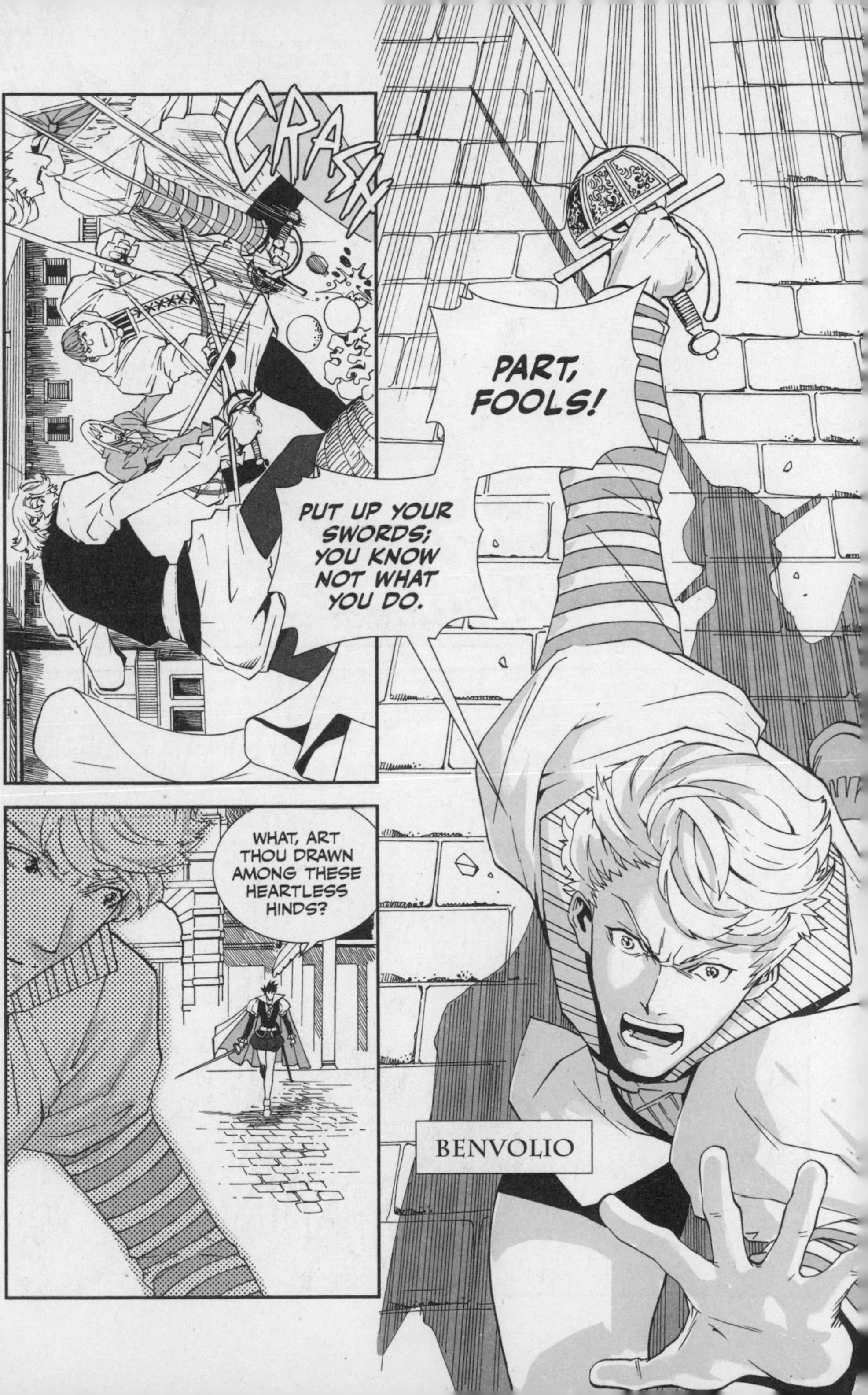
PART, FOOLS!
PUT UP YOUR SWORDS; YOU KNOW NOT WHAT YOU DO.
BENVOLIO
CRASH
WHAT, ART THOU DRAWN AMONG THESE HEARTLESS HINDS?

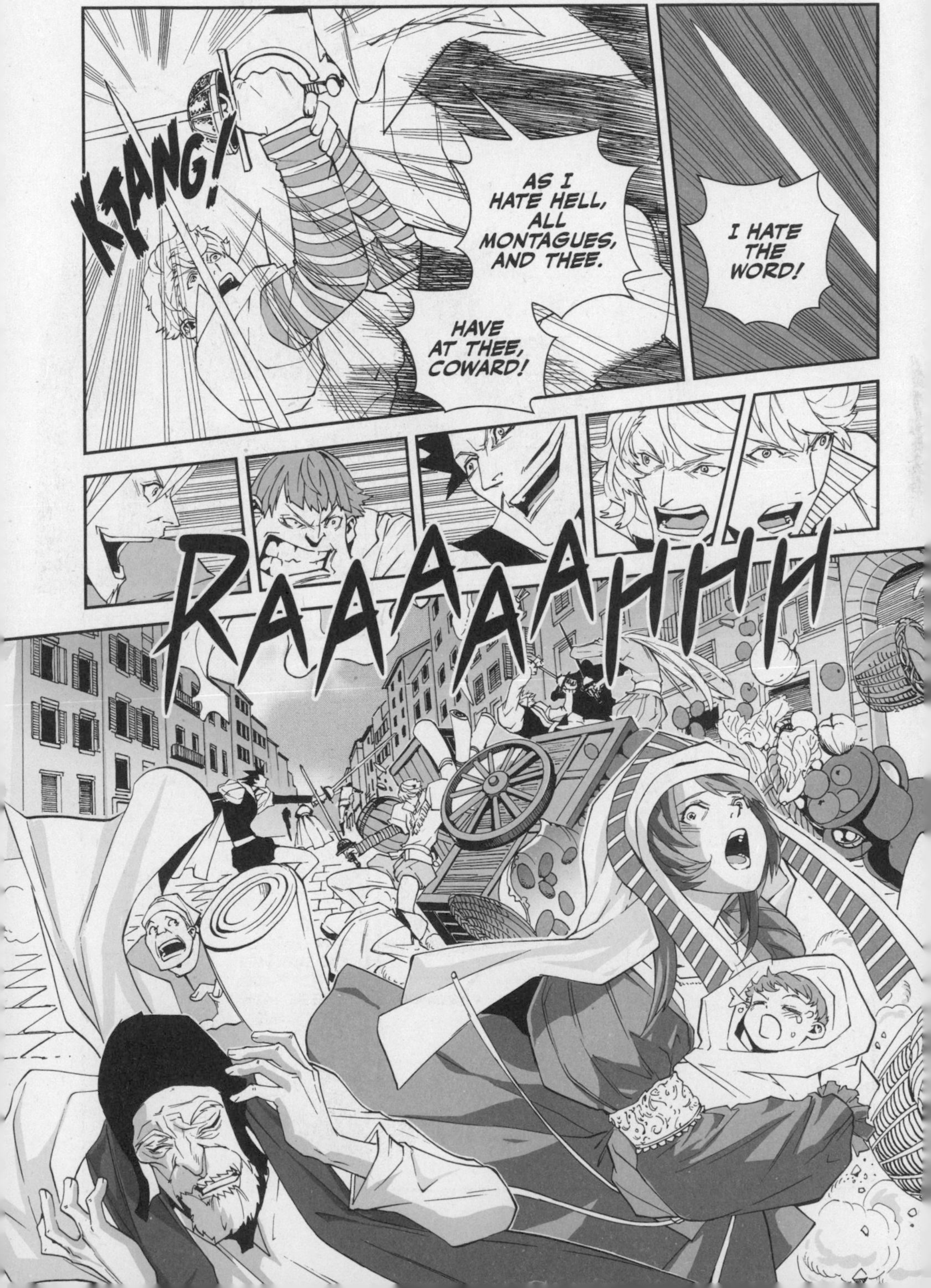
I HATE THE WORD!
AS I HATE HELL, ALL MONTAGUES, AND THEE.
HAVE AT THEE, COWARD!
KTANG!
RAAAAAHHH

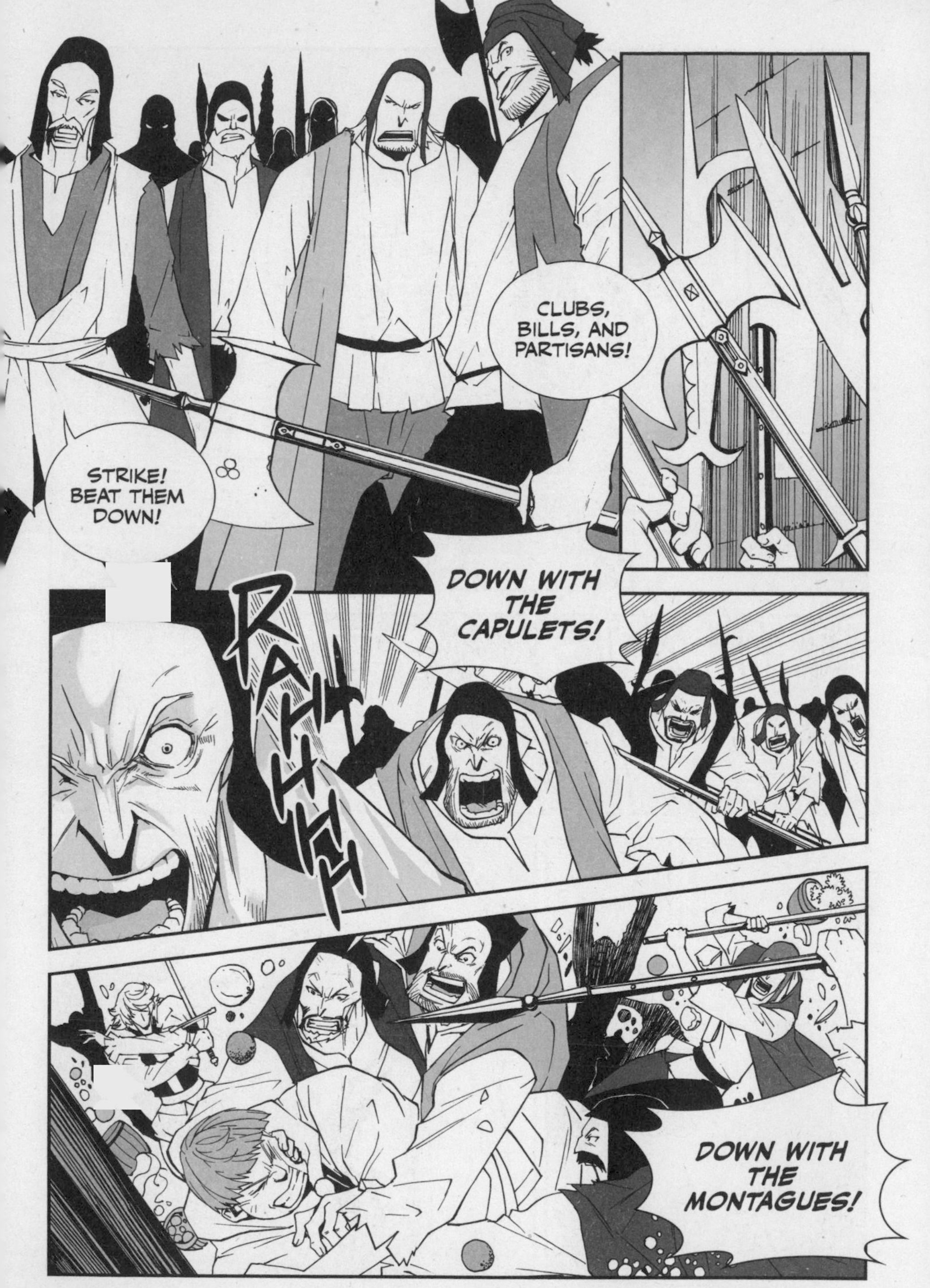
CLUBS, BILLS, AND PARTISANS!
STRIKE! BEAT THEM DOWN!
DOWN WITH THE CAPULETS!
RAHHHHH
DOWN WITH THE MONTAGUES!

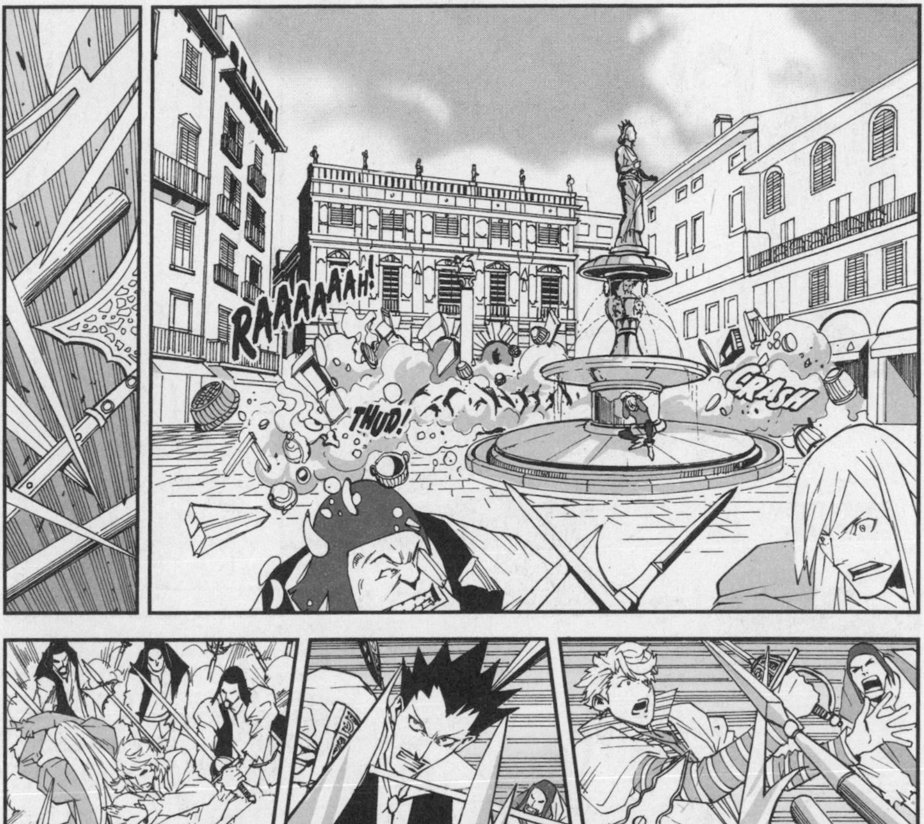
RAAAAAAH!
CRASH
THUD!
WHAT NOISE IS THIS?

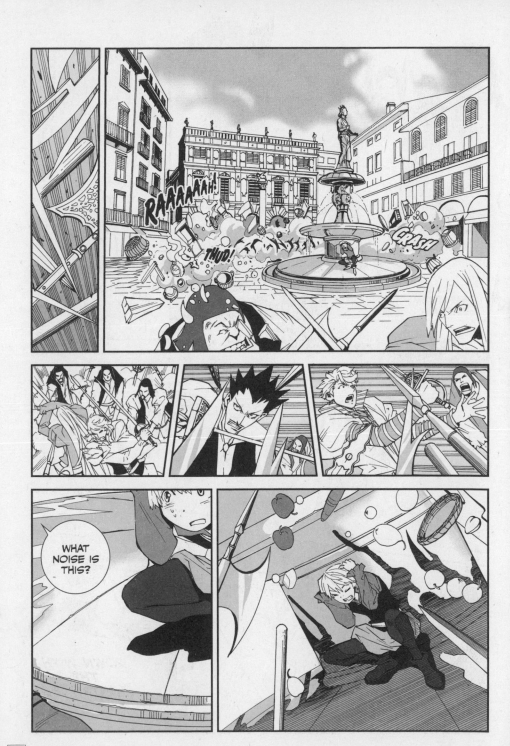

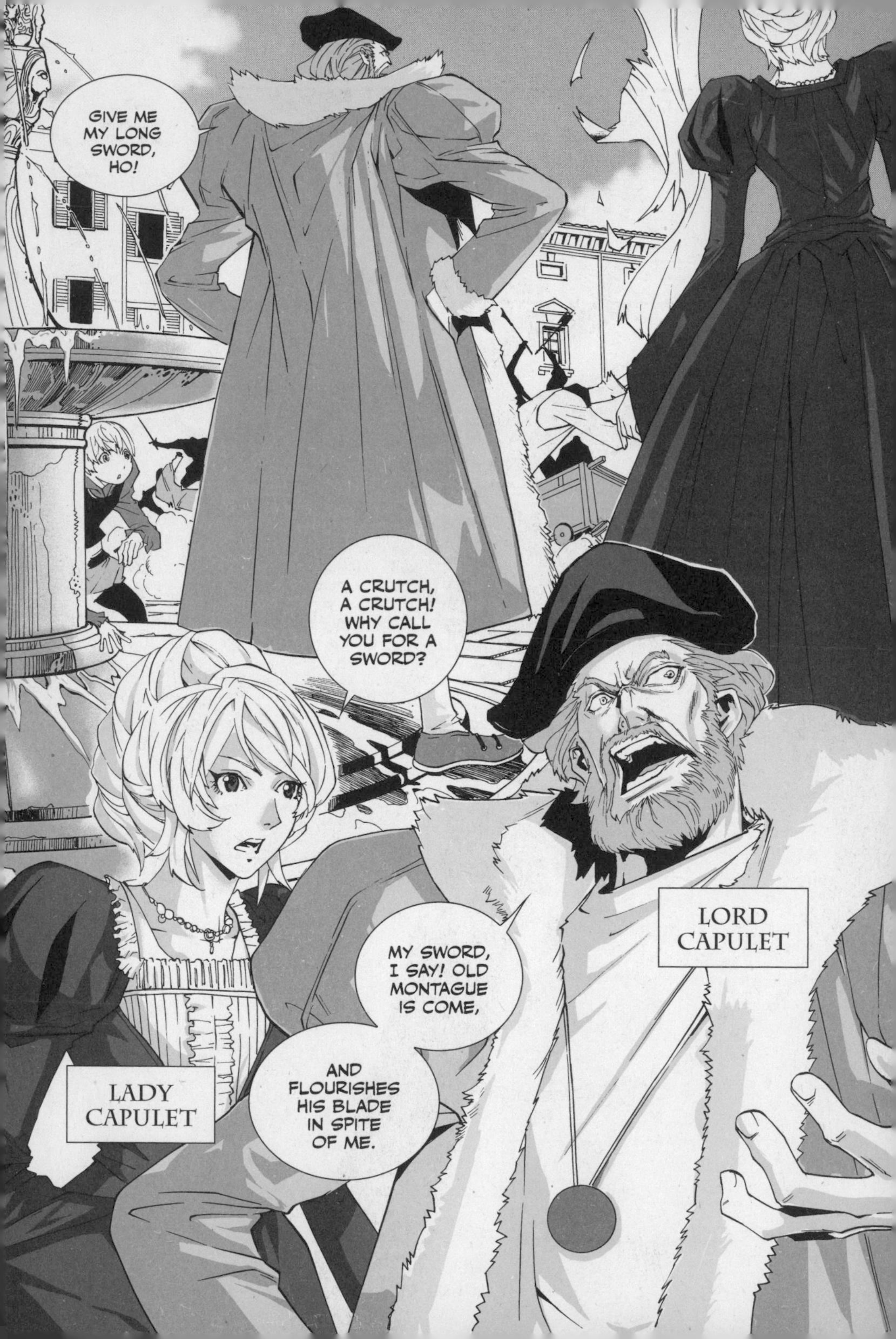
GIVE ME MY LONG SWORD, HO!
A CRUTCH, A CRUTCH! WHY CALL YOU FOR A SWORD?
LORD CAPULET
MY SWORD, I SAY! OLD MONTAGUE IS COME,
AND FLOURISHES HIS BLADE IN SPITE OF ME.
LADY CAPULET

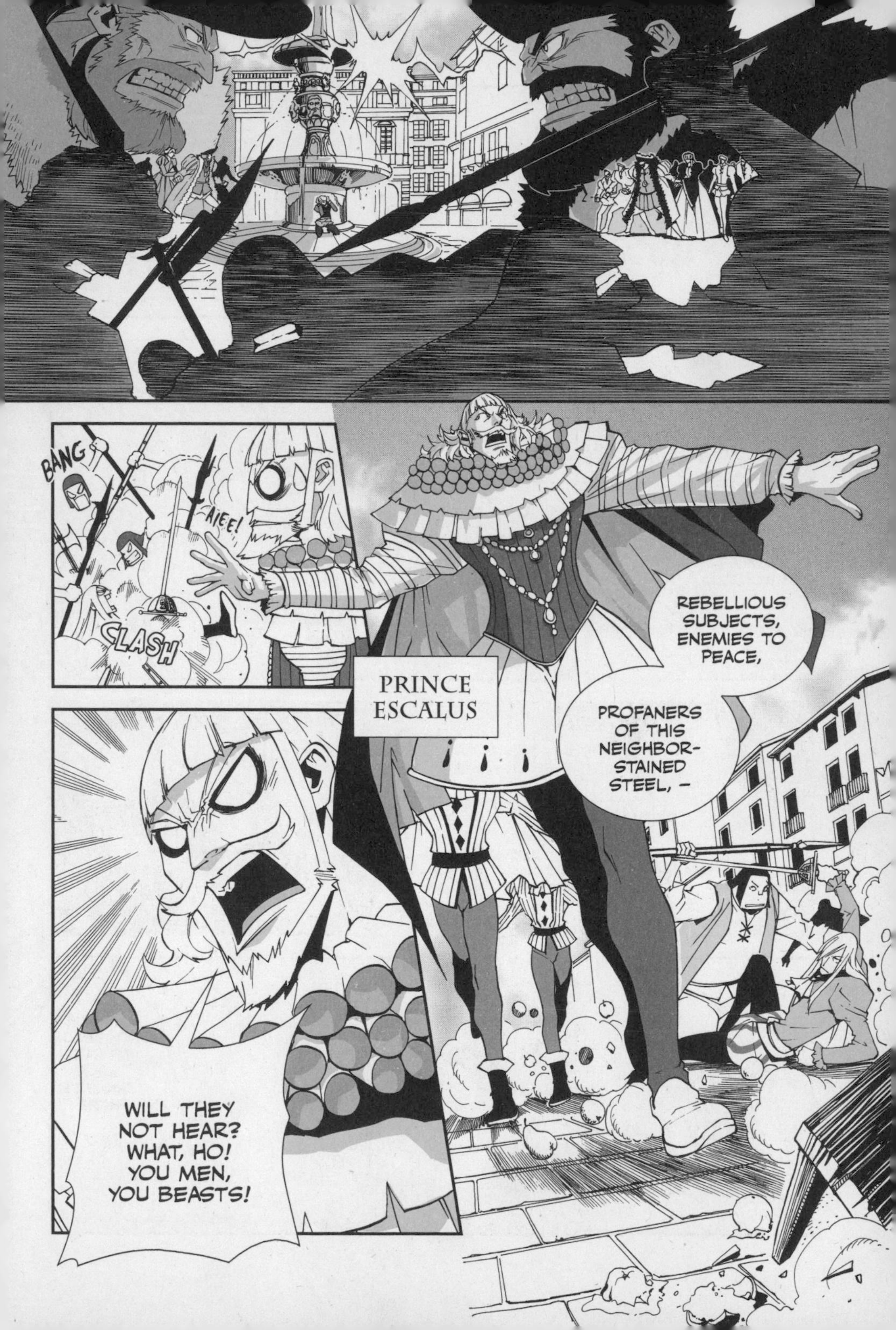
PRINCE ESCALUS
REBELLIOUS SUBJECTS, ENEMIES TO PEACE,
PROFANERS OF THIS NEIGHBOR-STAINED STEEL, –
BANG
AIEE!
CLASH
WILL THEY NOT HEAR? WHAT, HO! YOU MEN, YOU BEASTS!

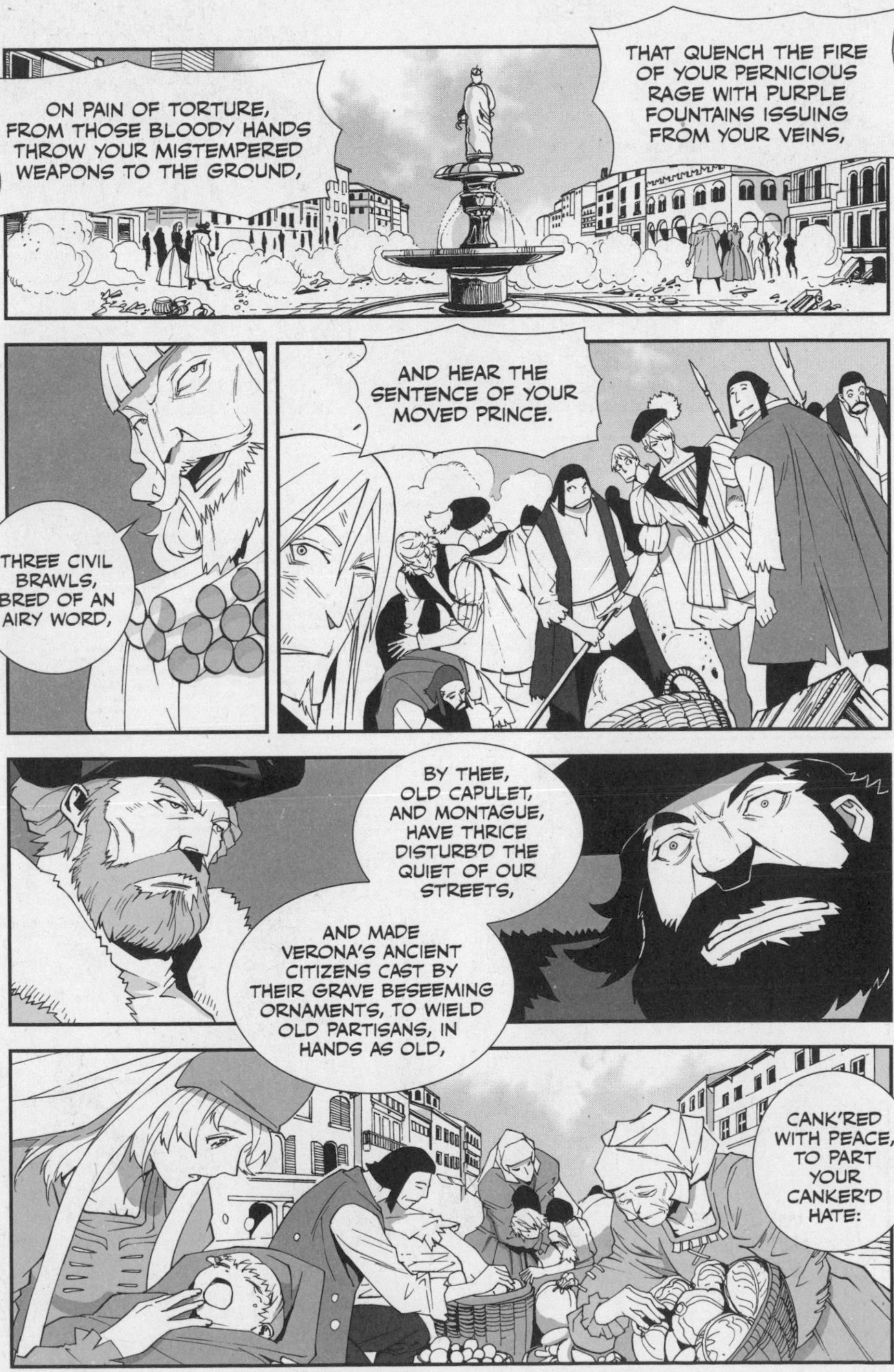

THAT QUENCH THE FIRE OF YOUR PERNICIOUS RAGE WITH PURPLE FOUNTAINS ISSUING FROM YOUR VEINS,
ON PAIN OF TORTURE, FROM THOSE BLOODY HANDS THROW YOUR MISTEMPERED WEAPONS TO THE GROUND,
AND HEAR THE SENTENCE OF YOUR MOVED PRINCE.
THREE CIVIL BRAWLS, BRED OF AN AIRY WORD,
BY THEE, OLD CAPULET, AND MONTAGUE, HAVE THRICE DISTURB'D THE QUIET OF OUR STREETS,
AND MADE VERONA'S ANCIENT CITIZENS CAST BY THEIR GRAVE BESEEMING ORNAMENTS, TO WIELD OLD PARTISANS, IN HANDS AS OLD,
CANK'RED WITH PEACE, TO PART YOUR CANKER'D HATE:

IF EVER YOU DISTURB OUR STREETS AGAIN, YOUR LIVES SHALL PAY THE FORFEIT OF THE PEACE.

FOR THIS TIME, ALL THE REST DEPART AWAY!

AND, MONTAGUE, COME YOU THIS AFTERNOON, TO KNOW OUR FURTHER PLEASURE IN THIS CASE,

YOU, CAPULET; SHALL GO ALONG WITH ME,

WHO SET THIS ANCIENT QUARREL NEW ABROACH?

SPEAK, NEPHEW, WERE YOU BY WHEN IT BEGAN?

HERE WERE THE SERVANTS OF YOUR ADVERSARY, AND YOURS, CLOSE FIGHTING ERE I DID APPROACH.

TO OLD FREE-TOWN, OUR COMMON JUDGMENT-PLACE. ONCE MORE, ON PAIN OF DEATH, ALL MEN DEPART.

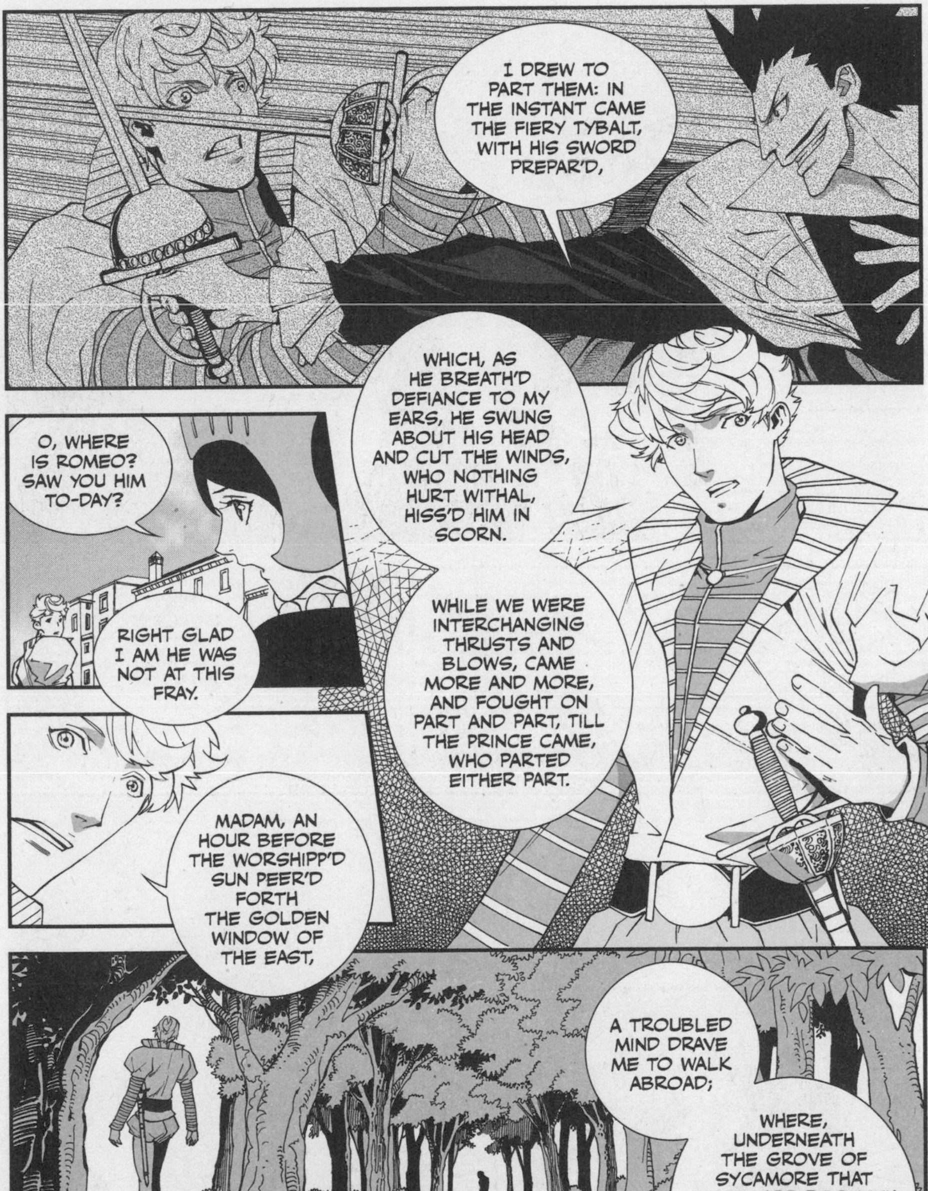
I DREW TO PART THEM: IN THE INSTANT CAME THE FIERY TYBALT, WITH HIS SWORD PREPAR'D,
WHICH, AS HE BREATH'D DEFIANCE TO MY EARS, HE SWUNG ABOUT HIS HEAD AND CUT THE WINDS, WHO NOTHING HURT WITHAL, HISS'D HIM IN SCORN.
WHILE WE WERE INTERCHANGING THRUSTS AND BLOWS, CAME MORE AND MORE, AND FOUGHT ON PART AND PART, TILL THE PRINCE CAME, WHO PARTED EITHER PART.
O, WHERE IS ROMEO? SAW YOU HIM TO-DAY?
RIGHT GLAD I AM HE WAS NOT AT THIS FRAY.
MADAM, AN HOUR BEFORE THE WORSHIPP'D SUN PEER'D FORTH THE GOLDEN WINDOW OF THE EAST,
A TROUBLED MIND DRAVE ME TO WALK ABROAD;
WHERE, UNDERNEATH THE GROVE OF SYCAMORE THAT WESTWARD ROOTETH FROM THIS CITY SIDE, SO EARLY WALKING DID I SEE YOUR SON.
TOWARDS HIM I MADE, BUT HE WAS WARE OF ME, AND STOLE INTO THE COVERT OF THE WOOD.

MY NOBLE UNCLE, DO YOU KNOW THE CAUSE?
I NEITHER KNOW IT NOR CAN LEARN OF HIM.
HAVE YOU IMPORTUN'D HIM BY ANY MEANS?
BOTH BY MYSELF AND MANY OTHER FRIENDS: BUT HE, HIS OWN AFFECTIONS' COUNSELLOR,
IS TO HIMSELF - I WILL NOT SAY HOW TRUE - BUT TO HIMSELF SO SECRET AND SO CLOSE,
SO FAR FROM SOUNDING AND DISCOVERY,
AS IS THE BUD BIT WITH AN ENVIOUS WORM, ERE HE CAN SPREAD HIS SWEET LEAVES TO THE AIR, OR DEDICATE HIS BEAUTY TO THE SUN.
COULD WE BUT LEARN FROM WHENCE HIS SORROWS GROW, WE WOULD AS WILLINGLY GIVE CURE AS KNOW.

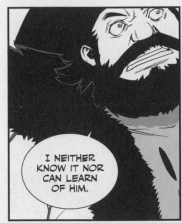

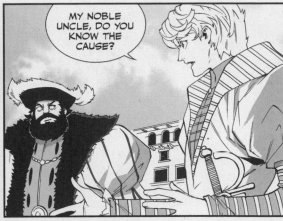

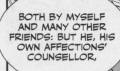

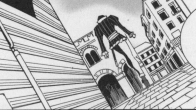

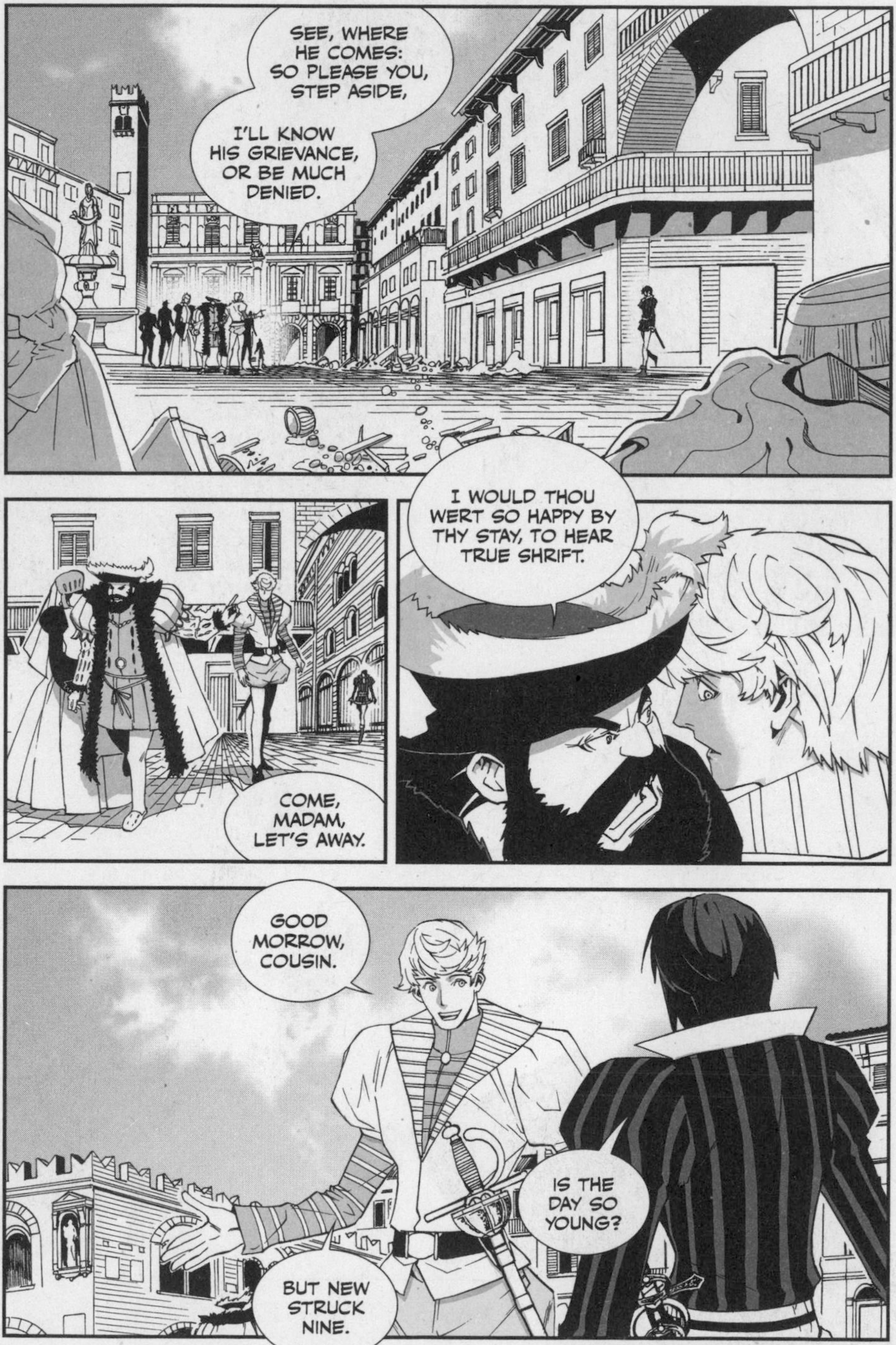
SEE, WHERE HE COMES: SO PLEASE YOU, STEP ASIDE,
I'LL KNOW HIS GRIEVANCE, OR BE MUCH DENIED.
I WOULD THOU WERT SO HAPPY BY THY STAY, TO HEAR TRUE SHRIFT.
COME, MADAM, LET'S AWAY.
GOOD MORROW, COUSIN.
IS THE DAY SO YOUNG?
BUT NEW STRUCK NINE.

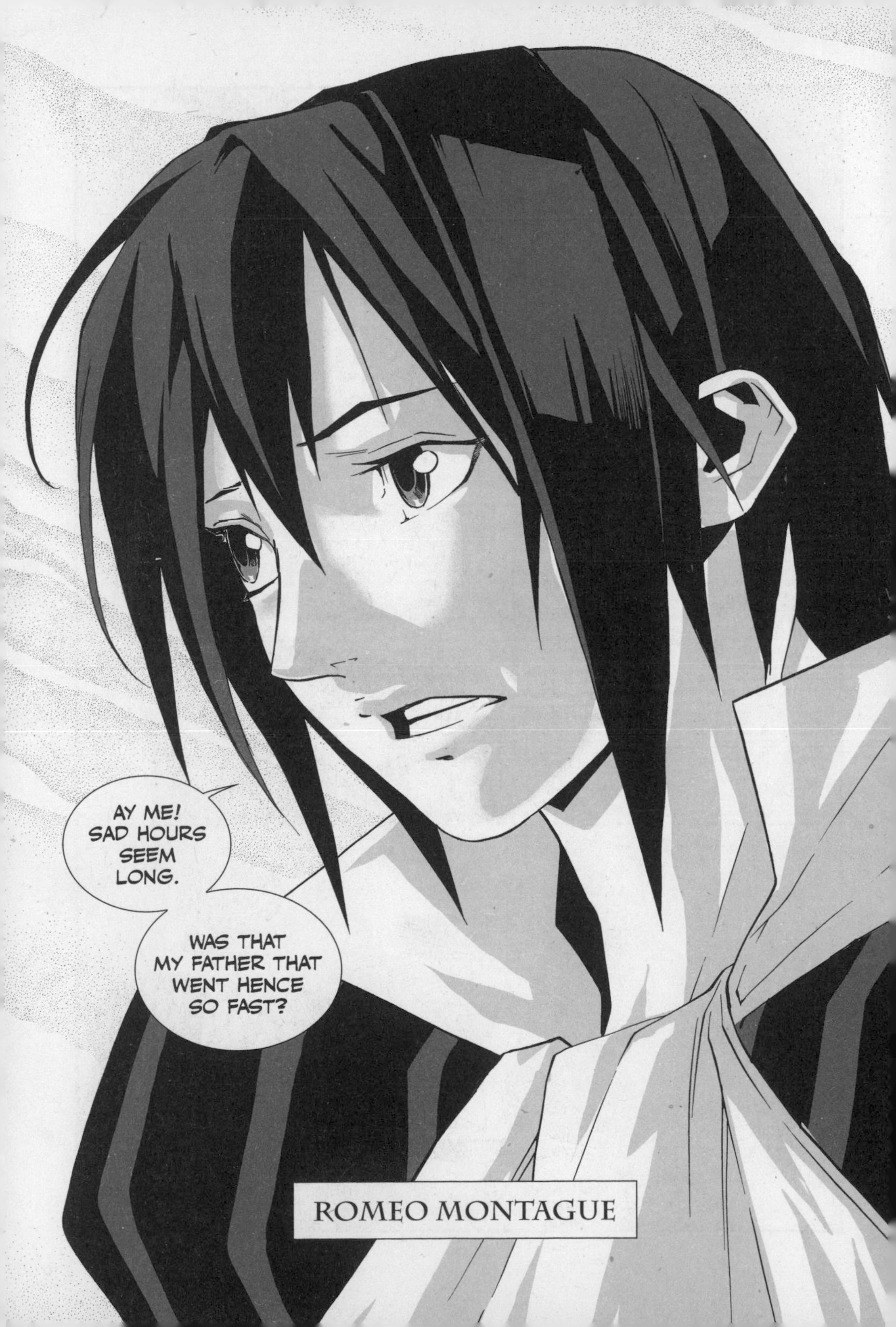
AY ME! SAD HOURS SEEM LONG.
WAS THAT MY FATHER THAT WENT HENCE SO FAST?
ROMEO MONTAGUE

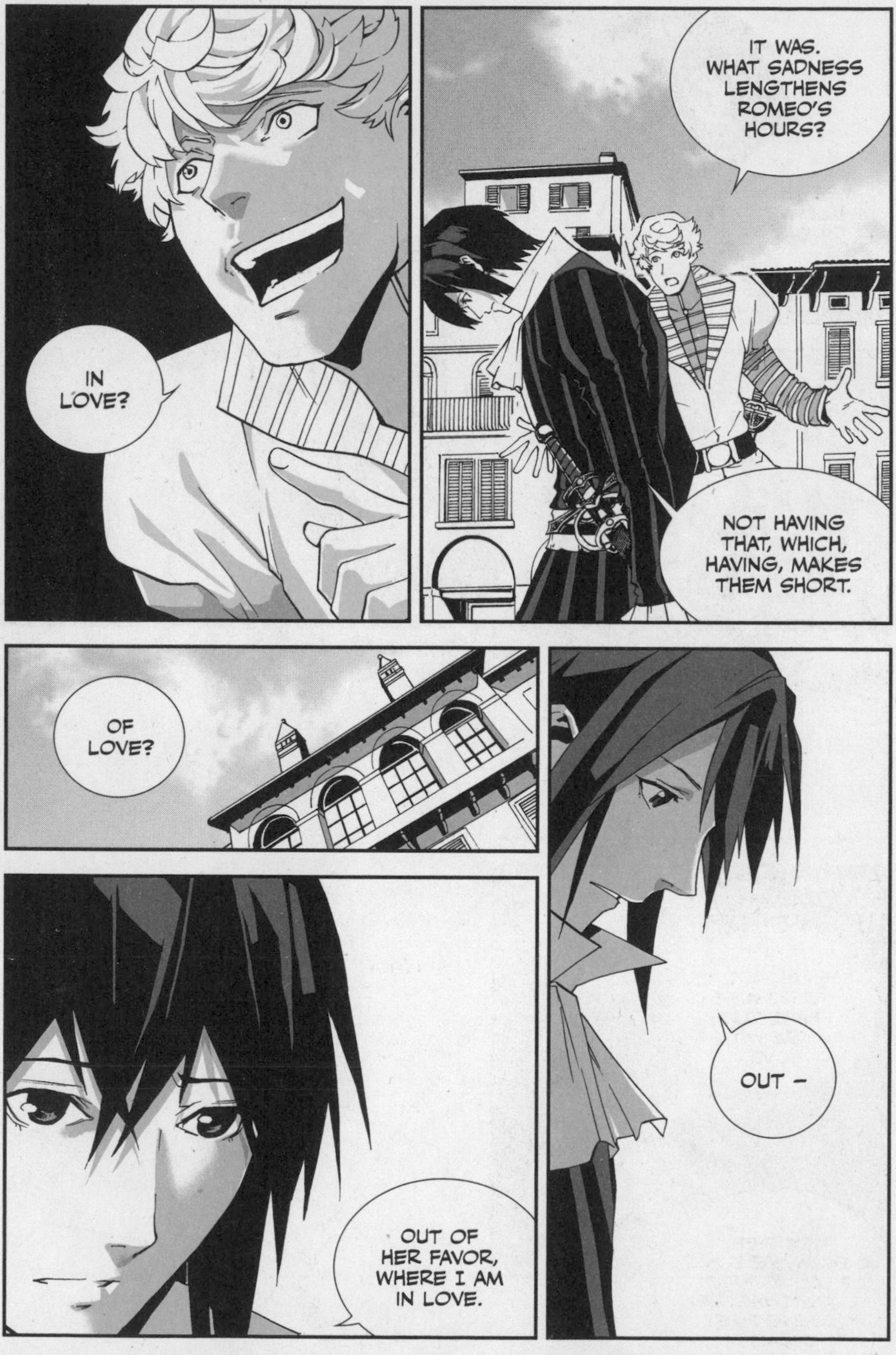
IT WAS. WHAT SADNESS LENGTHENS ROMEO'S HOURS?
NOT HAVING THAT, WHICH, HAVING, MAKES THEM SHORT.
IN LOVE?
OUT –
OF LOVE?
OUT OF HER FAVOR, WHERE I AM IN LOVE.

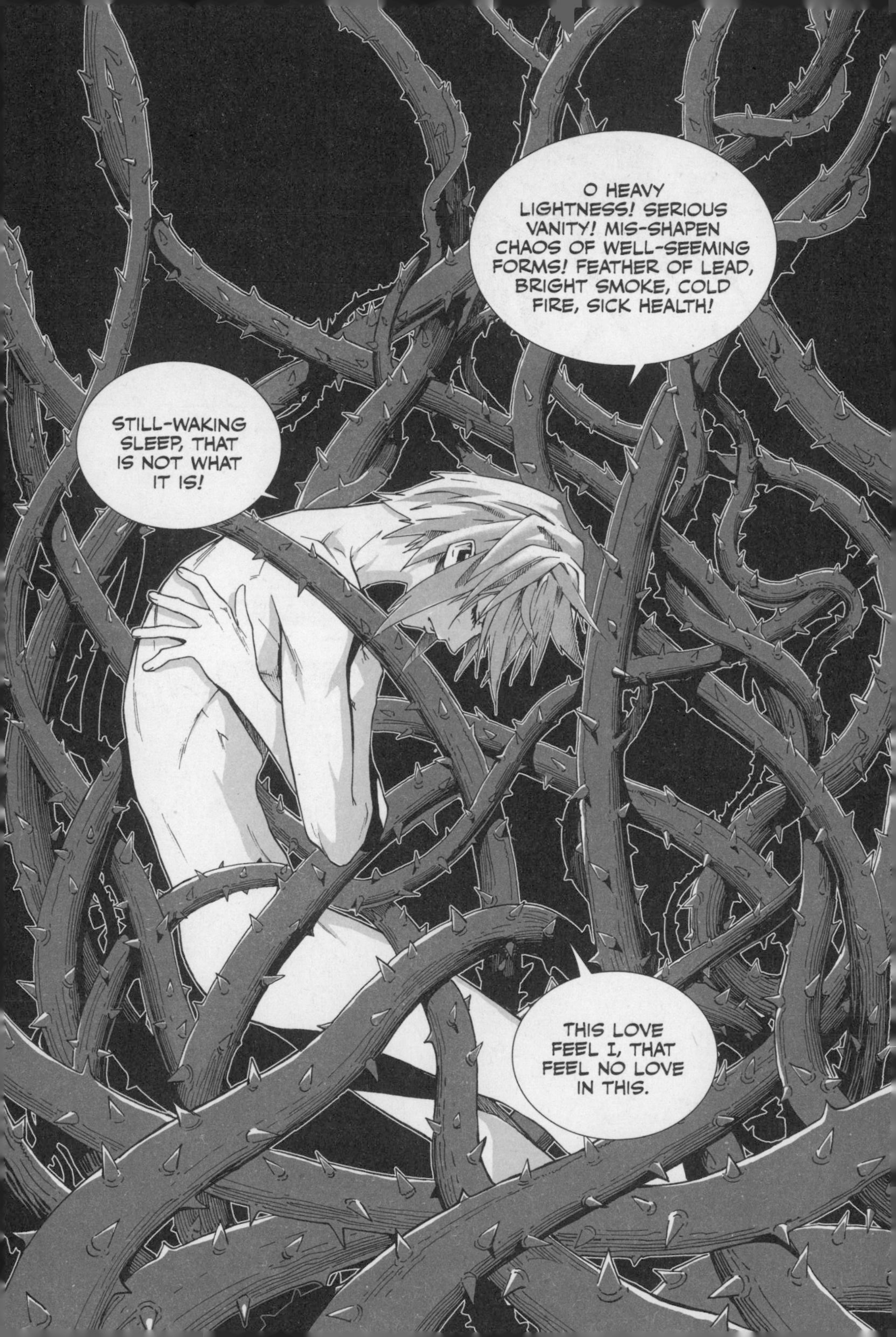
O HEAVY LIGHTNESS! SERIOUS VANITY! MIS-SHAPEN CHAOS OF WELL-SEEMING FORMS! FEATHER OF LEAD, BRIGHT SMOKE, COLD FIRE, SICK HEALTH!
STILL-WAKING SLEEP, THAT IS NOT WHAT IT IS!
THIS LOVE FEEL I, THAT FEEL NO LOVE IN THIS.

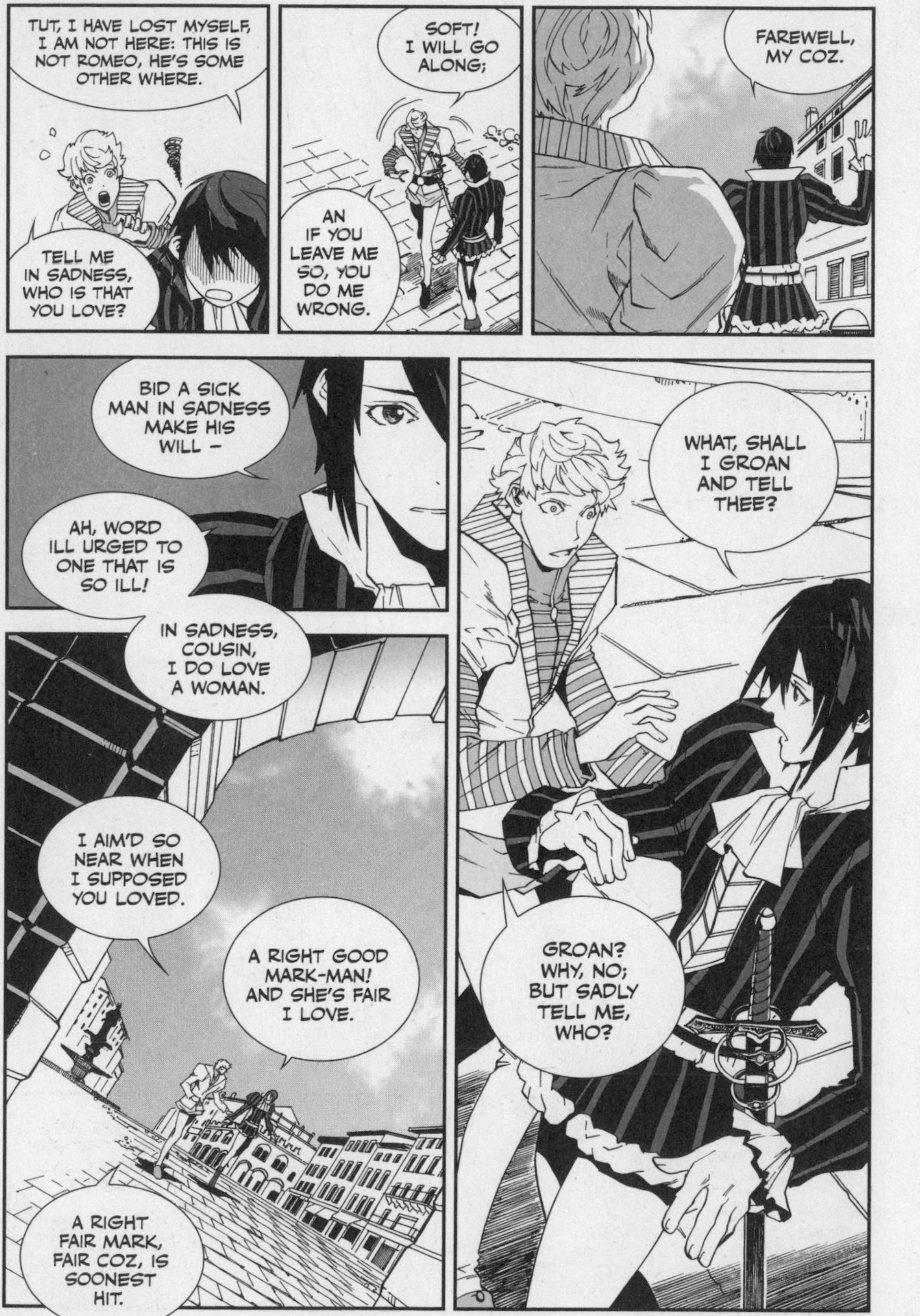
FAREWELL, MY COZ.
SOFT! I WILL GO ALONG;
AN IF YOU LEAVE ME SO, YOU DO ME WRONG.
TUT, I HAVE LOST MYSELF, I AM NOT HERE: THIS IS NOT ROMEO, HE'S SOME OTHER WHERE.
TELL ME IN SADNESS, WHO IS THAT YOU LOVE?
WHAT, SHALL I GROAN AND TELL THEE?
GROAN? WHY, NO; BUT SADLY TELL ME, WHO?
BID A SICK MAN IN SADNESS MAKE HIS WILL –
AH, WORD ILL URGED TO ONE THAT IS SO ILL!
IN SADNESS, COUSIN, I DO LOVE A WOMAN.
I AIM'D SO NEAR WHEN I SUPPOSED YOU LOVED.
A RIGHT GOOD MARK-MAN! AND SHE'S FAIR I LOVE.
A RIGHT FAIR MARK, FAIR COZ, IS SOONEST HIT.

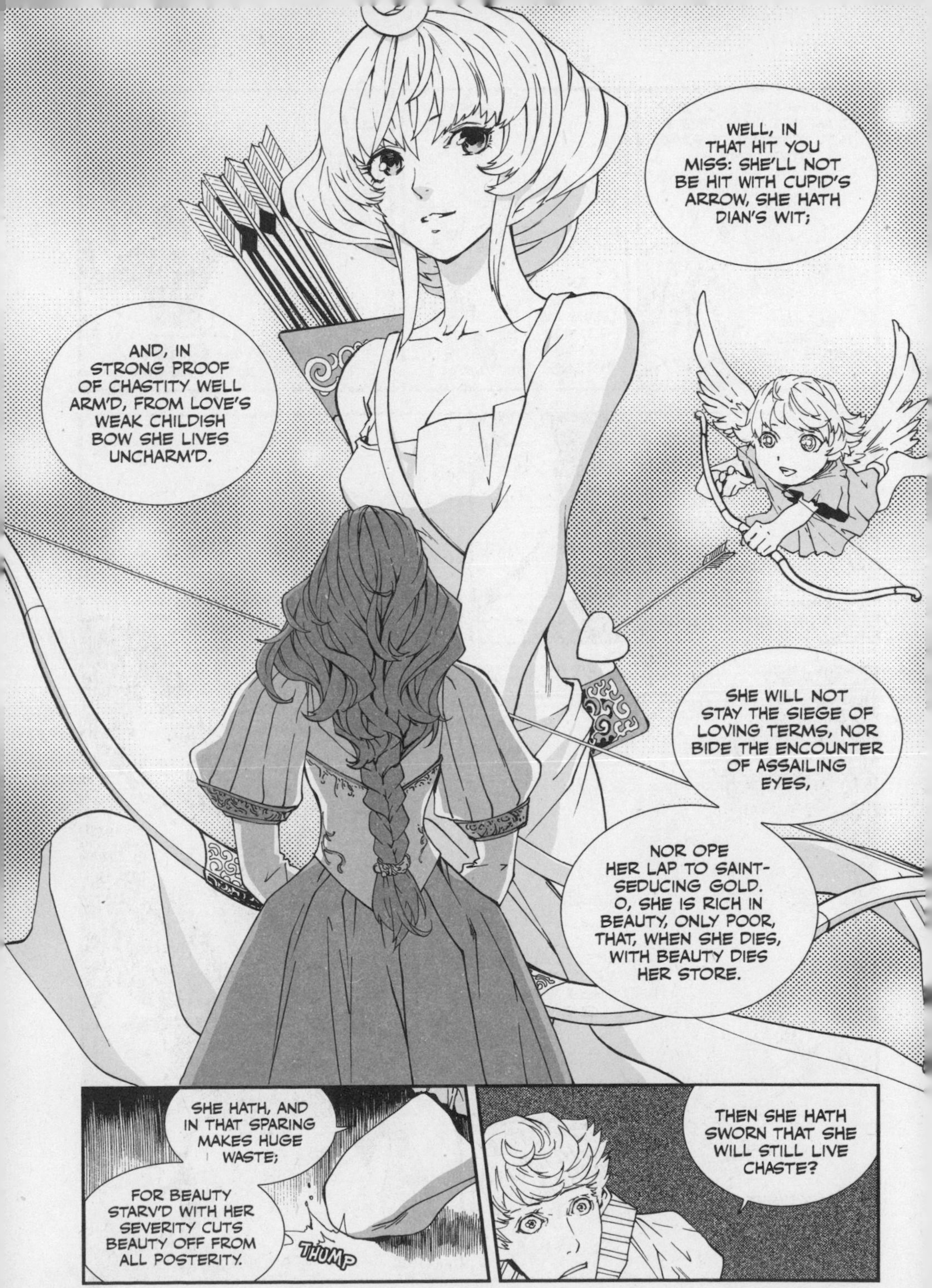
WELL, IN THAT HIT YOU MISS: SHE'LL NOT BE HIT WITH CUPID'S ARROW, SHE HATH DIAN'S WIT;
AND, IN STRONG PROOF OF CHASTITY WELL ARM'D, FROM LOVE'S WEAK CHILDISH BOW SHE LIVES UNCHARM'D.
SHE WILL NOT STAY THE SIEGE OF LOVING TERMS, NOR BIDE THE ENCOUNTER OF ASSAILING EYES,
NOR OPE HER LAP TO SAINT-SEDUCING GOLD. O, SHE IS RICH IN BEAUTY, ONLY POOR, THAT, WHEN SHE DIES, WITH BEAUTY DIES HER STORE.
THEN SHE HATH SWORN THAT SHE WILL STILL LIVE CHASTE?
SHE HATH, AND IN THAT SPARING MAKES HUGE WASTE;
FOR BEAUTY STARV'D WITH HER SEVERITY CUTS BEAUTY OFF FROM ALL POSTERITY.
THUMP

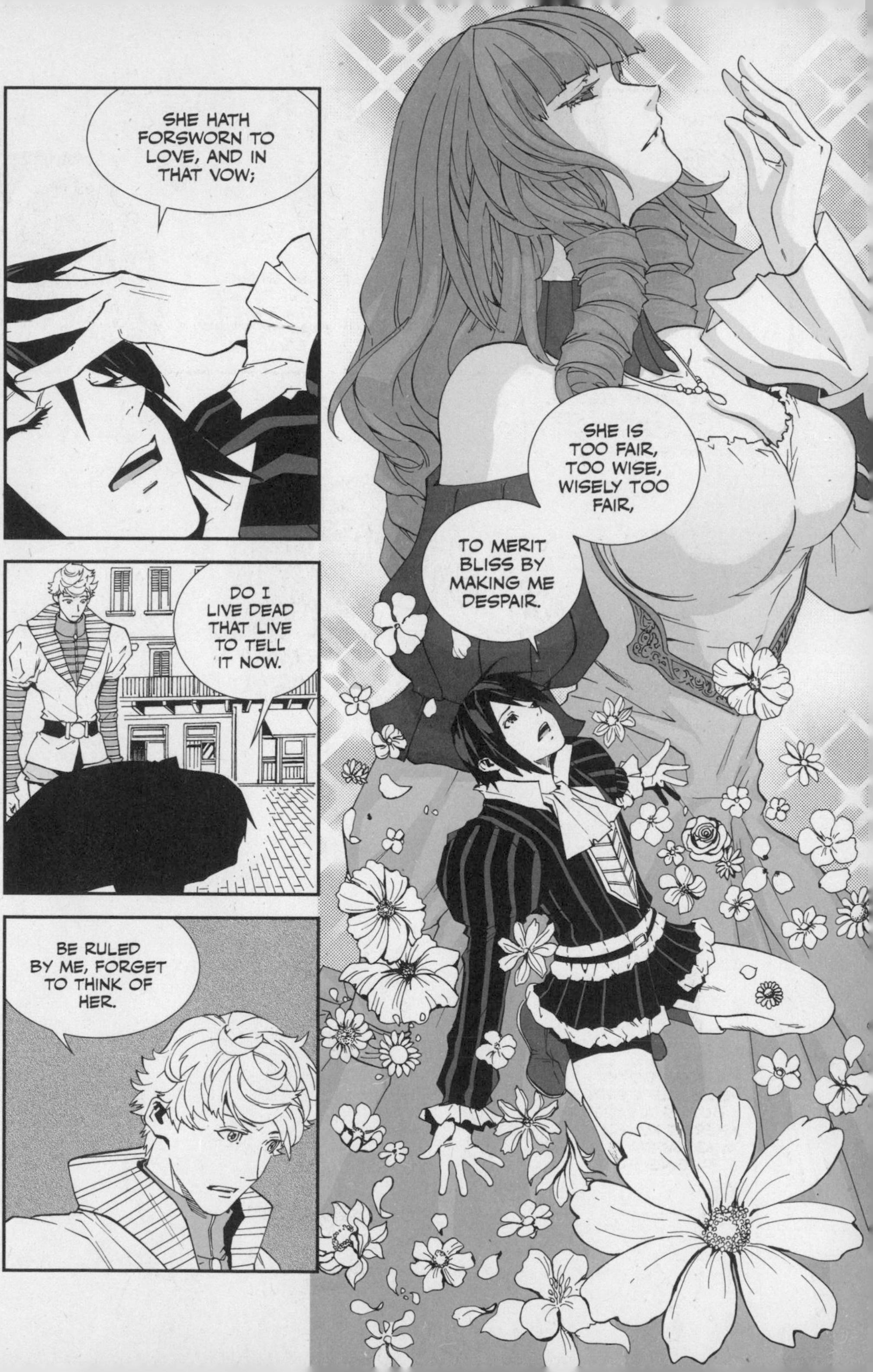
SHE IS TOO FAIR, TOO WISE, WISELY TOO FAIR,
TO MERIT BLISS BY MAKING ME DESPAIR.
SHE HATH FORSWORN TO LOVE, AND IN THAT VOW;
DO I LIVE DEAD THAT LIVE TO TELL IT NOW.
BE RULED BY ME, FORGET TO THINK OF HER.

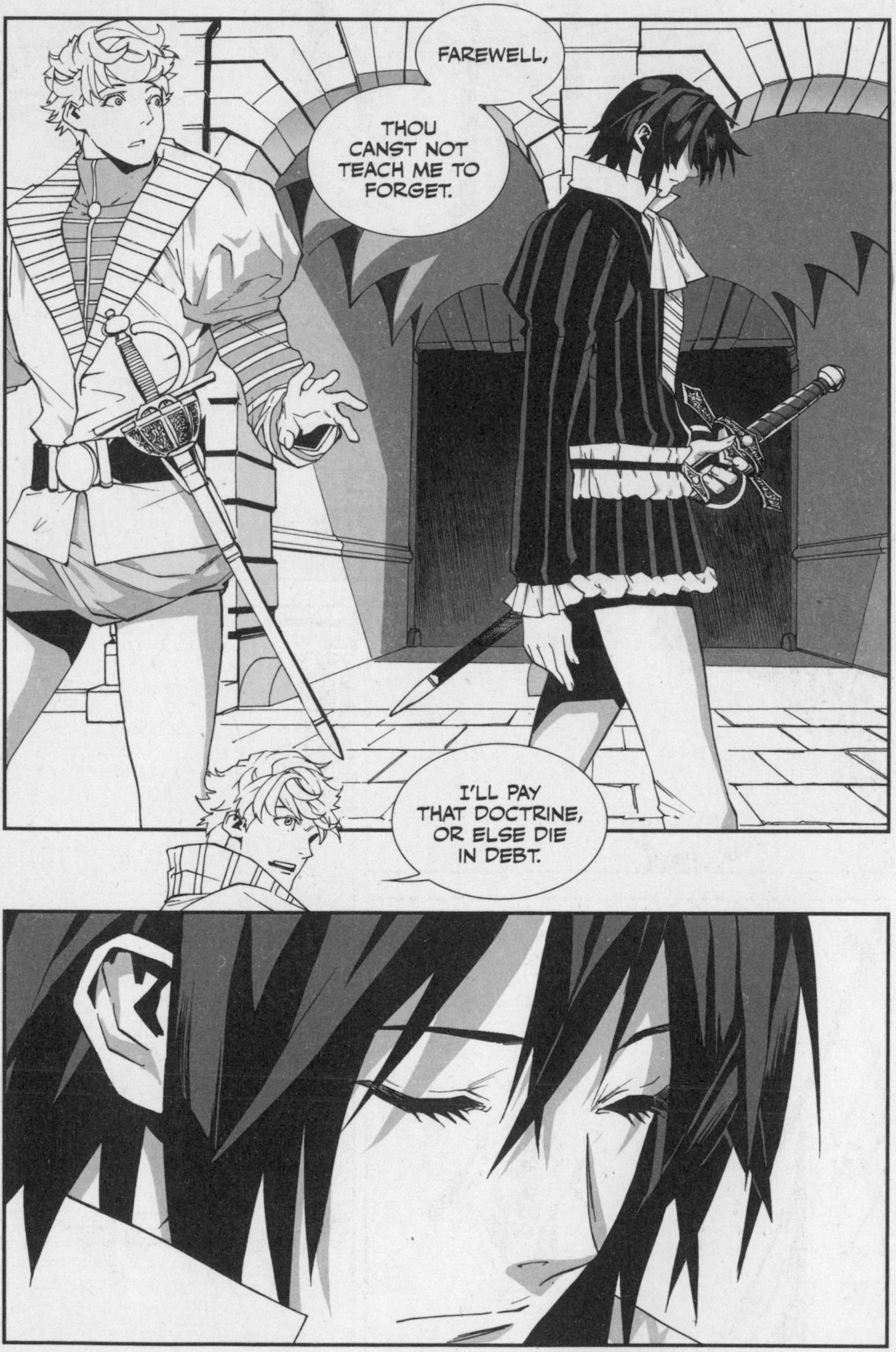
FAREWELL,
THOU CANST NOT TEACH ME TO FORGET.
I'LL PAY THAT DOCTRINE, OR ELSE DIE IN DEBT.

ACT I
SCENE II

FOR MEN SO OLD AS WE TO KEEP THE PEACE.

BUT MONTAGUE IS BOUND AS WELL AS I, IN PENALTY ALIKE; AND 'TIS NOT HARD, I THINK,

OF HONOURABLE RECKONING ARE YOU BOTH; AND PITY 'TIS YOU LIVED AT ODDS SO LONG.

YOUNGER THAN SHE ARE HAPPY MOTHERS MADE.

ERE WE MAY THINK HER RIPE TO BE A BRIDE.

BUT SAYING O'ER WHAT I HAVE SAID BEFORE: MY CHILD IS YET A STRANGER IN THE WORLD;

SHE HATH NOT SEEN THE CHANGE OF FOURTEEN YEARS, LET TWO MORE SUMMERS WITHER IN THEIR PRIDE,

BUT WOO HER, GENTLE PARIS, GET HER HEART, MY WILL TO HER CONSENT IS BUT A PART;

PAT

AN SHE AGREE, WITHIN HER SCOPE OF CHOICE LIES MY CONSENT AND FAIR ACCORDING VOICE.

AND TOO SOON MARR'D ARE THOSE SO EARLY MADE.

THE EARTH HATH SWALLOW'D ALL MY HOPES BUT SHE, SHE IS THE HOPEFUL LADY OF MY EARTH:

THIS NIGHT I HOLD AN OLD ACCUSTOM'D FEAST, WHERETO I HAVE INVITED MANY A GUEST, SUCH AS I LOVE; AND YOU, AMONG THE STORE,

ONE MORE, MOST WELCOME, MAKES MY NUMBER MORE.

SUCH COMFORT AS DO LUSTY YOUNG MEN FEEL WHEN WELL-APPARELL'D APRIL ON THE HEEL OF LIMPING WINTER TREADS,

AT MY POOR HOUSE LOOK TO BEHOLD THIS NIGHT EARTH-TREADING STARS THAT MAKE DARK HEAVEN LIGHT:

EVEN SUCH DELIGHT AMONG FRESH FEMALE BUDS SHALL YOU THIS NIGHT INHERIT AT MY HOUSE;

HEAR ALL, ALL SEE,

AND LIKE HER MOST WHOSE MERIT MOST SHALL BE: WHICH, ON MORE VIEW OF MANY, MINE BEING ONE, MAY STAND IN NUMBER,

THOUGH IN RECKONING NONE.

GO, SIRRAH, TRUDGE ABOUT THROUGH FAIR VERONA;

FIND THOSE PERSONS OUT WHOSE NAMES ARE WRITTEN THERE,

AND TO THEM SAY, MY HOUSE AND WELCOME ON THEIR PLEASURE STAY.

COME, GO WITH ME.

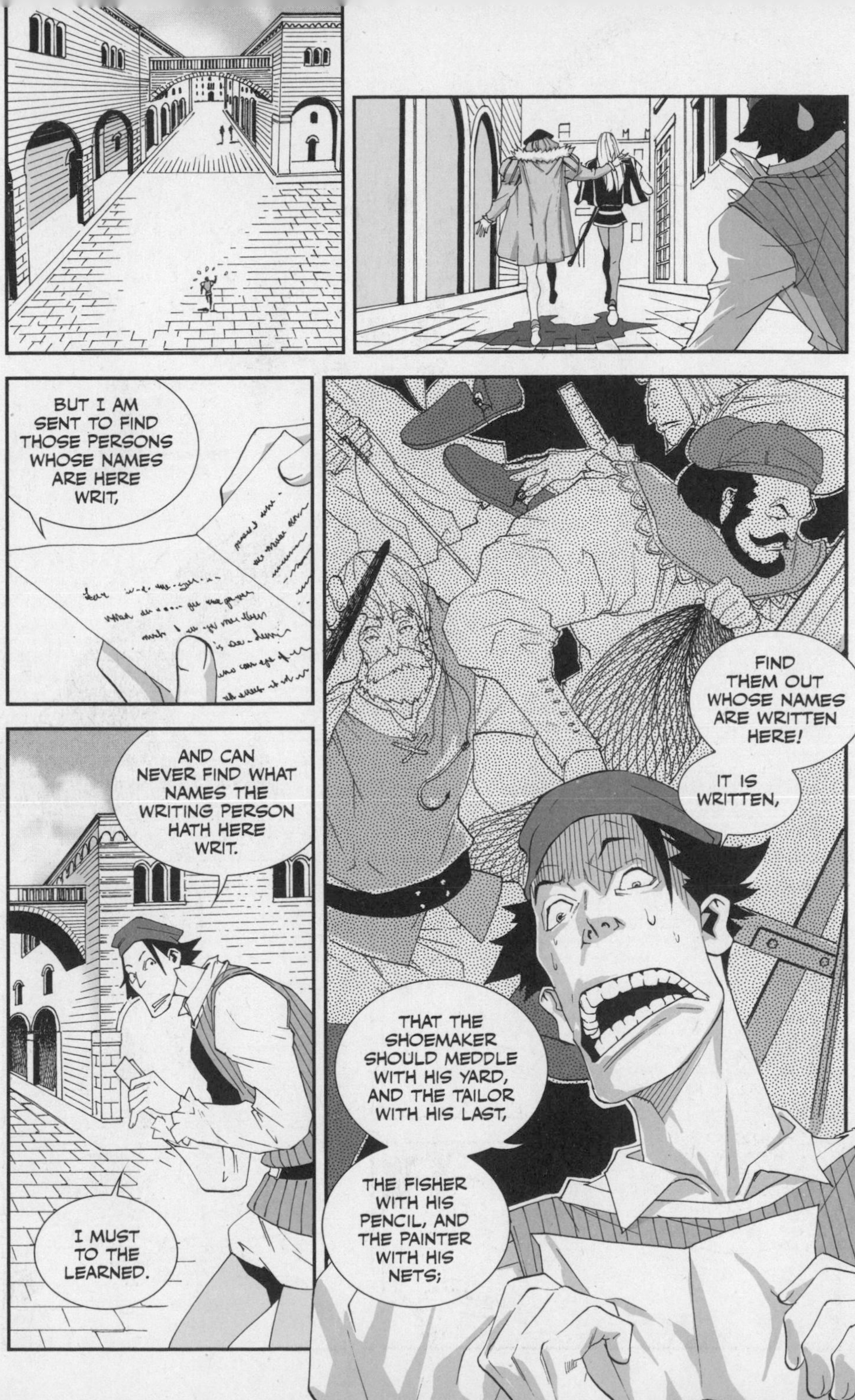
FIND THEM OUT WHOSE NAMES ARE WRITTEN HERE!
IT IS WRITTEN,
THAT THE SHOEMAKER SHOULD MEDDLE WITH HIS YARD, AND THE TAILOR WITH HIS LAST,
THE FISHER WITH HIS PENCIL, AND THE PAINTER WITH HIS NETS;
BUT I AM SENT TO FIND THOSE PERSONS WHOSE NAMES ARE HERE WRIT,
AND CAN NEVER FIND WHAT NAMES THE WRITING PERSON HATH HERE WRIT.
I MUST TO THE LEARNED.

IN GOOD TIME.

TUT, MAN, ONE FIRE BURNS OUT ANOTHER'S BURNING,

ONE DESPERATE GRIEF CURES WITH ANOTHER'S LANGUISH:

TAKE THOU SOME NEW INFECTION TO THY EYE,

AND THE RANK POISON OF THE OLD WILL DIE.

ONE PAIN IS LESSEN'D BY ANOTHER'S ANGUISH; TURN GIDDY, AND BE HOLP BY BACKWARD TURNING;

—S·TEP

YOUR PLAINTAIN-LEAF IS EXCELLENT FOR THAT.

NOT MAD, BUT BOUND MORE THAN A MAD-MAN IS; SHUT UP IN PRISON, KEPT WITHOUT MY FOOD, WHIPP'D AND TORMENTED AND —

GOD-DEN, GOOD FELLOW.

FOR YOUR BROKEN SHIN.

FOR WHAT, I PRAY THEE?

WHY, ROMEO, ART THOU MAD?

AY, MINE OWN FORTUNE IN MY MISERY.

GOD GI' GOD-DEN.

I PRAY, SIR, CAN YOU READ?

PERHAPS YOU HAVE LEARNED IT WITHOUT BOOK. BUT, I PRAY,

CAN YOU READ ANYTHING YOU SEE?

AY, IF I KNOW THE LETTERS AND THE LANGUAGE.

THWIP

STAY, FELLOW; I CAN READ.

YE SAY HONESTLY, REST YOU MERRY!

SIGNIOR MARTINO AND HIS WIFE AND DAUGHTERS; COUNTY ANSELME AND HIS BEAUTEOUS SISTERS;

THE LADY WIDOW OF VITRUVIO; SIGNIOR PLACENTIO AND HIS LOVELY NIECES; MERCUTIO AND HIS BROTHER VALENTINE;

MINE UNCLE CAPULET, HIS WIFE AND DAUGHTERS; MY FAIR NIECE ROSALINE;

LIVIA; SIGNIOR VALENTIO AND HIS COUSIN TYBALT, LUCIO AND THE LIVELY HELENA.

UP.

A FAIR ASSEMBLY: WHITHER SHOULD THEY COME?

WHITHER?

TO SUPPER; TO OUR HOUSE.

MY MASTER'S.

WHOSE HOUSE?

INDEED, I SHOULD HAVE ASK'D YOU THAT BEFORE.

AND SHE SHALL SCANT SHOW WELL THAT NOW SHOWS BEST.

I'LL GO ALONG, NO SUCH SIGHT TO BE SHOWN,

CAPULET'S HOUSE

BUT TO REJOICE IN SPLENDOR OF MINE OWN.

NURSE.

WHERE'S MY DAUGHTER? CALL HER FORTH TO ME.

ACT I
SCENE III

HM? HM? HM?

WHERE'S THIS GIRL?

FWIP

R-RIBBIT?

WHAT, JULIET!

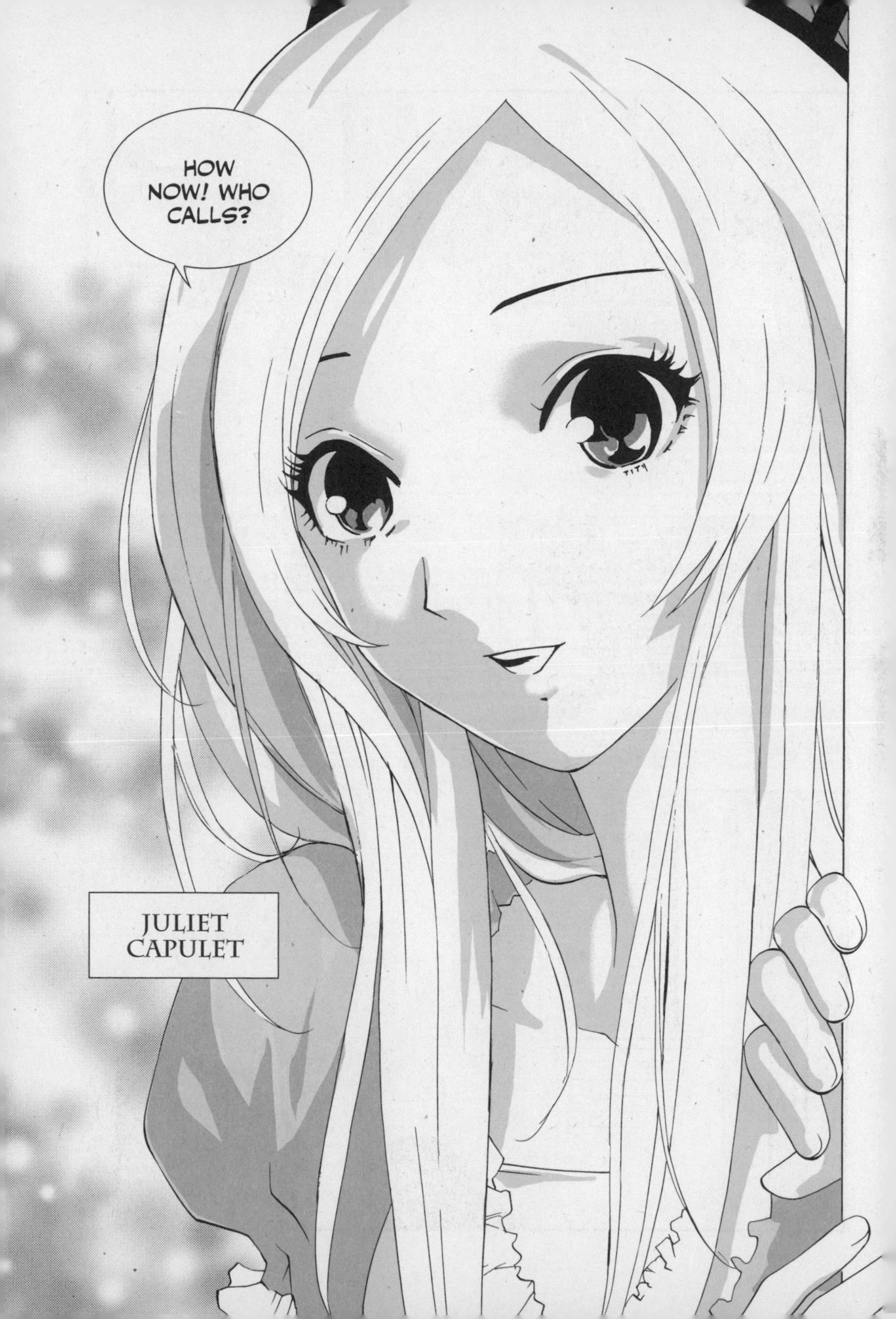
HOW NOW! WHO CALLS?
JULIET CAPULET

YOUR MOTHER.

MADAM, I AM HERE. WHAT IS YOUR WILL?

NURSE, GIVE LEAVE AWHILE, WE MUST TALK IN SECRET.

THIS IS THE MATTER —

NURSE, COME BACK AGAIN;

SLUMP

...

I HAVE REMEMBER'D ME, THOU'S HEAR OUR COUNSEL.

THOU KNOW'ST MY DAUGHTER'S OF A PRETTY AGE.

FAITH, I CAN TELL HER AGE UNTO AN HOUR.

I'LL LAY FOURTEEN OF MY TEETH —

AND YET, TO MY TEETH BE IT SPOKEN, I HAVE BUT FOUR —

SHE IS NOT FOURTEEN. HOW LONG IS IT NOW TO LAMMAS-TIDE?

SHE'S NOT FOURTEEN.

COME LAMMAS-EVE AT NIGHT SHALL SHE BE FOURTEEN. SUSAN AND SHE –

A FORTNIGHT AND ODD DAYS.

EVEN OR ODD, OF ALL DAYS IN THE YEAR,

BUT, AS I SAID, ON LAMMAS-EVE AT NIGHT SHALL SHE BE FOURTEEN; THAT SHALL SHE, MARRY; I REMEMBER IT WELL.

'TIS SINCE THE EARTHQUAKE NOW ELEVEN YEARS; AND SHE WAS WEAN'D –

I NEVER SHALL FORGET IT –

GOD REST ALL CHRISTIAN SOULS! –

WERE OF AN AGE: WELL, SUSAN IS WITH GOD;

SHE WAS TOO GOOD FOR ME:

MY LORD AND YOU WERE THEN AT MANTUA: NAY, I DO BEAR A BRAIN –

BUT, AS I SAID, WHEN IT DID TASTE THE WORMWOOD ON THE NIPPLE OF MY DUG AND FELT IT BITTER, PRETTY FOOL, TO SEE IT TETCHY AND FALL OUT WITH THE DUG!

OF ALL THE DAYS OF THE YEAR, UPON THAT DAY:

FOR I HAD THEN LAID WORMWOOD TO MY DUG, SITTING IN THE SUN UNDER THE DOVE-HOUSE WALL;

IT IS AN HONOUR THAT I DREAM NOT OF.

AN HONOUR!

LEAP!

TELL ME, DAUGHTER JULIET,

HOW STANDS YOUR DISPOSITION TO BE MARRIED?

WELL, THINK OF MARRIAGE NOW; YOUNGER THAN YOU,

WERE NOT I THINE ONLY NURSE, I WOULD SAY THOU HADST SUCK'D WISDOM FROM THY TEAT.

GRAB!

HERE IN VERONA, LADIES OF ESTEEM,

ARE MADE ALREADY MOTHERS:

THUS THEN IN BRIEF:

THE VALIANT PARIS SEEKS YOU FOR HIS LOVE.

BY MY COUNT, I WAS YOUR MOTHER MUCH UPON THESE YEARS THAT YOU ARE NOW A MAID.

LADY, SUCH A MAN AS ALL THE WORLD – WHY, HE'S A MAN OF WAX.

A MAN, YOUNG LADY!

NAY, HE'S A FLOWER; IN FAITH, A VERY FLOWER.

SNIFF

VERONA'S SUMMER HATH NOT SUCH A FLOWER.

WHAT SAY YOU? CAN YOU LOVE THE GENTLEMAN?

THIS NIGHT YOU SHALL BEHOLD HIM AT OUR FEAST;

READ O'ER THE VOLUME OF YOUNG PARIS' FACE, AND FIND DELIGHT WRIT THERE WITH BEAUTY'S PEN;

SPEAK BRIEFLY,
CAN YOU LIKE OF
PARIS' LOVE?

NO LESS!
NAY, BIGGER;
WOMEN GROW
BY MEN.

I'LL LOOK
TO LIKE, IF
LOOKING
LIKING
MOVE:

BUT NO
MORE DEEP WILL
I ENDART MINE
EYE THAN YOUR
CONSENT GIVES
STRENGTH TO
MAKE IT FLY.

MADAM, THE GUESTS ARE COME, SUPPER SERVED UP, YOU CALLED, MY YOUNG LADY ASKED FOR,

I MUST HENCE TO WAIT; I BESEECH YOU, FOLLOW STRAIGHT.

WE FOLLOW THEE.

THE NURSE CURSED IN THE PANTRY, AND EVERY THING IN EXTREMITY.

SHOVE!

YANK!

JULIET, THE COUNTY STAYS.

GO, GIRL, SEEK HAPPY NIGHTS TO HAPPY DAYS.

IS LOVE A TENDER THING?

AND, TO SINK IN IT, SHOULD YOU BURDEN LOVE;

TOO GREAT OPPRESSION FOR A TENDER THING.

IT IS TOO ROUGH,

TOO RUDE, TOO BOISTEROUS, AND IT PRICKS LIKE THORN.

PRICK LOVE FOR PRICKING, AND YOU BEAT LOVE DOWN.

IF LOVE BE ROUGH WITH YOU, BE ROUGH WITH LOVE;

SHUF
SHUF

SPRONG
SPRONG

'COME, KNOCK AND ENTER; AND NO SOONER IN,

BUT EVERY MAN BETAKE HIM TO HIS LEGS.

FOR I AM PROVERB'D WITH A GRANDSIRE PHRASE;

I'LL BE A CANDLE-HOLDER, AND LOOK ON. THE GAME WAS NE'ER SO FAIR, AND I AM DONE.

A TORCH FOR ME:

GRAB

LET WANTONS LIGHT OF HEART TICKLE THE SENSE-LESS RUSHES WITH THEIR HEELS,

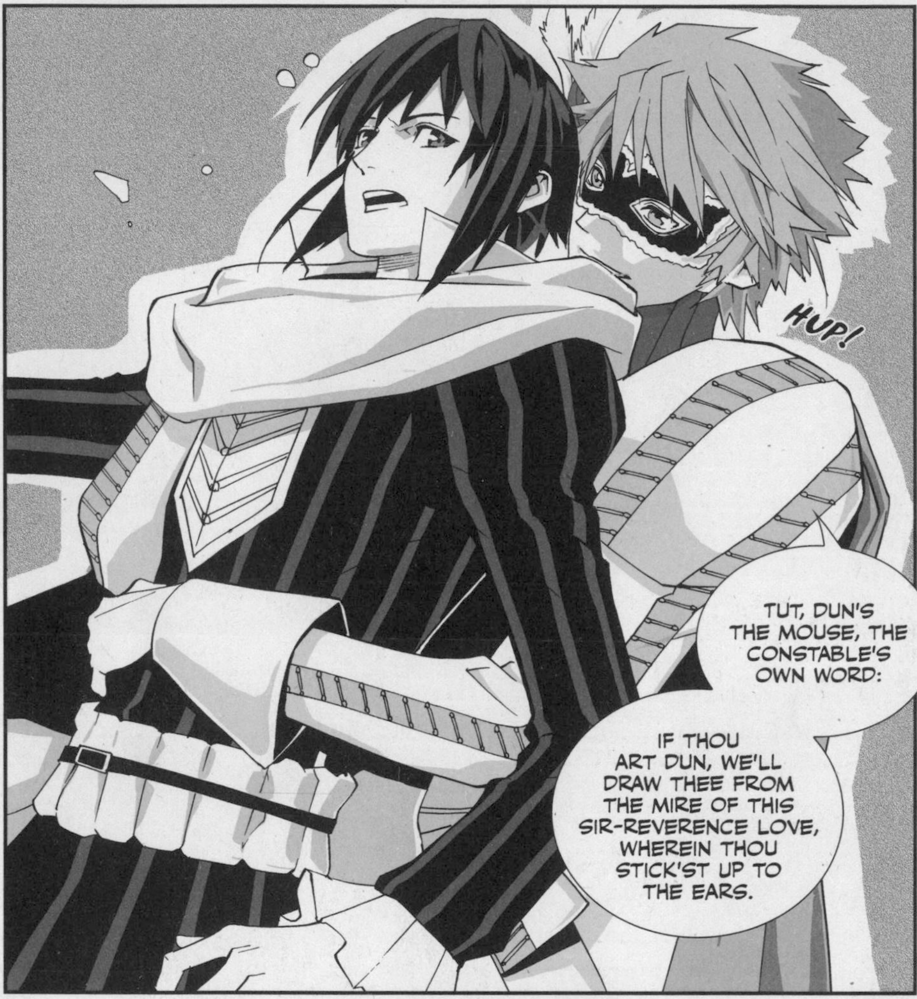
HUP!
TUT, DUN'S THE MOUSE, THE CONSTABLE'S OWN WORD:
IF THOU ART DUN, WE'LL DRAW THEE FROM THE MIRE OF THIS SIR-REVERENCE LOVE, WHEREIN THOU STICK'ST UP TO THE EARS.
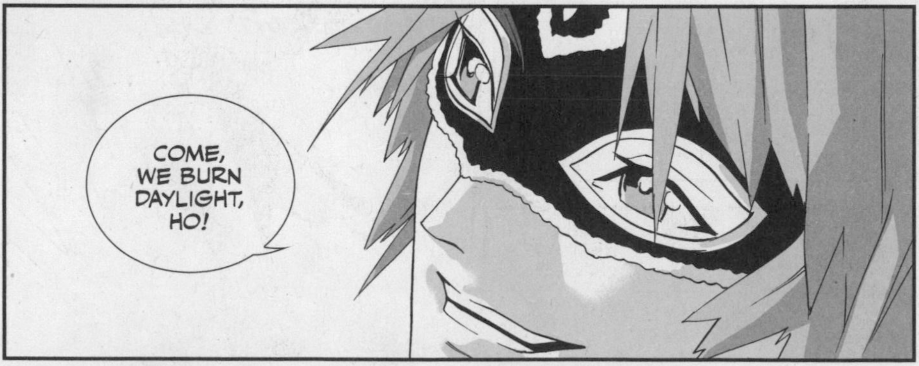
COME, WE BURN DAYLIGHT, HO!

NAY, THAT'S NOT SO.

I MEAN, SIR, IN DELAY WE WASTE OUR LIGHTS IN VAIN, LIKE LAMPS BY DAY.

FWIP

SHUFFLE

SHUFFLE

TAKE OUR GOOD MEANING, FOR OUR JUDGMENT SITS FIVE TIMES IN THAT ERE ONCE IN OUR FIVE WITS.

WHY, MAY ONE ASK?

I DREAM'D A DREAM TO-NIGHT.

AND SO DID I.

WELL, WHAT WAS YOURS?

AND WE MEAN WELL IN GOING TO THIS MASK; BUT 'TIS NO WIT TO GO.

PEACE, PEACE, MERCUTIO, PEACE!

THOU TALK'ST OF NOTHING.

POP!

THIS IS SHE —

TRUE, I TALK OF DREAMS, WHICH ARE THE CHILDREN OF AN IDLE BRAIN, BEGOT OF NOTHING BUT VAIN FANTASY,

WHICH IS AS THIN OF SUBSTANCE AS THE AIR AND MORE INCONSTANT THAN THE WIND,

WHO WOOES EVEN NOW THE FROZEN BOSOM OF THE NORTH, AND, BEING ANGER'D, PUFFS AWAY FROM THENCE,

TURNING HIS FACE TO THE DEW-DROPPING SOUTH.

SUPPER IS DONE, AND WE SHALL COME TOO LATE.

THIS WIND, YOU TALK OF BLOWS US FROM OURSELVES;

BUT HE, THAT HATH THE STEERAGE OF MY COURSE,

DIRECT MY SAIL! ON, LUSTY GENTLEMEN.

GRAB!

I FEAR, TOO EARLY: FOR MY MIND MISGIVES SOME CONSEQUENCE YET HANGING IN THE STARS SHALL BITTERLY BEGIN HIS FEARFUL DATE WITH THIS NIGHT'S REVELS AND EXPIRE THE TERM OF A DESPISED LIFE CLOSED IN MY BREAST BY SOME VILE FORFEIT OF UNTIMELY DEATH.

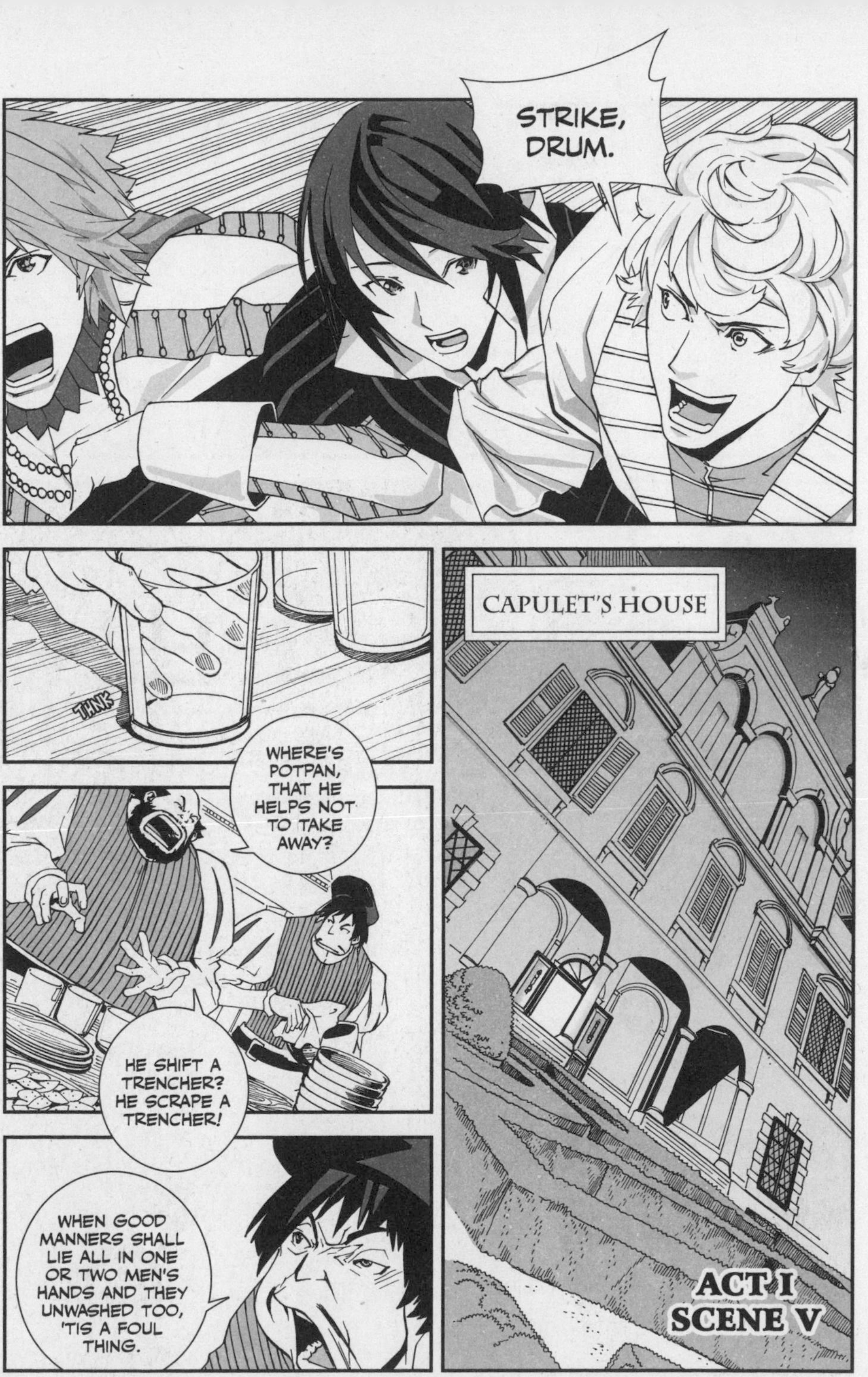
STRIKE, DRUM.
CAPULET'S HOUSE
ACT I SCENE V
THNK
WHERE'S POTPAN, THAT HE HELPS NOT TO TAKE AWAY?
HE SHIFT A TRENCHER? HE SCRAPE A TRENCHER!
WHEN GOOD MANNERS SHALL LIE ALL IN ONE OR TWO MEN'S HANDS AND THEY UNWASHED TOO, 'TIS A FOUL THING.

GOOD THOU, SAVE ME A PIECE OF MARCHPANE;

AND, AS THOU LOVEST ME, LET THE PORTER LET IN SUSAN GRINDSTONE AND NELL.

AWAY WITH THE JOINT-STOOLS, REMOVE THE COURT-CUPBOARD, LOOK TO THE PLATE.

AY, BOY, READY.

ANTONY, AND POTPAN!

WELCOME, GENTLEMEN! LADIES THAT HAVE THEIR TOES UNPLAGUED WITH CORNS WILL HAVE A BOUT WITH YOU.

AH HA, MY MISTRESSES! WHICH OF YOU ALL WILL NOW DENY TO DANCE?

SHE THAT MAKES DAINTY, SHE, I'LL SWEAR, HATH CORNS;

WE CANNOT BE HERE AND THERE TOO. CHEERLY, BOYS; BE BRISK AWHILE, AND THE LONGER LIVER TAKE ALL.

YOU ARE LOOKED FOR AND CALLED FOR, ASKED FOR AND SOUGHT FOR, IN THE GREAT CHAMBER.

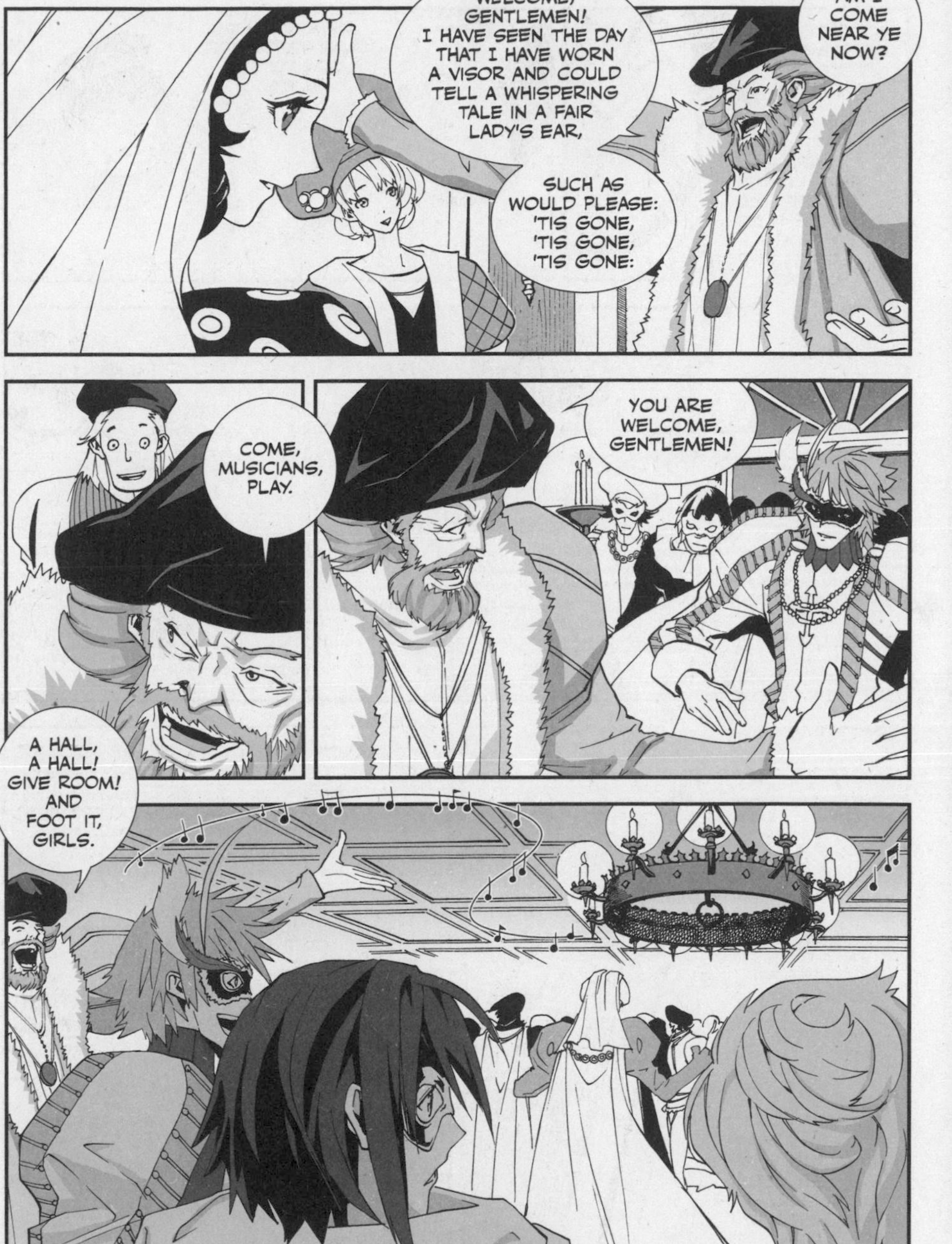
AM I COME NEAR YE NOW?
WELCOME, GENTLEMEN! I HAVE SEEN THE DAY THAT I HAVE WORN A VISOR AND COULD TELL A WHISPERING TALE IN A FAIR LADY'S EAR,
SUCH AS WOULD PLEASE: 'TIS GONE, 'TIS GONE, 'TIS GONE:
YOU ARE WELCOME, GENTLEMEN!
COME, MUSICIANS, PLAY.
A HALL, A HALL! GIVE ROOM! AND FOOT IT, GIRLS.

AH, SIRRAH, THIS UNLOOK'D-FOR SPORT COMES WELL.

MORE LIGHT, YOU KNAVES; AND TURN THE TABLES UP,

AND QUENCH THE FIRE, THE ROOM IS GROWN TOO HOT.

FOR YOU AND I ARE PAST OUR DANCING DAYS: HOW LONG IS'T NOW SINCE LAST YOURSELF AND I WERE IN A MASK?

BY'R LADY, THIRTY YEARS.

NAY, SIT, NAY, SIT, GOOD COUSIN CAPULET;

'TIS MORE, 'TIS MORE, HIS SON IS ELDER, SIR; HIS SON IS THIRTY.

WILL YOU TELL ME THAT? HIS SON WAS BUT A WARD TWO YEARS AGO.

WHAT, MAN! 'TIS NOT SO MUCH, 'TIS NOT SO MUCH:

'TIS SINCE THE NUPTIALS OF LUCENTIO, COME PENTECOST AS QUICKLY AS IT WILL,

SOME FIVE AND TWENTY YEARS; AND THEN WE MASK'D.

FOR I NE'ER SAW TRUE BEAUTY TILL THIS NIGHT.

THIS, BY HIS VOICE, SHOULD BE A MONTAGUE.

FETCH ME MY RAPIER, BOY.

WHAT DARES THE SLAVE COME HITHER, COVER'D WITH AN ANTIC FACE, TO FLEER AND SCORN AT OUR SOLEMNITY?

WHY, HOW NOW, KINSMAN! WHEREFORE STORM YOU SO?

NOW, BY THE STOCK AND HONOUR OF MY KIN, TO STRIKE HIM DEAD, I HOLD IT NOT A SIN.

SHING

UNCLE, THIS IS A MONTAGUE, OUR FOE,

A VILLAIN THAT IS HITHER COME IN SPITE, TO SCORN AT OUR SOLEMNITY THIS NIGHT.

YOUNG ROMEO IS IT?

'TIS HE, THAT VILLAIN ROMEO.

PAT

CONTENT THEE, GENTLE COZ, LET HIM ALONE; HE BEARS HIM LIKE A PORTLY GENTLEMAN;

AND, TO SAY TRUTH, VERONA BRAGS OF HIM TO BE A VIRTUOUS AND WELL-GOVERN'D YOUTH:

I WOULD NOT FOR THE WEALTH OF ALL THE TOWN HERE IN MY HOUSE DO HIM DISPARAGEMENT:

THEREFORE BE PATIENT, TAKE NO NOTE OF HIM:

IT IS MY WILL,

THE WHICH IF THOU RESPECT, SHOW A FAIR PRESENCE AND PUT OFF THESE FROWNS, AN ILL-BESEEMING SEMBLANCE FOR A FEAST.

IT FITS, WHEN SUCH A VILLAIN IS A GUEST: I'LL NOT ENDURE HIM.

HE SHALL BE ENDURED:

WHAT, GOODMAN BOY! I SAY, HE SHALL: GO TO;

TREMBLE

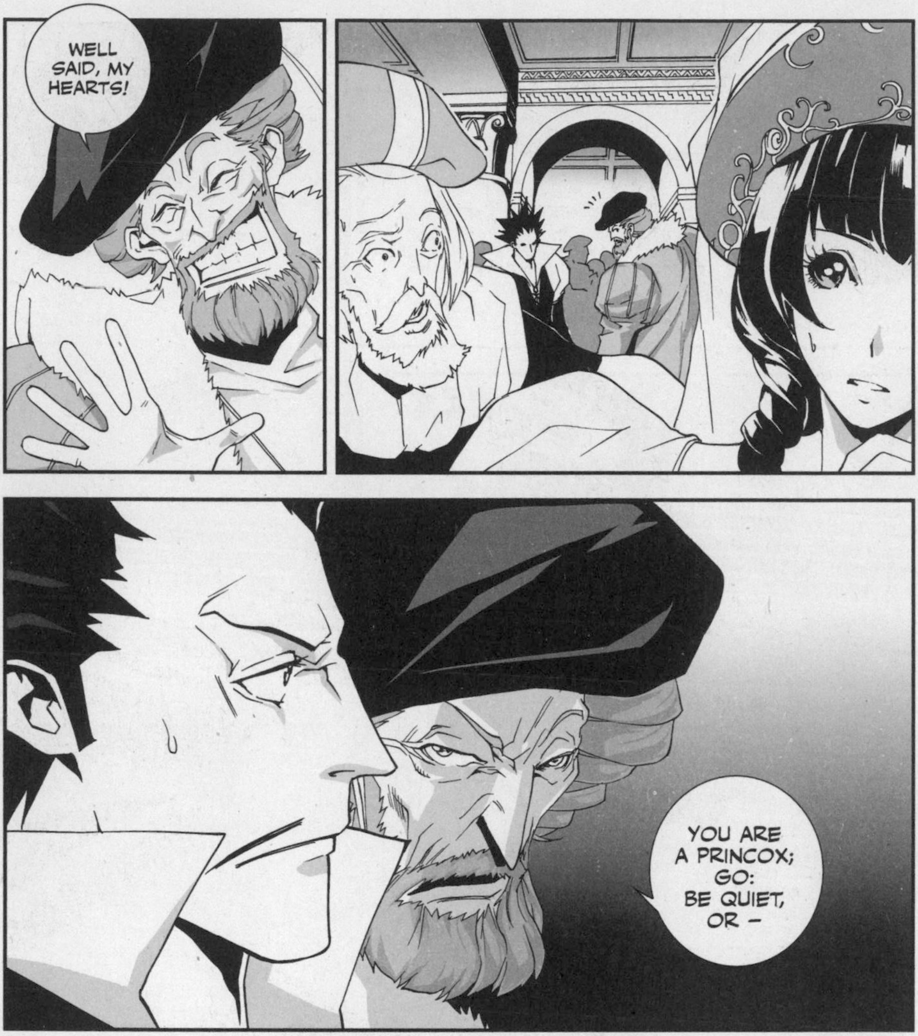
WELL SAID, MY HEARTS!
YOU ARE A PRINCOX; GO: BE QUIET, OR –
MORE LIGHT, MORE LIGHT!
...

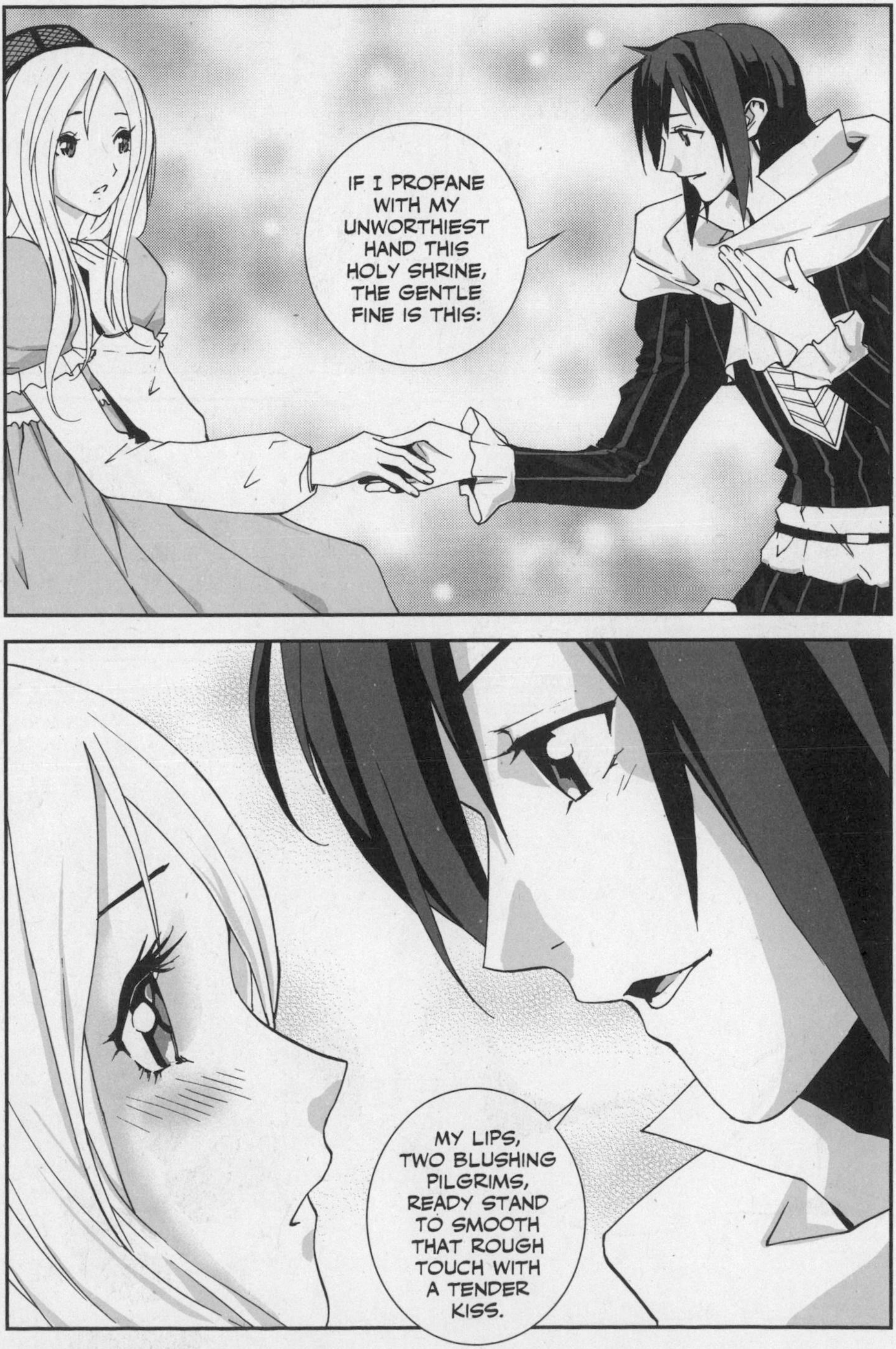
IF I PROFANE WITH MY UNWORTHIEST HAND THIS HOLY SHRINE, THE GENTLE FINE IS THIS:
MY LIPS, TWO BLUSHING PILGRIMS, READY STAND TO SMOOTH THAT ROUGH TOUCH WITH A TENDER KISS.

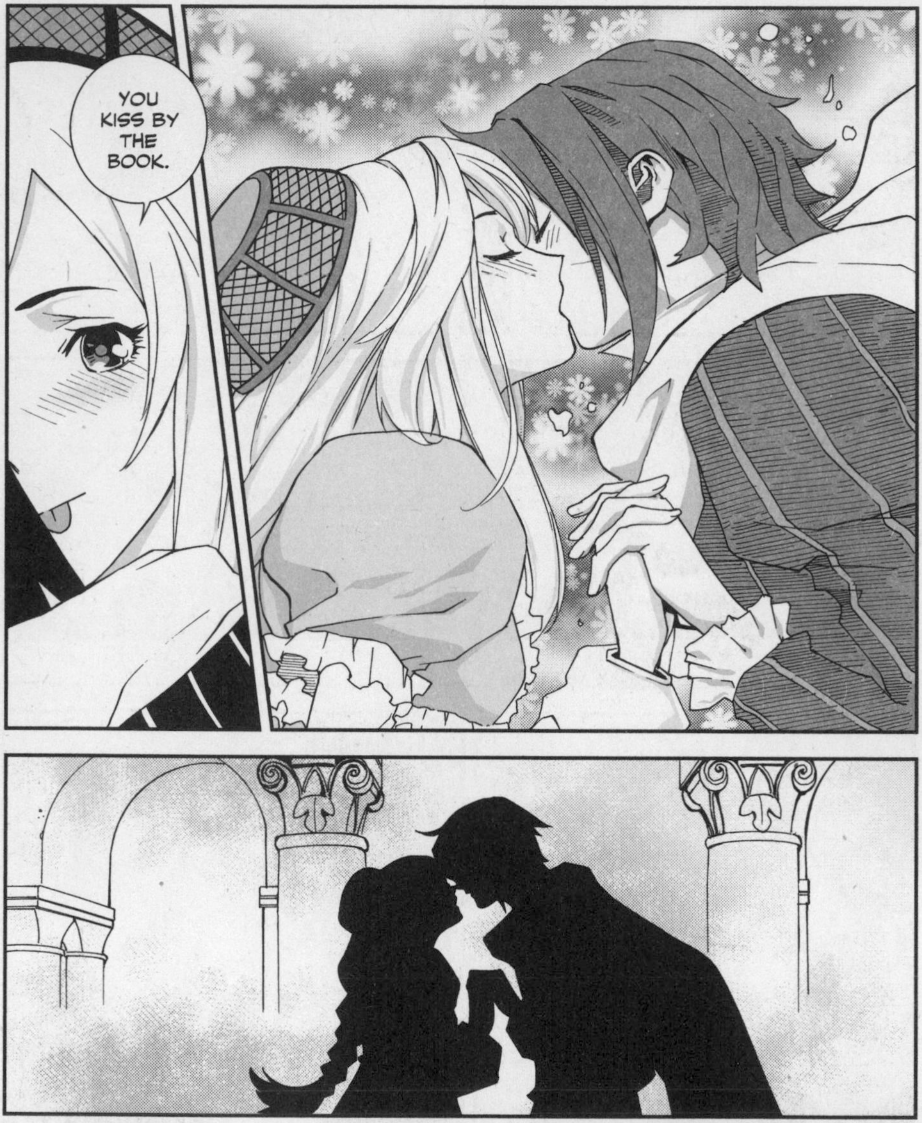
YOU KISS BY THE BOOK.
MADAM,
OH!

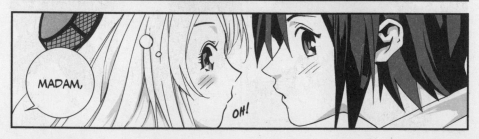

...

HUSTLE HUSTLE!

YOUR MOTHER CRAVES A WORD WITH YOU.

......

MARRY, BACHELOR, HER MOTHER IS THE LADY OF THE HOUSE, AND A GOOD LADY,

AND A WISE AND VIRTUOUS I NURSED HER DAUGHTER,

THAT YOU TALK'D WITHAL;

WHAT IS HER MOTHER?

I TELL YOU, HE THAT CAN LAY HOLD OF HER SHALL HAVE THE CHINKS.

WHUMP!

AWAY, BEGONE; THE SPORT IS AT THE BEST.

IS SHE A CAPULET? O DEAR ACCOUNT! MY LIFE IS MY FOE'S DEBT.

AY, SO I FEAR; THE MORE IS MY UNREST.

COME HITHER, NURSE. WHAT IS YOND GENTLEMAN?

GOODBYE!

FAREWELL!

THE SON AND HEIR OF OLD TIBERIO.

WHAT'S HE THAT FOLLOWS THERE, THAT WOULD NOT DANCE?

WHAT'S HE THAT NOW IS GOING OUT OF DOOR?

MARRY, THAT, I THINK, BE YOUNG PETRUCIO.

I KNOW NOT.

MY GRAVE IS LIKE TO BE MY WEDDING BED.

GO ASK HIS NAME: IF HE BE MARRIED,

HIS NAME IS ROMEO, AND A MONTAGUE;

THE ONLY SON OF YOUR GREAT ENEMY.

ACT II

NOW OLD DESIRE DOTH IN HIS DEATH-BED LIE,
AND YOUNG AFFECTION GAPES TO BE HIS HEIR;
THAT FAIR FOR WHICH LOVE GROAN'D FOR, AND WOULD DIE,
WITH TENDER JULIET MATCH'D, IS NOW NOT FAIR.

NOW ROMEO IS BELOVED AND LOVES AGAIN,
ALIKE BEWITCHED BY THE CHARM OF LOOKS;
BUT TO HIS FOE SUPPOSED HE MUST COMPLAIN,
AND SHE STEAL LOVE'S SWEET BAIT FROM FEARFUL HOOKS:

BEING HELD A FOE, HE MAY NOT HAVE ACCESS
TO BREATHE SUCH VOWS AS LOVERS USED TO SWEAR;
AND SHE AS MUCH IN LOVE, HER MEANS MUCH LESS
TO MEET HER NEW BELOVED ANYWHERE:

BUT PASSION LENDS THEM POWER, TIME MEANS, TO MEET,
TEMPERING EXTREMITIES WITH EXTREME SWEET.

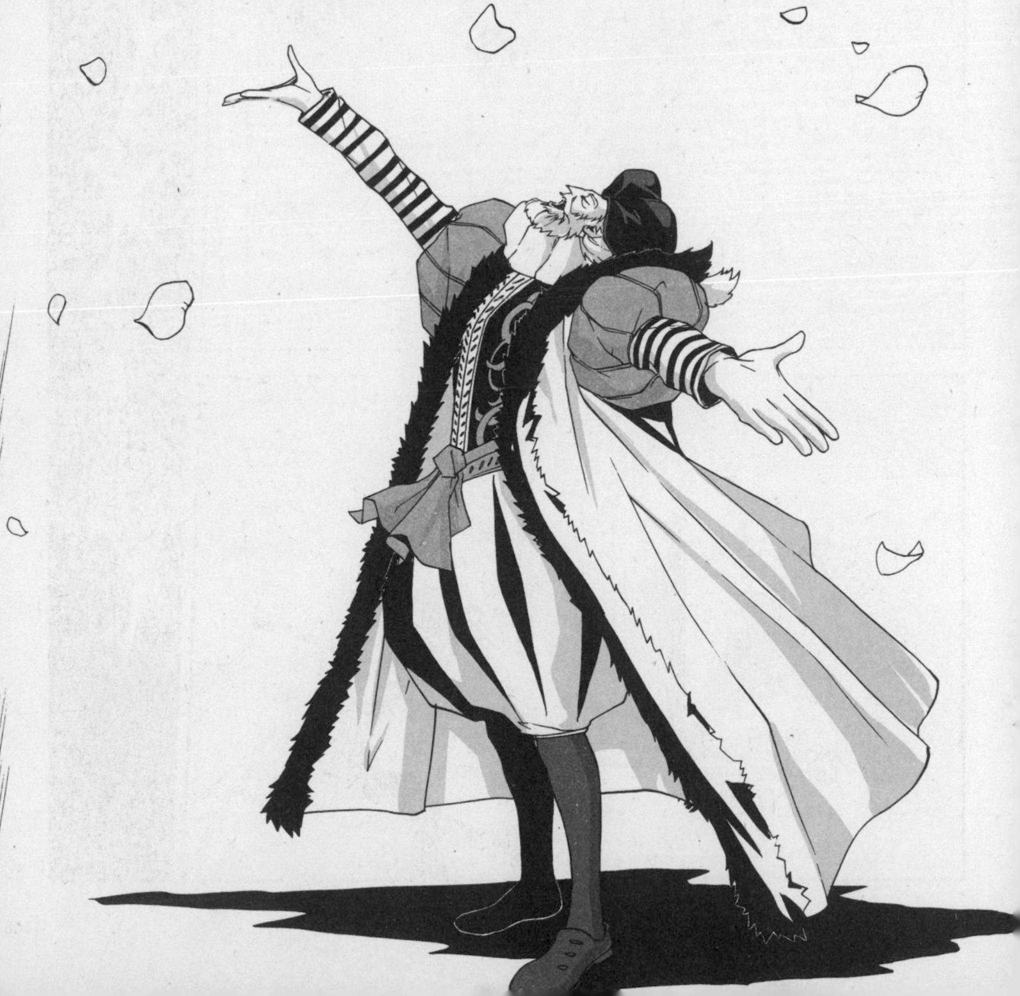

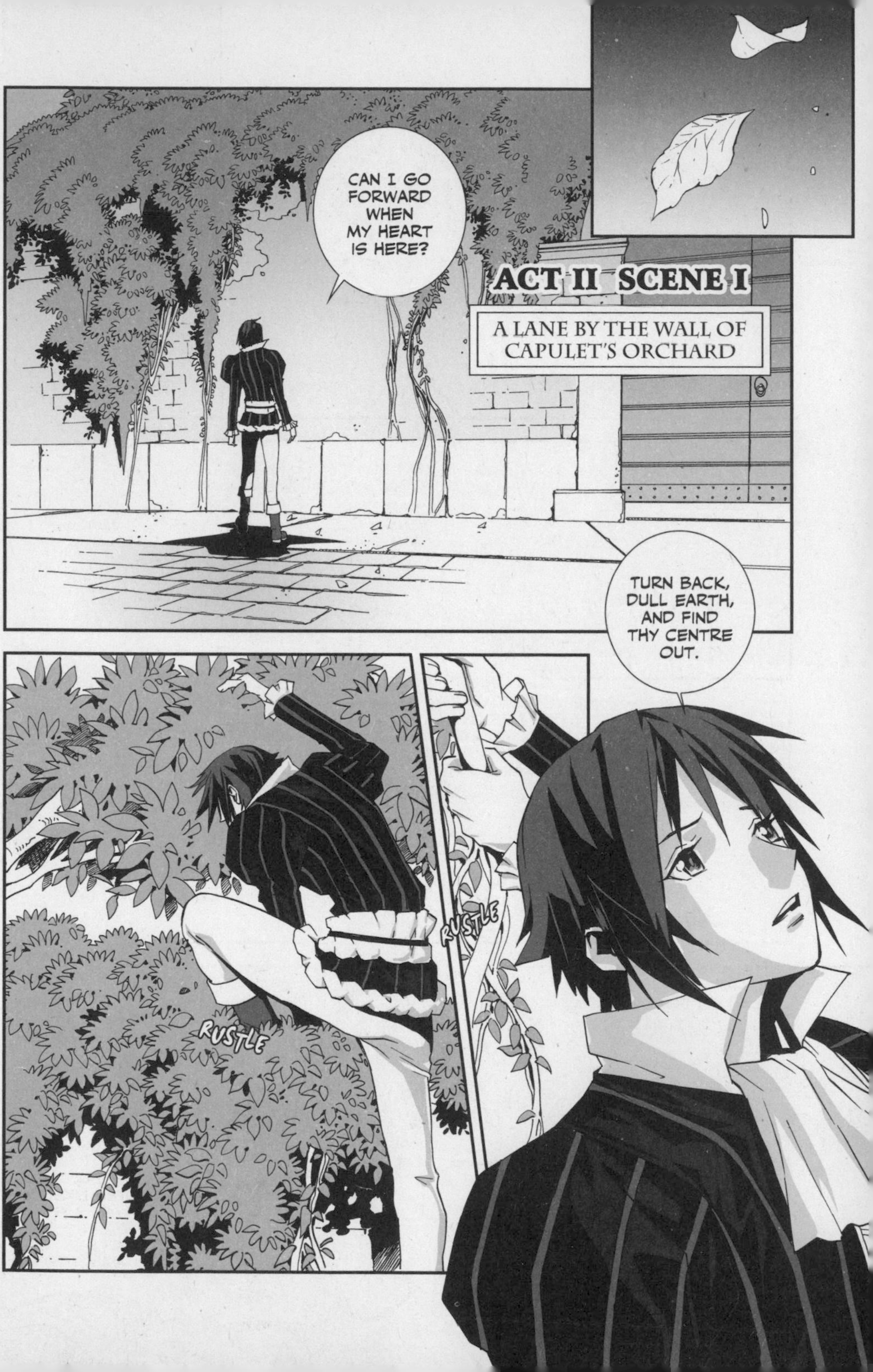
ACT II SCENE I
A LANE BY THE WALL OF CAPULET'S ORCHARD
CAN I GO FORWARD WHEN MY HEART IS HERE?
TURN BACK, DULL EARTH, AND FIND THY CENTRE OUT.
RUSTLE
RUSTLE

HE THAT SHOT SO TRIM, WHEN KING COPHETUA LOVED THE BEGGAR-MAID!

I CONJURE THEE BY ROSALINE'S BRIGHT EYES, BY HER HIGH FOREHEAD AND HER SCARLET LIP,

BY HER FINE FOOT, STRAIGHT LEG AND QUIVERING THIGH AND THE DEMESNES THAT THERE ADJACENT LIE,

THAT IN THY LIKENESS THOU APPEAR TO US!

AND IF HE HEAR THEE, THOU WILT ANGER HIM.

HE HEARETH NOT, HE STIRRETH NOT, HE MOVETH NOT; THE APE IS DEAD, AND I MUST CONJURE HIM.

114

HE JESTS AT SCARS THAT NEVER FELT A WOUND.

BUT, SOFT! WHAT LIGHT THROUGH YONDER WINDOW BREAKS?

IT IS THE EAST, AND JULIET IS THE SUN.

ACT II SCENE II

SIIIGH

RUSTLE...

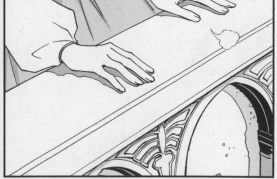

O ROMEO, ROMEO! WHEREFORE ART THOU ROMEO?

DENY THY FATHER AND REFUSE THY NAME; OR, IF THOU WILT NOT, BE BUT SWORN MY LOVE,

AND I'LL NO LONGER BE A CAPULET.

'TIS BUT THY NAME THAT IS MY ENEMY; THOU ART THYSELF, THOUGH NOT A MONTAGUE.

WHAT'S MONTAGUE?

IT IS NOR HAND, NOR FOOT, NOR ARM, NOR FACE, NOR ANY OTHER PART BELONGING TO A MAN. O, BE SOME OTHER NAME!

SHALL I HEAR MORE, OR SHALL I SPEAK AT THIS?

WHAT'S IN A NAME? THAT WHICH WE CALL A ROSE BY ANY OTHER NAME WOULD SMELL AS SWEET;

SO ROMEO WOULD, WERE HE NOT ROMEO CALL'D, RETAIN THAT DEAR PERFECTION WHICH HE OWES WITHOUT THAT TITLE.

ROMEO, DOFF THY NAME,

AND FOR THAT NAME WHICH IS NO PART OF THEE, TAKE ALL MYSELF.

I WOULD NOT FOR THE WORLD THEY SAW THEE HERE.

CLANCE CLANCE

OHH...

I HAVE NIGHT'S CLOAK TO HIDE ME FROM THEIR SIGHT; AND BUT THOU LOVE ME, LET THEM FIND ME HERE:

MY LIFE WERE BETTER ENDED BY THEIR HATE, THAN DEATH PROROGUED, WANTING OF THY LOVE.

BY WHOSE DIRECTION FOUND'ST THOU OUT THIS PLACE?

BY LOVE, WHO FIRST DID PROMPT ME TO INQUIRE; HE LENT ME COUNSEL AND I LENT HIM EYES.

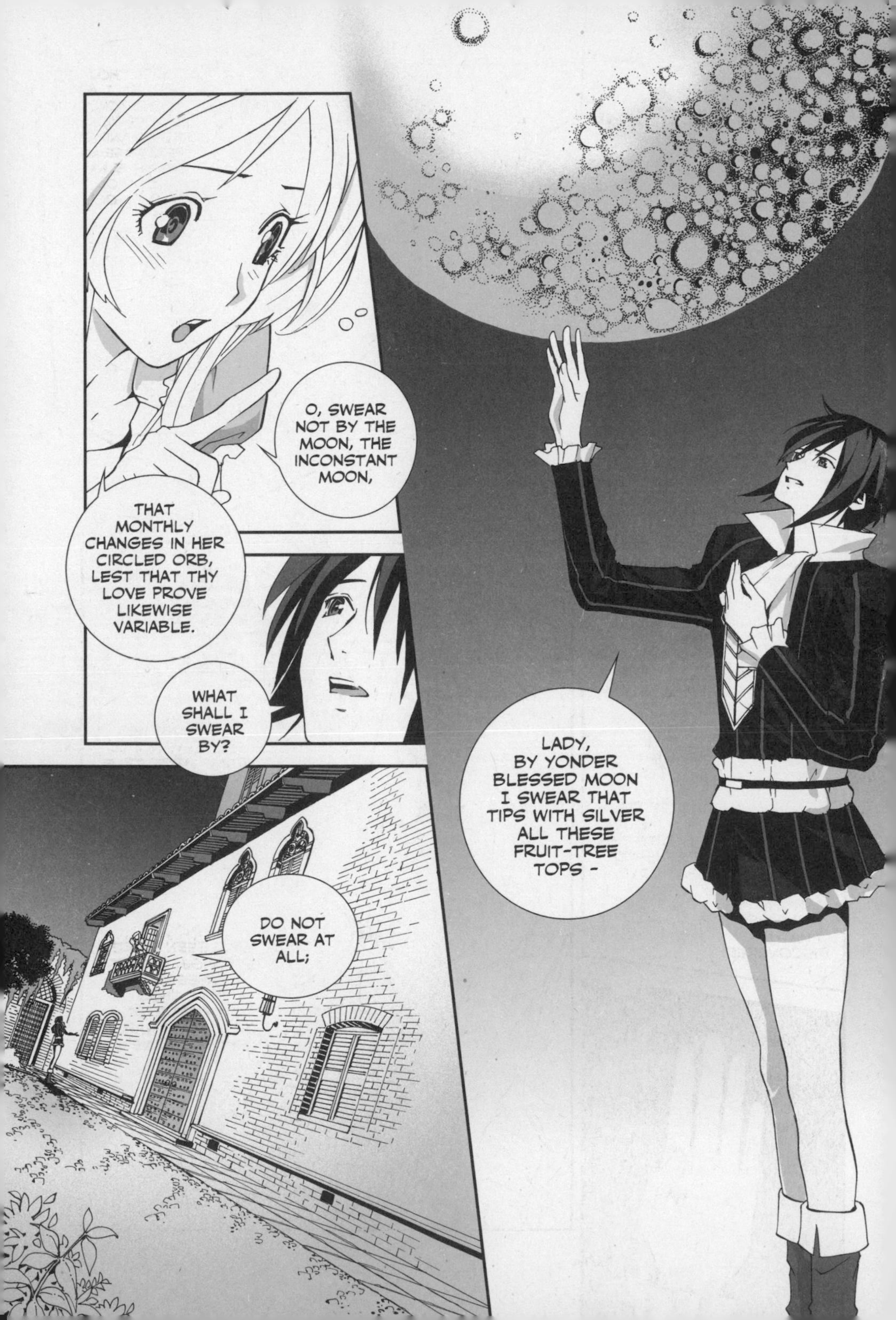
LADY, BY YONDER BLESSED MOON I SWEAR THAT TIPS WITH SILVER ALL THESE FRUIT-TREE TOPS -
O, SWEAR NOT BY THE MOON, THE INCONSTANT MOON,
THAT MONTHLY CHANGES IN HER CIRCLED ORB, LEST THAT THY LOVE PROVE LIKEWISE VARIABLE.
WHAT SHALL I SWEAR BY?
DO NOT SWEAR AT ALL;

SWEET, GOOD NIGHT! THIS BUD OF LOVE, BY SUMMER'S RIPENING BREATH,

MAY PROVE A BEAUTEOUS FLOWER WHEN NEXT WE MEET.

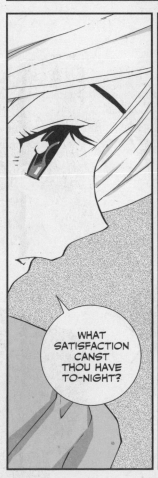

WHAT SATISFACTION CANST THOU HAVE TO-NIGHT?

O, WILT THOU LEAVE ME SO UNSATISFIED?

SHUT

GOOD NIGHT, GOOD NIGHT!

AS SWEET REPOSE AND REST COME TO THY HEART AS THAT WITHIN MY BREAST!

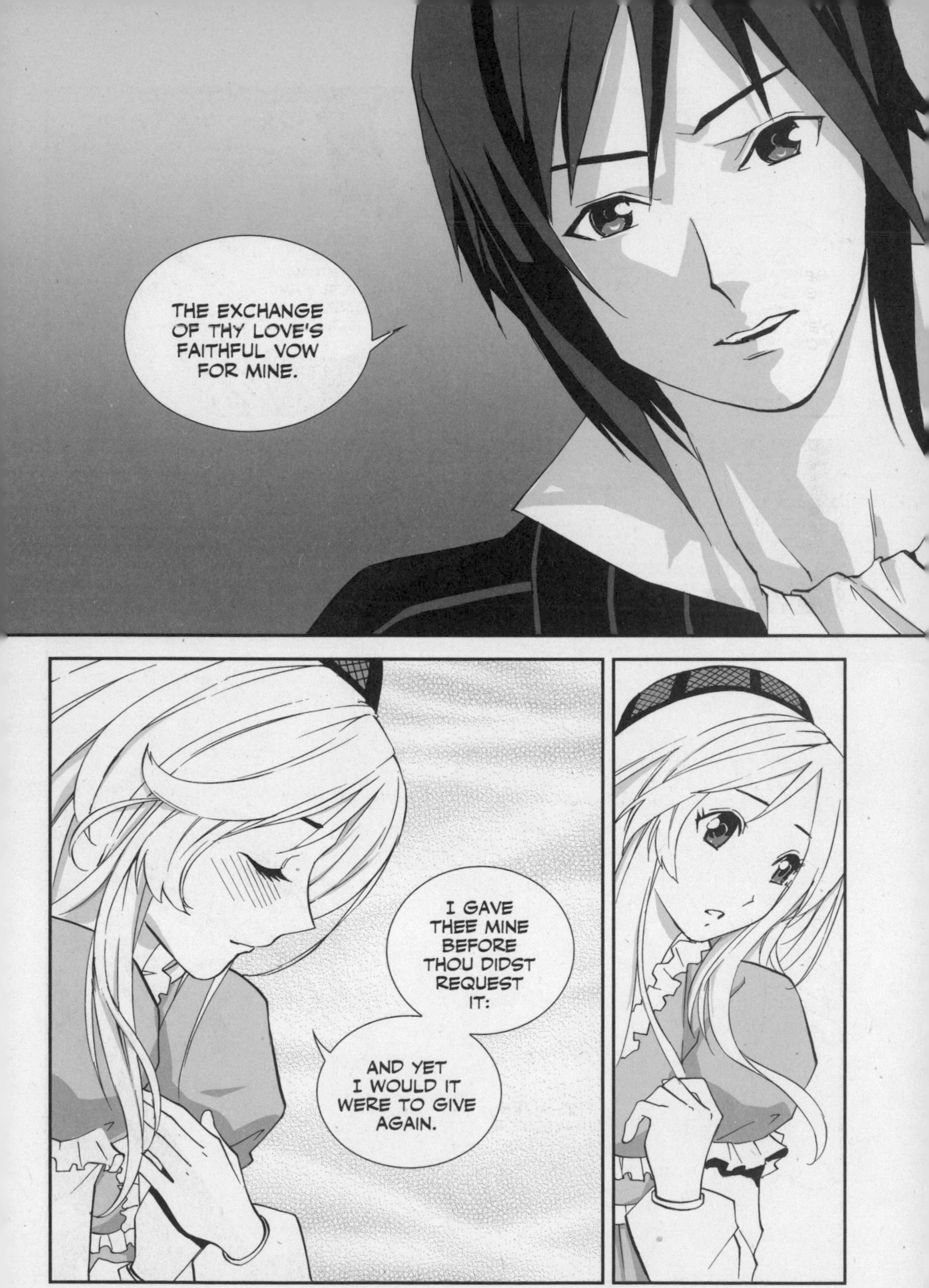
THE EXCHANGE OF THY LOVE'S FAITHFUL VOW FOR MINE.
I GAVE THEE MINE BEFORE THOU DIDST REQUEST IT:
AND YET I WOULD IT WERE TO GIVE AGAIN.

BUT TO BE FRANK, AND GIVE IT THEE AGAIN. AND YET I WISH BUT FOR THE THING I HAVE:

WOULDST THOU WITHDRAW IT? FOR WHAT PURPOSE, LOVE?

MY BOUNTY IS AS BOUNDLESS AS THE SEA,

MY LOVE AS DEEP; THE MORE I GIVE TO THEE,

THE MORE I HAVE, FOR BOTH ARE INFINITE.

SO THRIVE MY SOUL —

TO CEASE THY STRIFE AND LEAVE ME TO MY GRIEF: TO-MORROW WILL I SEND.

A THOUSAND TIMES GOOD NIGHT!

DASH

A THOUSAND TIMES THE WORSE, TO WANT THY LIGHT.

LOVE GOES TOWARD LOVE, AS SCHOOLBOYS FROM THEIR BOOKS,

BUT LOVE FROM LOVE, TOWARD SCHOOL WITH HEAVY LOOKS.

FOR THIS, BEING SMELT, WITH THAT PART CHEERS EACH PART; BEING TASTED, SLAYS ALL SENSES WITH THE HEART.

URGH!

SNIFF

TWO SUCH OPPOSED KINGS ENCAMP THEM STILL, IN MAN AS WELL AS HERBS, GRACE AND RUDE WILL;

AND WHERE THE WORSER IS PREDOMINANT, FULL SOON THE CANKER DEATH EATS UP THAT PLANT.

WITHIN THE INFANT RIND OF THIS SMALL FLOWER, POISON HATH RESIDENCE AND MEDICINE POWER:

GOOD MORROW, FATHER.

YOUNG SON, IT ARGUES A DISTEMPER'D HEAD SO SOON TO BID GOOD MORROW TO THY BED:

BENEDICITE!

WHAT EARLY TONGUE SO SWEET SALUTETH ME?

BUT WHERE UNBRUISED YOUTH WITH UNSTUFF'D BRAIN DOTH COUCH HIS LIMBS, THERE GOLDEN SLEEP DOTH REIGN:

CARE KEEPS HIS WATCH IN EVERY OLD MAN'S EYE, AND WHERE CARE LODGES, SLEEP WILL NEVER LIE;

GRASP

GOD PARDON SIN! WAST THOU WITH ROSALINE?

THEREFORE THY EARLINESS DOTH ME ASSURE THOU ART UP-ROUSED BY SOME DISTEMPERATURE;

AHEH...

OR IF NOT SO, THEN HERE I HIT IT RIGHT,

OUR ROMEO HATH NOT BEEN IN BED TO-NIGHT.

THAT LAST IS TRUE; THE SWEETER REST WAS MINE.

WITH ROSALINE, MY GHOSTLY FATHER?

NO; I HAVE FORGOT THAT NAME, AND THAT NAME'S WOE.

THAT'S MY GOOD SON: BUT WHERE HAST THOU BEEN, THEN?

I'LL TELL THEE, ERE THOU ASK IT ME AGAIN.

PAT

BOTH OUR REMEDIES WITHIN THY HELP AND HOLY PHYSIC LIES:

I BEAR NO HATRED, BLESSED MAN, FOR, LO, MY INTERCESSION LIKEWISE STEADS MY FOE.

I HAVE BEEN FEASTING WITH MINE ENEMY, WHERE ON A SUDDEN ONE HATH WOUNDED ME, THAT'S BY ME WOUNDED:

BE PLAIN, GOOD SON, AND HOMELY IN THY DRIFT;

EH?

RIDDLING CONFESSION FINDS BUT RIDDLING SHRIFT.

THOU CHID'ST ME OFT FOR LOVING ROSALINE.

PRONOUNCE THIS SENTENCE THEN, WOMEN MAY FALL, WHEN THERE'S NO STRENGTH IN MEN.

AND BAD'ST ME BURY LOVE.

FOR DOTING, NOT FOR LOVING, PUPIL MINE.

TWEET!

I PRAY THEE, 'CHIDE NOT; SHE WHOM I LOVE NOW DOTH GRACE FOR GRACE AND LOVE FOR LOVE ALLOW;

THE OTHER DID NOT SO.

BONK!

NOT IN A GRAVE, TO LAY ONE IN, ANOTHER OUT TO HAVE.

BUT COME, YOUNG WAVERER, COME, GO WITH ME, IN ONE RESPECT I'LL THY ASSISTANT BE;

FOR THIS ALLIANCE MAY SO HAPPY PROVE, TO TURN YOUR HOUSEHOLDS' RANCOUR TO PURE LOVE.

O, SHE KNEW WELL THY LOVE DID READ BY ROTE AND COULD NOT SPELL.

WISELY AND SLOW; THEY STUMBLE THAT RUN FAST.

ZOOOOOOM~

O, LET US HENCE; I STAND ON SUDDEN HASTE.

ZWIP!

NOT TO HIS FATHER'S; I SPOKE WITH HIS MAN.

WHERE THE DEVIL SHOULD THIS ROMEO BE?

CAME HE NOT HOME TONIGHT?

ACT II
SCENE IV

AH, THAT SAME PALE HARD-HEARTED WENCH, THAT ROSALINE,

TORMENTS HIM SO THAT HE WILL SURE RUN MAD.

TYBALT, THE KINSMAN OF OLD CAPULET, HATH SENT A LETTER TO HIS FATHER'S HOUSE.

A CHALLENGE, ON MY LIFE.

NAY, HE WILL ANSWER THE LETTER'S MASTER, HOW HE DARES, BEING DARED.

PSSH!

ANY MAN THAT CAN WRITE MAY ANSWER A LETTER.

ROMEO WILL ANSWER IT.

THE VERY PIN OF HIS HEART CLEFT WITH THE BLIND BOW-BOY'S BUTT-SHAFT: AND IS HE A MAN TO ENCOUNTER TYBALT?

ALAS, POOR ROMEO! HE IS ALREADY DEAD; STABBED WITH A WHITE WENCH'S BLACK EYE; SHOT THROUGH THE EAR WITH A LOVE-SONG;

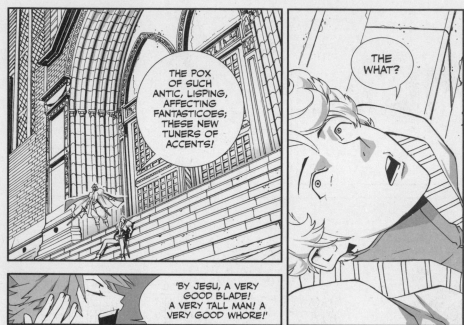

THE POX OF SUCH ANTIC, LISPING, AFFECTING FANTASTICOES; THESE NEW TUNERS OF ACCENTS!

THE WHAT?

'BY JESU, A VERY GOOD BLADE! A VERY TALL MAN! A VERY GOOD WHORE!'

WHY, IS NOT THIS A LAMENTABLE THING, GRANDSIRE,

THAT WE SHOULD BE THUS AFFLICTED WITH THESE STRANGE FLIES, THESE FASHION-MONGERS, THESE PARDON-ME'S,

WHO STAND SO MUCH ON THE NEW FORM, THAT THEY CANNOT SIT AT EASE ON THE OLD BENCH? O, THEIR BONES, THEIR BONES!

WITHOUT HIS ROE, LIKE A DRIED HERRING: O FLESH, FLESH, HOW ART THOU FISHIFIED!

HERE COMES ROMEO, HERE COMES ROMEO!

NOW IS HE FOR THE NUMBERS THAT PETRARCH FLOWED IN: LAURA TO HIS LADY WAS BUT A KITCHEN-WENCH;

DIDO A DOWDY; CLEOPATRA A GIPSY; HELEN AND HERO HILDINGS AND HARLOTS;

THISBE A GREY EYE OR SO, BUT NOT TO THE PURPOSE.

MARRY, SHE HAD A BETTER LOVE TO BE-RHYME HER;

THE SLIP, SIR, THE SLIP; CAN YOU NOT CONCEIVE?

PARDON, GOOD MERCUTIO, MY BUSINESS WAS GREAT; AND IN SUCH A CASE AS MINE A MAN MAY STRAIN COURTESY.

MWAH!

GOOD MORROW TO YOU BOTH. WHAT COUNTERFEIT DID I GIVE YOU?

SIGNIOR ROMEO, BONJOUR.

THERE'S A FRENCH SALUTATION TO YOUR FRENCH SLOP. YOU GAVE US THE COUNTERFEIT FAIRLY LAST NIGHT.

MEANING, TO COURT'SY.

DOKE

THOU HAST MOST KINDLY HIT IT.

SUCH A CASE AS YOURS CONSTRAINS A MAN TO BOW IN THE HAMS.

THAT'S AS MUCH AS TO SAY,

HYUP

A MOST COURTEOUS EXPOSITION.

NAY, I AM THE VERY PINK OF COURTESY.

THOU WAST NEVER WITH ME FOR ANYTHING WHEN THOU WAST NOT THERE FOR THE GOOSE.

I WILL BITE THEE BY THE EAR FOR THAT JEST.

THY WIT IS A VERY BITTER SWEETING; IT IS A MOST SHARP SAUCE.

NAY, GOOD GOOSE, BITE NOT.

AND IS IT NOT WELL SERVED IN TO A SWEET GOOSE?

CHOMP

O HERE'S A WIT OF CHEVERIL, THAT STRETCHES FROM AN INCH NARROW TO AN ELL BROAD!

I STRETCH IT OUT FOR THAT WORD BROAD: WHICH ADDED TO THE GOOSE,

PROVES THEE FAR AND WIDE A BROAD GOOSE.

NOW ART THOU SOCIABLE, NOW ART THOU ROMEO; NOW ART THOU WHAT THOU ART, BY ART AS WELL AS BY NATURE:

WHY, IS NOT THIS BETTER NOW THAN GROANING FOR LOVE?

STOP THERE, STOP THERE.

FOR THIS DRIVELING LOVE IS LIKE A GREAT NATURAL,

THAT RUNS LOLLING UP AND DOWN TO HIDE HIS BAUBLE IN A HOLE.

BAM!

THOU DESIREST ME TO STOP IN MY TALE AGAINST THE HAIR.

O, THOU ART DECEIVED; I WOULD HAVE MADE IT SHORT:

FOR I WAS COME TO THE WHOLE DEPTH OF MY TALE; AND MEANT, INDEED, TO OCCUPY THE ARGUMENT NO LONGER.

FWIP

THOU WOULDST ELSE HAVE MADE THY TALE LARGE.

A BAWD, A BAWD, A BAWD! SO HO!

SHE WILL INDITE HIM TO SOME SUPPER.

IF YOU BE HE, SIR, I DESIRE SOME CONFIDENCE WITH YOU.

NO HARE, SIR; UNLESS A HARE, SIR, IN A LENTEN PIE, THAT IS SOMETHING STALE AND HOAR ERE IT BE SPENT.

WHAT HAST THOU FOUND?

SHH!

AN OLD HARE HOAR, AND AN OLD HARE HOAR, IS VERY GOOD MEAT IN LENT BUT A HARE THAT IS HOAR IS TOO MUCH FOR A SCORE,

WHEN IT HOARS ERE IT BE SPENT.

ROMEO, WILL YOU COME TO YOUR FATHER'S? WE'LL TO DINNER, THITHER.

I WILL FOLLOW YOU.

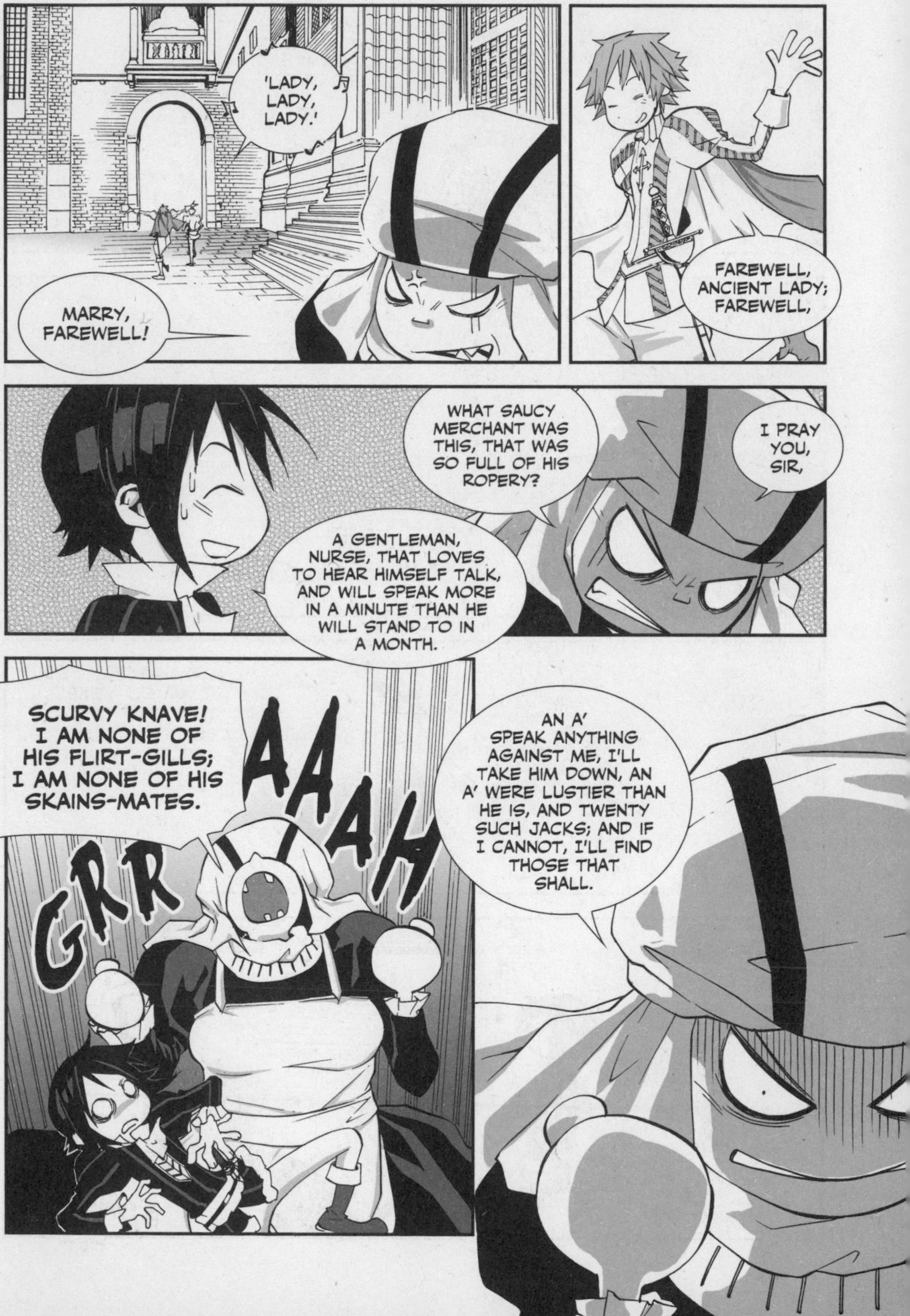
FAREWELL, ANCIENT LADY; FAREWELL,
'LADY, LADY, LADY.'
MARRY, FAREWELL!
I PRAY YOU, SIR,
WHAT SAUCY MERCHANT WAS THIS, THAT WAS SO FULL OF HIS ROPERY?
A GENTLEMAN, NURSE, THAT LOVES TO HEAR HIMSELF TALK, AND WILL SPEAK MORE IN A MINUTE THAN HE WILL STAND TO IN A MONTH.
AN A' SPEAK ANYTHING AGAINST ME, I'LL TAKE HIM DOWN, AN A' WERE LUSTIER THAN HE IS, AND TWENTY SUCH JACKS; AND IF I CANNOT, I'LL FIND THOSE THAT SHALL.
SCURVY KNAVE! I AM NONE OF HIS FLIRT-GILLS; I AM NONE OF HIS SKAINS-MATES.
GRR
AAAH

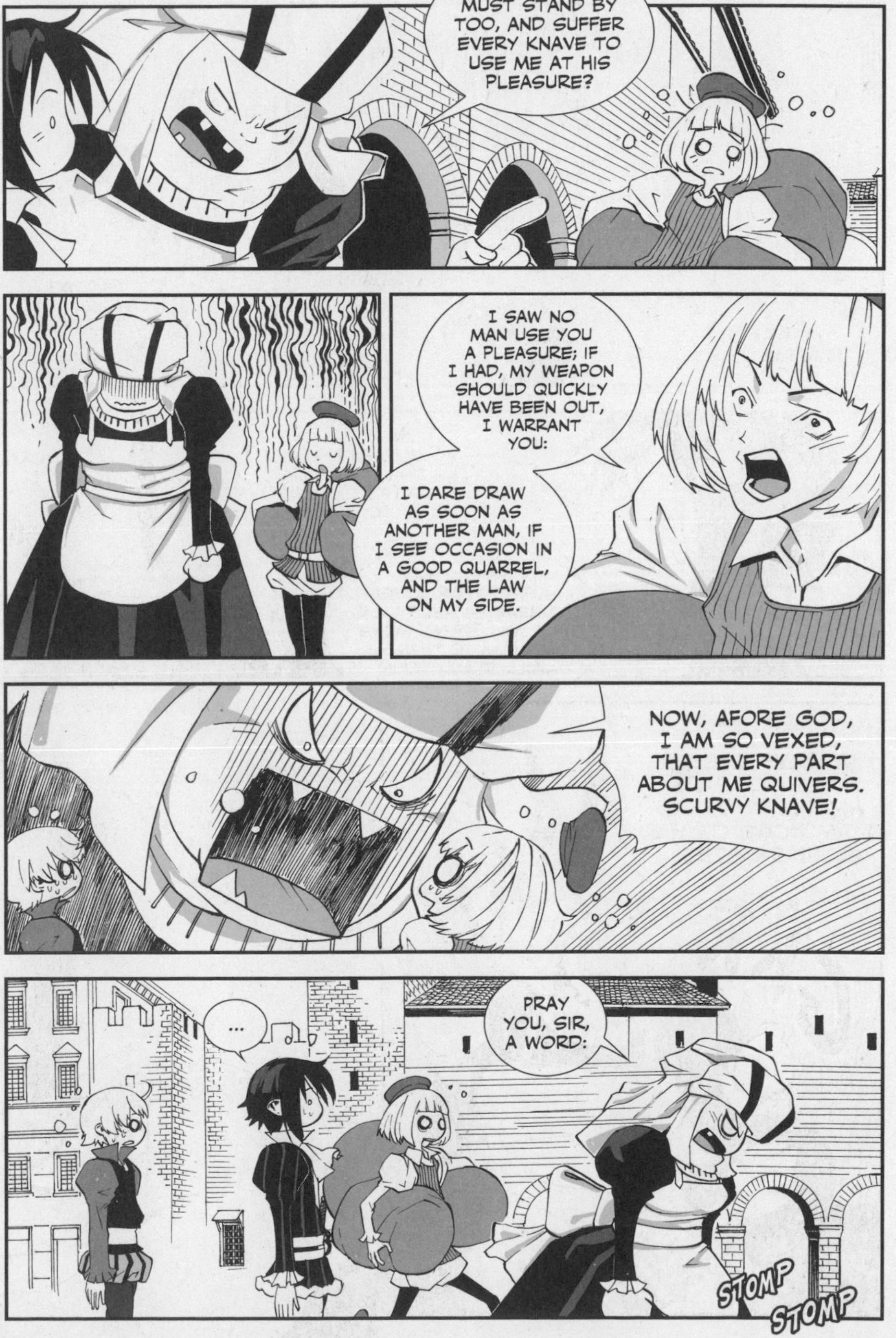
AND THOU MUST STAND BY TOO, AND SUFFER EVERY KNAVE TO USE ME AT HIS PLEASURE?
I SAW NO MAN USE YOU A PLEASURE; IF I HAD, MY WEAPON SHOULD QUICKLY HAVE BEEN OUT, I WARRANT YOU:
I DARE DRAW AS SOON AS ANOTHER MAN, IF I SEE OCCASION IN A GOOD QUARREL, AND THE LAW ON MY SIDE.
NOW, AFORE GOD, I AM SO VEXED, THAT EVERY PART ABOUT ME QUIVERS. SCURVY KNAVE!
PRAY YOU, SIR, A WORD:
...
STOMP
STOMP

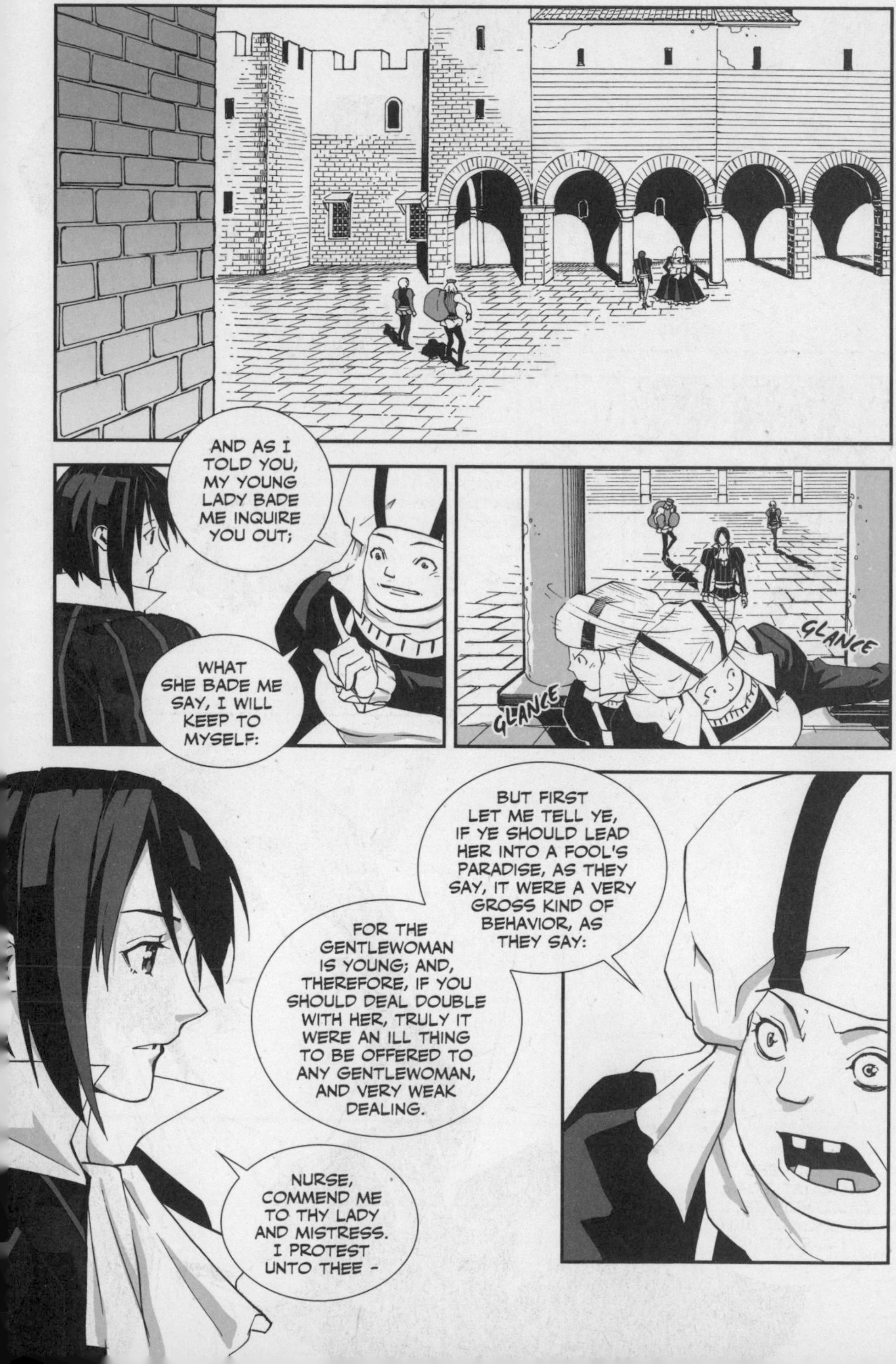
GLANCE
GLANCE
AND AS I TOLD YOU, MY YOUNG LADY BADE ME INQUIRE YOU OUT;
WHAT SHE BADE ME SAY, I WILL KEEP TO MYSELF:
BUT FIRST LET ME TELL YE, IF YE SHOULD LEAD HER INTO A FOOL'S PARADISE, AS THEY SAY, IT WERE A VERY GROSS KIND OF BEHAVIOR, AS THEY SAY:
FOR THE GENTLEWOMAN IS YOUNG; AND, THEREFORE, IF YOU SHOULD DEAL DOUBLE WITH HER, TRULY IT WERE AN ILL THING TO BE OFFERED TO ANY GENTLEWOMAN, AND VERY WEAK DEALING.
NURSE, COMMEND ME TO THY LADY AND MISTRESS. I PROTEST UNTO THEE -

NOW GOD IN HEAVEN BLESS THEE! HARK YOU, SIR.

FAREWELL; COMMEND ME TO THY MISTRESS.

FAREWELL; BE TRUSTY, AND I'LL QUIT THY PAINS:

WHAT SAY'ST THOU, MY DEAR NURSE?

HEH

I WARRANT THEE, MY MAN'S AS TRUE AS STEEL.

IS YOUR MAN SECRET?

DID YOU NE'ER HEAR SAY, TWO MAY KEEP COUNSEL, PUTTING ONE AWAY?

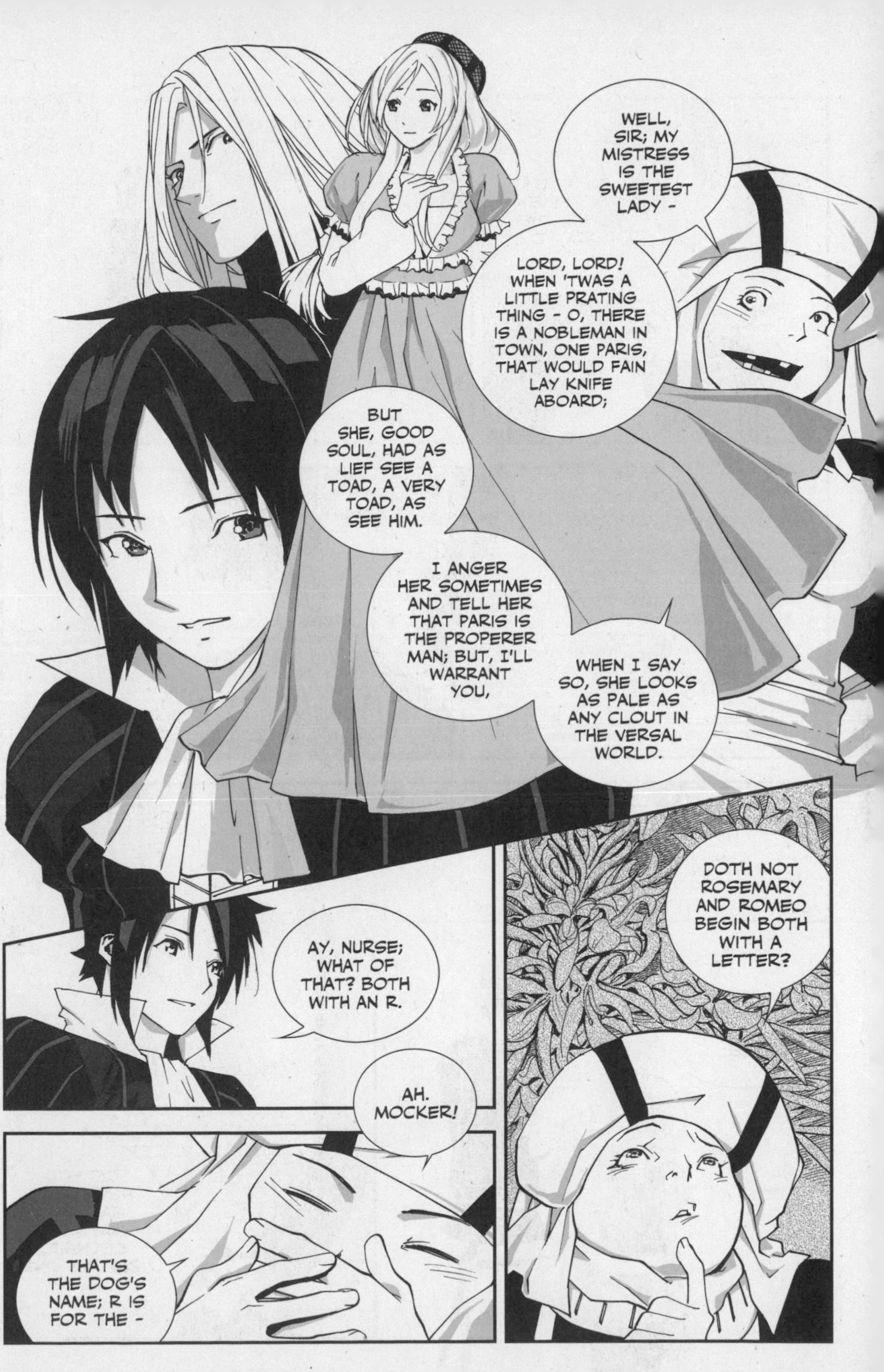
WELL, SIR; MY MISTRESS IS THE SWEETEST LADY -
LORD, LORD! WHEN 'TWAS A LITTLE PRATING THING - O, THERE IS A NOBLEMAN IN TOWN, ONE PARIS, THAT WOULD FAIN LAY KNIFE ABOARD;
BUT SHE, GOOD SOUL, HAD AS LIEF SEE A TOAD, A VERY TOAD, AS SEE HIM.
I ANGER HER SOMETIMES AND TELL HER THAT PARIS IS THE PROPERER MAN; BUT, I'LL WARRANT YOU,
WHEN I SAY SO, SHE LOOKS AS PALE AS ANY CLOUT IN THE VERSAL WORLD.
DOTH NOT ROSEMARY AND ROMEO BEGIN BOTH WITH A LETTER?
AY, NURSE; WHAT OF THAT? BOTH WITH AN R.
AH. MOCKER!
THAT'S THE DOG'S NAME; R IS FOR THE -

WHAP!

NO; I KNOW IT BEGINS WITH SOME OTHER LETTER –

AND SHE HATH THE PRETTIEST SENTENTIOUS OF IT, OF YOU AND ROSEMARY, THAT IT WOULD DO YOU GOOD TO HEAR IT.

AY, A THOUSAND TIMES.

COMMEND ME TO THY LADY.

PETER!

Z Z Z

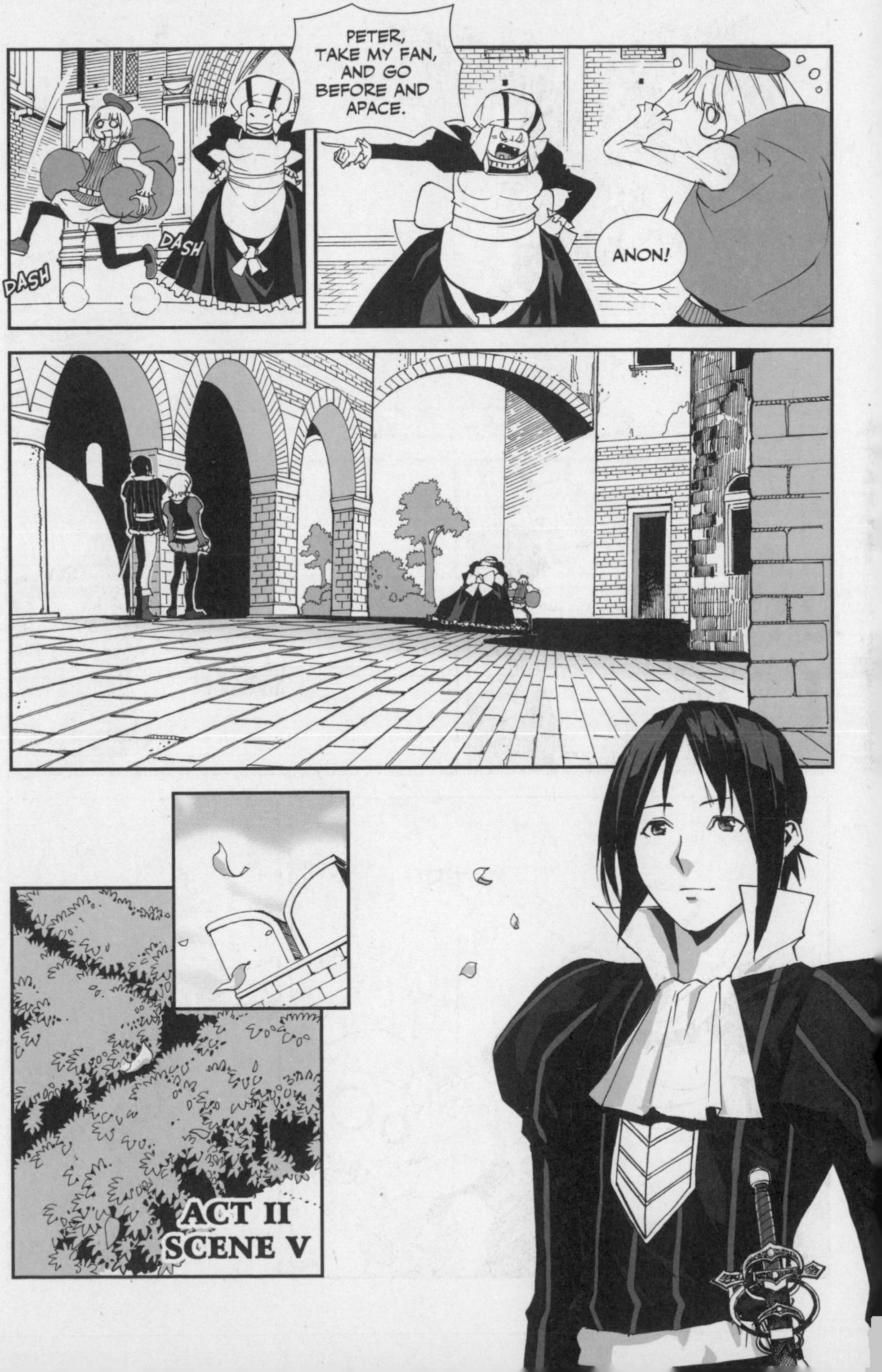
PETER, TAKE MY FAN, AND GO BEFORE AND APACE.
ANON!
DASH
DASH
ACT II
SCENE V

THE CLOCK STRUCK NINE WHEN I DID SEND THE NURSE; IN HALF AN HOUR SHE PROMISED TO RETURN.

CAPULET'S ORCHARD

PERCHANCE SHE CANNOT MEET HIM: THAT'S NOT SO. O, SHE IS LAME!

SHE

DRIVING BACK SHADOWS OVER LOURING HILLS:

LOVE'S HERALDS SHOULD BE THOUGHTS,

WHICH TEN TIMES FASTER GLIDE THAN THE SUN'S BEAMS,

170

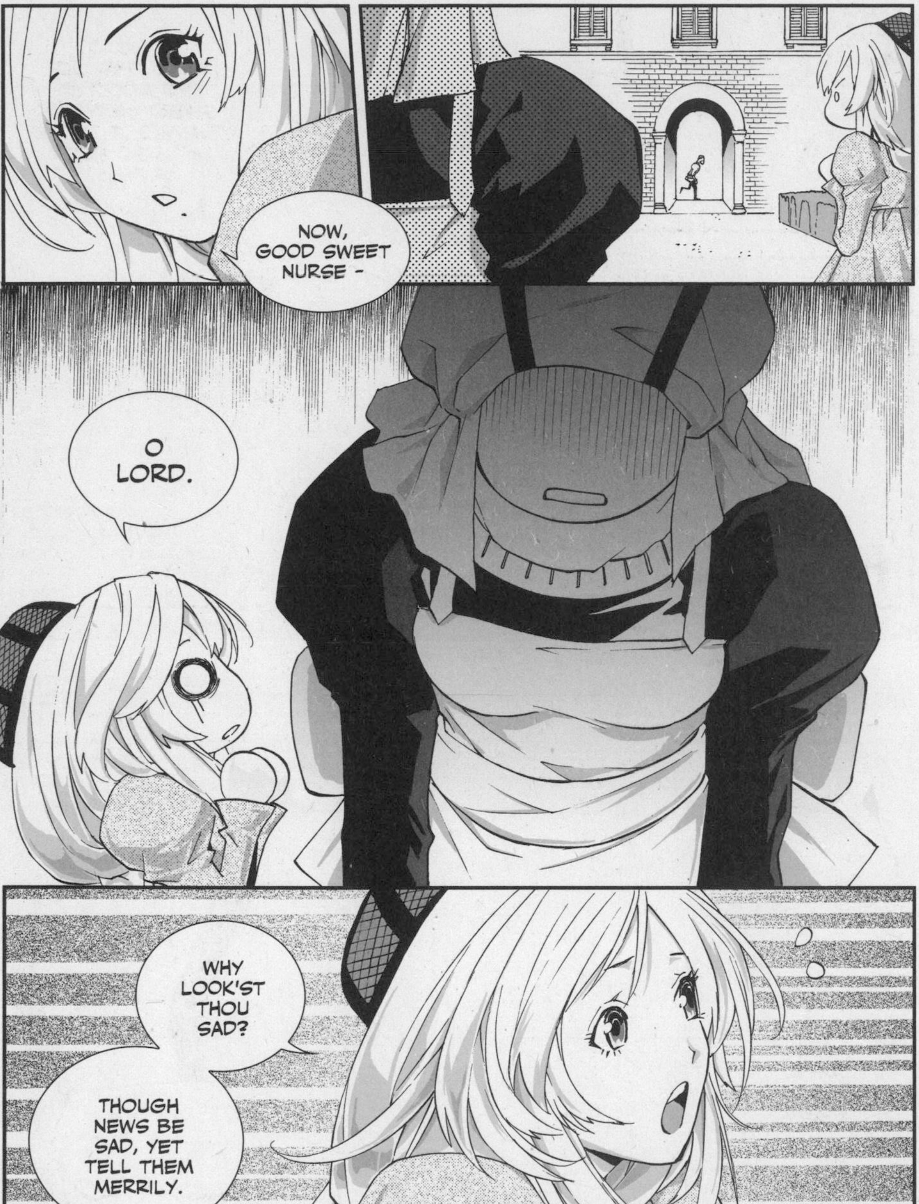
NOW, GOOD SWEET NURSE -
O LORD.
WHY LOOK'ST THOU SAD?
THOUGH NEWS BE SAD, YET TELL THEM MERRILY.

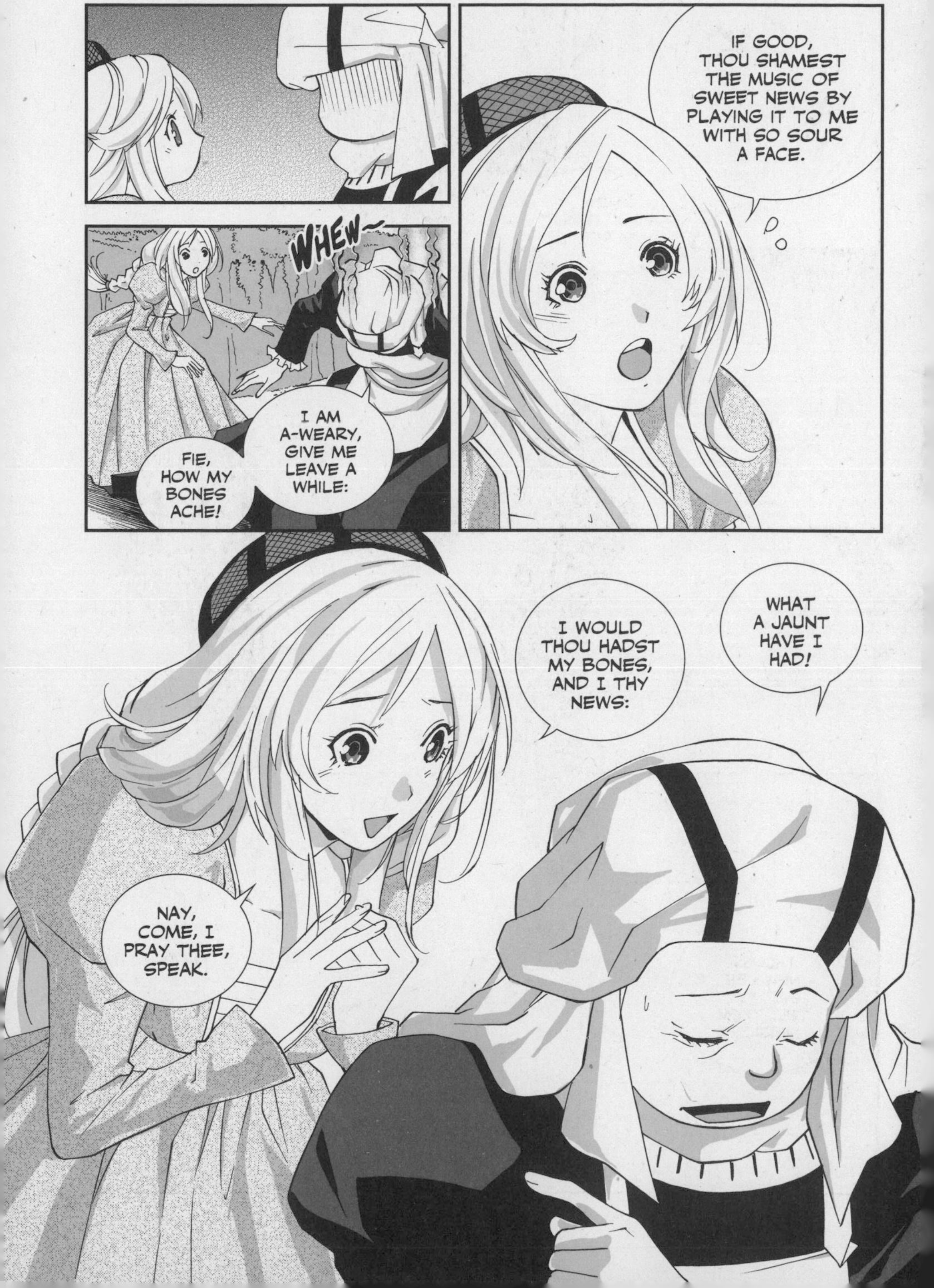
IF GOOD, THOU SHAMEST THE MUSIC OF SWEET NEWS BY PLAYING IT TO ME WITH SO SOUR A FACE.
WHEW~
I AM A-WEARY, GIVE ME LEAVE A WHILE:
FIE, HOW MY BONES ACHE!
WHAT A JAUNT HAVE I HAD!
I WOULD THOU HADST MY BONES, AND I THY NEWS:
NAY, COME, I PRAY THEE, SPEAK.

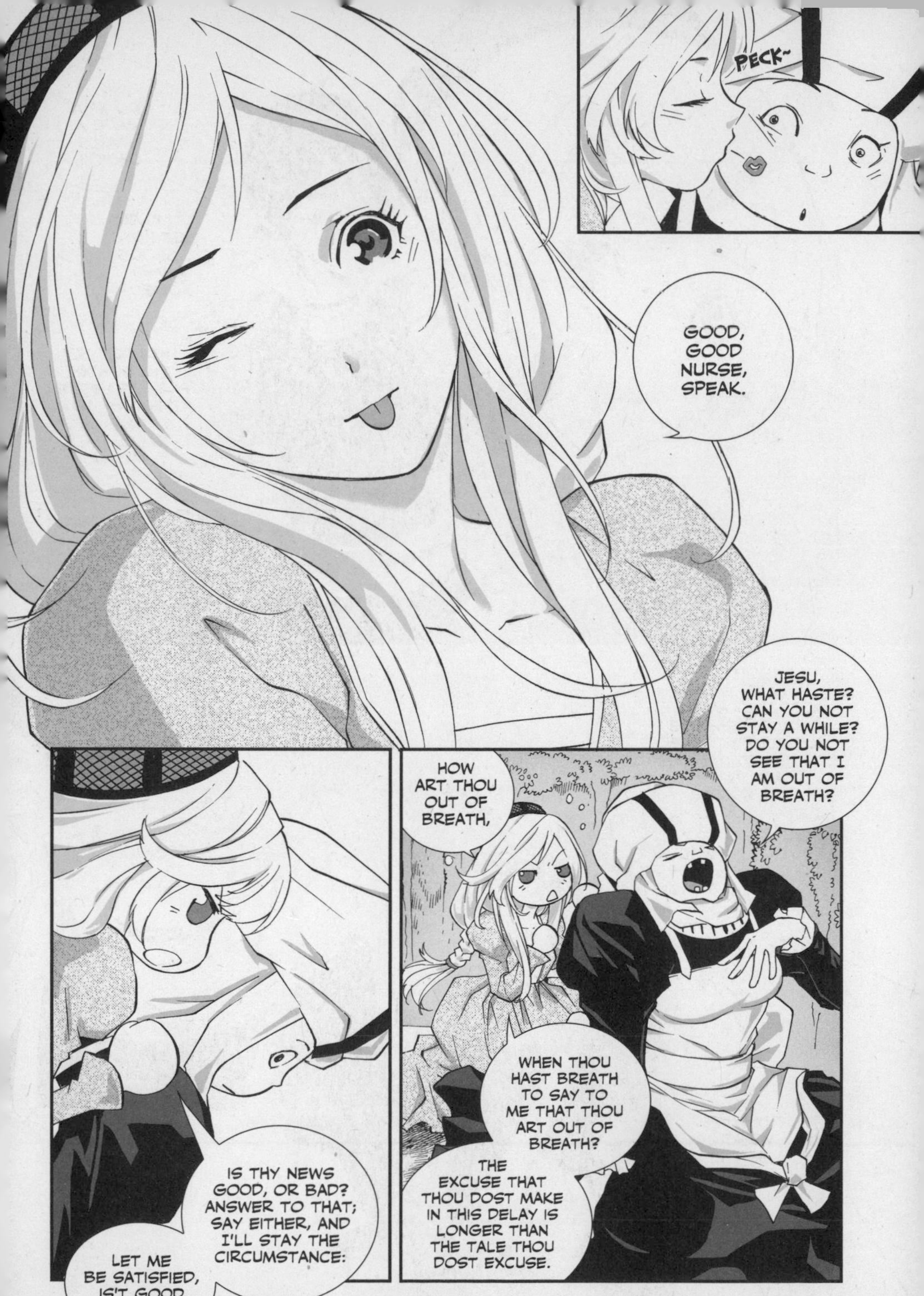
PECK~
GOOD, GOOD NURSE, SPEAK.
JESU, WHAT HASTE? CAN YOU NOT STAY A WHILE? DO YOU NOT SEE THAT I AM OUT OF BREATH?
HOW ART THOU OUT OF BREATH,
WHEN THOU HAST BREATH TO SAY TO ME THAT THOU ART OUT OF BREATH?
THE EXCUSE THAT THOU DOST MAKE IN THIS DELAY IS LONGER THAN THE TALE THOU DOST EXCUSE.
IS THY NEWS GOOD, OR BAD? ANSWER TO THAT; SAY EITHER, AND I'LL STAY THE CIRCUMSTANCE:
LET ME BE SATISFIED, IS'T GOOD OR BAD?

178

HIE TO HIGH FORTUNE!

HONEST NURSE, FAREWELL.

SO SMILE THE HEAVENS UPON THIS HOLY ACT, THAT AFTER HOURS WITH SORROW CHIDE US NOT!

AMEN, AMEN!

ACT II SCENE VI

FRIAR LAURENCE'S CELL

BUT COME WHAT SORROW CAN, IT CANNOT COUNTERVAIL THE EXCHANGE OF JOY THAT ONE SHORT MINUTE GIVES ME IN HER SIGHT.

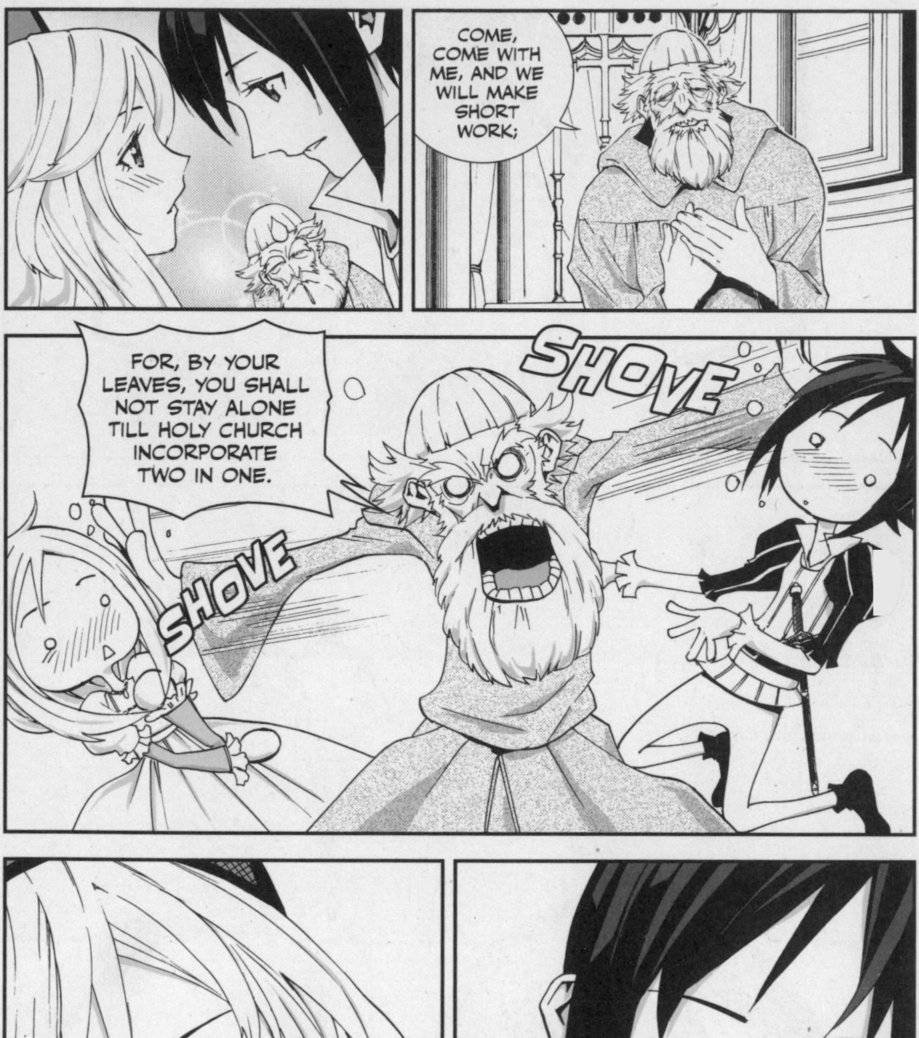
COME, COME WITH ME, AND WE WILL MAKE SHORT WORK;
SHOVE
FOR, BY YOUR LEAVES, YOU SHALL NOT STAY ALONE TILL HOLY CHURCH INCORPORATE TWO IN ONE.
SHOVE

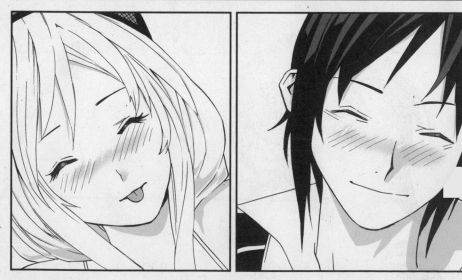

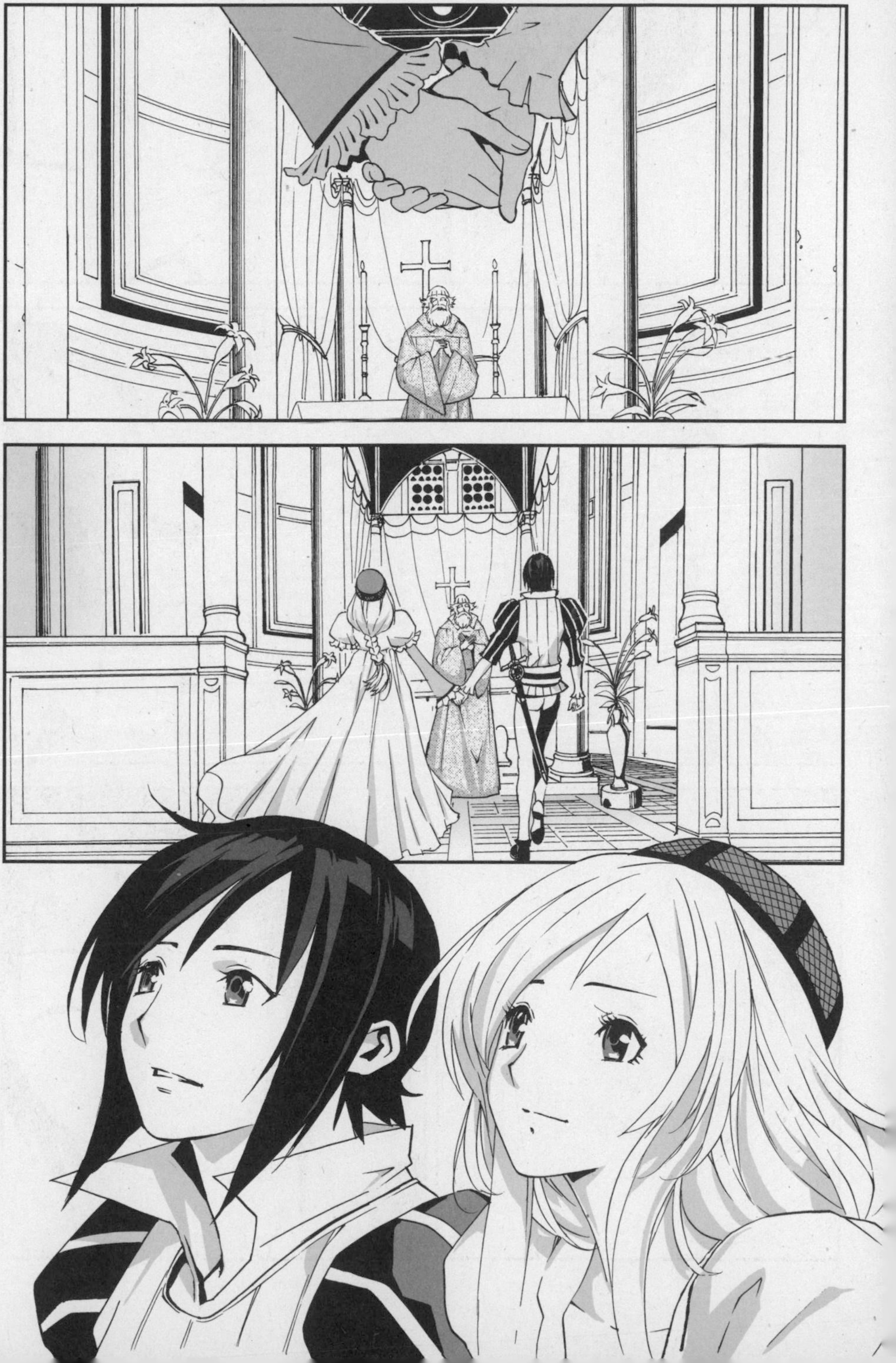

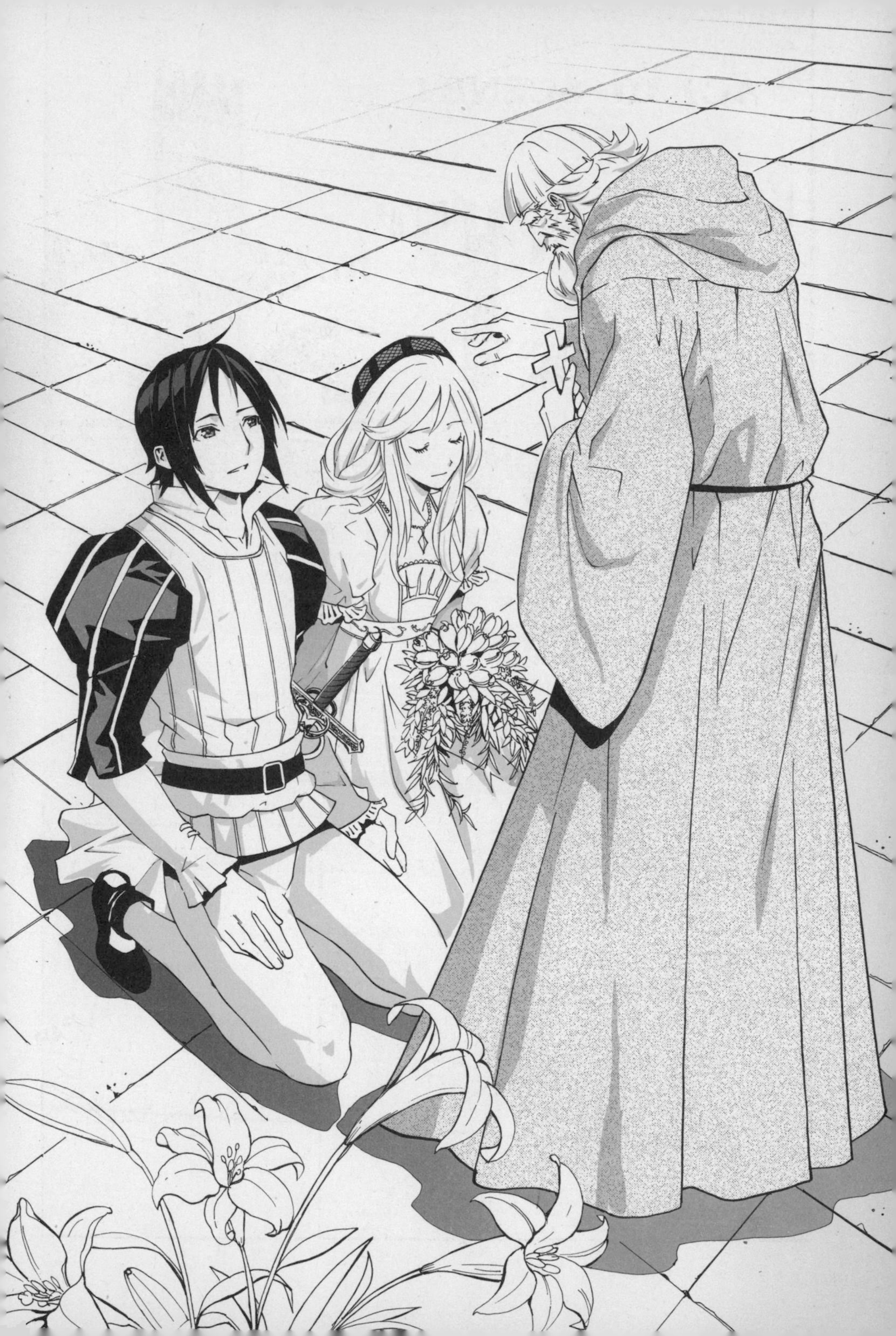

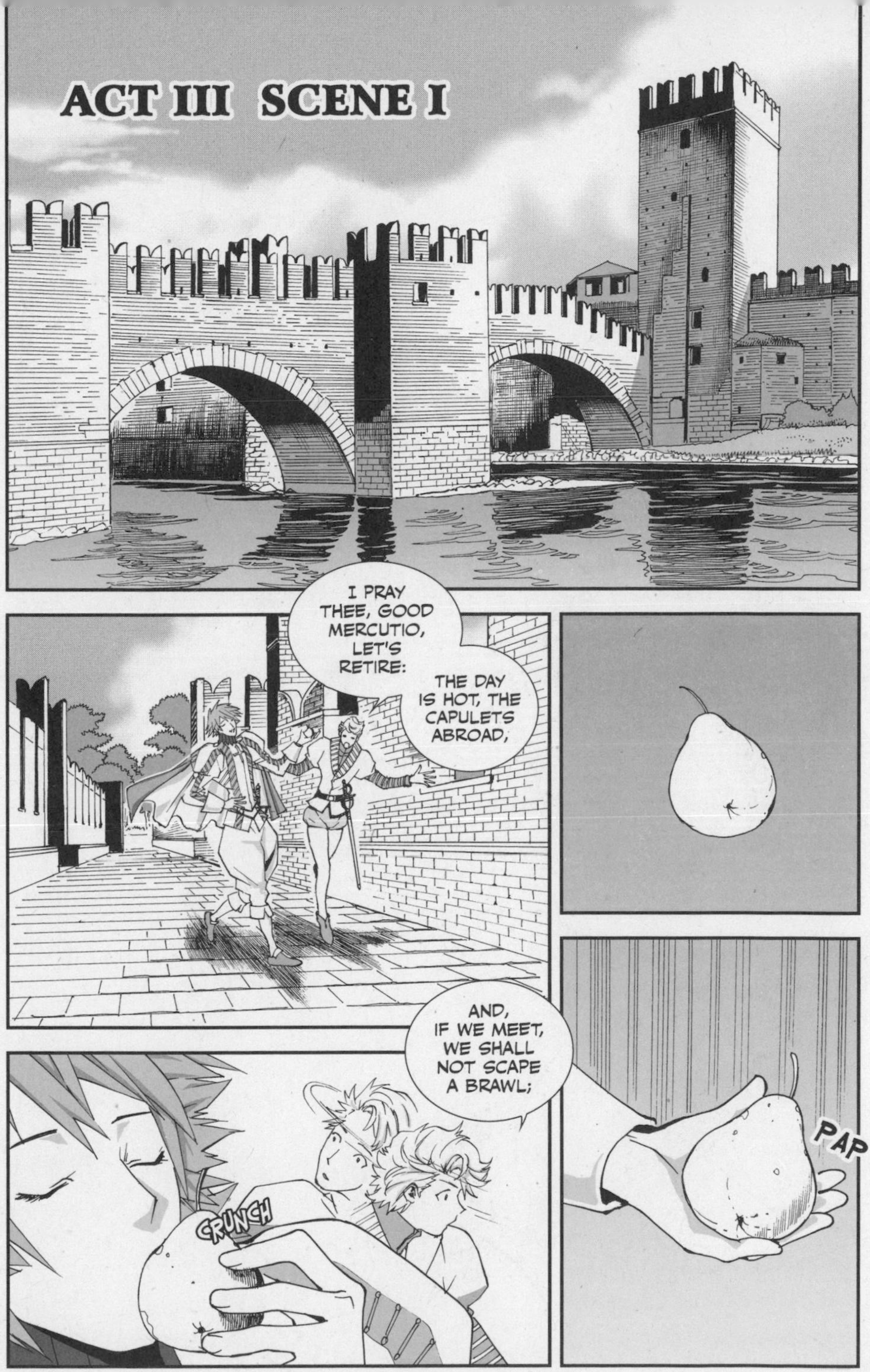
ACT III SCENE I
I PRAY THEE, GOOD MERCUTIO, LET'S RETIRE:
THE DAY IS HOT, THE CAPULETS ABROAD,
PAP
AND, IF WE MEET, WE SHALL NOT SCAPE A BRAWL;
CRUNCH

THOU ART LIKE ONE OF THOSE FELLOWS THAT WHEN HE ENTERS THE CONFINES OF A TAVERN CLAPS ME HIS SWORD UPON THE TABLE AND SAYS 'GOD SEND ME NO NEED OF THEE!'

AND BY THE OPERATION OF THE SECOND CUP DRAWS IT ON THE DRAWER, WHEN INDEED THERE IS NO NEED.

FOR NOW, THESE HOT DAYS, IS THE MAD BLOOD STIRRING -

MRMPH!

THOU ART AS HOT A JACK IN THY MOOD AS ANY IN ITALY,

COME, COME,

AND AS SOON MOVED TO BE MOODY, AND AS SOON MOODY TO BE MOVED.

AND WHAT TO?

AM I LIKE SUCH A FELLOW?

THOU WILT QUARREL WITH A MAN FOR CRACKING NUTS, HAVING NO OTHER REASON BUT BECAUSE THOU HAST HAZEL EYES: WHAT EYE BUT SUCH AN EYE WOULD SPY OUT SUCH A QUARREL?

THY HEAD IS AS FUN OF QUARRELS AS AN EGG IS FULL OF MEAT, AND YET THY HEAD HATH BEEN BEATEN AS ADDLE AS AN EGG FOR QUARRELLING:

NAY, AN THERE WERE TWO SUCH, WE SHOULD HAVE NONE SHORTLY, FOR ONE WOULD KILL THE OTHER. THOU!

WHY, THOU WILT QUARREL WITH A MAN THAT HATH A HAIR MORE, OR A HAIR LESS, IN HIS BEARD, THAN THOU HAST:

PINCH

BOY, THIS SHALL NOT EXCUSE THE INJURIES THAT THOU HAST DONE ME; THEREFORE TURN AND DRAW.

AND SO, GOOD CAPULET – WHICH NAME I TENDER AS DEARLY AS MY OWN – BE SATISFIED.

I DO PROTEST, I NEVER INJURED THEE, BUT LOVE THEE BETTER THAN THOU CANST DEVISE, TILL THOU SHALT KNOW THE REASON OF MY LOVE:

SHIING

TYBALT, YOU RAT-CATCHER, WILL YOU WALK?

O CALM, DISHONOURABLE, VILE SUBMISSION! ALLA STOCCATA CARRIES IT AWAY.

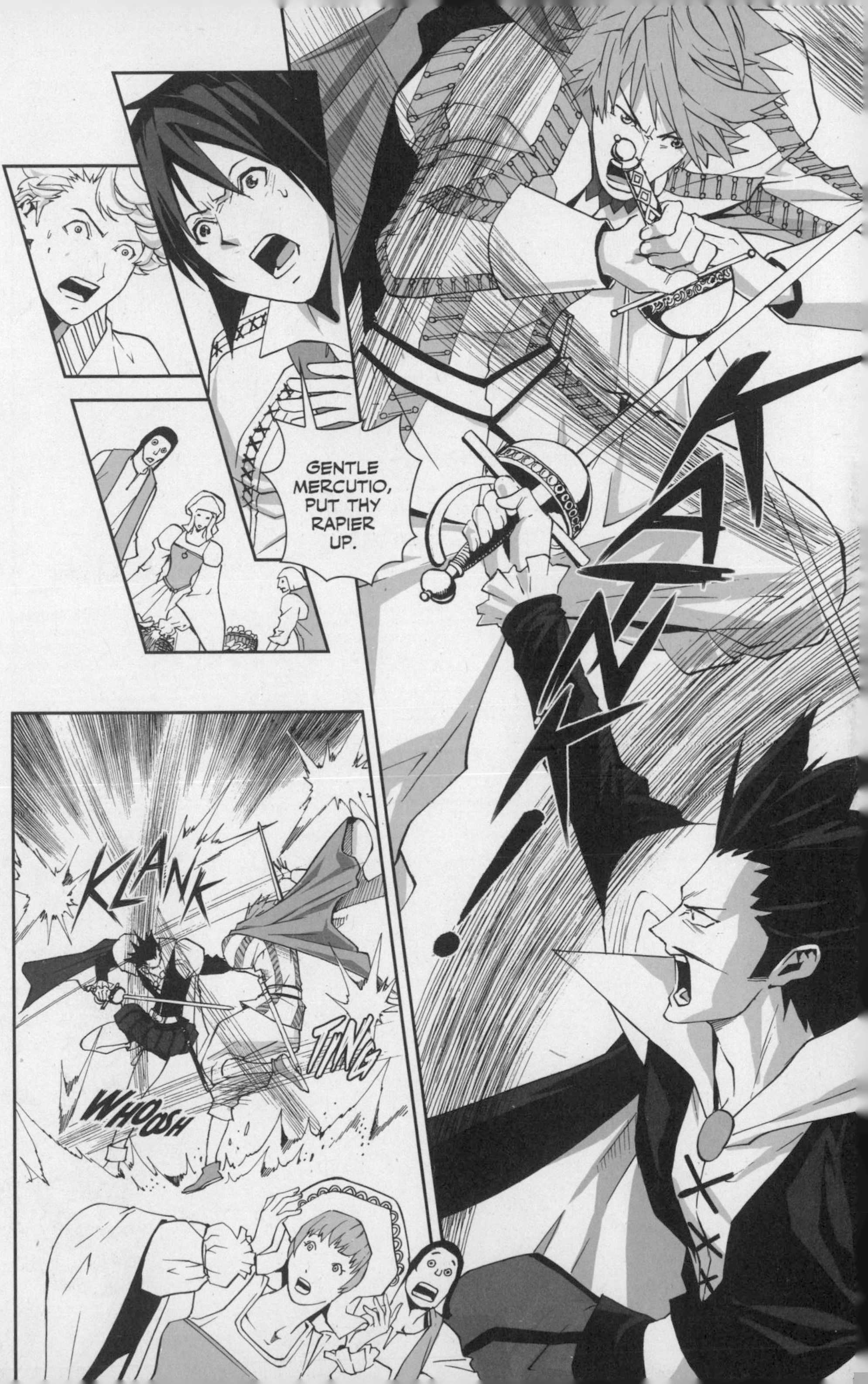
GENTLE MERCUTIO, PUT THY RAPIER UP.
ANK!
KLANK
TING
WHOOSH

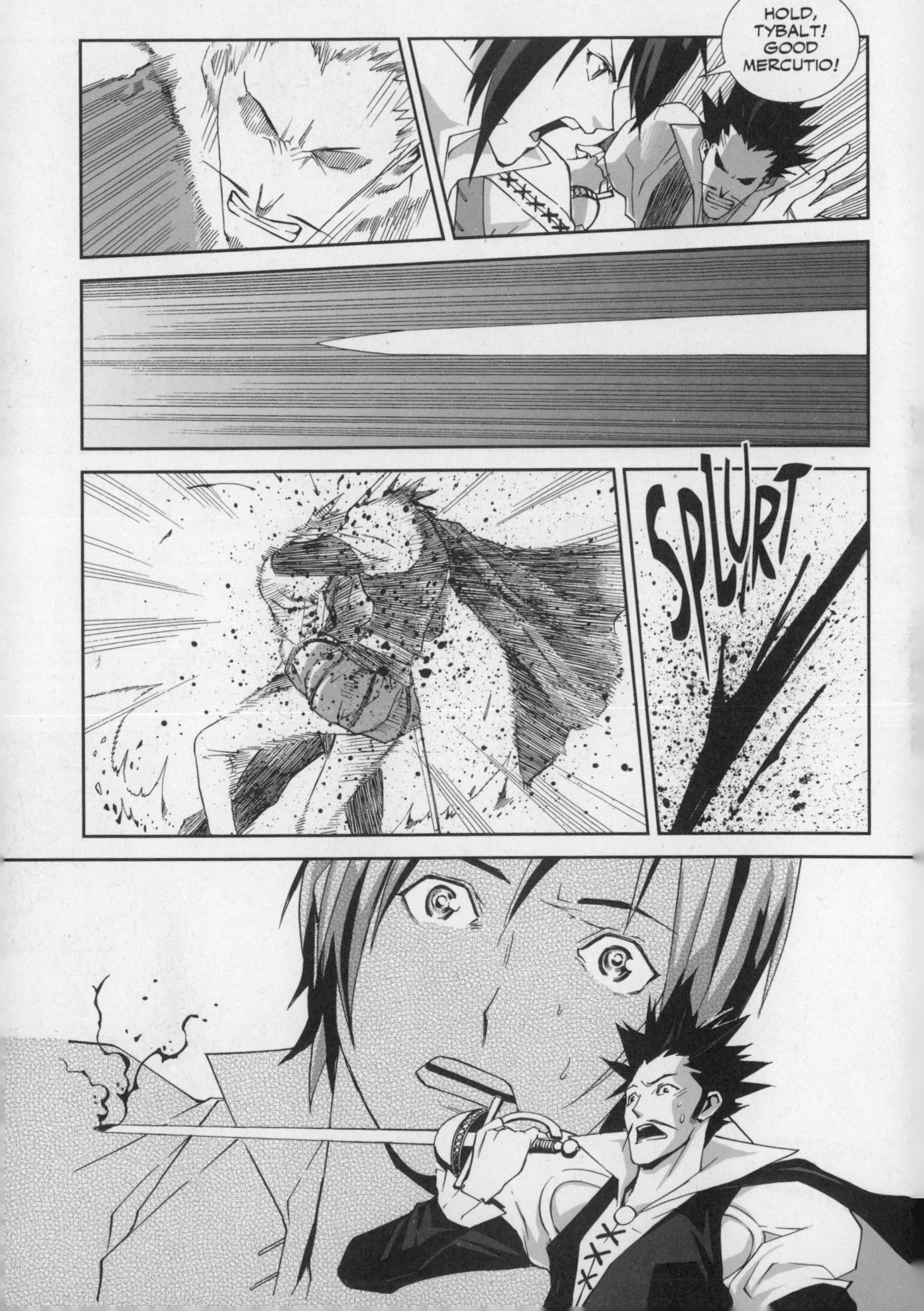
HOLD, TYBALT! GOOD MERCUTIO!
SPLURT

WHERE IS MY PAGE?

GO, VILLAIN, FETCH A SURGEON.

AY, AY, A SCRATCH, A SCRATCH; MARRY, 'TIS ENOUGH.

WHAT, ART THOU HURT?

SHUDDER

COURAGE, MAN; THE HURT CANNOT BE MUCH.

THUD

KOFF

202

NO, 'TIS NOT SO DEEP AS A WELL, NOR SO WIDE AS A CHURCH-DOOR; BUT 'TIS ENOUGH, 'TWILL SERVE:

ASK FOR ME TO-MORROW, AND YOU SHALL FIND ME A GRAVE MAN. I AM PEPPERED, I WARRANT, FOR THIS WORLD.

HACK

WHY THE DEVIL CAME YOU BETWEEN US? I WAS HURT UNDER YOUR ARM.

A BRAGGART, A ROGUE, A VILLAIN, THAT FIGHTS BY THE BOOK OF ARITHMETIC!

'ZOUNDS, A DOG, A RAT, A MOUSE, A CAT, TO SCRATCH A MAN TO DEATH!

A PLAGUE O' BOTH YOUR HOUSES!

I THOUGHT ALL FOR THE BEST.

THEY HAVE MADE WORMS' MEAT OF ME: I HAVE IT, AND SOUNDLY TOO: YOUR HOUSES!

HELP ME INTO SOME HOUSE, BENVOLIO, OR I SHALL FAINT. A PLAGUE O' BOTH YOUR HOUSES!

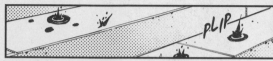

PLIP

THIS GENTLEMAN, THE PRINCE'S NEAR ALLY, MY VERY FRIEND, HATH GOT HIS MORTAL HURT IN MY BEHALF;

MY REPUTATION STAINED WITH TYBALT'S SLANDER - TYBALT, THAT AN HOUR HATH BEEN MY KINSMAN!

O SWEET JULIET, THY BEAUTY HATH MADE ME EFFEMINATE AND IN MY TEMPER SOFTENED VALOR'S STEEL!

THAT GALLANT SPIRIT HATH ASPIRED THE CLOUDS,

WHICH TOO UNTIMELY HERE DID SCORN THE EARTH.

BRAVE MERCUTIO'S DEAD!

O ROMEO, ROMEO,

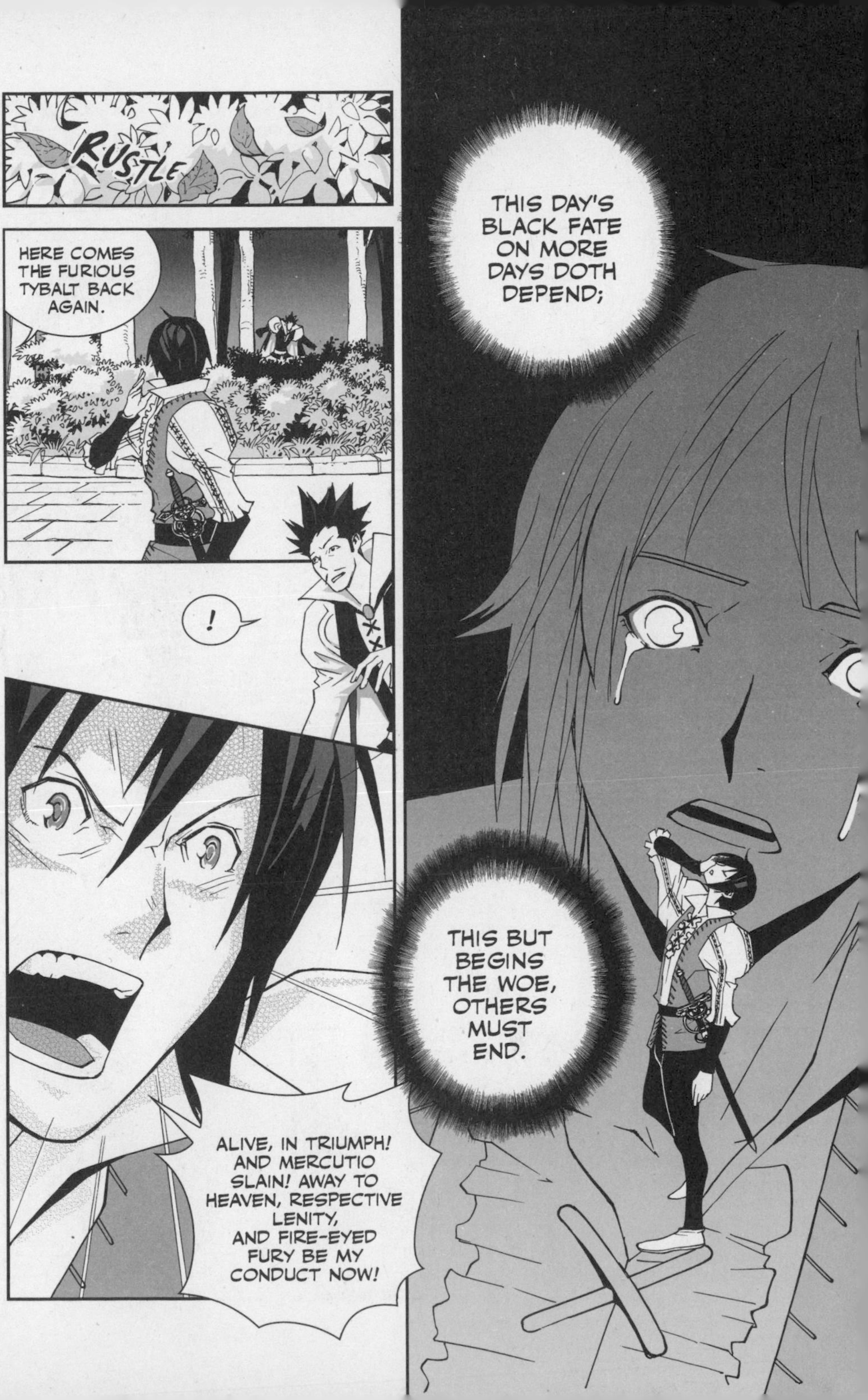
THIS DAY'S BLACK FATE ON MORE DAYS DOTH DEPEND;
THIS BUT BEGINS THE WOE, OTHERS MUST END.
RUSTLE
HERE COMES THE FURIOUS TYBALT BACK AGAIN.
!
ALIVE, IN TRIUMPH! AND MERCUTIO SLAIN! AWAY TO HEAVEN, RESPECTIVE LENITY, AND FIRE-EYED FURY BE MY CONDUCT NOW!

WHO ALL AS HOT, TURNS DEADLY POINT TO POINT, AND, WITH A MARTIAL SCORN, WITH ONE HAND BEATS COLD DEATH ASIDE,

ROMEO HE CRIES ALOUD, 'HOLD, FRIENDS! FRIENDS, PART!'

AND, SWIFTER THAN HIS TONGUE, HIS AGILE ARM BEATS DOWN THEIR FATAL POINTS,

AND WITH THE OTHER SENDS IT BACK TO TYBALT, WHOSE DEXTERITY, RETORTS IT:

THIS IS THE TRUTH, OR LET BENVOLIO DIE.

AND 'TWIXT THEM RUSHES; UNDERNEATH WHOSE ARM AN ENVIOUS THRUST FROM TYBALT HIT THE LIFE OF STOUT MERCUTIO, AND THEN TYBALT FLED;

BUT BY AND BY COMES BACK TO ROMEO,

HE IS A KINSMAN TO THE MONTAGUE; AFFECTION MAKES HIM FALSE; HE SPEAKS NOT TRUE:

SOME TWENTY OF THEM FOUGHT IN THIS BLACK STRIFE, AND ALL THOSE TWENTY COULD BUT KILL ONE LIFE.

I BEG FOR JUSTICE, WHICH THOU, PRINCE, MUST GIVE; ROMEO SLEW TYBALT,

ROMEO MUST NOT LIVE.

WHO HAD BUT NEWLY ENTERTAINED REVENGE, AND TO 'T THEY GO LIKE LIGHTNING, FOR, ERE I COULD DRAW TO PART THEM, WAS STOUT TYBALT SLAIN.

AND, AS HE FELL, DID ROMEO TURN AND FLY.

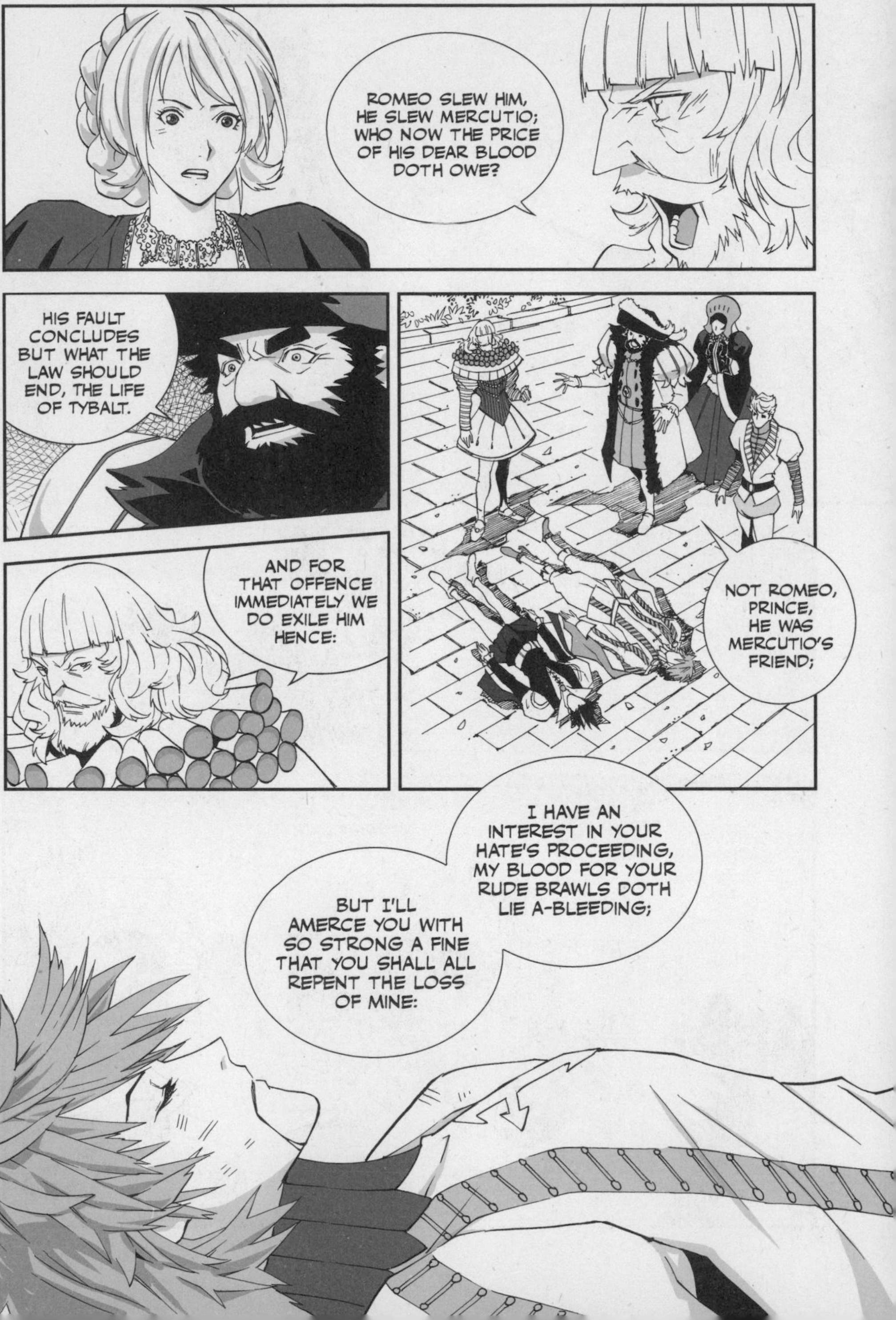
ROMEO SLEW HIM, HE SLEW MERCUTIO; WHO NOW THE PRICE OF HIS DEAR BLOOD DOTH OWE?
NOT ROMEO, PRINCE, HE WAS MERCUTIO'S FRIEND;
HIS FAULT CONCLUDES BUT WHAT THE LAW SHOULD END, THE LIFE OF TYBALT.
AND FOR THAT OFFENCE IMMEDIATELY WE DO EXILE HIM HENCE:
I HAVE AN INTEREST IN YOUR HATE'S PROCEEDING, MY BLOOD FOR YOUR RUDE BRAWLS DOTH LIE A-BLEEDING;
BUT I'LL AMERCE YOU WITH SO STRONG A FINE THAT YOU SHALL ALL REPENT THE LOSS OF MINE:

THEREFORE USE NONE: LET ROMEO HENCE IN HASTE, ELSE, WHEN HE'S FOUND, THAT HOUR IS HIS LAST.

I WILL BE DEAF TO PLEADING AND EXCUSES; NOR TEARS NOR PRAYERS SHALL PURCHASE OUT ABUSES:

OHH...

MERCY BUT MURDERS, PARDONING THOSE THAT KILL.

BEAR HENCE THIS BODY AND ATTEND OUR WILL:

THE CORDS THAT ROMEO BID THEE FETCH?

TOSS~

AY, AY, THE CORDS.

AY ME! WHAT NEWS? WHY DOST THOU WRING THY HANDS?

...

TREMBLE

THUD

219

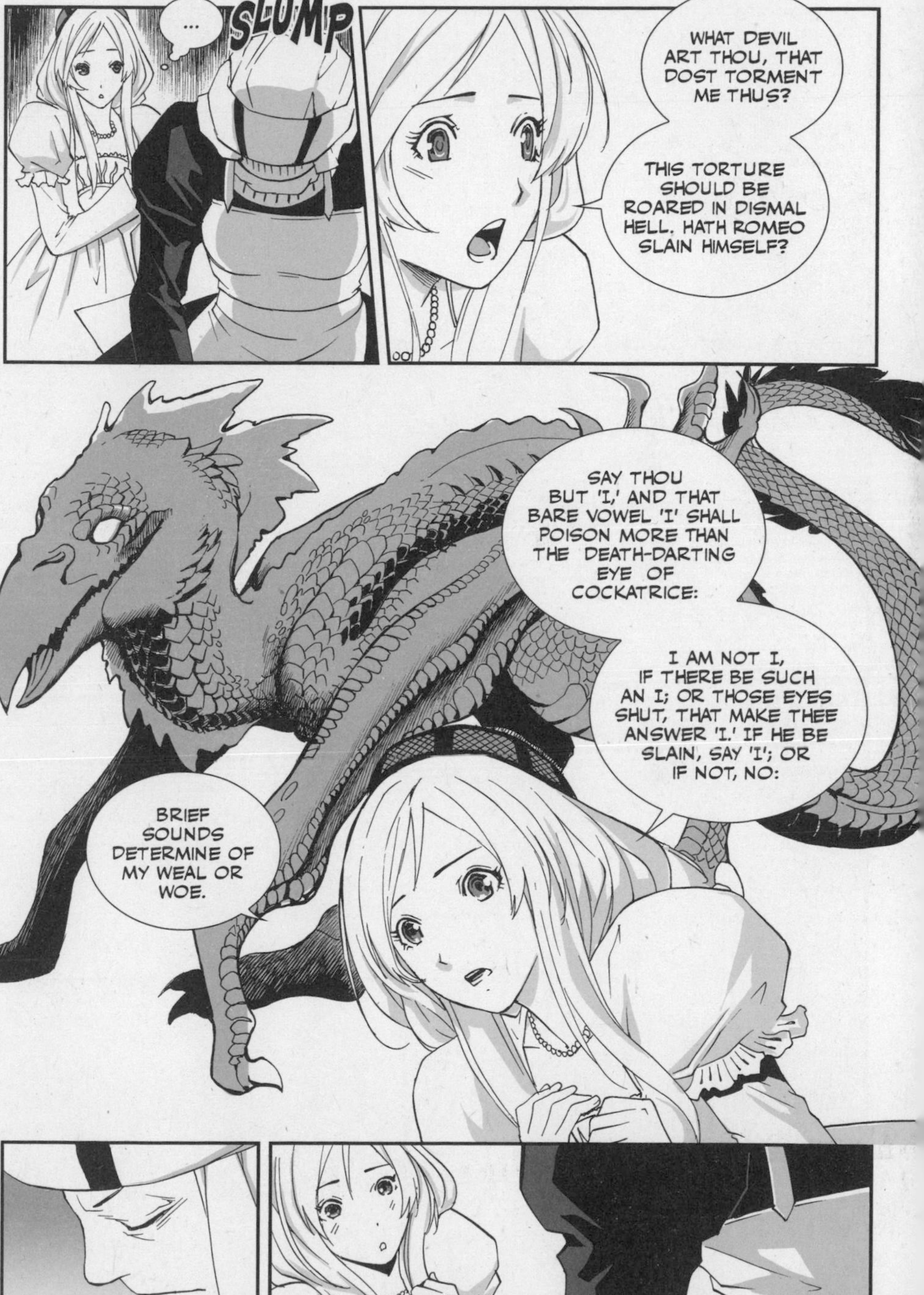
WHAT DEVIL ART THOU, THAT DOST TORMENT ME THUS?
THIS TORTURE SHOULD BE ROARED IN DISMAL HELL. HATH ROMEO SLAIN HIMSELF?
...
SLUMP
SAY THOU BUT 'I,' AND THAT BARE VOWEL 'I' SHALL POISON MORE THAN THE DEATH-DARTING EYE OF COCKATRICE:
I AM NOT I, IF THERE BE SUCH AN I; OR THOSE EYES SHUT, THAT MAKE THEE ANSWER 'I.' IF HE BE SLAIN, SAY 'I'; OR IF NOT, NO:
BRIEF SOUNDS DETERMINE OF MY WEAL OR WOE.

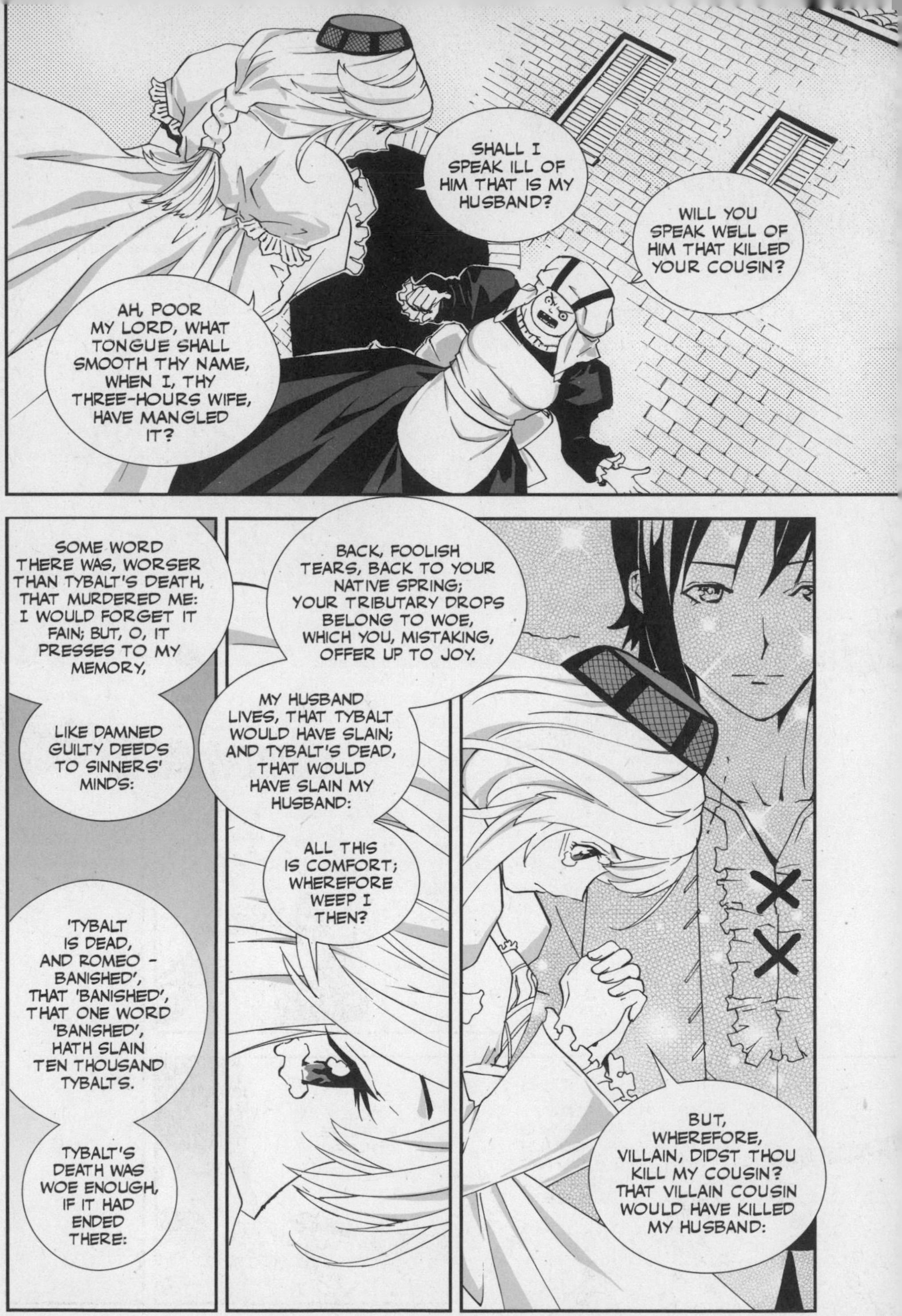
WILL YOU SPEAK WELL OF HIM THAT KILLED YOUR COUSIN?
SHALL I SPEAK ILL OF HIM THAT IS MY HUSBAND?
AH, POOR MY LORD, WHAT TONGUE SHALL SMOOTH THY NAME, WHEN I, THY THREE-HOURS WIFE, HAVE MANGLED IT?
BUT, WHEREFORE, VILLAIN, DIDST THOU KILL MY COUSIN? THAT VILLAIN COUSIN WOULD HAVE KILLED MY HUSBAND:
BACK, FOOLISH TEARS, BACK TO YOUR NATIVE SPRING; YOUR TRIBUTARY DROPS BELONG TO WOE, WHICH YOU, MISTAKING, OFFER UP TO JOY.
MY HUSBAND LIVES, THAT TYBALT WOULD HAVE SLAIN; AND TYBALT'S DEAD, THAT WOULD HAVE SLAIN MY HUSBAND:
ALL THIS IS COMFORT; WHEREFORE WEEP I THEN?
SOME WORD THERE WAS, WORSER THAN TYBALT'S DEATH, THAT MURDERED ME: I WOULD FORGET IT FAIN; BUT, O, IT PRESSES TO MY MEMORY,
LIKE DAMNED GUILTY DEEDS TO SINNERS' MINDS:
'TYBALT IS DEAD, AND ROMEO - BANISHED', THAT 'BANISHED', THAT ONE WORD 'BANISHED', HATH SLAIN TEN THOUSAND TYBALTS.
TYBALT'S DEATH WAS WOE ENOUGH, IF IT HAD ENDED THERE:

ROMEO, COME FORTH; COME FORTH, THOU FEARFUL MAN:

AFFLICTION IS ENAMORED OF THY PARTS, AND THOU ART WEDDED TO CALAMITY.

ACT III SCENE III

FRIAR LAURENCE'S CELL

WHAT SORROW CRAVES ACQUAINTANCE AT MY HAND, THAT I YET KNOW NOT?

FATHER, WHAT NEWS? WHAT IS THE PRINCE'S DOOM?

A GENTLER JUDGMENT VANISHED FROM HIS LIPS, NOT BODY'S DEATH, BUT BODY'S BANISHMENT.

WHAT LESS THAN DOOMS-DAY IS THE PRINCE'S DOOM?

TOO FAMILIAR IS MY DEAR SON WITH SUCH SOUR COMPANY:

I BRING THEE TIDINGS OF THE PRINCE'S DOOM.

HENCE FROM VERONA ART THOU BANISHED:

BE PATIENT, FOR THE WORLD IS BROAD AND WIDE.

HA, BANISHMENT! BE MERCIFUL, SAY 'DEATH'; FOR EXILE HATH MORE TERROR IN HIS LOOK,

MUCH MORE THAN DEATH: DO NOT SAY 'BANISHMENT'.

THERE IS NO WORLD WITHOUT VERONA WALLS, BUT PURGATORY, TORTURE, HELL ITSELF.

HENCE "BANISHED" IS "BANISHED FROM THE WORLD", AND WORLD'S EXILE IS DEATH:

THEN BANISHED, IS DEATH MISTERMED: CALLING DEATH BANISHMENT, THOU CUTT'ST MY HEAD OFF WITH A GOLDEN AXE, AND SMILEST UPON THE STROKE THAT MURDERS ME.

O DEADLY SIN! O RUDE UNTHANKFULNESS! THY FAULT OUR LAW CALLS DEATH;

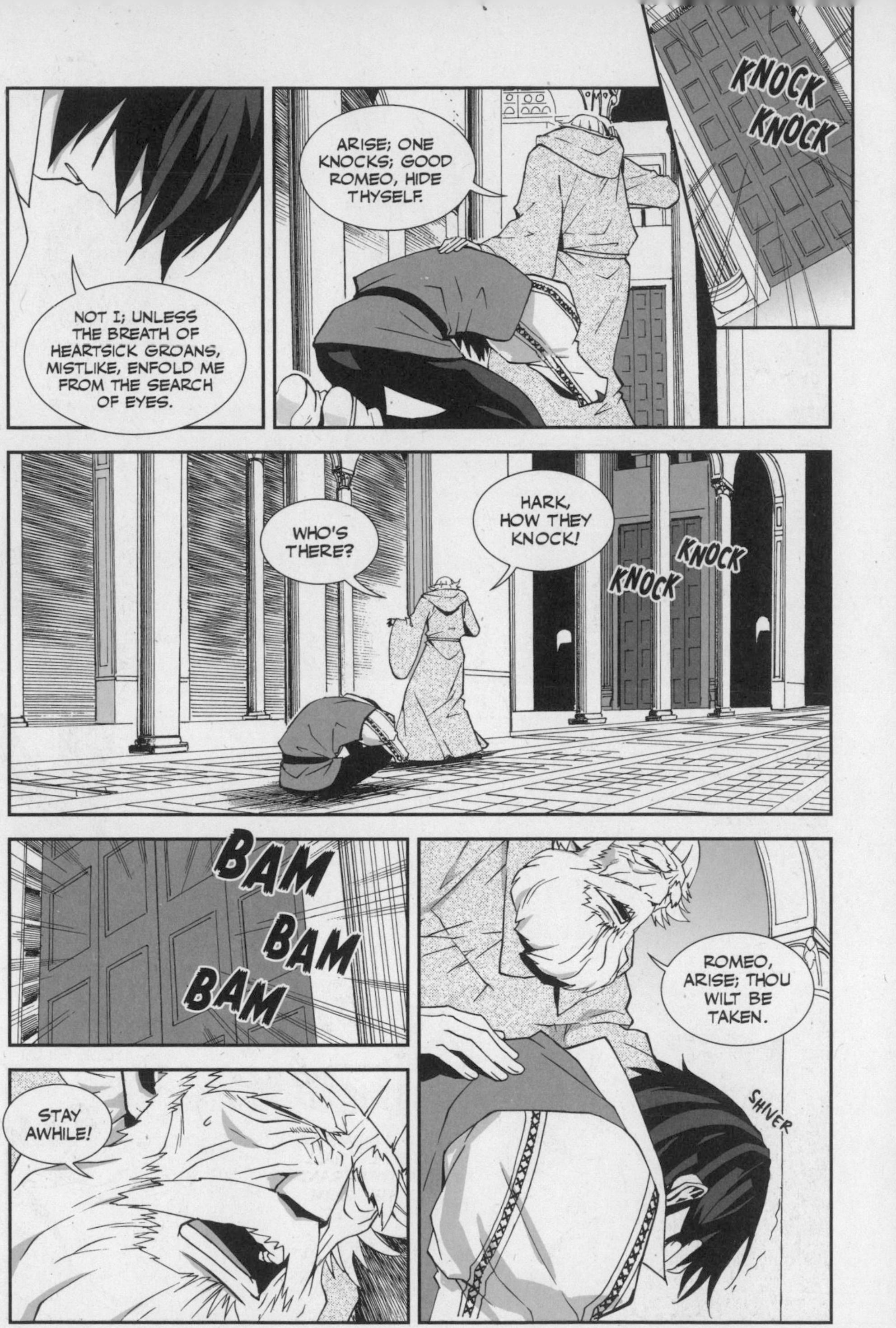
KNOCK KNOCK
ARISE; ONE KNOCKS; GOOD ROMEO, HIDE THYSELF.
NOT I; UNLESS THE BREATH OF HEARTSICK GROANS, MISTLIKE, ENFOLD ME FROM THE SEARCH OF EYES.
HARK, HOW THEY KNOCK!
KNOCK KNOCK
WHO'S THERE?
ROMEO, ARISE; THOU WILT BE TAKEN.
SHIVER
BAM BAM BAM
STAY AWHILE!

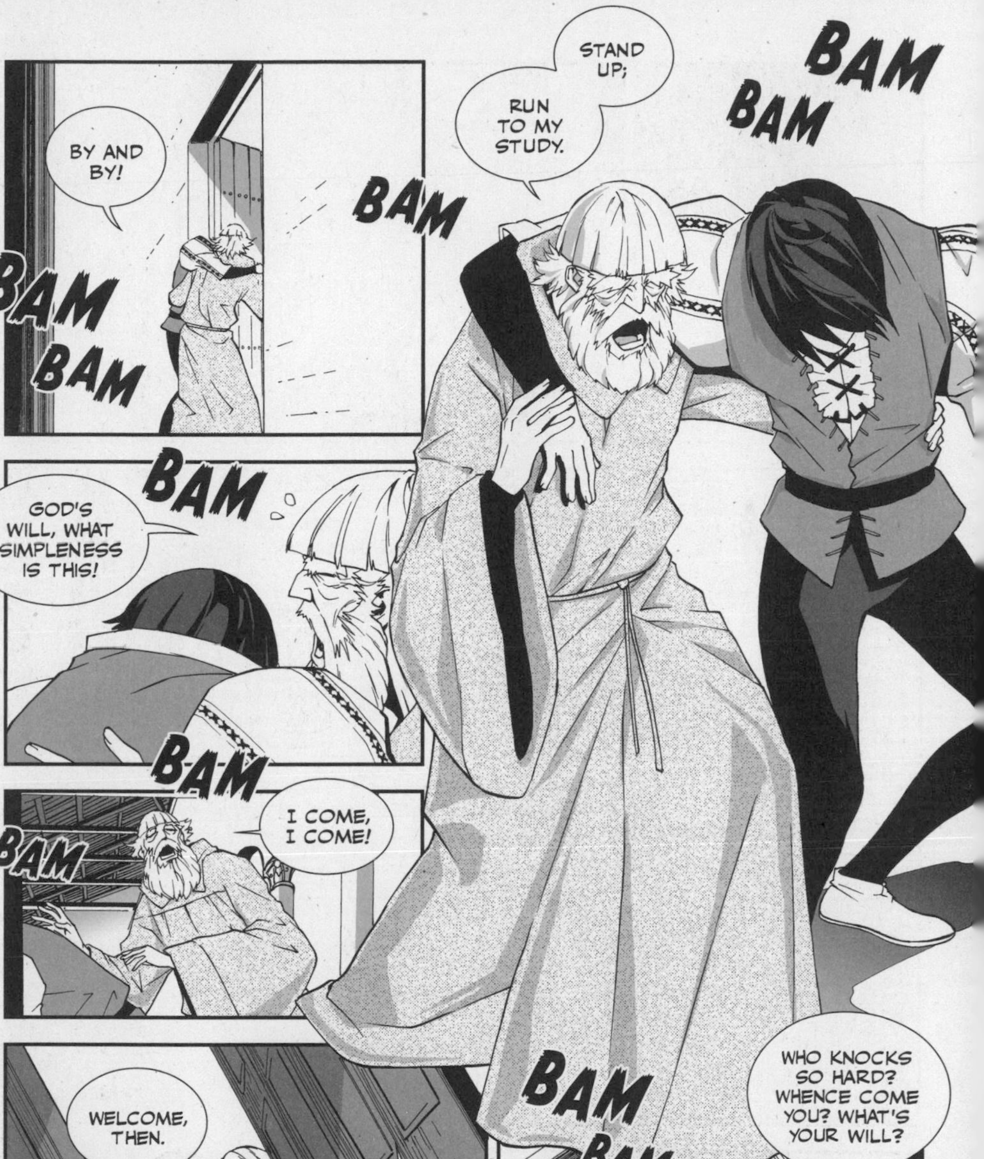
BAM
BAM
STAND UP;
RUN TO MY STUDY.
BAM
BAM
BAM
BY AND BY!
BAM
BAM
GOD'S WILL, WHAT SIMPLENESS IS THIS!
BAM
BAM
I COME, I COME!
BAM
WHO KNOCKS SO HARD? WHENCE COME YOU? WHAT'S YOUR WILL?
BAM
LET ME COME IN, AND YOU SHALL KNOW MY ERRAND; I COME FROM LADY JULIET.
WELCOME, THEN.

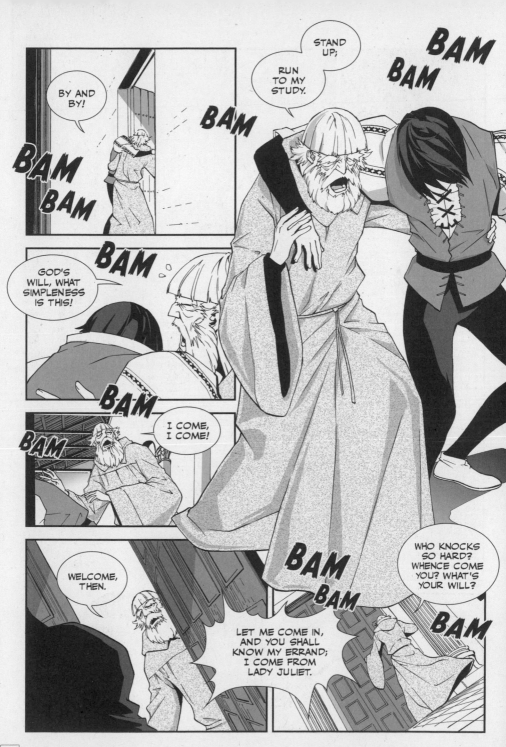

THY JULIET IS ALIVE, FOR WHOSE DEAR SAKE THOU WAST BUT LATELY DEAD; THERE ART THOU HAPPY:

TYBALT WOULD KILL THEE, BUT THOU SLEW'ST TYBALT; THERE ARE THOU HAPPY TOO:

THE LAW THAT THREATENED DEATH BECOMES THY FRIEND AND TURNS IT TO EXILE; THERE ART THOU HAPPY:

A PACK OF BLESSINGS LIGHTS UP UPON THY BACK; HAPPINESS COURTS THEE IN HER BEST ARRAY;

BUT, LIKE A MISBEHAVED AND SULLEN WENCH, THOU POUT'ST UPON THY FORTUNE AND THY LOVE: TAKE HEED, TAKE HEED, FOR SUCH DIE MISERABLE.

BUT LOOK THOU STAY NOT TILL THE WATCH BE SET, FOR THEN THOU CANST NOT PASS TO MANTUA; WHERE THOU SHALT LIVE, TILL WE CAN FIND A TIME TO BLAZE YOUR MARRIAGE, RECONCILE YOUR FRIENDS,

BEG PARDON OF THE PRINCE, AND CALL THEE BACK WITH TWENTY HUNDRED THOUSAND TIMES MORE JOY THAN THOU WENT'ST FORTH IN LAMENTATION.

GO, GET THEE TO THY LOVE, AS WAS DECREED, ASCEND HER CHAMBER, HENCE AND COMFORT HER:

GO BEFORE, NURSE: COMMEND ME TO THY LADY; AND BID HER HASTEN ALL THE HOUSE TO BED, WHICH HEAVY SORROW MAKES THEM APT UNTO: ROMEO IS COMING.

O LORD, I COULD HAVE STAYED HERE ALL THE NIGHT TO HEAR GOOD COUNSEL: O, WHAT LEARNING IS!

MY LORD, I'LL TELL MY LADY YOU WILL COME.

242

HERE, SIR, A RING SHE BID ME GIVE YOU, SIR: HIE YOU, MAKE HASTE, FOR IT GROWS VERY LATE.

PAP

DO SO, AND BID MY SWEET PREPARE TO CHIDE.

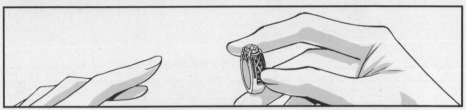

HOW WELL MY COMFORT IS REVIVED BY THIS!

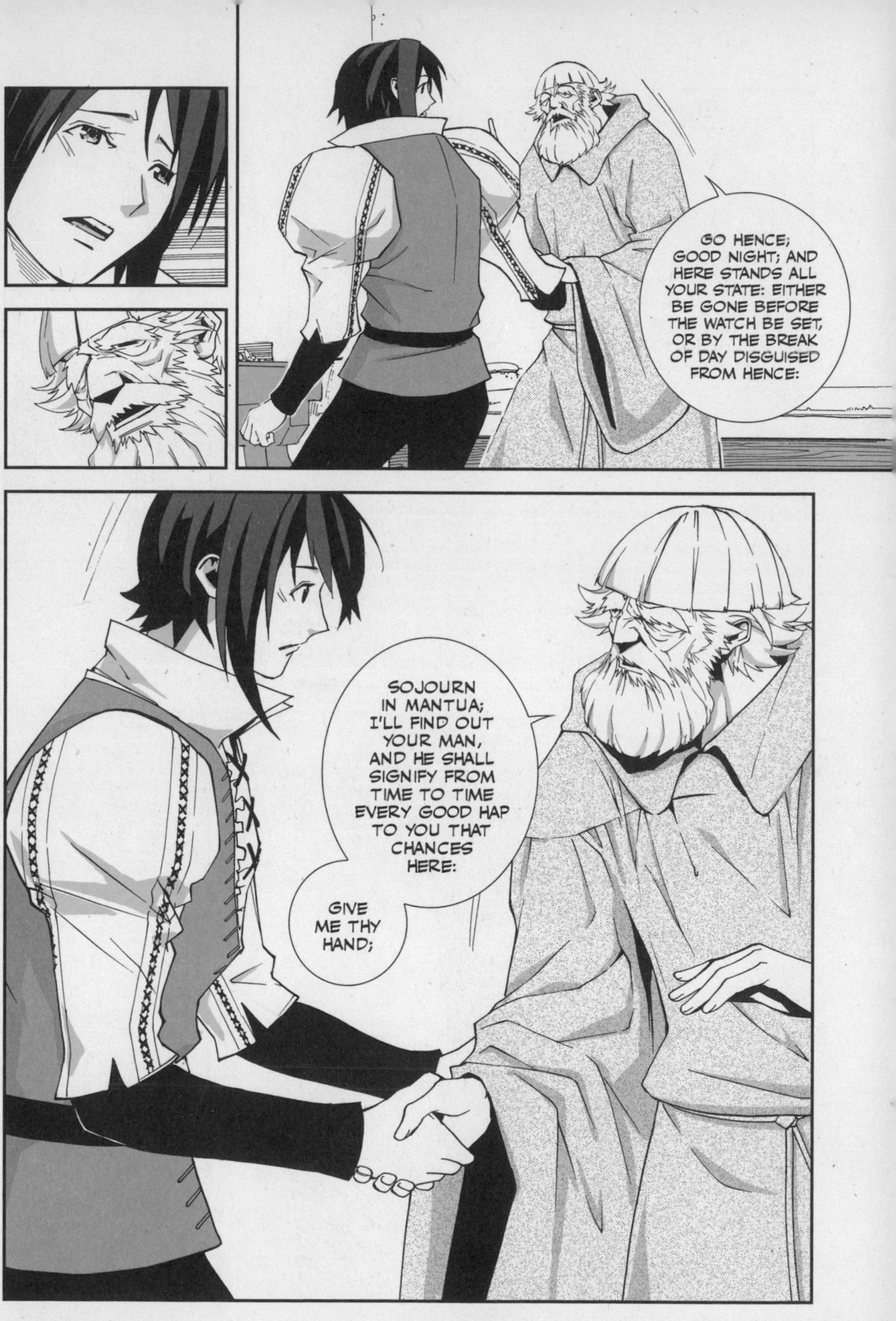
GO HENCE; GOOD NIGHT; AND HERE STANDS ALL YOUR STATE: EITHER BE GONE BEFORE THE WATCH BE SET, OR BY THE BREAK OF DAY DISGUISED FROM HENCE:
SOJOURN IN MANTUA; I'LL FIND OUT YOUR MAN, AND HE SHALL SIGNIFY FROM TIME TO TIME EVERY GOOD HAP TO YOU THAT CHANCES HERE:
GIVE ME THY HAND;

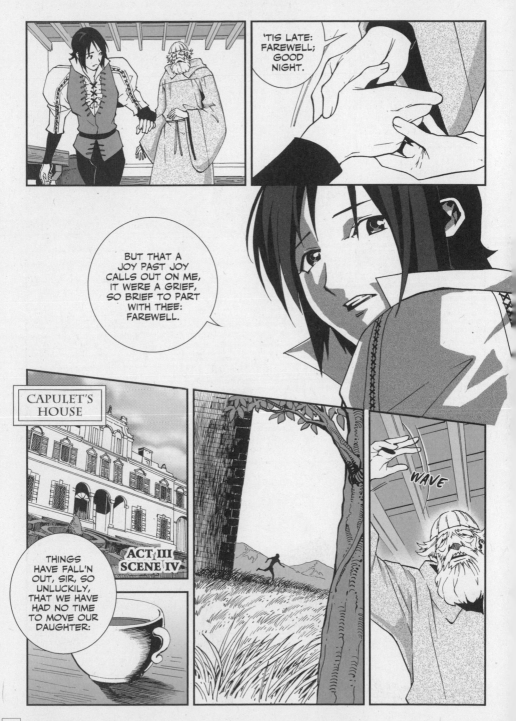

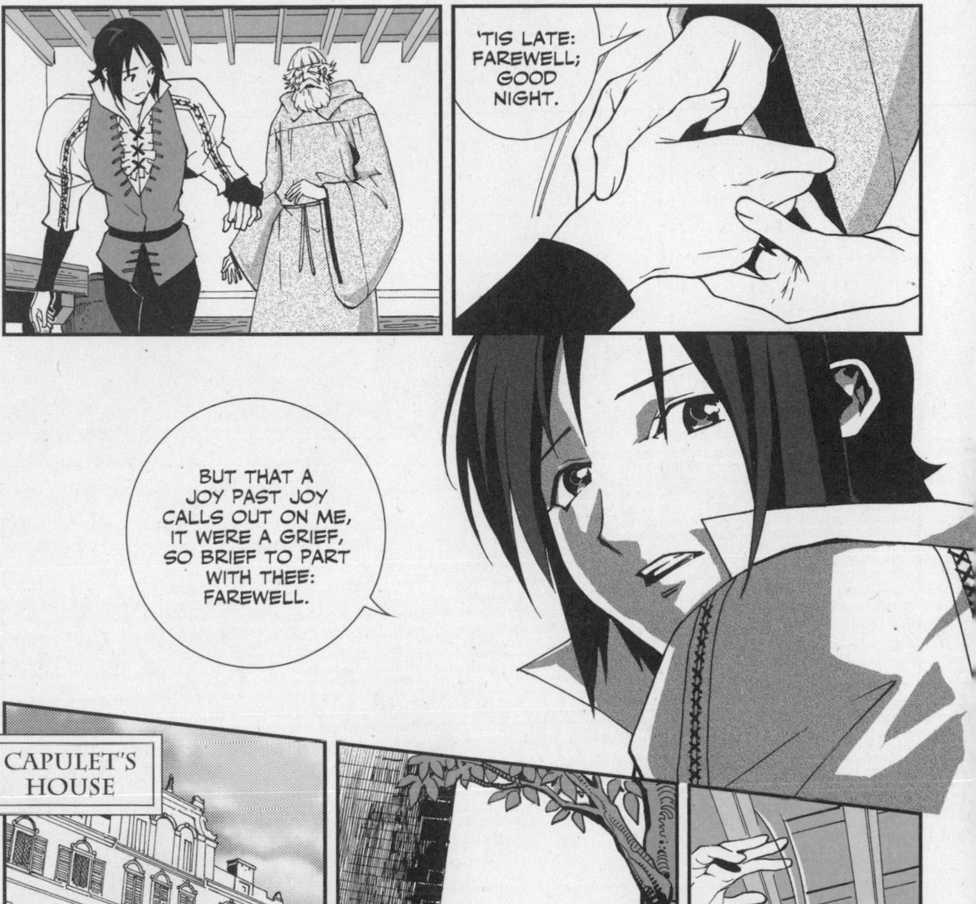
'TIS LATE: FAREWELL; GOOD NIGHT.
BUT THAT A JOY PAST JOY CALLS OUT ON ME, IT WERE A GRIEF, SO BRIEF TO PART WITH THEE: FAREWELL.
WAVE
CAPULET'S HOUSE
ACT III SCENE IV
THINGS HAVE FALL'N OUT, SIR, SO UNLUCKILY, THAT WE HAVE HAD NO TIME TO MOVE OUR DAUGHTER:

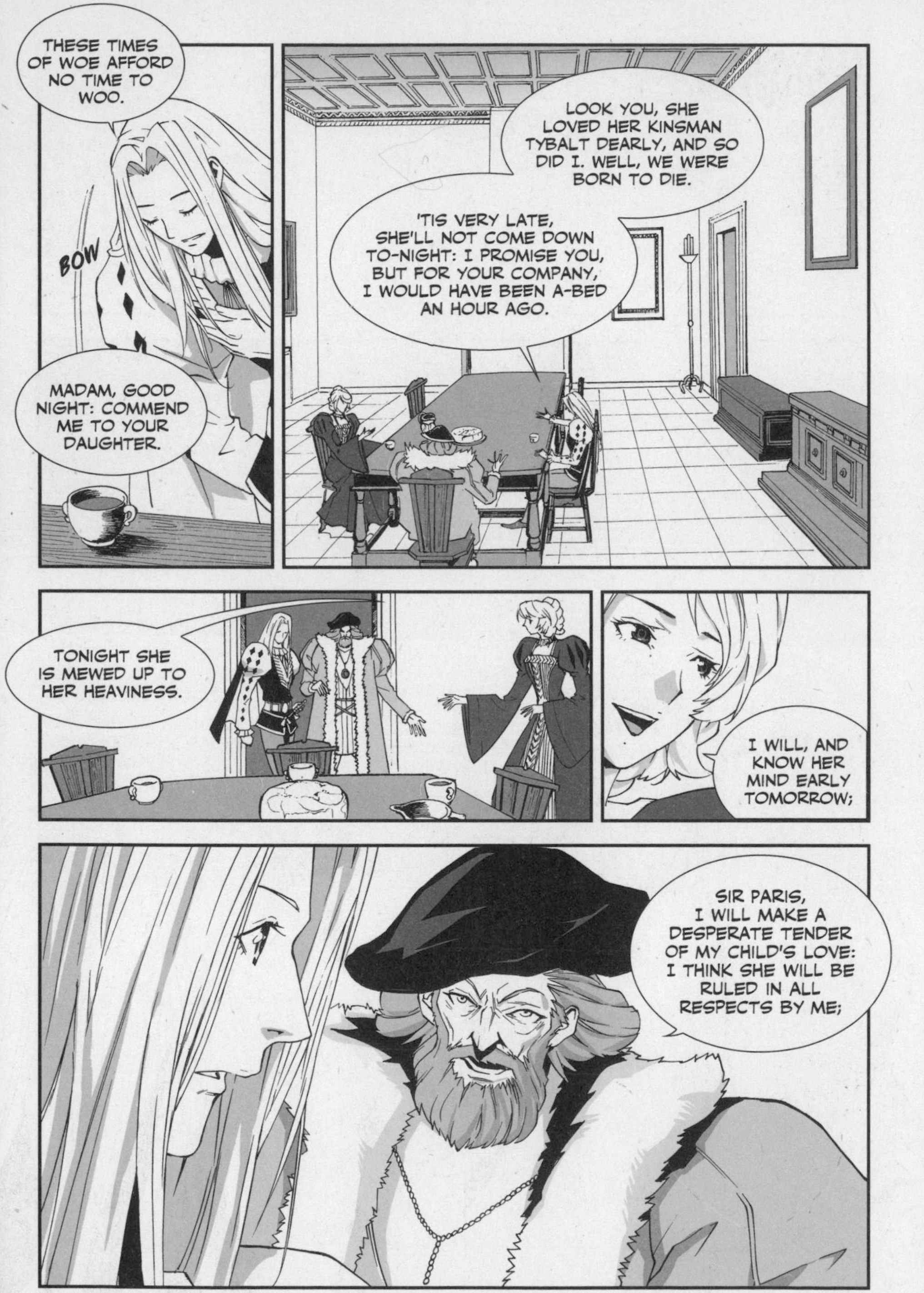
THESE TIMES OF WOE AFFORD NO TIME TO WOO.
BOW
MADAM, GOOD NIGHT: COMMEND ME TO YOUR DAUGHTER.
LOOK YOU, SHE LOVED HER KINSMAN TYBALT DEARLY, AND SO DID I. WELL, WE WERE BORN TO DIE.
'TIS VERY LATE, SHE'LL NOT COME DOWN TO-NIGHT: I PROMISE YOU, BUT FOR YOUR COMPANY, I WOULD HAVE BEEN A-BED AN HOUR AGO.
TONIGHT SHE IS MEWED UP TO HER HEAVINESS.
I WILL, AND KNOW HER MIND EARLY TOMORROW;
SIR PARIS, I WILL MAKE A DESPERATE TENDER OF MY CHILD'S LOVE: I THINK SHE WILL BE RULED IN ALL RESPECTS BY ME;

O' THURSDAY, TELL HER, SHE SHALL BE MARRIED TO THIS NOBLE EARL.

FOR, HARK YOU, TYBALT BEING SLAIN SO LATE, IT MAY BE THOUGHT WE HELD HIM CARELESSLY, BEING OUR KINSMAN, IF WE REVEL MUCH:

WILL YOU BE READY? DO YOU LIKE THIS HASTE? WE'LL KEEP NO GREAT ADO - A FRIEND OR TWO;

MY LORD, I WOULD THAT THURSDAY WERE TO-MORROW.

THEREFORE WE'LL HAVE SOME HALF A DOZEN FRIENDS, AND THERE AN END. BUT WHAT SAY YOU TO THURSDAY?

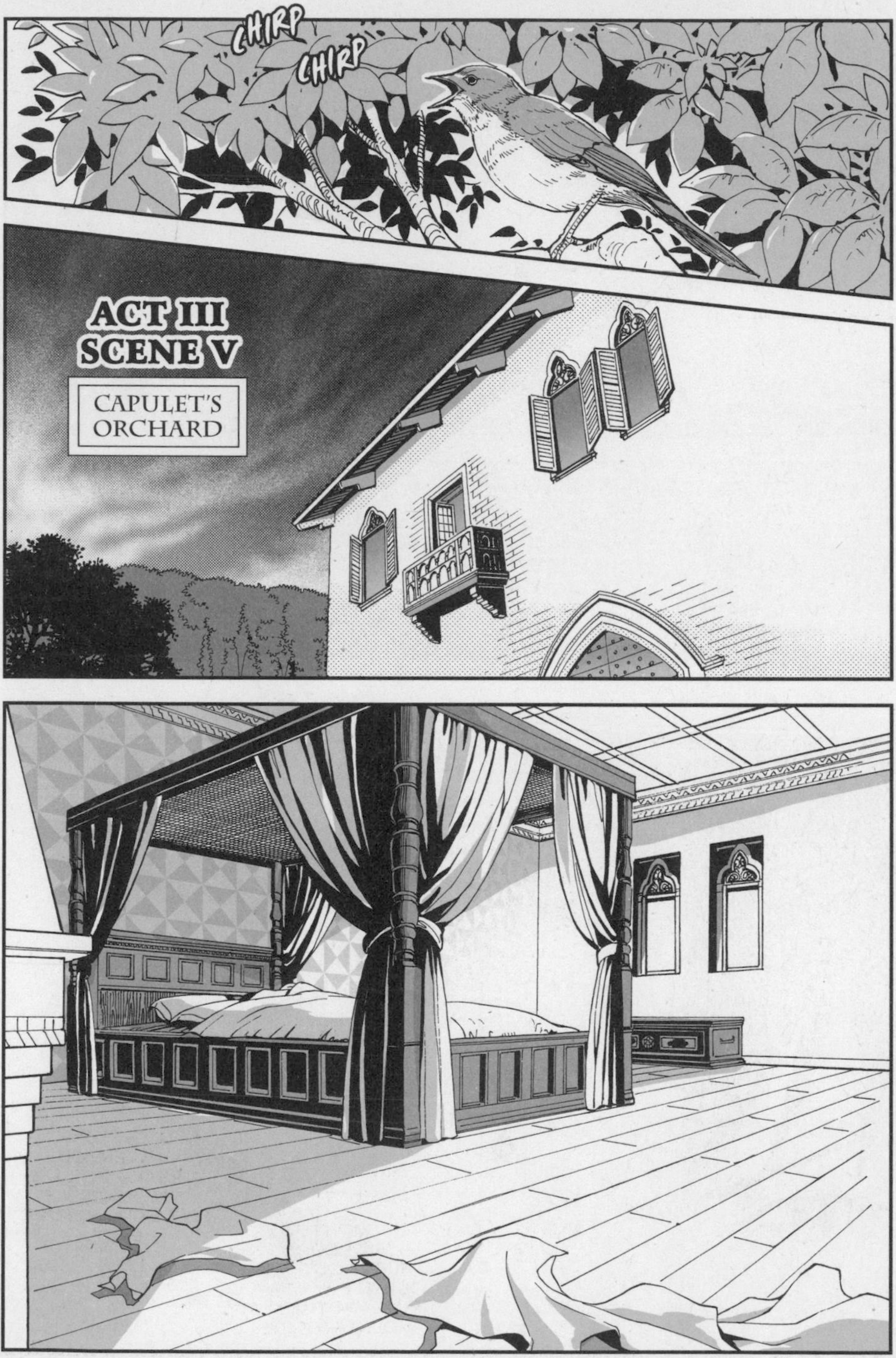
CHIRP
CHIRP
ACT III
SCENE V
CAPULET'S
ORCHARD

WILT THOU BE GONE? IT IS NOT YET NEAR DAY:

...

RUSTLE

IT WAS THE NIGHTINGALE, AND NOT THE LARK, THAT PIERCED THE FEARFUL HOLLOW OF THINE EAR;

NIGHTLY SHE SINGS ON YON POMEGRANATE-TREE: BELIEVE ME, LOVE, IT WAS THE NIGHTINGALE.

I MUST BE GONE AND LIVE, OR STAY AND DIE.

IT WAS THE LARK, THE HERALD OF THE MORN, NO NIGHTINGALE.

LOOK, LOVE, WHAT ENVIOUS STREAKS DO LACE THE SEVERING CLOUDS IN YONDER EAST.

NIGHT'S CANDLES ARE BURNT OUT, AND JOCUND DAY STANDS TIPTOE ON THE MISTY MOUNTAIN TOPS.

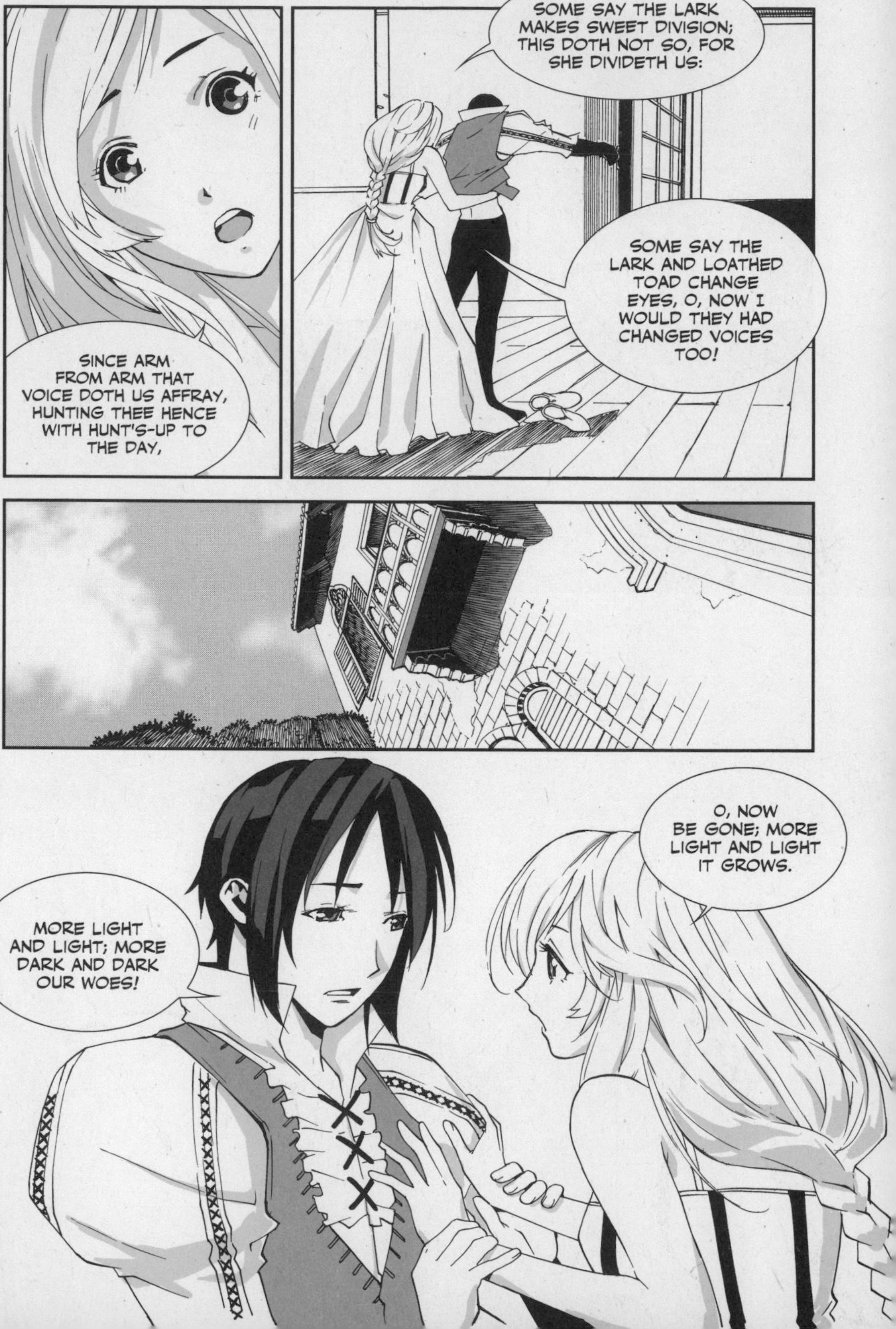
SOME SAY THE LARK MAKES SWEET DIVISION; THIS DOTH NOT SO, FOR SHE DIVIDETH US:
SOME SAY THE LARK AND LOATHED TOAD CHANGE EYES, O, NOW I WOULD THEY HAD CHANGED VOICES TOO!
SINCE ARM FROM ARM THAT VOICE DOTH US AFFRAY, HUNTING THEE HENCE WITH HUNT'S-UP TO THE DAY,
O, NOW BE GONE; MORE LIGHT AND LIGHT IT GROWS.
MORE LIGHT AND LIGHT; MORE DARK AND DARK OUR WOES!

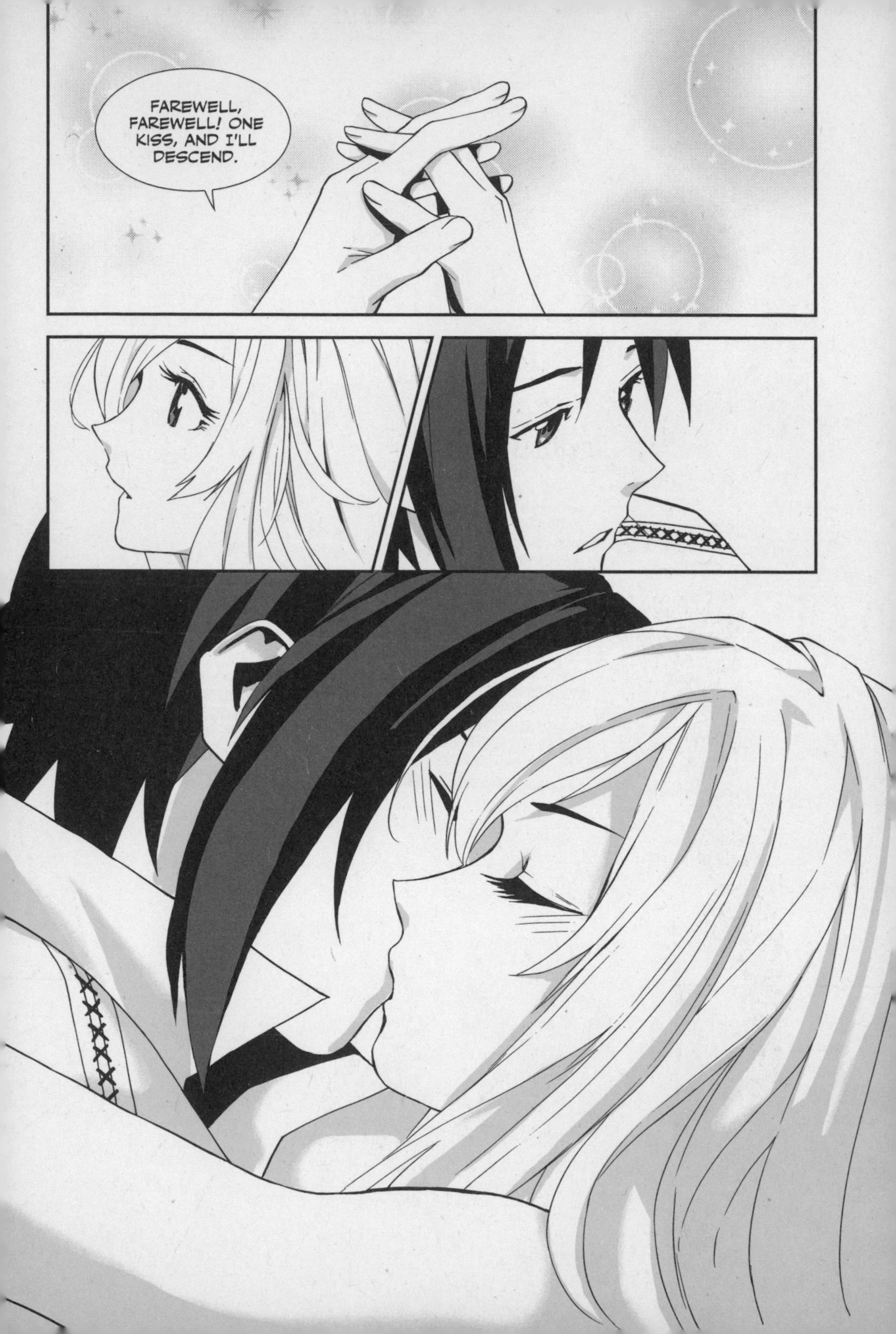
FAREWELL, FAREWELL! ONE KISS, AND I'LL DESCEND.

FAREWELL!

I WILL OMIT NO OPPORTUNITY THAT MAY CONVEY MY GREETINGS, LOVE, TO THEE.

I DOUBT IT NOT; AND ALL THESE WOES SHALL SERVE FOR SWEET DISCOURSES IN OUR TIME TO COME.

O THINK'ST THOU WE SHALL EVER MEET AGAIN?

DASH

HO, DAUGHTER! ARE YOU UP?

SNIVER

SNIFF

WHO IS'T THAT CALLS? IS IT MY LADY MOTHER?

IS SHE NOT DOWN SO LATE, OR UP SO EARLY? WHAT UNACCUSTOMED CAUSE PROCURES HER HITHER?

MADAM, I AM NOT WELL.

WHY, HOW NOW, JULIET!

THEREFORE, HAVE DONE: SOME GRIEF SHOWS MUCH OF LOVE; BUT MUCH OF GRIEF SHOWS STILL SOME WANT OF WIT.

EVERMORE WEEPING FOR YOUR COUSIN'S DEATH? WHAT, WILT THOU WASH HIM FROM HIS GRAVE WITH TEARS?

AN IF THOU COULDST, THOU COULDST NOT MAKE HIM LIVE;

SO SHALL YOU FEEL THE LOSS, BUT NOT THE FRIEND WHICH YOU WEEP FOR.

YET LET ME WEEP FOR SUCH A FEELING LOSS.

WELL, GIRL, THOU WEEP'ST NOT SO MUCH FOR HIS DEATH, AS THAT THE VILLAIN LIVES WHICH SLAUGHTERED HIM.

FEELING SO THE LOSS, CANNOT CHOOSE BUT EVER WEEP THE FRIEND.

SHALL GIVE HIM SUCH AN UNACCUSTOMED DRAM, THAT HE SHALL SOON KEEP TYBALT COMPANY: AND THEN, I HOPE, THOU WILT BE SATISFIED.

THEN WEEP NO MORE. I'LL SEND TO ONE IN MANTUA, WHERE THAT SAME BANISHED RUNAGATE DOTH LIVE,

INDEED, I NEVER SHALL BE SATISFIED WITH ROMEO, TILL I BEHOLD HIM – DEAD – IS MY POOR HEART FOR A KINSMAN VEX'D.

MADAM, IF YOU COULD FIND OUT BUT A MAN TO BEAR A POISON, I WOULD TEMPER IT; THAT ROMEO SHOULD, UPON RECEIPT THEREOF, SOON SLEEP IN QUIET.

FIND THOU THE MEANS, AND I'LL FIND SUCH A MAN.

O, HOW MY HEART ABHORS TO HEAR HIM NAMED, AND CANNOT COME TO HIM.

BUT NOW I'LL TELL THEE JOYFUL TIDINGS, GIRL.

TO WREAK THE LOVE I BORE MY COUSIN UPON HIS BODY THAT SLAUGHTERED HIM!

AND JOY COMES WELL IN SUCH A NEEDY TIME: WHAT ARE THEY, I BESEECH YOUR LADYSHIP?

WELL, WELL, THOU HAST A CAREFUL FATHER, CHILD; ONE WHO, TO PUT THEE FROM THY HEAVINESS, HATH SORTED OUT A SUDDEN DAY OF JOY,

THAT THOU EXPECTS NOT NOR I LOOKED NOT FOR.

MARRY, MY CHILD, EARLY NEXT THURSDAY MORN, THE GALLANT, YOUNG AND NOBLE GENTLEMAN, THE COUNTY PARIS, AT SAINT PETER'S CHURCH, SHALL HAPPILY MAKE THEE THERE A JOYFUL BRIDE.

MADAM, IN HAPPY TIME, WHAT DAY IS THAT?

NOW, BY SAINT PETER'S CHURCH AND PETER TOO, HE SHALL NOT MAKE ME THERE A JOYFUL BRIDE.

I WONDER AT THIS HASTE; THAT I MUST WED ERE HE, THAT SHOULD BE HUSBAND, COMES TO WOO.

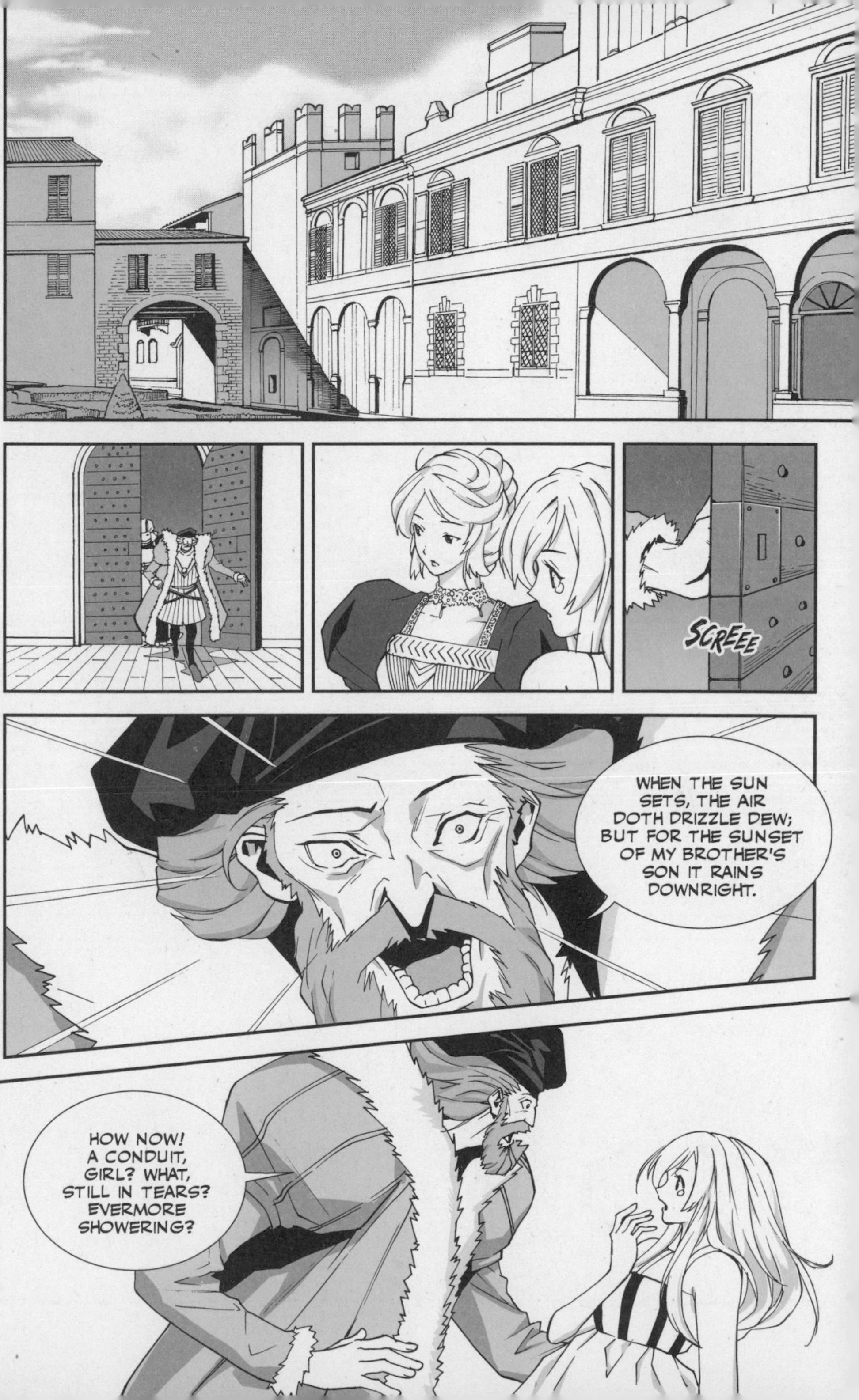
SCREEE
WHEN THE SUN SETS, THE AIR DOTH DRIZZLE DEW; BUT FOR THE SUNSET OF MY BROTHER'S SON IT RAINS DOWNRIGHT.
HOW NOW! A CONDUIT, GIRL? WHAT, STILL IN TEARS? EVERMORE SHOWERING?

HUFF

HUFF

FLINCH

BUT NOW I SEE THIS ONE IS ONE TOO MUCH, AND THAT WE HAVE A CURSE IN HAVING HER:

OUT ON HER, HILDING!

GRAB!

WIFE, WE SCARCE THOUGHT US BLEST THAT GOD HAD LENT US BUT THIS ONLY CHILD;

AND WHY, MY LADY WISDOM?

HOLD YOUR TONGUE, GOOD PRUDENCE; SMATTER WITH YOUR GOSSIPS, GO.

GOD IN HEAVEN BLESS HER! YOU ARE TO BLAME, MY LORD, TO RATE HER SO.

O, GOD YE GOD-DEN.

MAY NOT ONE SPEAK?

I SPEAK NO TREASON.

PEACE, YOU MUMBLING FOOL!

UTTER YOUR GRAVITY O'ER A GOSSIP'S BOWL; FOR HERE WE NEED IT NOT.

275

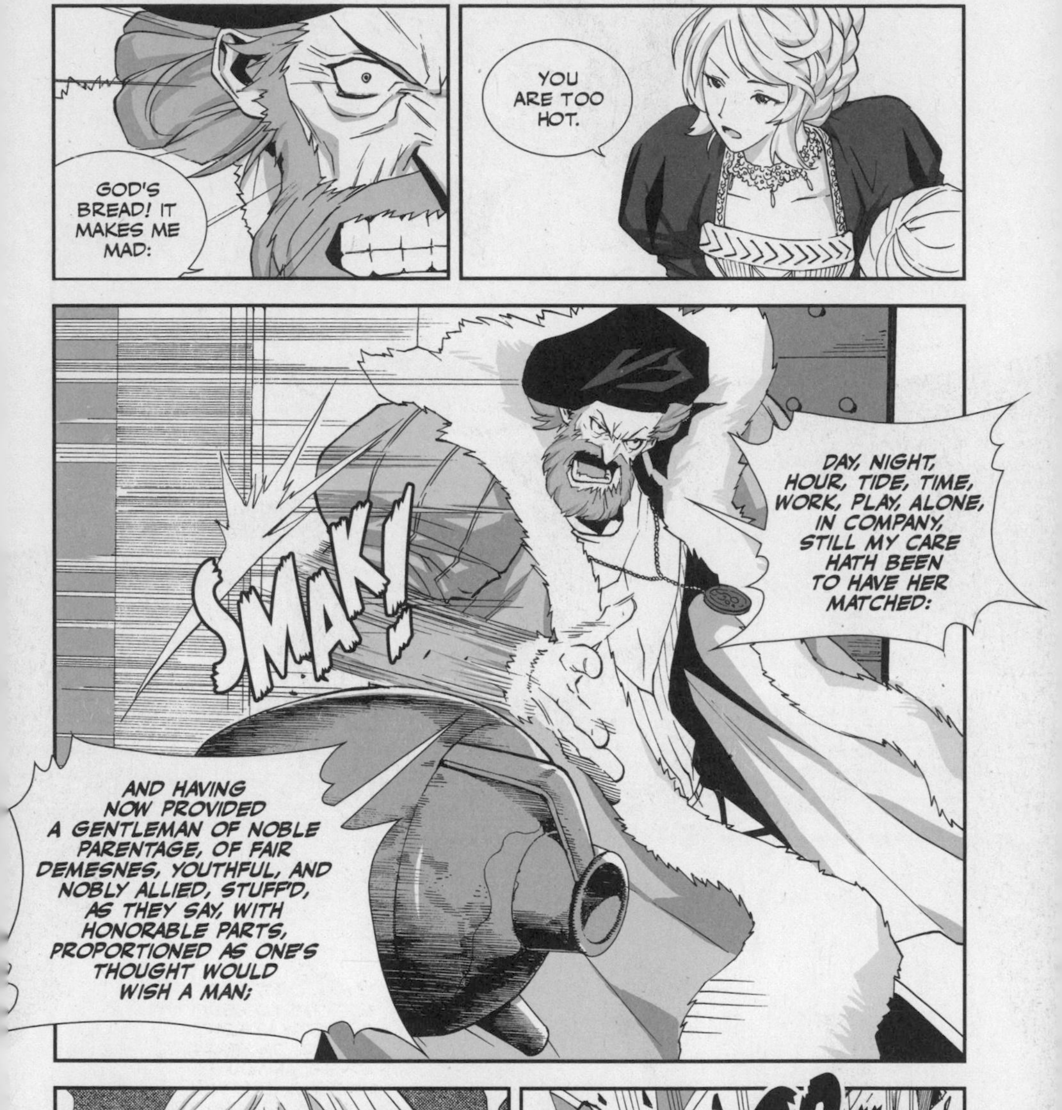
YOU ARE TOO HOT.
GOD'S BREAD! IT MAKES ME MAD:
DAY, NIGHT, HOUR, TIDE, TIME, WORK, PLAY, ALONE, IN COMPANY, STILL MY CARE HATH BEEN TO HAVE HER MATCHED:
SMAK!
AND HAVING NOW PROVIDED A GENTLEMAN OF NOBLE PARENTAGE, OF FAIR DEMESNES, YOUTHFUL, AND NOBLY ALLIED, STUFF'D, AS THEY SAY, WITH HONORABLE PARTS, PROPORTIONED AS ONE'S THOUGHT WOULD WISH A MAN;
CRAASH
SOB

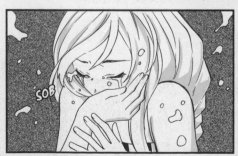

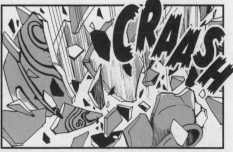

DO AS THOU WILT, FOR I HAVE DONE WITH THEE.

TALK NOT TO ME, FOR I'LL NOT SPEAK A WORD:

SNATCH

O GOD!

SHH!

O NURSE, HOW SHALL THIS BE PREVENTED?

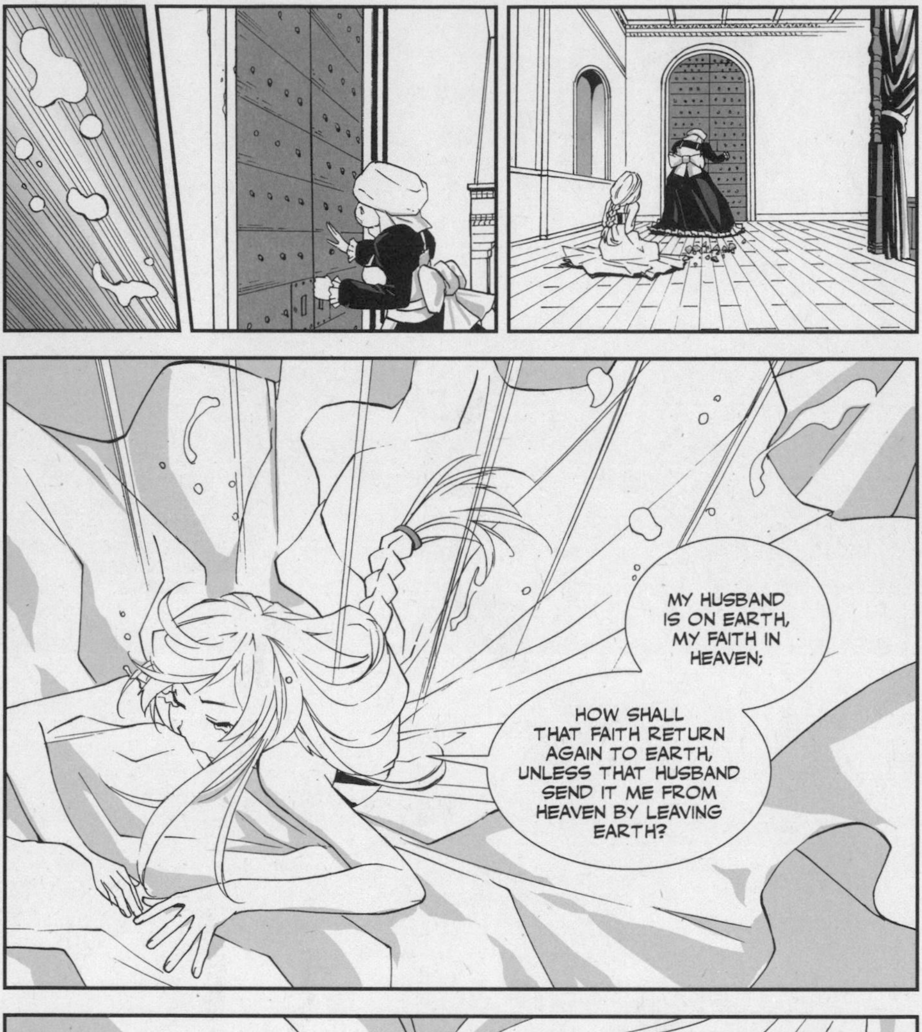
MY HUSBAND IS ON EARTH, MY FAITH IN HEAVEN;
HOW SHALL THAT FAITH RETURN AGAIN TO EARTH, UNLESS THAT HUSBAND SEND IT ME FROM HEAVEN BY LEAVING EARTH?
COMFORT ME, COUNSEL ME. ALACK, ALACK, THAT HEAVEN SHOULD PRACTICE STRATAGEMS
UPON SO SOFT A SUBJECT AS MYSELF!

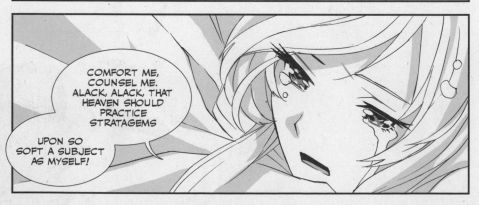

WHAT?

WELL, THOU HAST COMFORTED ME MARVELLOUS MUCH. GO IN:

AND TELL MY LADY I AM GONE, HAVING DISPLEASED MY FATHER, TO LAURENCE' CELL, TO MAKE CONFESSION AND TO BE ABSOLVED.

CLICK

MARRY, I WILL;

AND THIS IS WISELY DONE.

ON THURSDAY, SIR? THE TIME IS VERY SHORT.

ACT IV SCENE I

FRIAR LAURENCE'S CELL

YOU SAY YOU DO NOT KNOW THE LADY'S MIND: UNEVEN IS THE COURSE, I LIKE IT NOT.

MY FATHER CAPULET WILL HAVE IT SO; AND I AM NOTHING SLOW TO SLACK HIS HASTE.

IMMODERATELY SHE WEEPS FOR TYBALT'S DEATH, AND THEREFORE HAVE I LITTLE TALK'D OF LOVE;

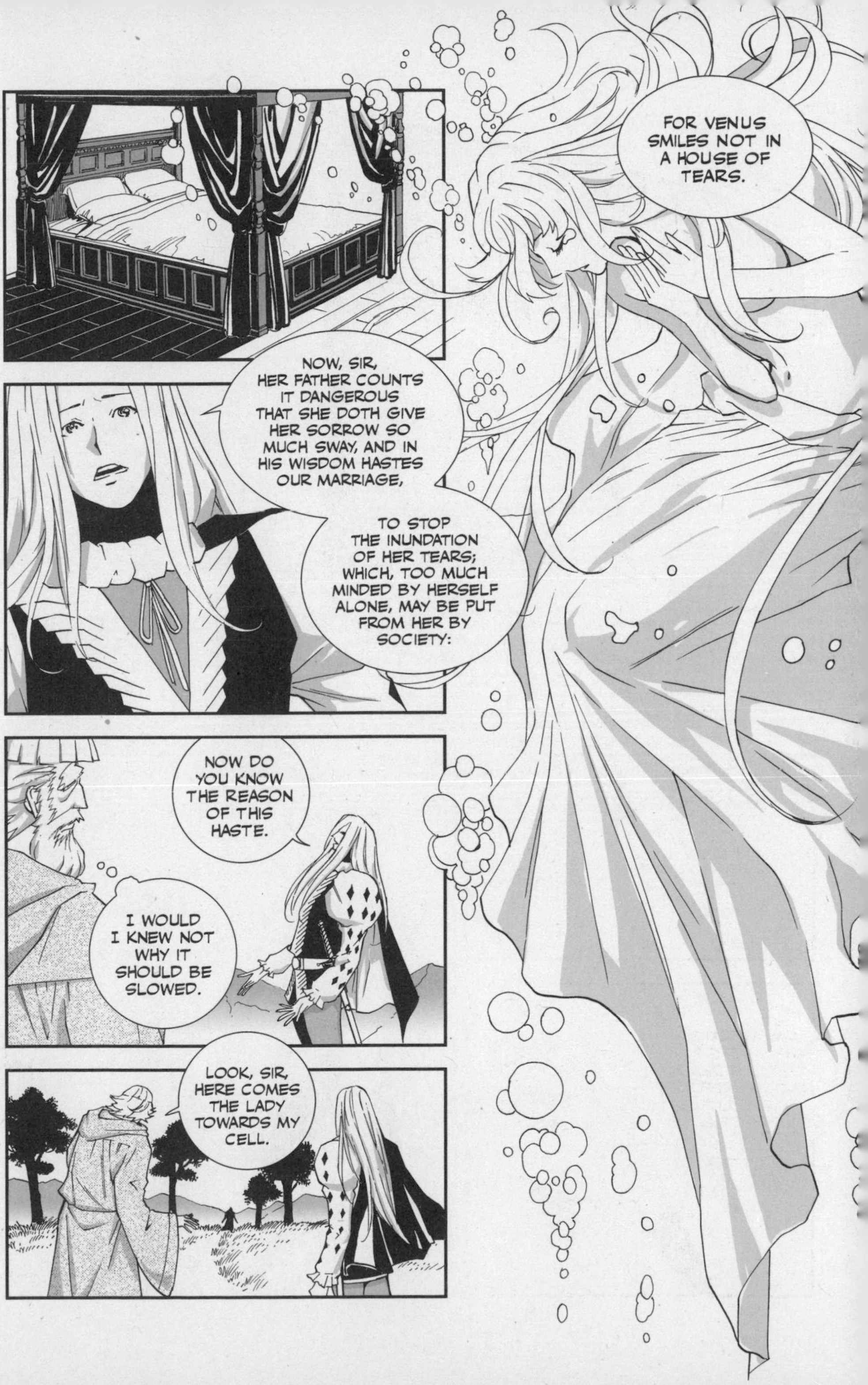
FOR VENUS SMILES NOT IN A HOUSE OF TEARS.
NOW, SIR, HER FATHER COUNTS IT DANGEROUS THAT SHE DOTH GIVE HER SORROW SO MUCH SWAY, AND IN HIS WISDOM HASTES OUR MARRIAGE,
TO STOP THE INUNDATION OF HER TEARS; WHICH, TOO MUCH MINDED BY HERSELF ALONE, MAY BE PUT FROM HER BY SOCIETY:
NOW DO YOU KNOW THE REASON OF THIS HASTE.
I WOULD I KNEW NOT WHY IT SHOULD BE SLOWED.
LOOK, SIR, HERE COMES THE LADY TOWARDS MY CELL.

COME YOU TO MAKE CONFESSION TO THIS FATHER?

THAT'S A CERTAIN TEXT.

I WILL CONFESS TO YOU THAT I LOVE HIM.

DO NOT DENY TO HIM THAT YOU LOVE ME.

TO ANSWER THAT, I SHOULD CONFESS TO YOU.

IF I DO SO, IT WILL BE OF MORE PRICE, BEING SPOKE BEHIND YOUR BACK, THAN TO YOUR FACE.

SO WILL YE, I AM SURE, THAT YOU LOVE ME.

IT MAY BE SO, FOR IT IS NOT MINE OWN.

THY FACE IS MINE, AND THOU HAST SLANDERED IT.

MY LEISURE SERVES ME, PENSIVE DAUGHTER, NOW.

MY LORD, WE MUST ENTREAT THE TIME ALONE.

ARE YOU AT LEISURE, HOLY FATHER, NOW; OR SHALL I COME TO YOU AT EVENING MASS?

JULIET, ON THURSDAY EARLY WILL I ROUSE YE:

GOD SHIELD I SHOULD DISTURB DEVOTION!

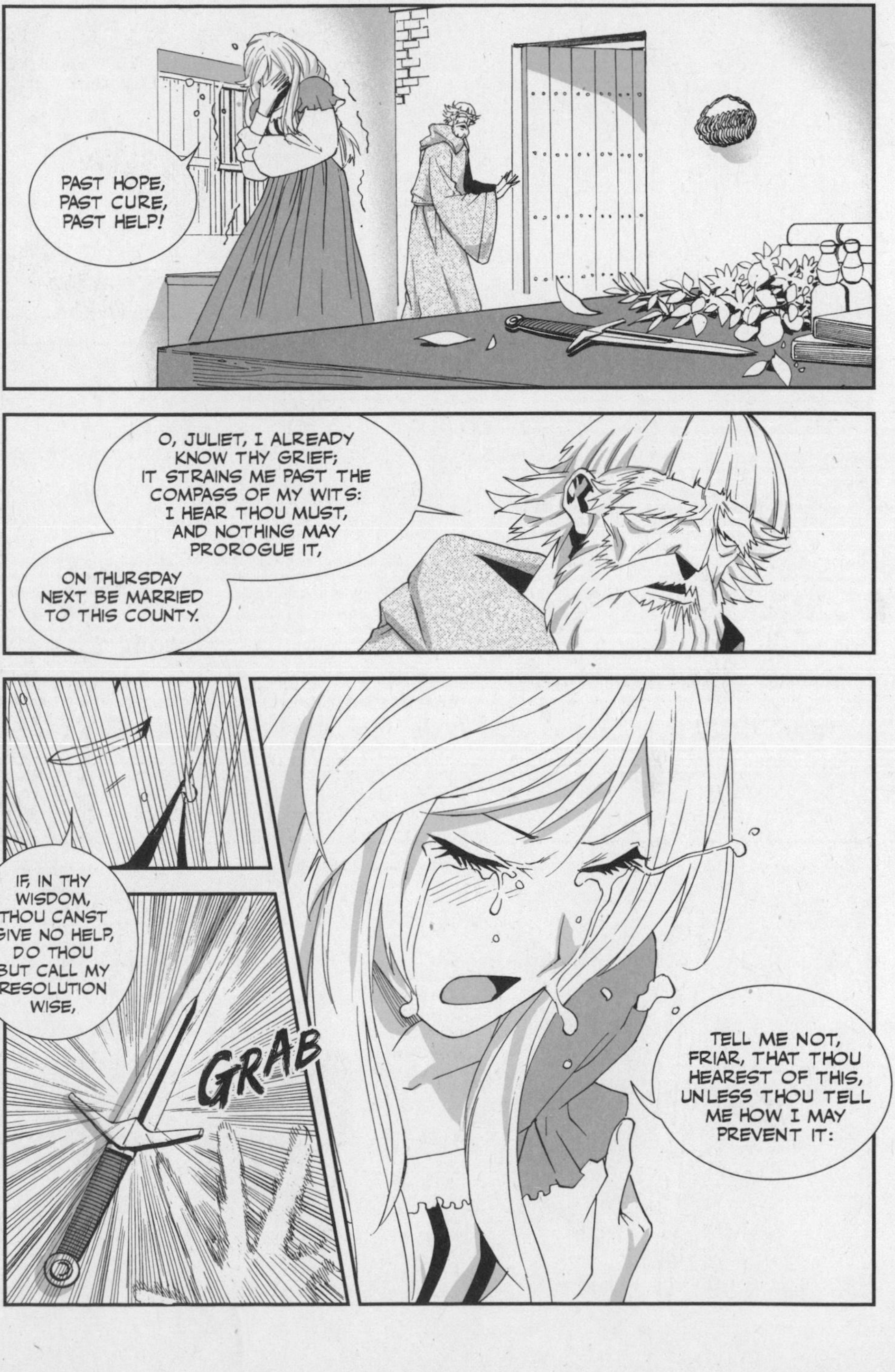
PAST HOPE, PAST CURE, PAST HELP!
O, JULIET, I ALREADY KNOW THY GRIEF; IT STRAINS ME PAST THE COMPASS OF MY WITS: I HEAR THOU MUST, AND NOTHING MAY PROROGUE IT,
ON THURSDAY NEXT BE MARRIED TO THIS COUNTY.
TELL ME NOT, FRIAR, THAT THOU HEAREST OF THIS, UNLESS THOU TELL ME HOW I MAY PREVENT IT:
IF, IN THY WISDOM, THOU CANST GIVE NO HELP, DO THOU BUT CALL MY RESOLUTION WISE,
GRAB

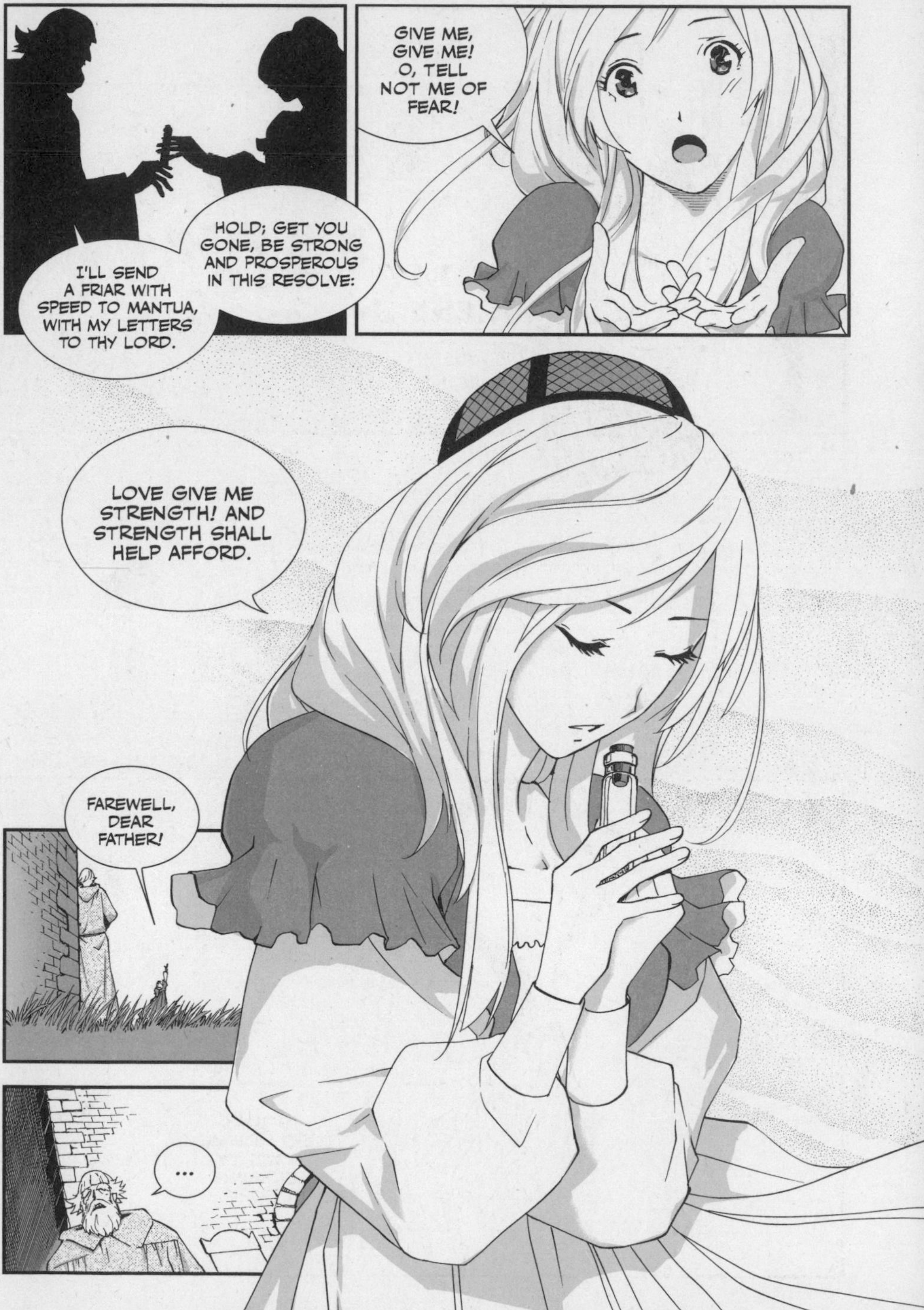
GIVE ME, GIVE ME! O, TELL NOT ME OF FEAR!
HOLD; GET YOU GONE, BE STRONG AND PROSPEROUS IN THIS RESOLVE:
I'LL SEND A FRIAR WITH SPEED TO MANTUA, WITH MY LETTERS TO THY LORD.
LOVE GIVE ME STRENGTH! AND STRENGTH SHALL HELP AFFORD.
FAREWELL, DEAR FATHER!
...

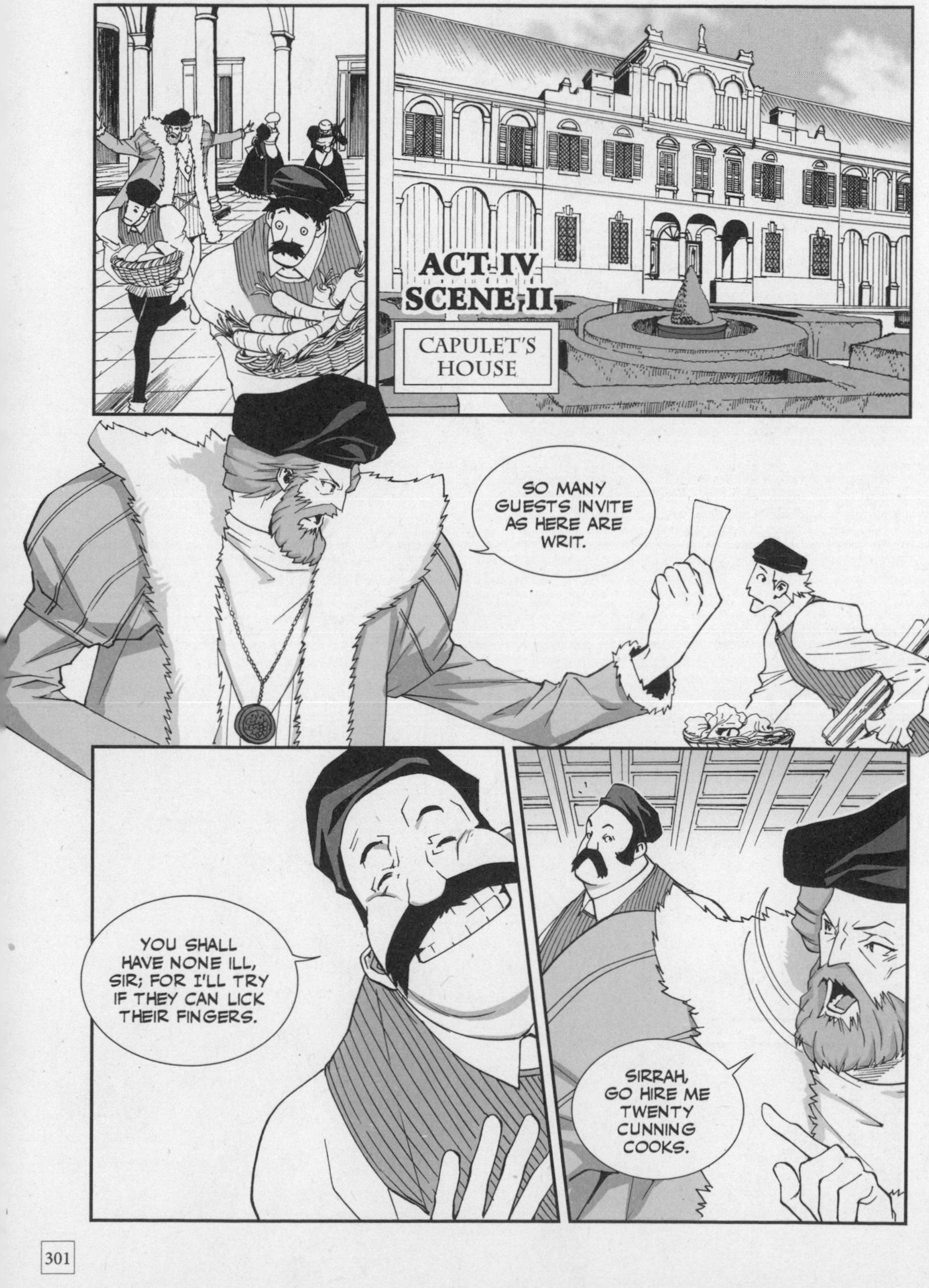
ACT IV
SCENE II
CAPULET'S HOUSE
SO MANY GUESTS INVITE AS HERE ARE WRIT.
SIRRAH, GO HIRE ME TWENTY CUNNING COOKS.
YOU SHALL HAVE NONE ILL, SIR; FOR I'LL TRY IF THEY CAN LICK THEIR FINGERS.

MARRY, SIR, 'TIS AN ILL COOK THAT CANNOT LICK HIS OWN FINGERS: THEREFORE HE THAT CANNOT LICK HIS FINGERS GOES NOT WITH ME.

HOW CANST THOU TRY THEM SO?

GO, BE GONE.

POFF POFF

WE SHALL BE MUCH UNFURNISHED FOR THIS TIME.

WHAT, IS MY DAUGHTER GONE TO FRIAR LAURENCE?

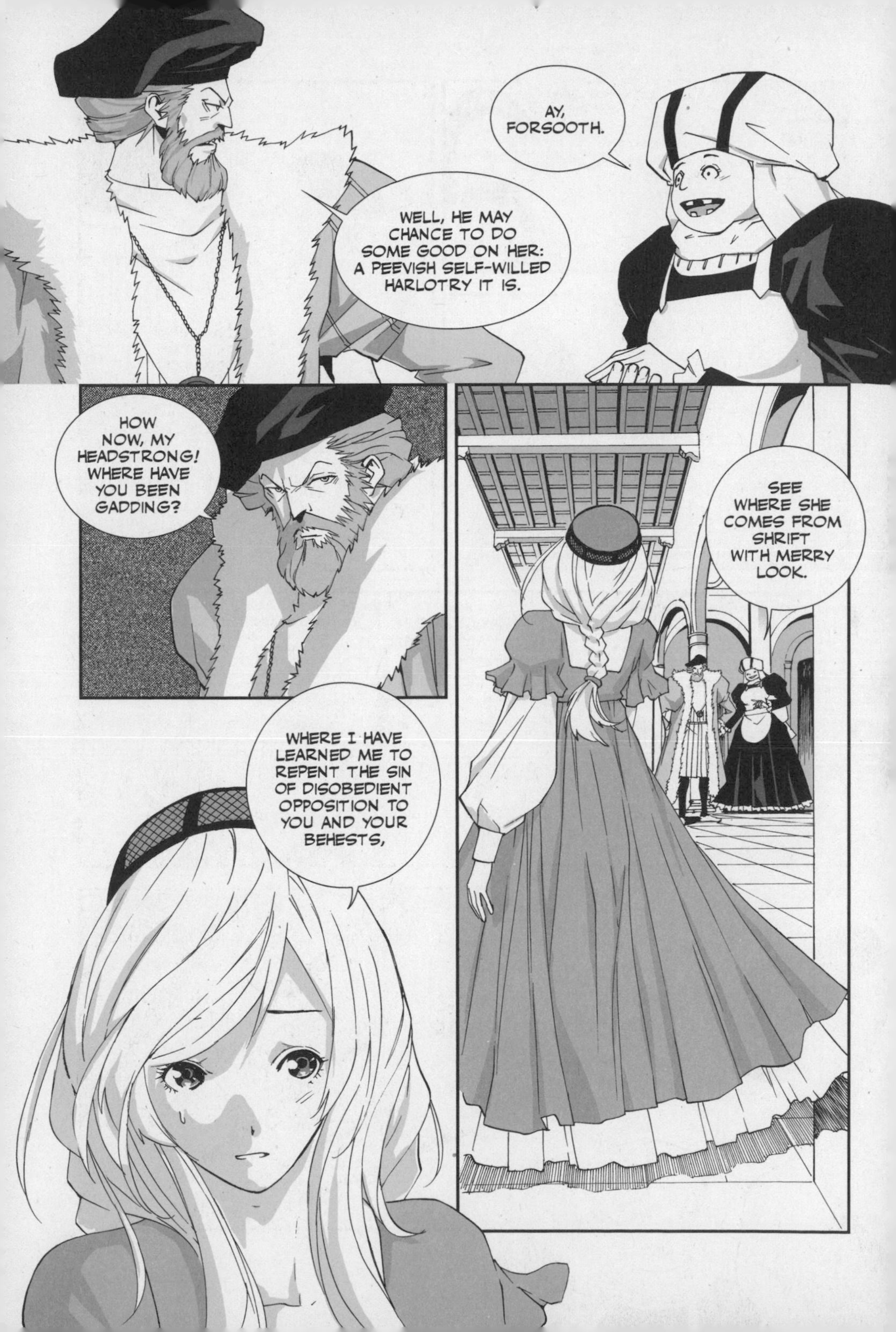
AY, FORSOOTH.
WELL, HE MAY CHANCE TO DO SOME GOOD ON HER: A PEEVISH SELF-WILLED HARLOTRY IT IS.
SEE WHERE SHE COMES FROM SHRIFT WITH MERRY LOOK.
HOW NOW, MY HEADSTRONG! WHERE HAVE YOU BEEN GADDING?
WHERE I HAVE LEARNED ME TO REPENT THE SIN OF DISOBEDIENT OPPOSITION TO YOU AND YOUR BEHESTS,

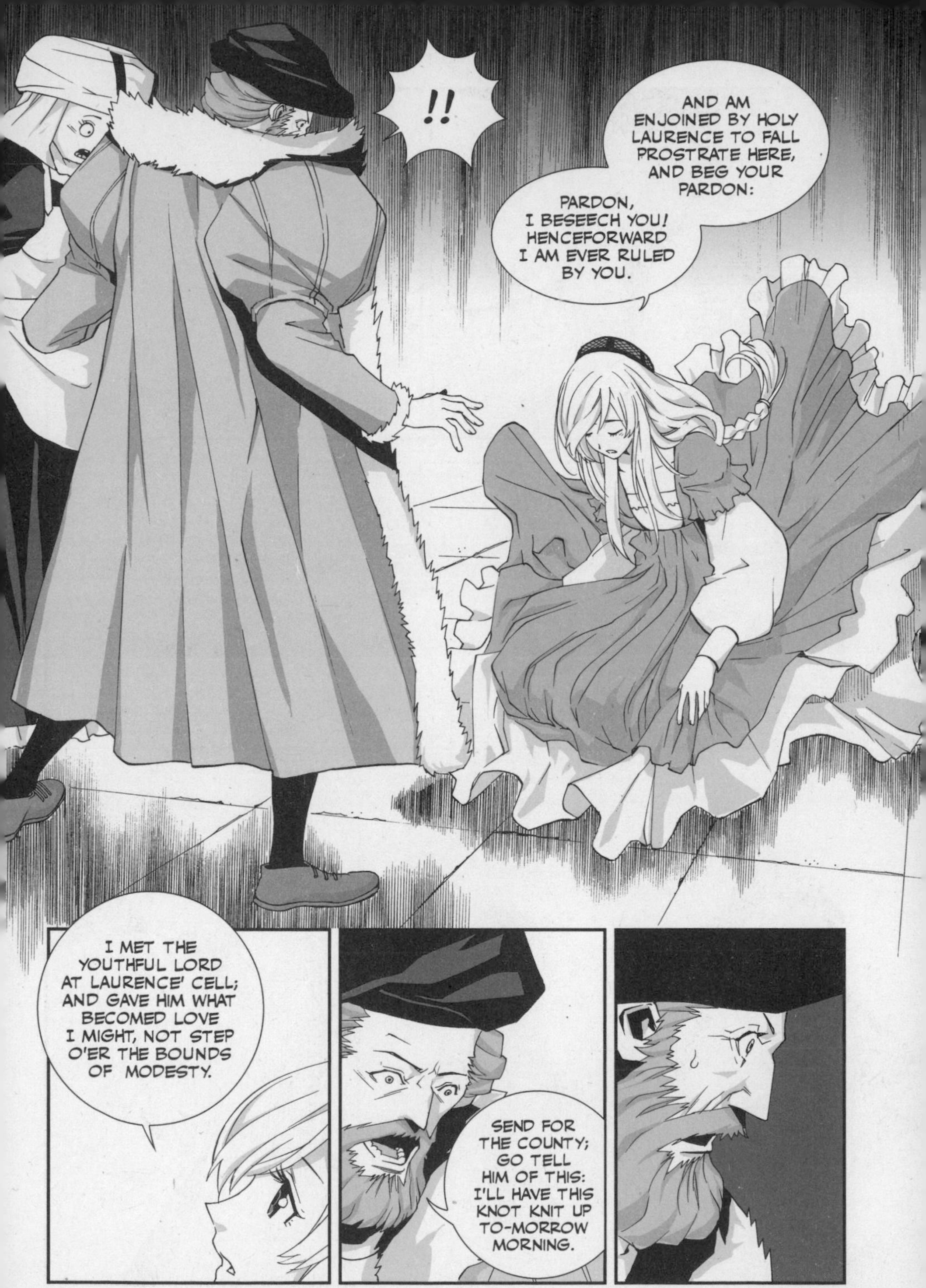
AND AM ENJOINED BY HOLY LAURENCE TO FALL PROSTRATE HERE, AND BEG YOUR PARDON:
!!
PARDON, I BESEECH YOU! HENCEFORWARD I AM EVER RULED BY YOU.
SEND FOR THE COUNTY; GO TELL HIM OF THIS: I'LL HAVE THIS KNOT KNIT UP TO-MORROW MORNING.
I MET THE YOUTHFUL LORD AT LAURENCE' CELL; AND GAVE HIM WHAT BECOMED LOVE I MIGHT, NOT STEP O'ER THE BOUNDS OF MODESTY.

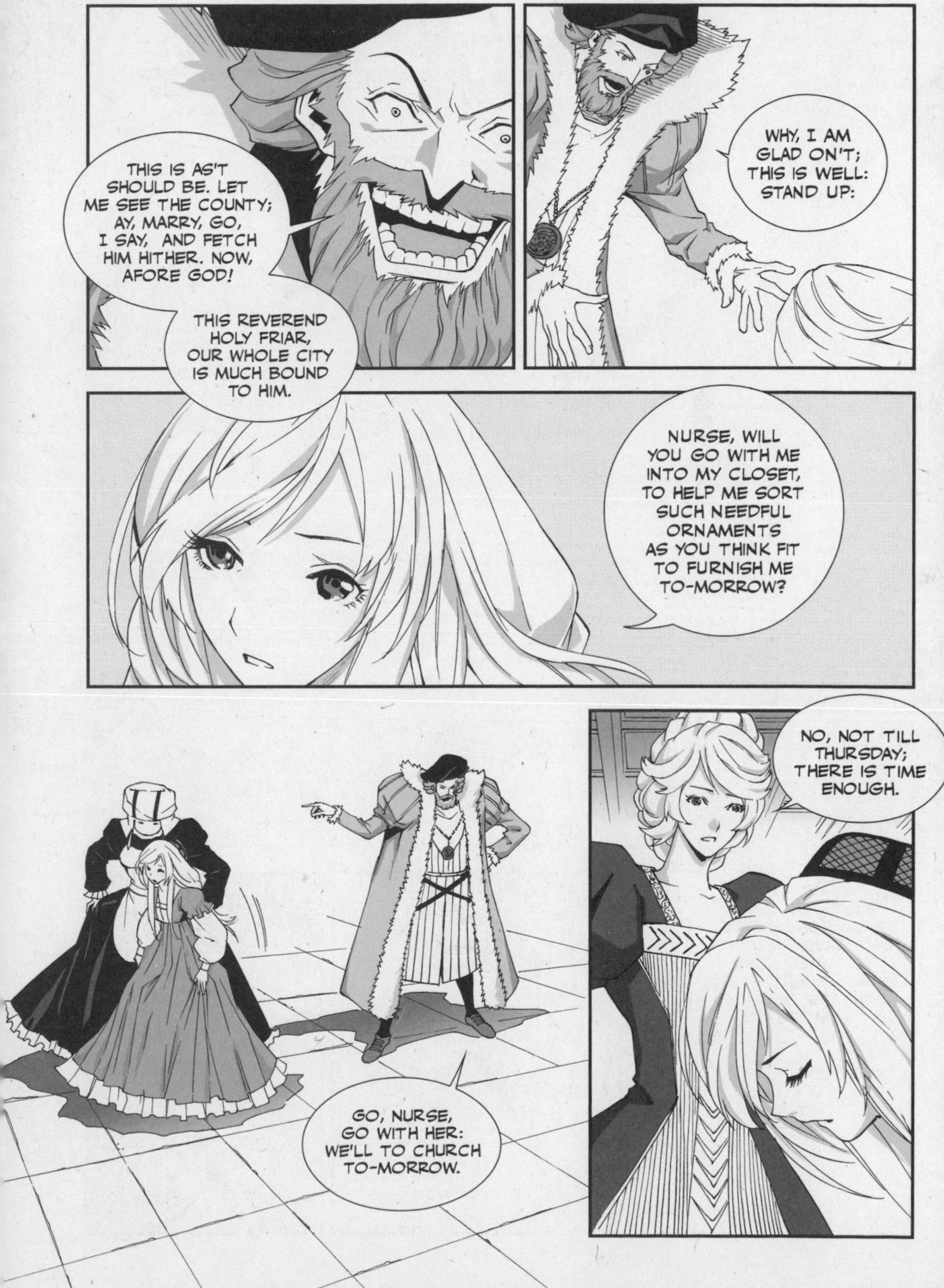
WHY, I AM GLAD ON'T; THIS IS WELL: STAND UP:
THIS IS AS'T SHOULD BE. LET ME SEE THE COUNTY; AY, MARRY, GO, I SAY, AND FETCH HIM HITHER. NOW, AFORE GOD!
THIS REVEREND HOLY FRIAR, OUR WHOLE CITY IS MUCH BOUND TO HIM.
NURSE, WILL YOU GO WITH ME INTO MY CLOSET, TO HELP ME SORT SUCH NEEDFUL ORNAMENTS AS YOU THINK FIT TO FURNISH ME TO-MORROW?
NO, NOT TILL THURSDAY; THERE IS TIME ENOUGH.
GO, NURSE, GO WITH HER: WE'LL TO CHURCH TO-MORROW.

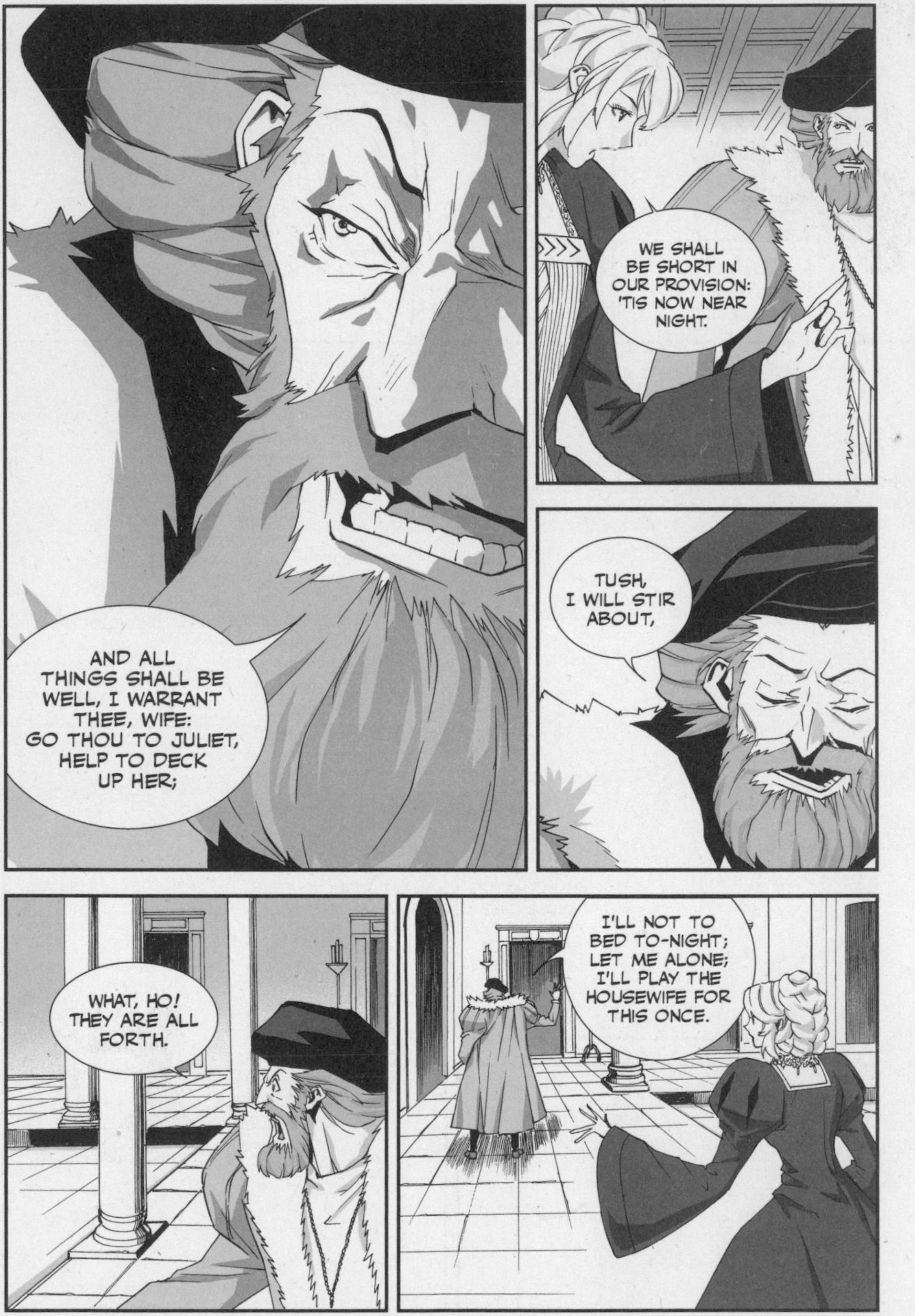
WE SHALL BE SHORT IN OUR PROVISION: 'TIS NOW NEAR NIGHT.
TUSH, I WILL STIR ABOUT,
AND ALL THINGS SHALL BE WELL, I WARRANT THEE, WIFE: GO THOU TO JULIET, HELP TO DECK UP HER;
I'LL NOT TO BED TO-NIGHT; LET ME ALONE; I'LL PLAY THE HOUSEWIFE FOR THIS ONCE.
WHAT, HO! THEY ARE ALL FORTH.

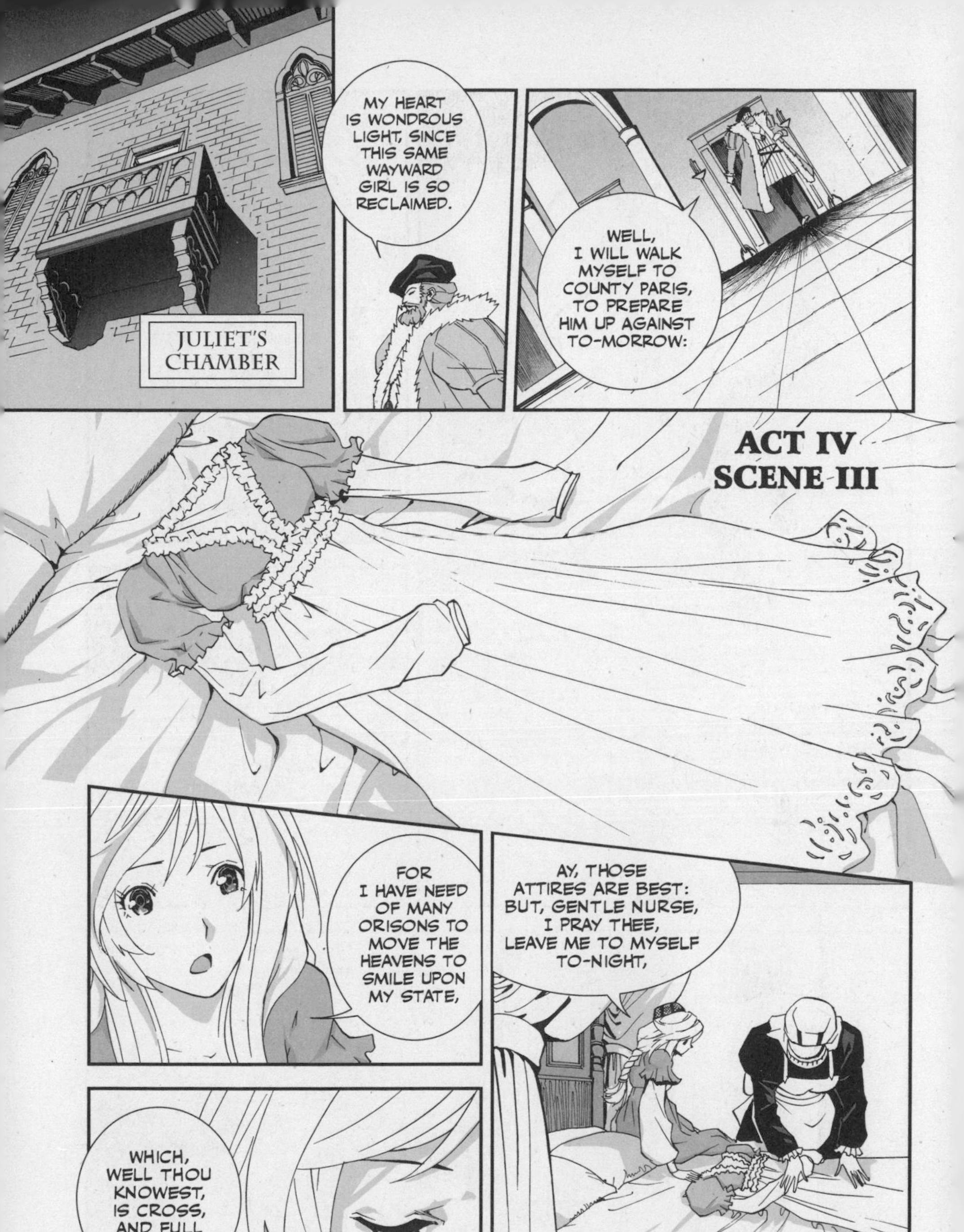
WELL, I WILL WALK MYSELF TO COUNTY PARIS, TO PREPARE HIM UP AGAINST TO-MORROW:
MY HEART IS WONDROUS LIGHT, SINCE THIS SAME WAYWARD GIRL IS SO RECLAIMED.
JULIET'S CHAMBER
ACT IV SCENE III
AY, THOSE ATTIRES ARE BEST: BUT, GENTLE NURSE, I PRAY THEE, LEAVE ME TO MYSELF TO-NIGHT,
FOR I HAVE NEED OF MANY ORISONS TO MOVE THE HEAVENS TO SMILE UPON MY STATE,
WHICH, WELL THOU KNOWEST, IS CROSS, AND FULL OF SIN.

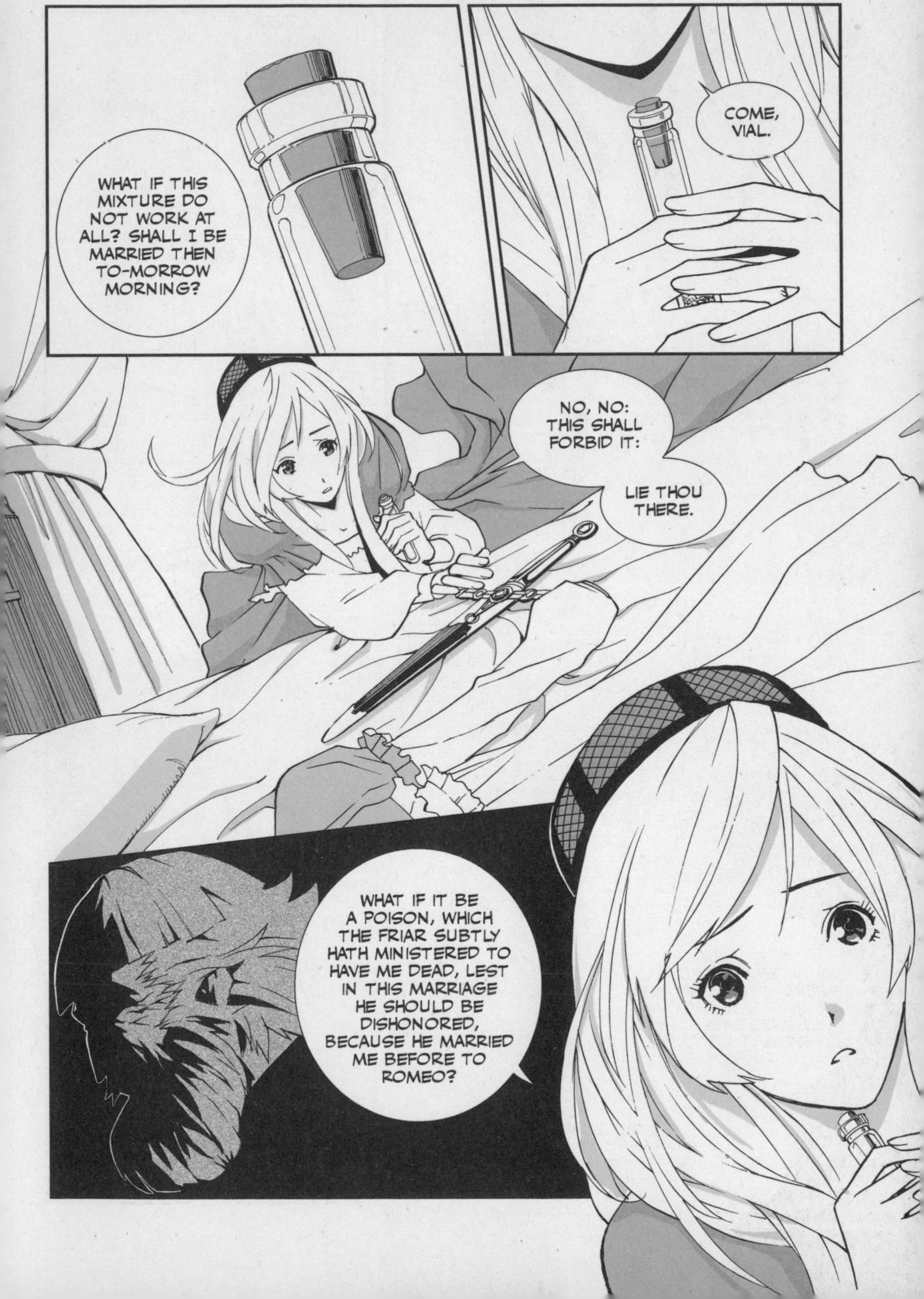
COME, VIAL.
WHAT IF THIS MIXTURE DO NOT WORK AT ALL? SHALL I BE MARRIED THEN TO-MORROW MORNING?
NO, NO: THIS SHALL FORBID IT:
LIE THOU THERE.
WHAT IF IT BE A POISON, WHICH THE FRIAR SUBTLY HATH MINISTERED TO HAVE ME DEAD, LEST IN THIS MARRIAGE HE SHOULD BE DISHONORED, BECAUSE HE MARRIED ME BEFORE TO ROMEO?

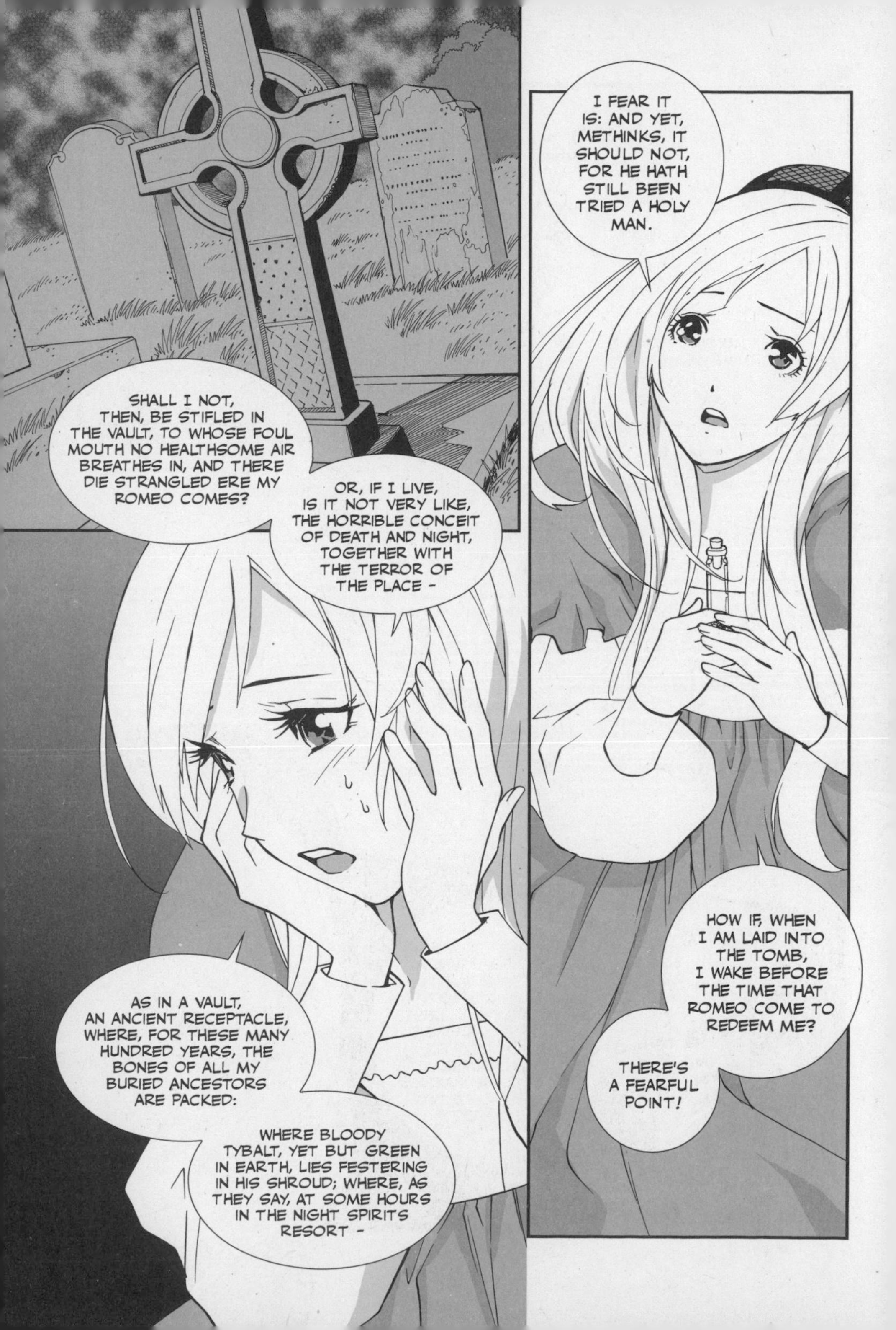
I FEAR IT IS: AND YET, METHINKS, IT SHOULD NOT, FOR HE HATH STILL BEEN TRIED A HOLY MAN.
HOW IF, WHEN I AM LAID INTO THE TOMB, I WAKE BEFORE THE TIME THAT ROMEO COME TO REDEEM ME?
THERE'S A FEARFUL POINT!
SHALL I NOT, THEN, BE STIFLED IN THE VAULT, TO WHOSE FOUL MOUTH NO HEALTHSOME AIR BREATHES IN, AND THERE DIE STRANGLED ERE MY ROMEO COMES?
OR, IF I LIVE, IS IT NOT VERY LIKE, THE HORRIBLE CONCEIT OF DEATH AND NIGHT, TOGETHER WITH THE TERROR OF THE PLACE -
AS IN A VAULT, AN ANCIENT RECEPTACLE, WHERE, FOR THESE MANY HUNDRED YEARS, THE BONES OF ALL MY BURIED ANCESTORS ARE PACKED:
WHERE BLOODY TYBALT, YET BUT GREEN IN EARTH, LIES FESTERING IN HIS SHROUD; WHERE, AS THEY SAY, AT SOME HOURS IN THE NIGHT SPIRITS RESORT -

ROMEO,
ROMEO,
ROMEO!

HERE'S DRINK.
I DRINK TO
THEE.

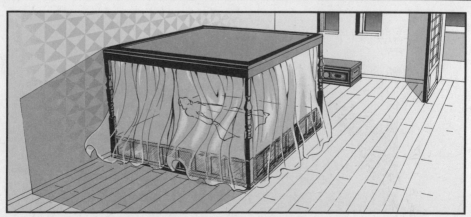

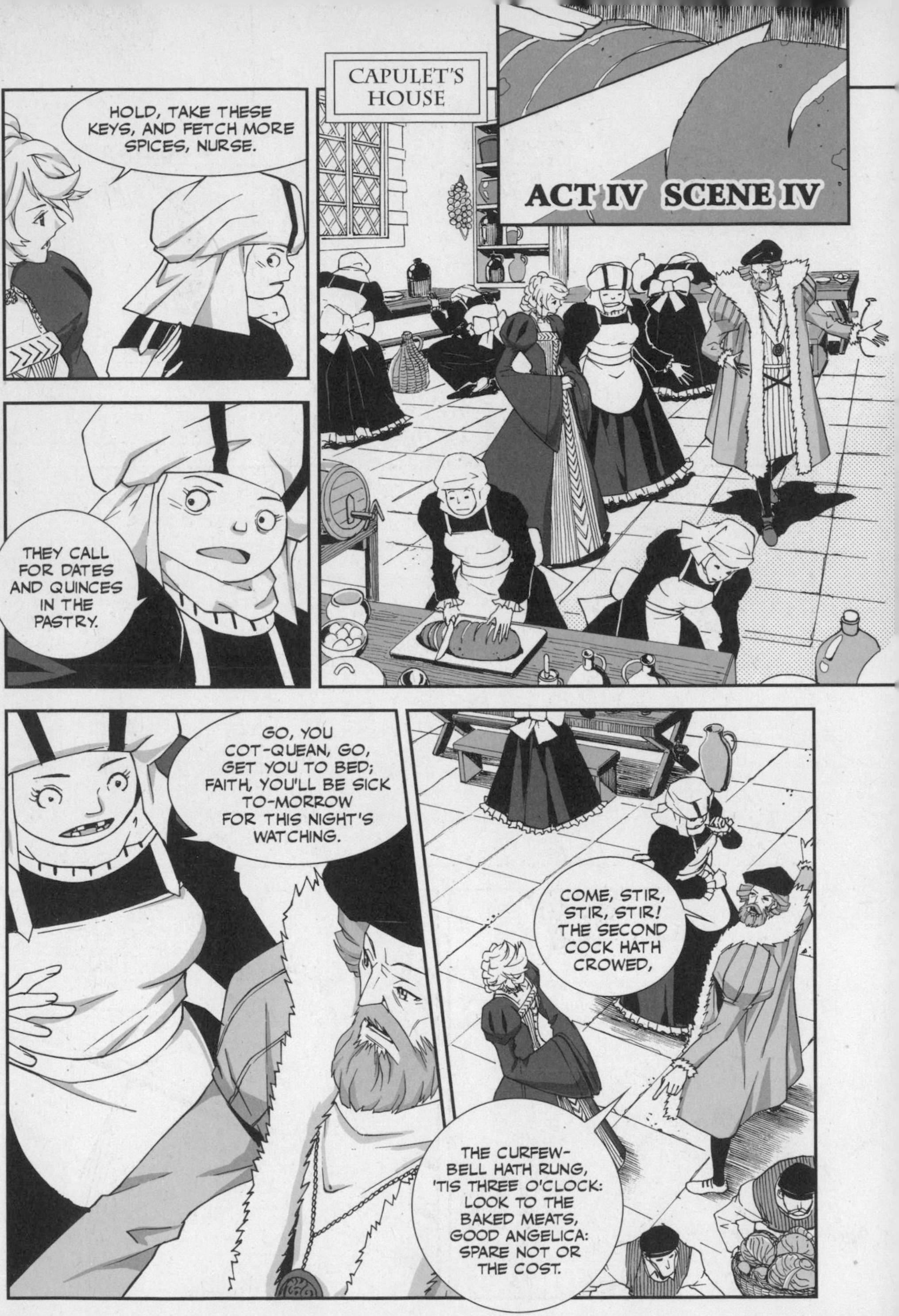
ACT IV SCENE IV
CAPULET'S HOUSE
HOLD, TAKE THESE KEYS, AND FETCH MORE SPICES, NURSE.
THEY CALL FOR DATES AND QUINCES IN THE PASTRY.
COME, STIR, STIR, STIR! THE SECOND COCK HATH CROWED,
THE CURFEW-BELL HATH RUNG, 'TIS THREE O'CLOCK: LOOK TO THE BAKED MEATS, GOOD ANGELICA: SPARE NOT OR THE COST.
GO, YOU COT-QUEAN, GO, GET YOU TO BED; FAITH, YOU'LL BE SICK TO-MORROW FOR THIS NIGHT'S WATCHING.

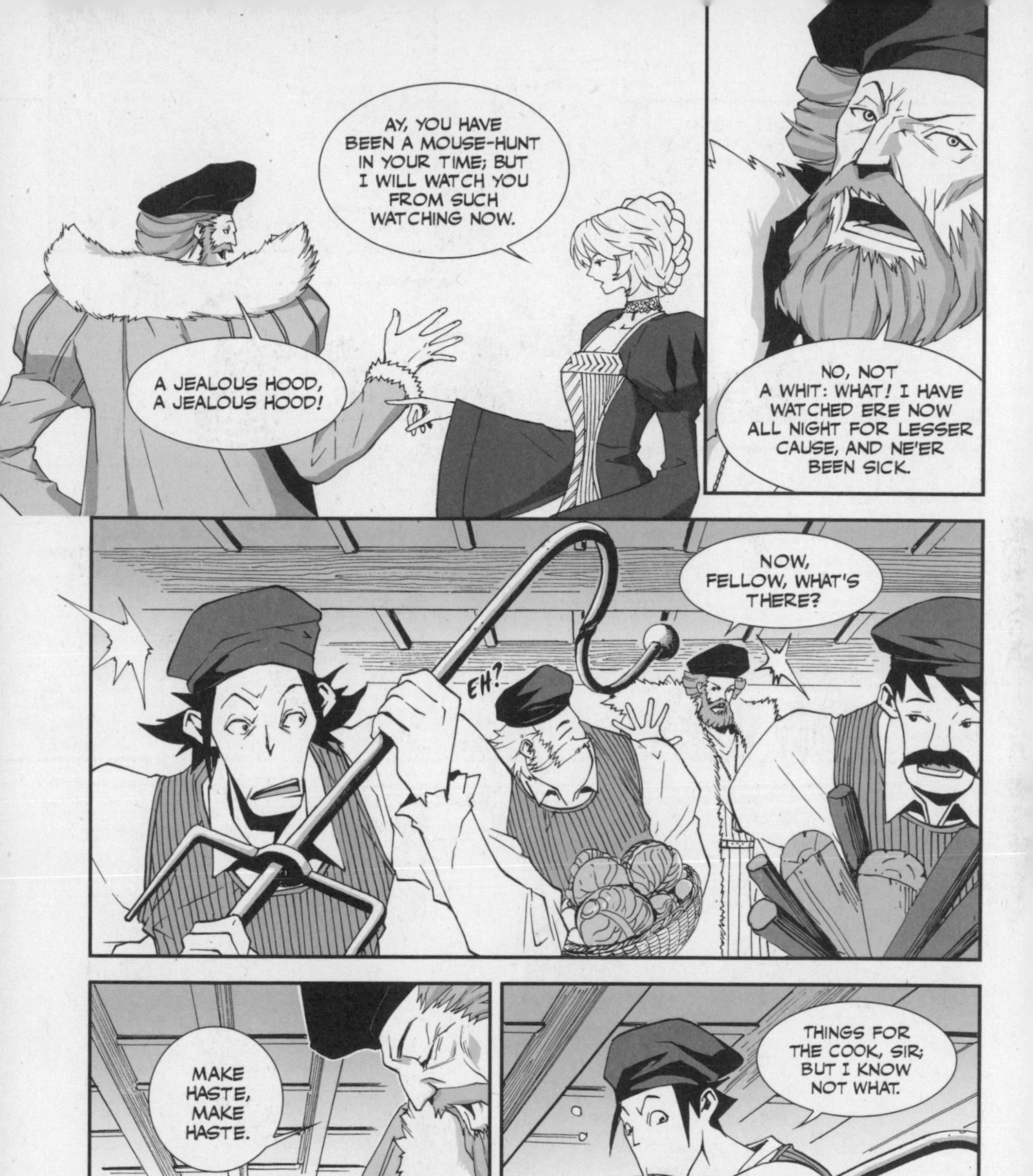
NO, NOT A WHIT: WHAT! I HAVE WATCHED ERE NOW ALL NIGHT FOR LESSER CAUSE, AND NE'ER BEEN SICK.
AY, YOU HAVE BEEN A MOUSE-HUNT IN YOUR TIME; BUT I WILL WATCH YOU FROM SUCH WATCHING NOW.
A JEALOUS HOOD, A JEALOUS HOOD!
NOW, FELLOW, WHAT'S THERE?
EH?
THINGS FOR THE COOK, SIR; BUT I KNOW NOT WHAT.
MAKE HASTE, MAKE HASTE.

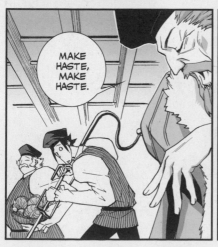

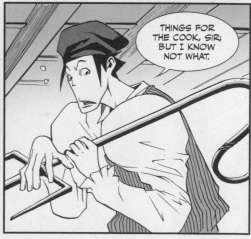

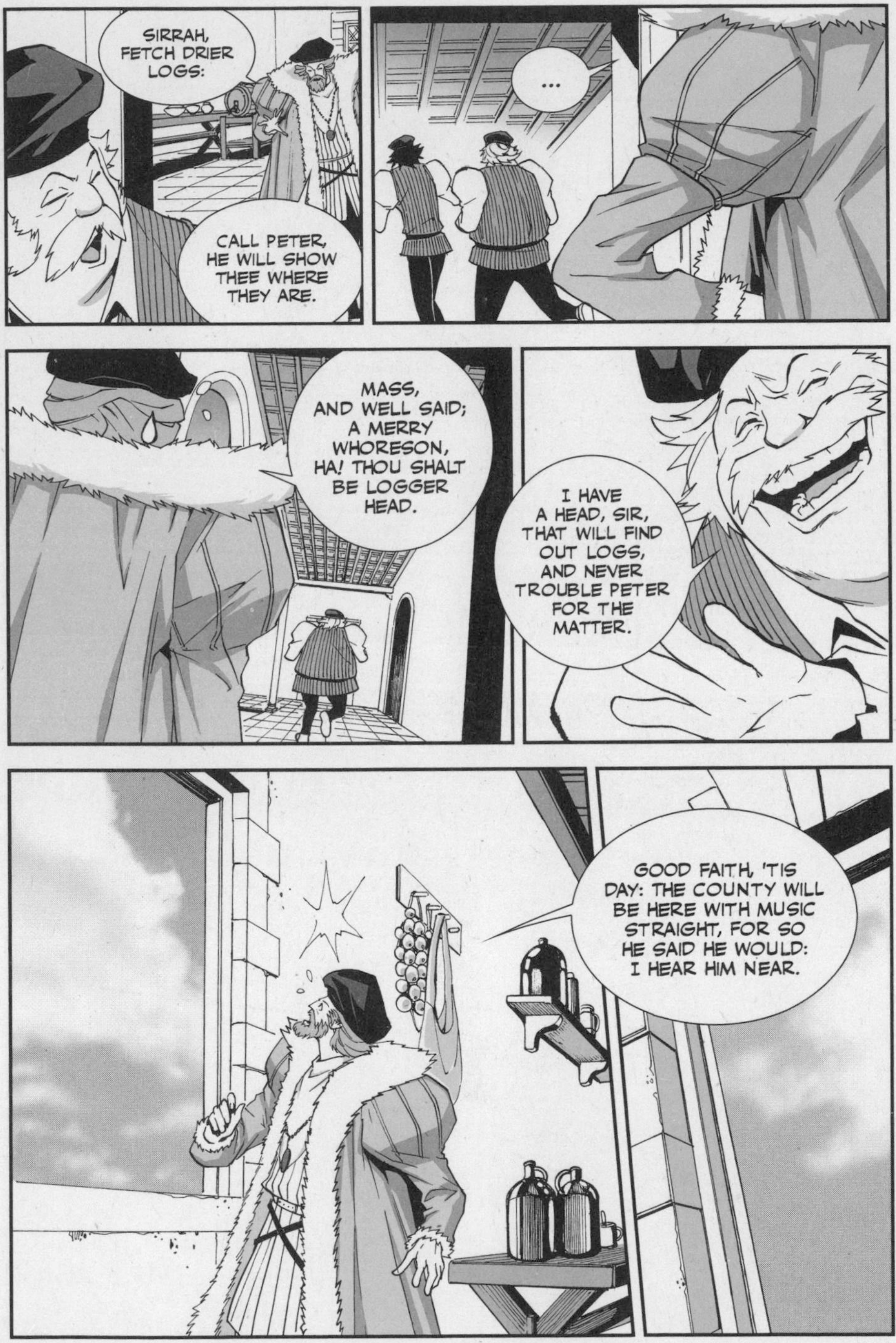
...
SIRRAH, FETCH DRIER LOGS:
CALL PETER, HE WILL SHOW THEE WHERE THEY ARE.
I HAVE A HEAD, SIR, THAT WILL FIND OUT LOGS, AND NEVER TROUBLE PETER FOR THE MATTER.
MASS, AND WELL SAID; A MERRY WHORESON, HA! THOU SHALT BE LOGGER HEAD.
GOOD FAITH, 'TIS DAY: THE COUNTY WILL BE HERE WITH MUSIC STRAIGHT, FOR SO HE SAID HE WOULD: I HEAR HIM NEAR.

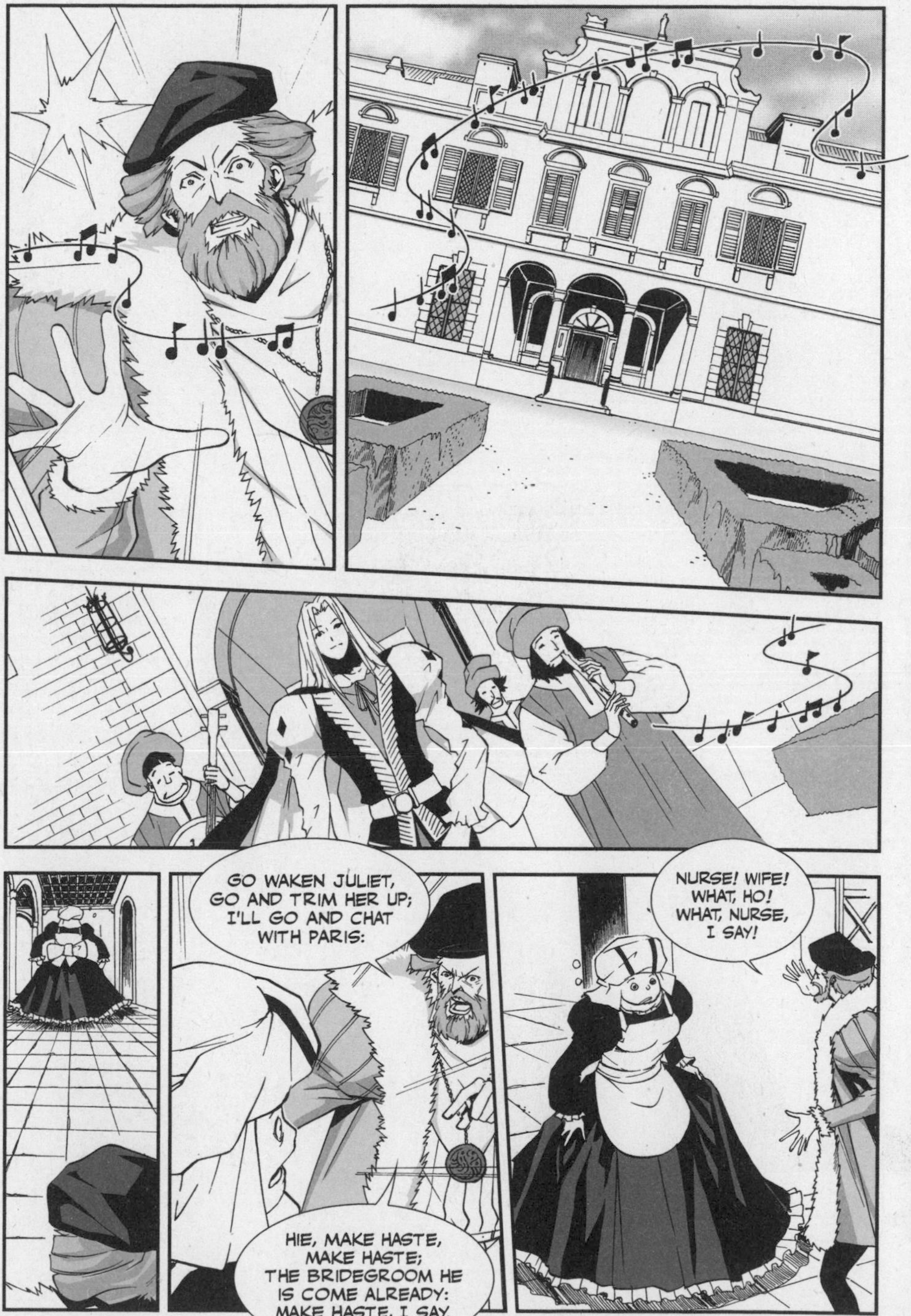
NURSE! WIFE! WHAT, HO! WHAT, NURSE, I SAY!
GO WAKEN JULIET, GO AND TRIM HER UP; I'LL GO AND CHAT WITH PARIS:
HIE, MAKE HASTE, MAKE HASTE; THE BRIDEGROOM HE IS COME ALREADY: MAKE HASTE, I SAY.

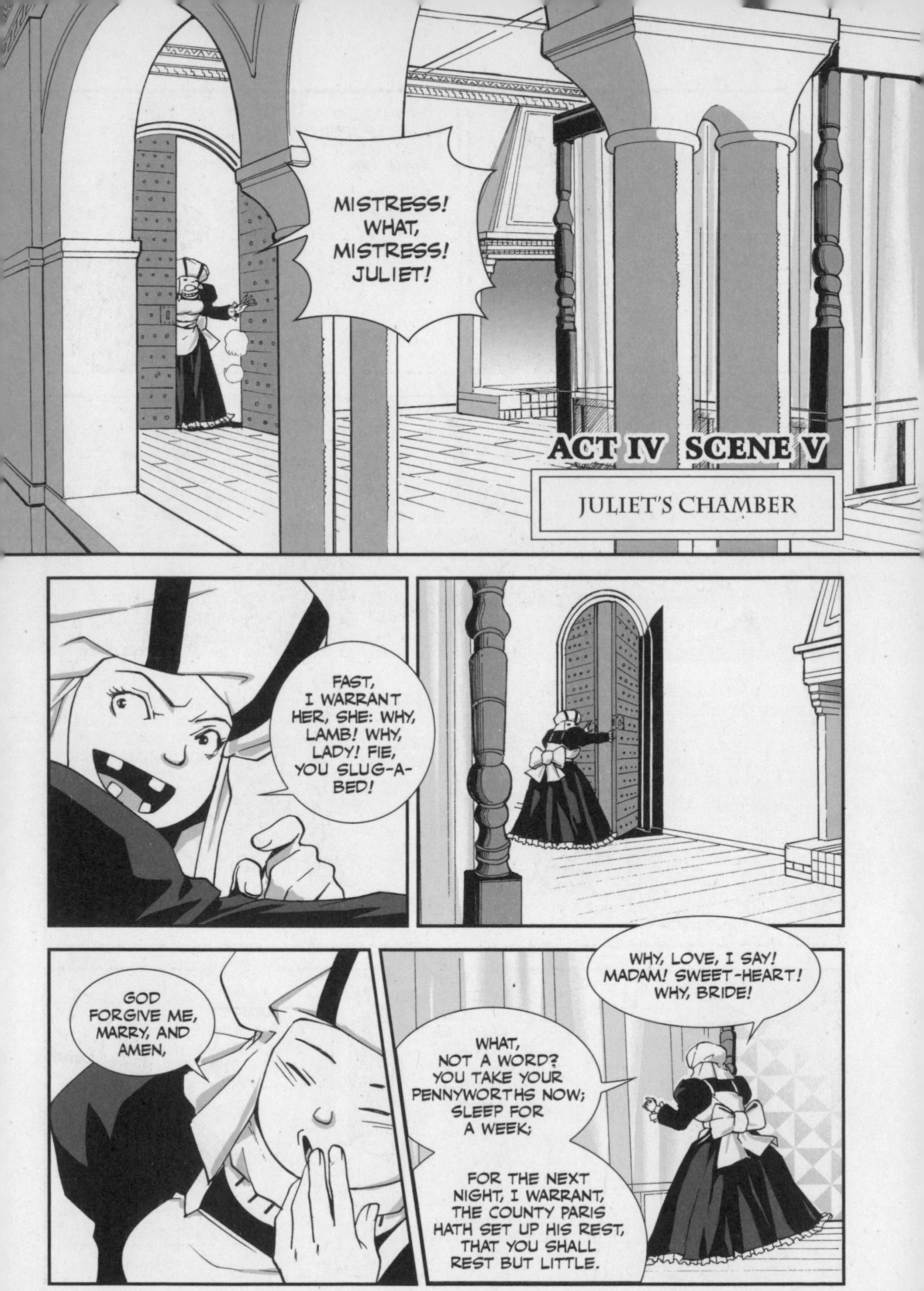
MISTRESS! WHAT, MISTRESS! JULIET!
ACT IV SCENE V
JULIET'S CHAMBER
FAST, I WARRANT HER, SHE: WHY, LAMB! WHY, LADY! FIE, YOU SLUG-A-BED!
WHY, LOVE, I SAY! MADAM! SWEET-HEART! WHY, BRIDE!
WHAT, NOT A WORD? YOU TAKE YOUR PENNYWORTHS NOW; SLEEP FOR A WEEK;
FOR THE NEXT NIGHT, I WARRANT, THE COUNTY PARIS HATH SET UP HIS REST, THAT YOU SHALL REST BUT LITTLE.
GOD FORGIVE ME, MARRY, AND AMEN,

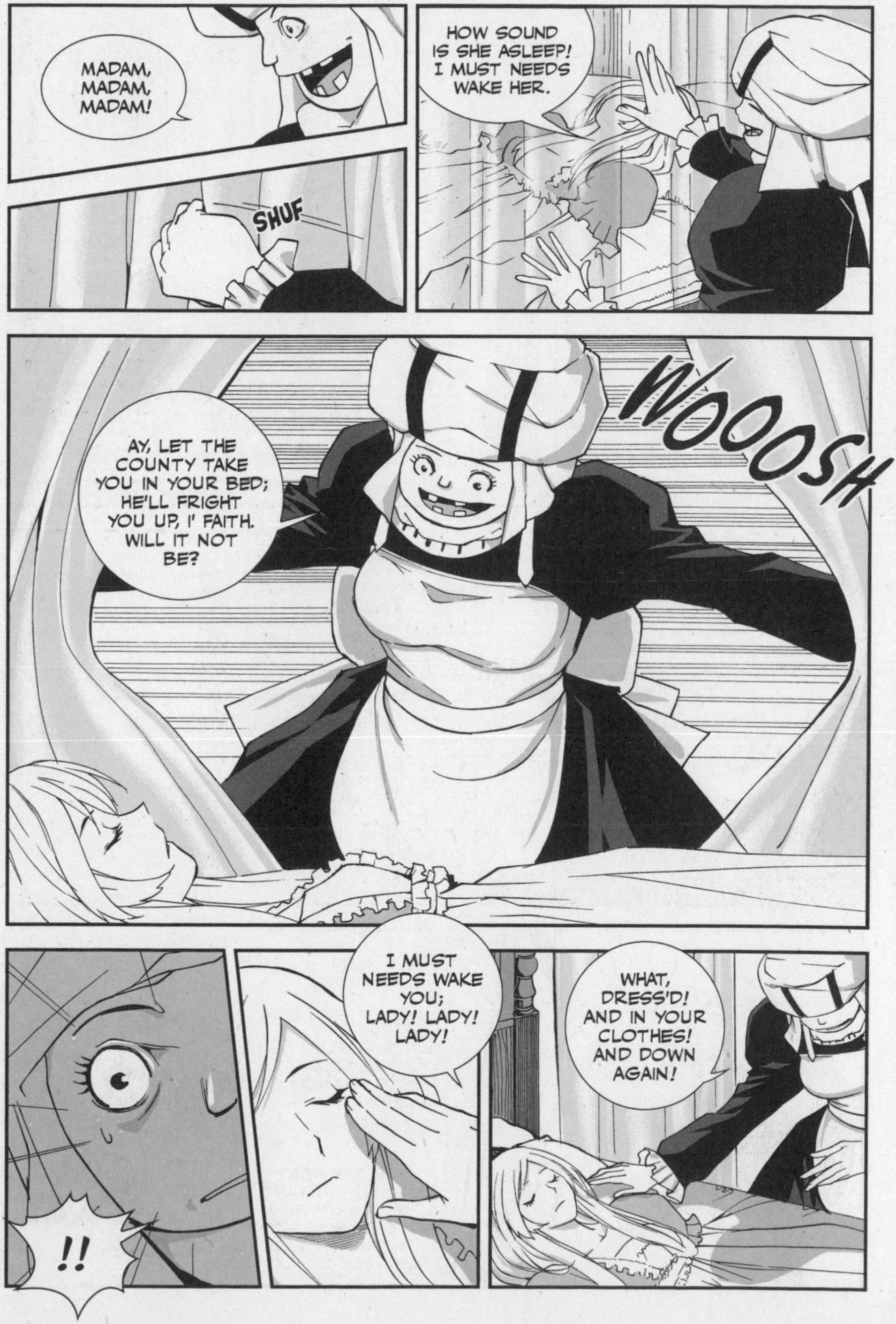
HOW SOUND IS SHE ASLEEP! I MUST NEEDS WAKE HER.
MADAM, MADAM, MADAM!
SHUF
WOOOSH
AY, LET THE COUNTY TAKE YOU IN YOUR BED; HE'LL FRIGHT YOU UP, I' FAITH. WILL IT NOT BE?
WHAT, DRESS'D! AND IN YOUR CLOTHES! AND DOWN AGAIN!
I MUST NEEDS WAKE YOU; LADY! LADY! LADY!
!!

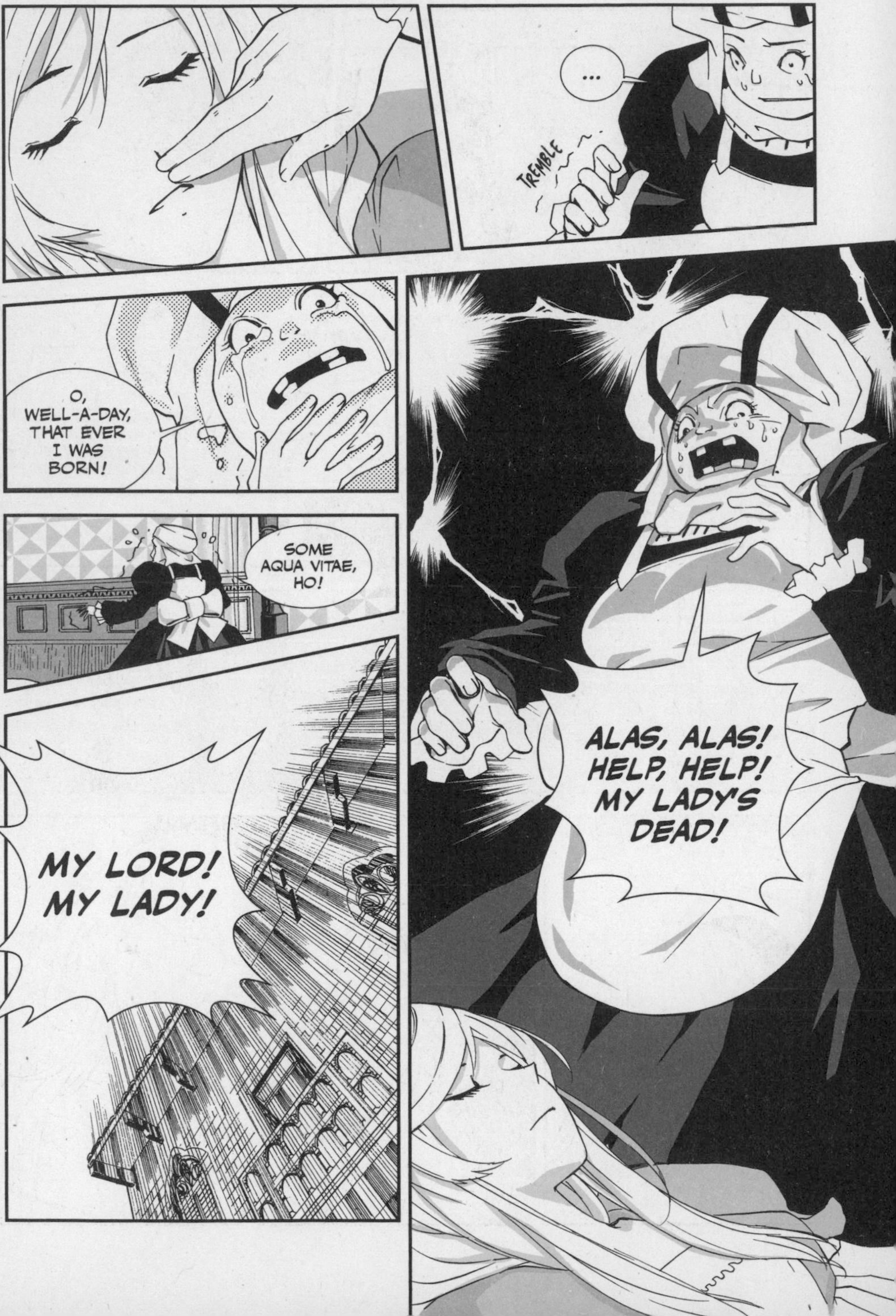
...
TREMBLE
ALAS, ALAS! HELP, HELP! MY LADY'S DEAD!
O, WELL-A-DAY, THAT EVER I WAS BORN!
SOME AQUA VITAE, HO!
MY LORD! MY LADY!

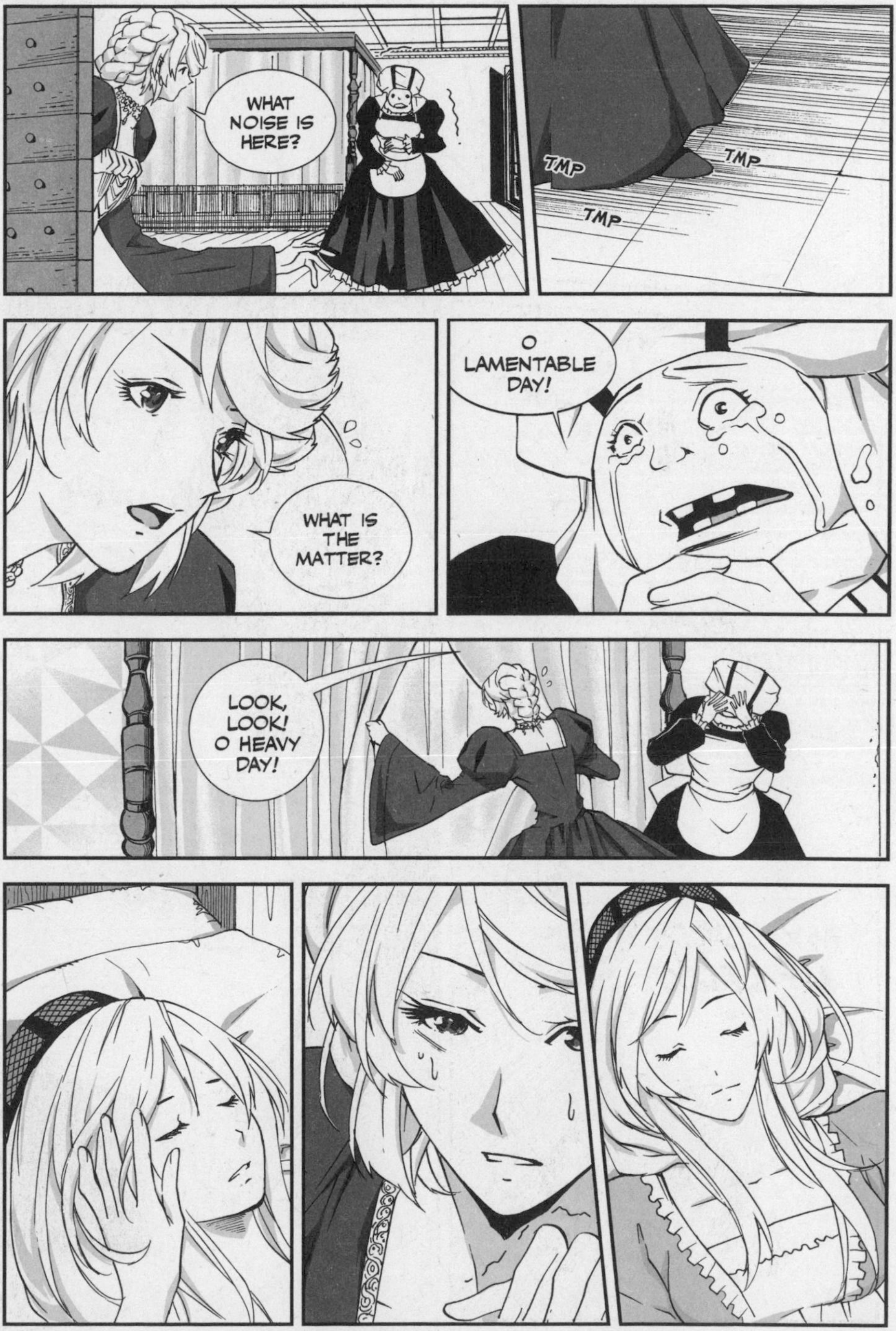
TMP
TMP
TMP
WHAT NOISE IS HERE?
O LAMENTABLE DAY!
WHAT IS THE MATTER?
LOOK, LOOK! O HEAVY DAY!

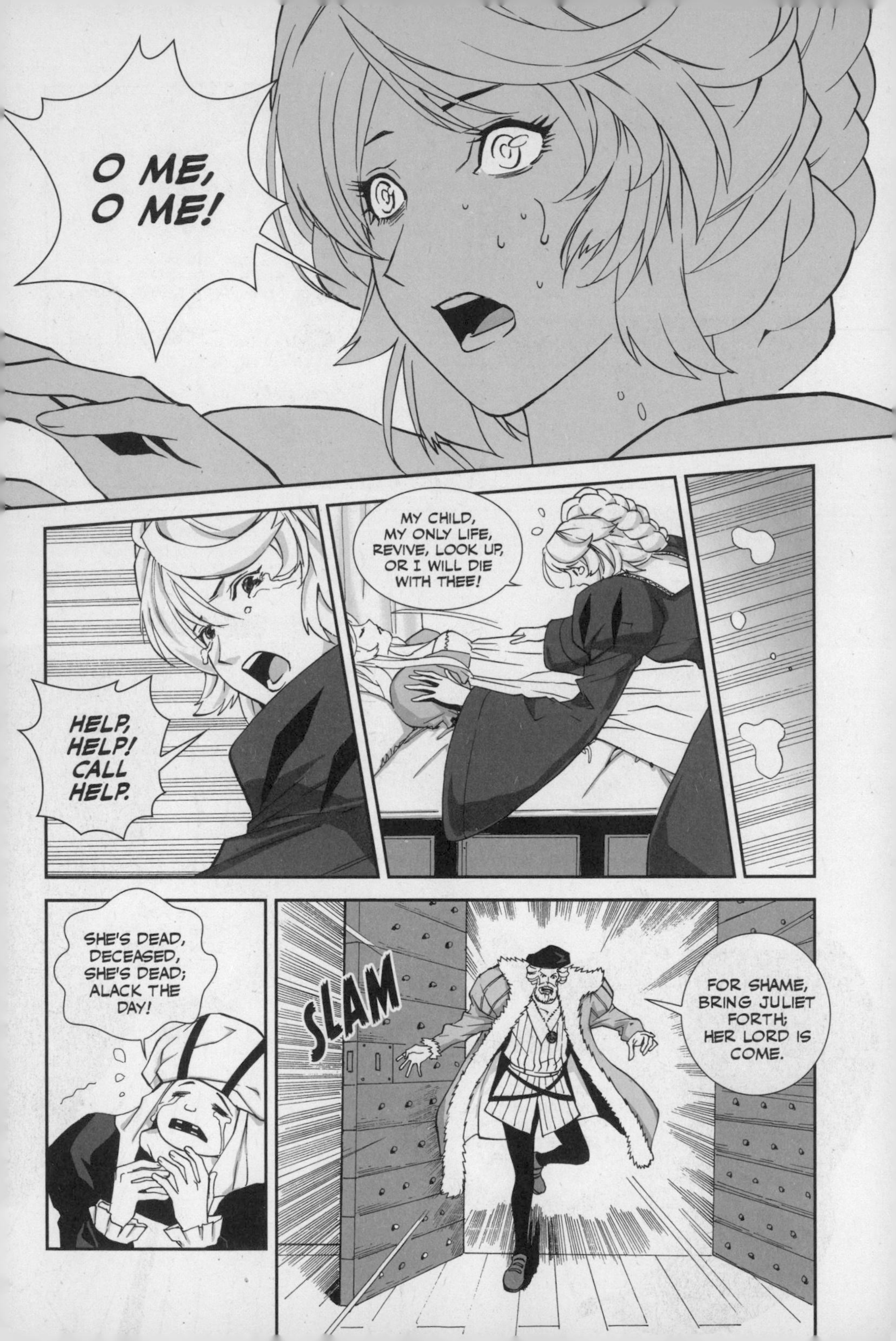
O ME, O ME!
MY CHILD, MY ONLY LIFE, REVIVE, LOOK UP, OR I WILL DIE WITH THEE!
HELP, HELP! CALL HELP.
FOR SHAME, BRING JULIET FORTH; HER LORD IS COME.
SLAM
SHE'S DEAD, DECEASED, SHE'S DEAD; ALACK THE DAY!

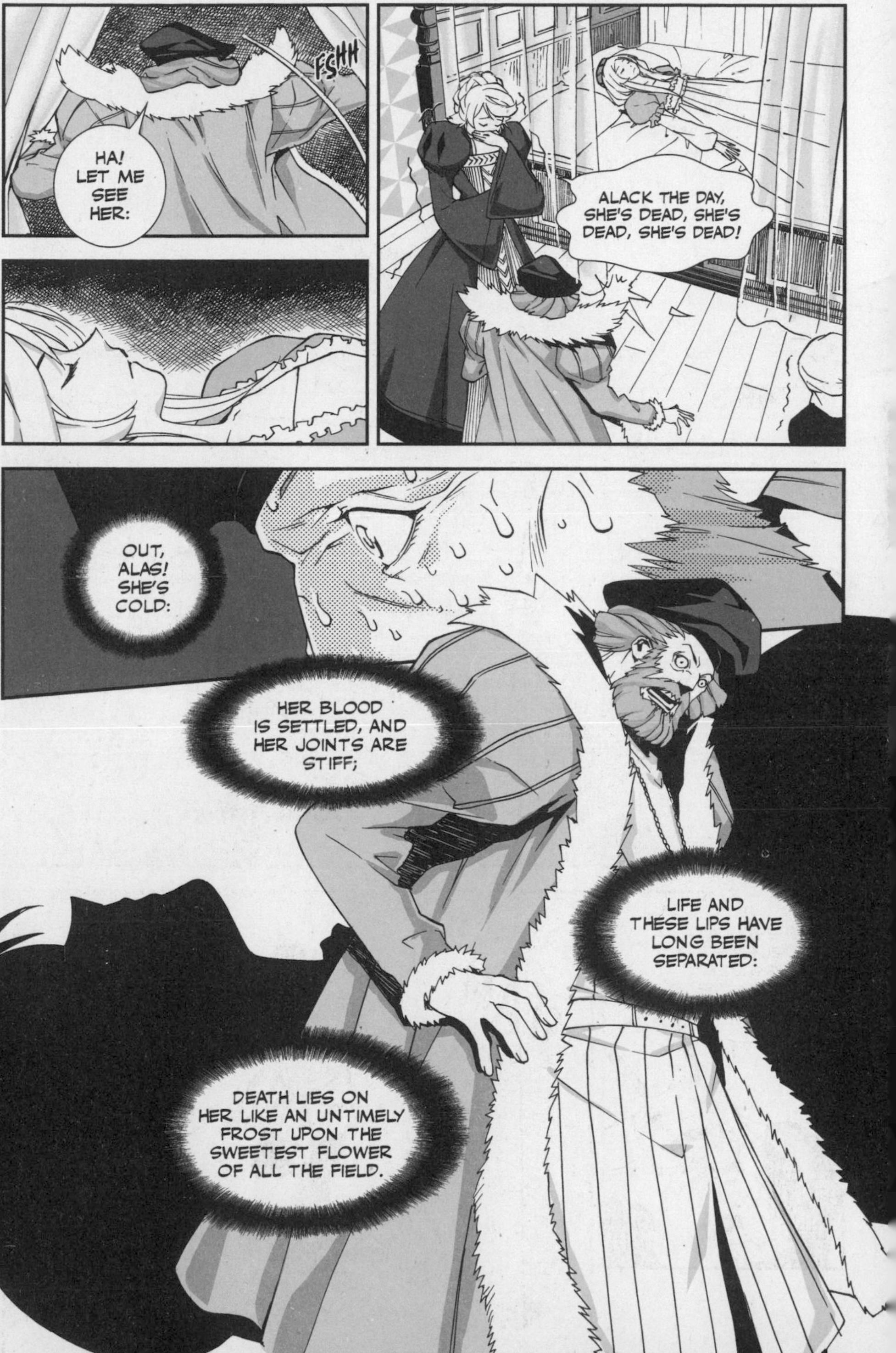
ALACK THE DAY, SHE'S DEAD, SHE'S DEAD, SHE'S DEAD!
FSHH
HA! LET ME SEE HER:
OUT, ALAS! SHE'S COLD:
HER BLOOD IS SETTLED, AND HER JOINTS ARE STIFF;
LIFE AND THESE LIPS HAVE LONG BEEN SEPARATED:
DEATH LIES ON HER LIKE AN UNTIMELY FROST UPON THE SWEETEST FLOWER OF ALL THE FIELD.

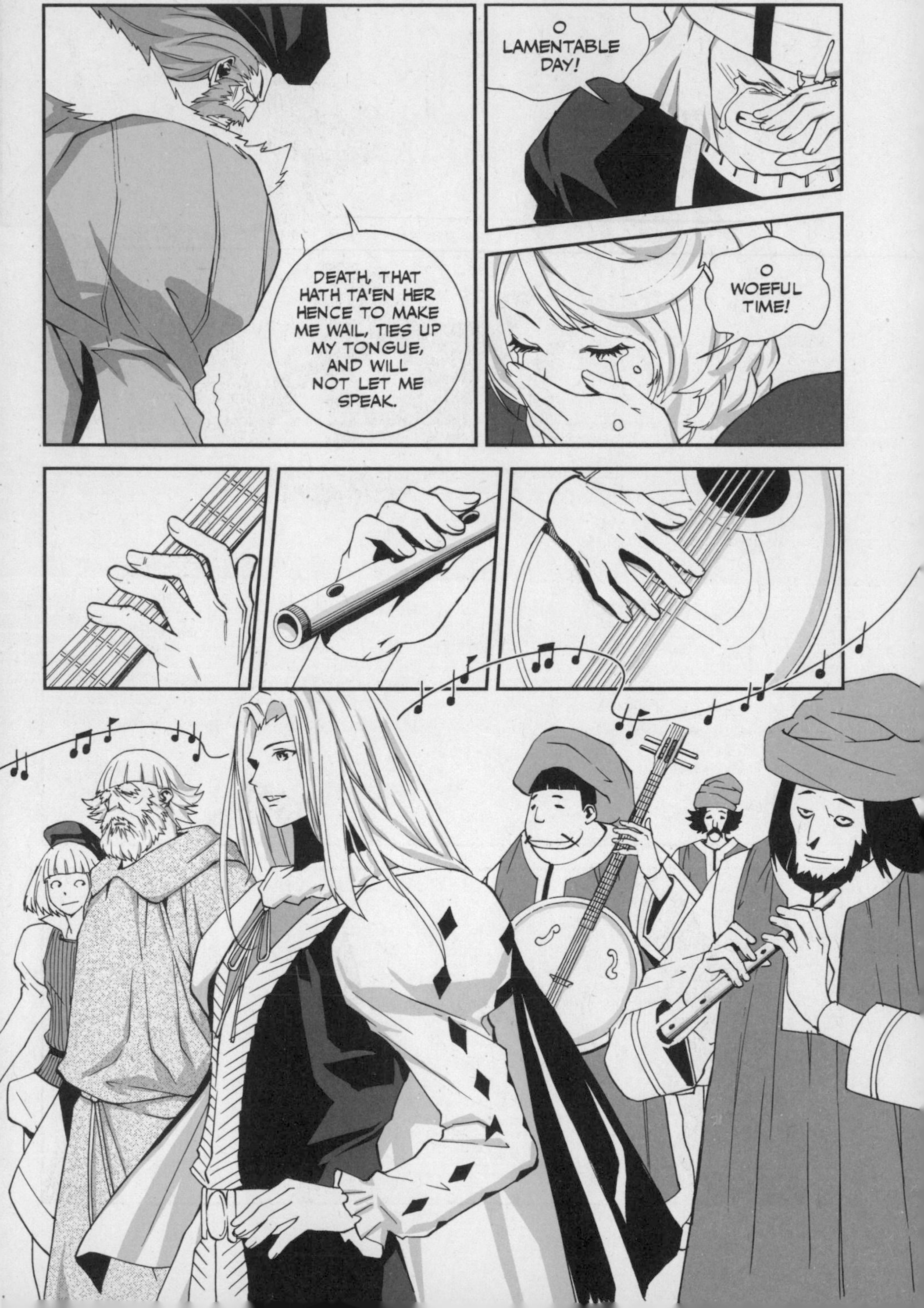

O LAMENTABLE DAY!
O WOEFUL TIME!
DEATH, THAT HATH TA'EN HER HENCE TO MAKE ME WAIL, TIES UP MY TONGUE, AND WILL NOT LET ME SPEAK.

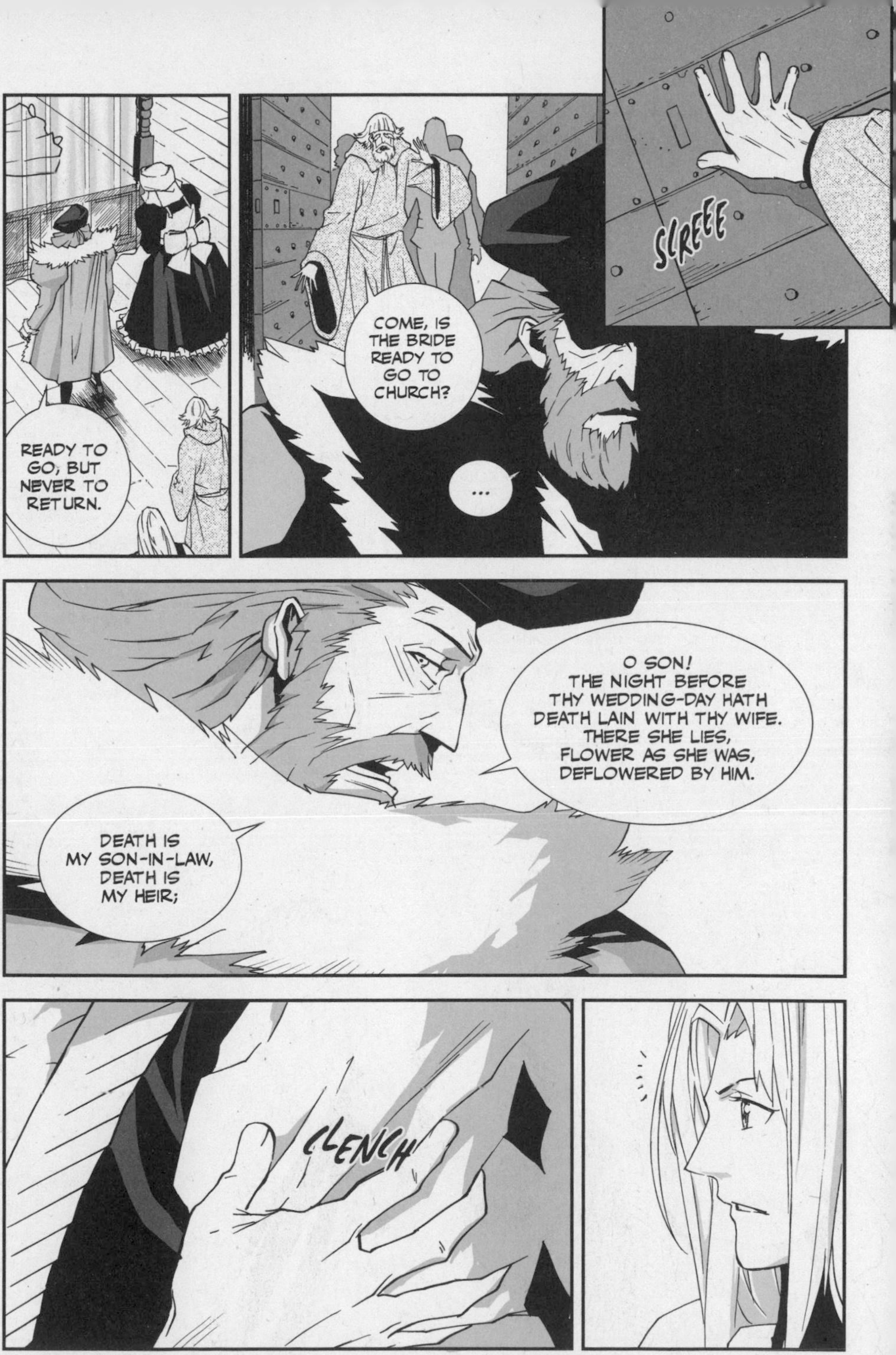
SCREEE
COME, IS THE BRIDE READY TO GO TO CHURCH?
...
READY TO GO; BUT NEVER TO RETURN.
O SON! THE NIGHT BEFORE THY WEDDING-DAY HATH DEATH LAIN WITH THY WIFE. THERE SHE LIES, FLOWER AS SHE WAS, DEFLOWERED BY HIM.
DEATH IS MY SON-IN-LAW, DEATH IS MY HEIR;
CLENCH

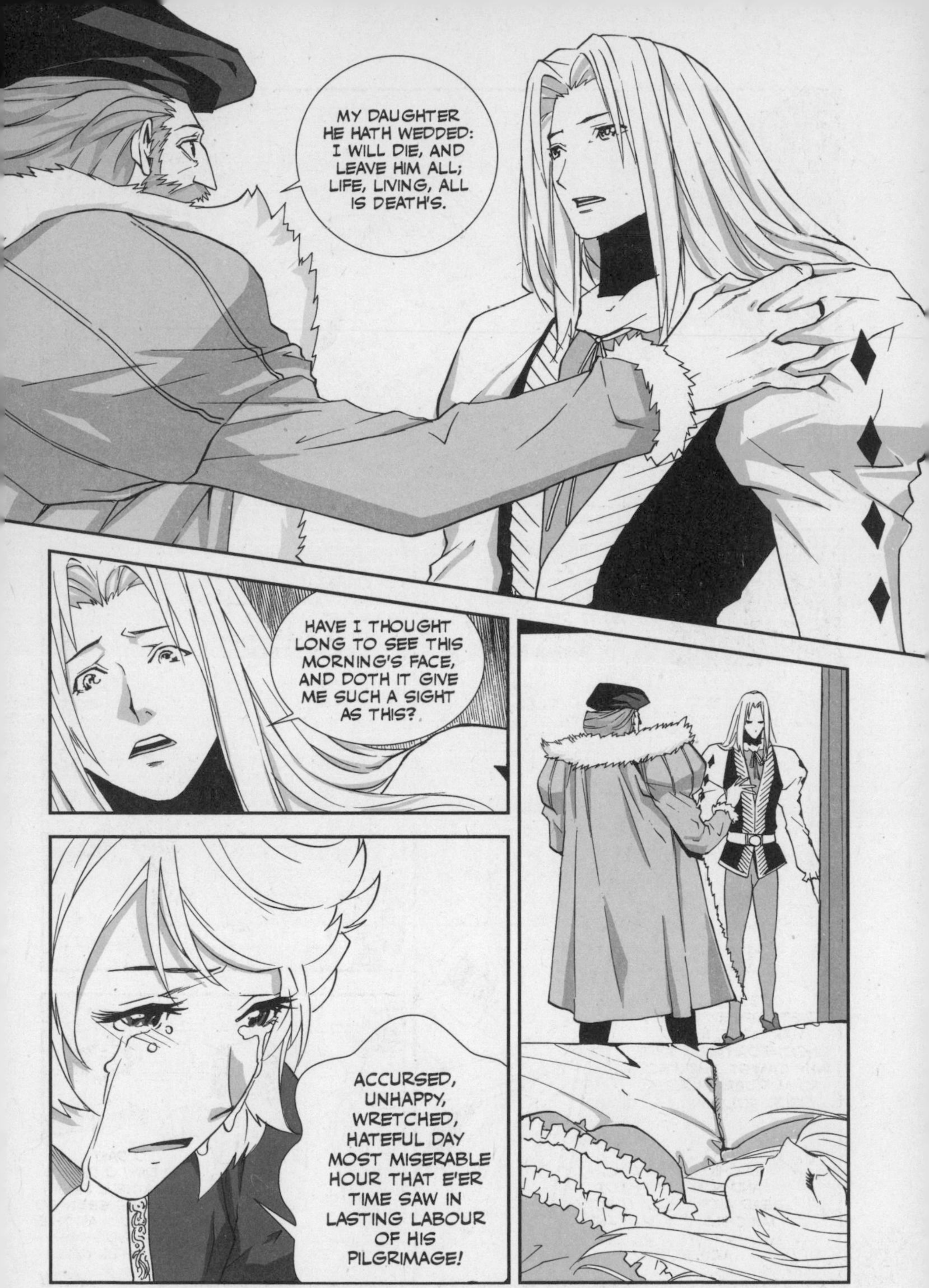
MY DAUGHTER HE HATH WEDDED: I WILL DIE, AND LEAVE HIM ALL; LIFE, LIVING, ALL IS DEATH'S.
HAVE I THOUGHT LONG TO SEE THIS MORNING'S FACE, AND DOTH IT GIVE ME SUCH A SIGHT AS THIS?
ACCURSED, UNHAPPY, WRETCHED, HATEFUL DAY MOST MISERABLE HOUR THAT E'ER TIME SAW IN LASTING LABOUR OF HIS PILGRIMAGE!

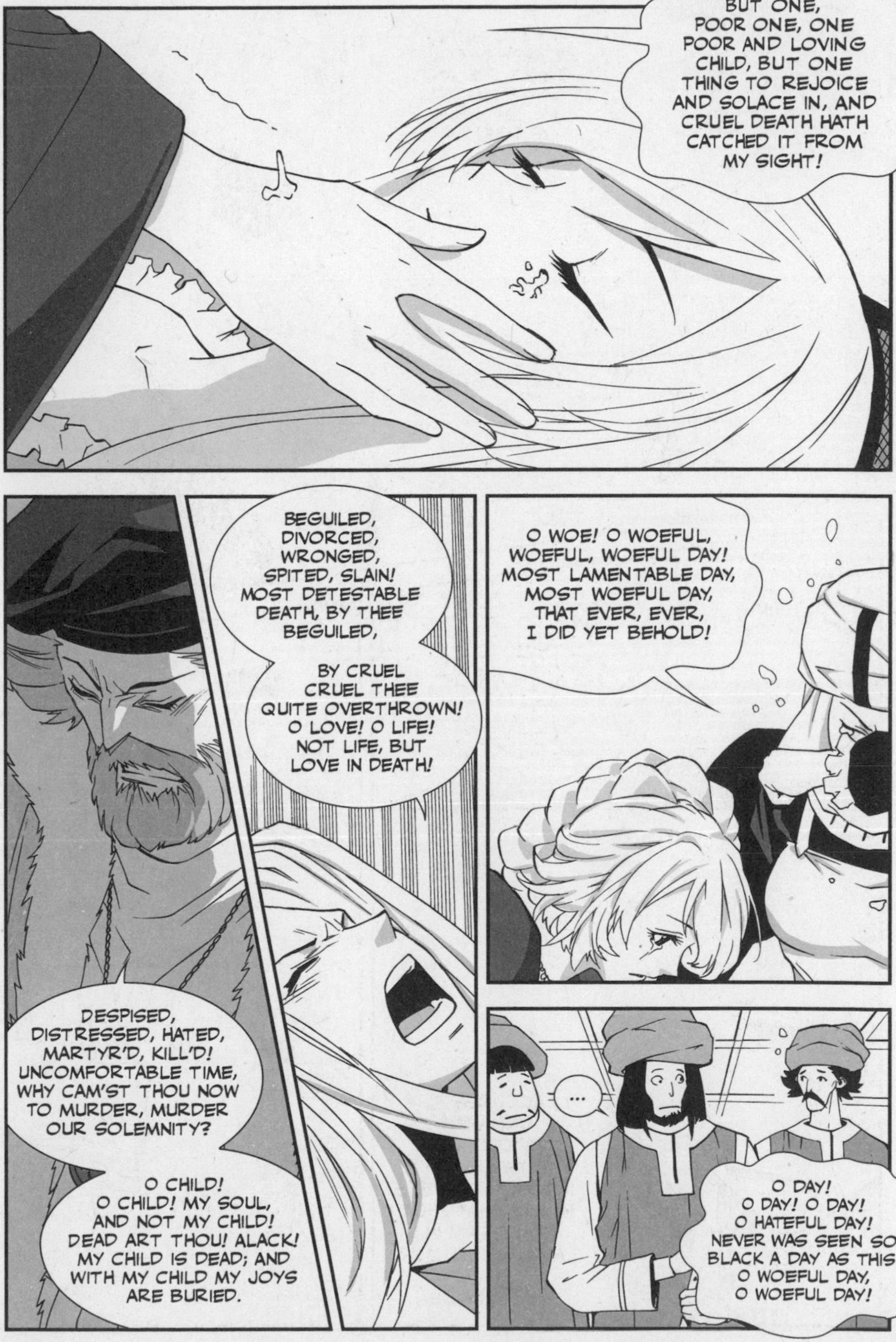
BUT ONE, POOR ONE, ONE POOR AND LOVING CHILD, BUT ONE THING TO REJOICE AND SOLACE IN, AND CRUEL DEATH HATH CATCHED IT FROM MY SIGHT!
O WOE! O WOEFUL, WOEFUL, WOEFUL DAY! MOST LAMENTABLE DAY, MOST WOEFUL DAY, THAT EVER, EVER, I DID YET BEHOLD!
...
O DAY! O DAY! O DAY! O HATEFUL DAY! NEVER WAS SEEN SO BLACK A DAY AS THIS: O WOEFUL DAY, O WOEFUL DAY!
BEGUILED, DIVORCED, WRONGED, SPITED, SLAIN! MOST DETESTABLE DEATH, BY THEE BEGUILED,
BY CRUEL CRUEL THEE QUITE OVERTHROWN! O LOVE! O LIFE! NOT LIFE, BUT LOVE IN DEATH!
DESPISED, DISTRESSED, HATED, MARTYR'D, KILL'D! UNCOMFORTABLE TIME, WHY CAM'ST THOU NOW TO MURDER, MURDER OUR SOLEMNITY?
O CHILD! O CHILD! MY SOUL, AND NOT MY CHILD! DEAD ART THOU! ALACK! MY CHILD IS DEAD; AND WITH MY CHILD MY JOYS ARE BURIED.

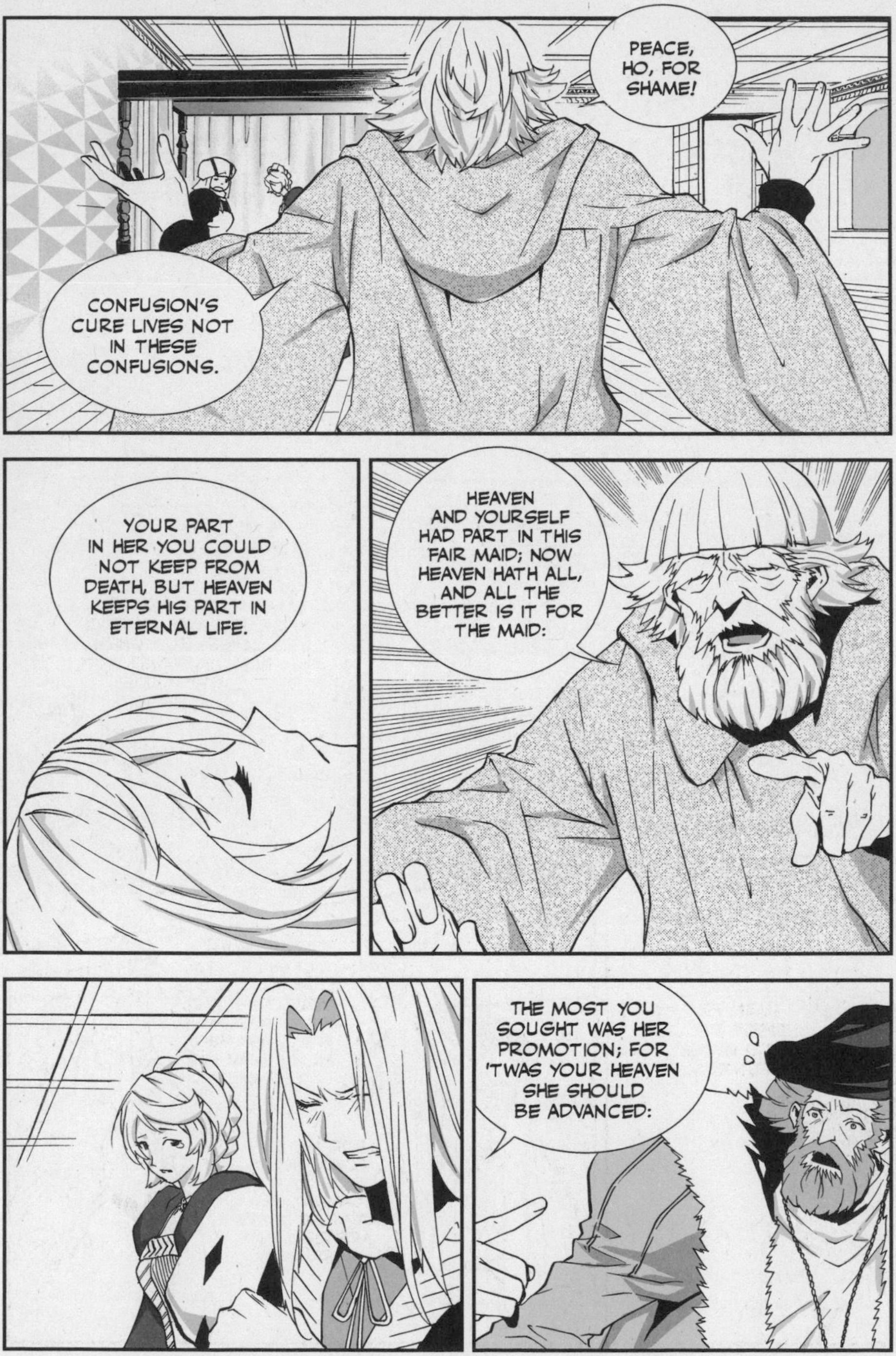
PEACE, HO, FOR SHAME!
CONFUSION'S CURE LIVES NOT IN THESE CONFUSIONS.
HEAVEN AND YOURSELF HAD PART IN THIS FAIR MAID; NOW HEAVEN HATH ALL, AND ALL THE BETTER IS IT FOR THE MAID:
YOUR PART IN HER YOU COULD NOT KEEP FROM DEATH, BUT HEAVEN KEEPS HIS PART IN ETERNAL LIFE.
THE MOST YOU SOUGHT WAS HER PROMOTION; FOR 'TWAS YOUR HEAVEN SHE SHOULD BE ADVANCED:

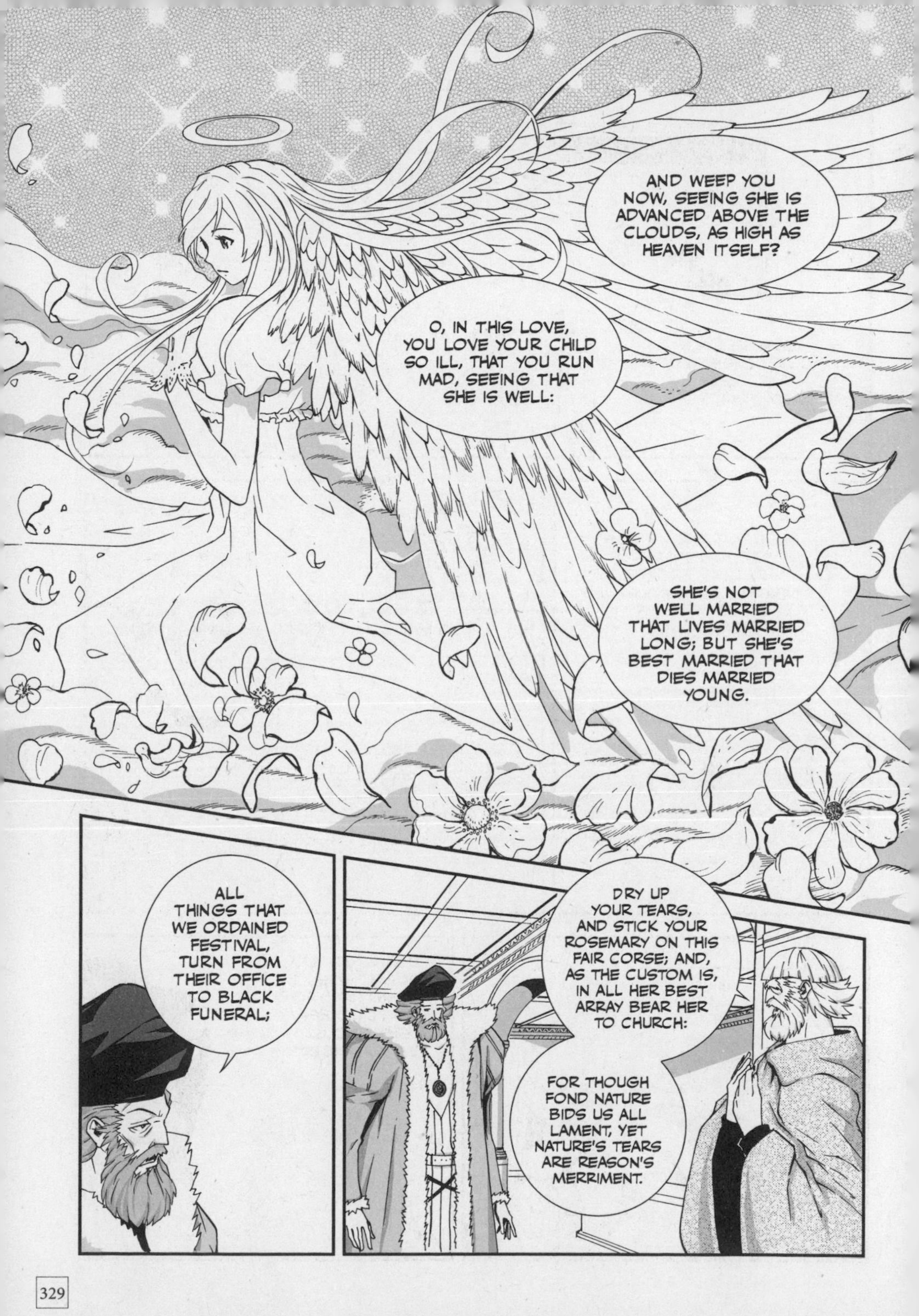
AND WEEP YOU NOW, SEEING SHE IS ADVANCED ABOVE THE CLOUDS, AS HIGH AS HEAVEN ITSELF?
O, IN THIS LOVE, YOU LOVE YOUR CHILD SO ILL, THAT YOU RUN MAD, SEEING THAT SHE IS WELL:
SHE'S NOT WELL MARRIED THAT LIVES MARRIED LONG; BUT SHE'S BEST MARRIED THAT DIES MARRIED YOUNG.
DRY UP YOUR TEARS, AND STICK YOUR ROSEMARY ON THIS FAIR CORSE; AND, AS THE CUSTOM IS, IN ALL HER BEST ARRAY BEAR HER TO CHURCH:
FOR THOUGH FOND NATURE BIDS US ALL LAMENT, YET NATURE'S TEARS ARE REASON'S MERRIMENT.
ALL THINGS THAT WE ORDAINED FESTIVAL, TURN FROM THEIR OFFICE TO BLACK FUNERAL;

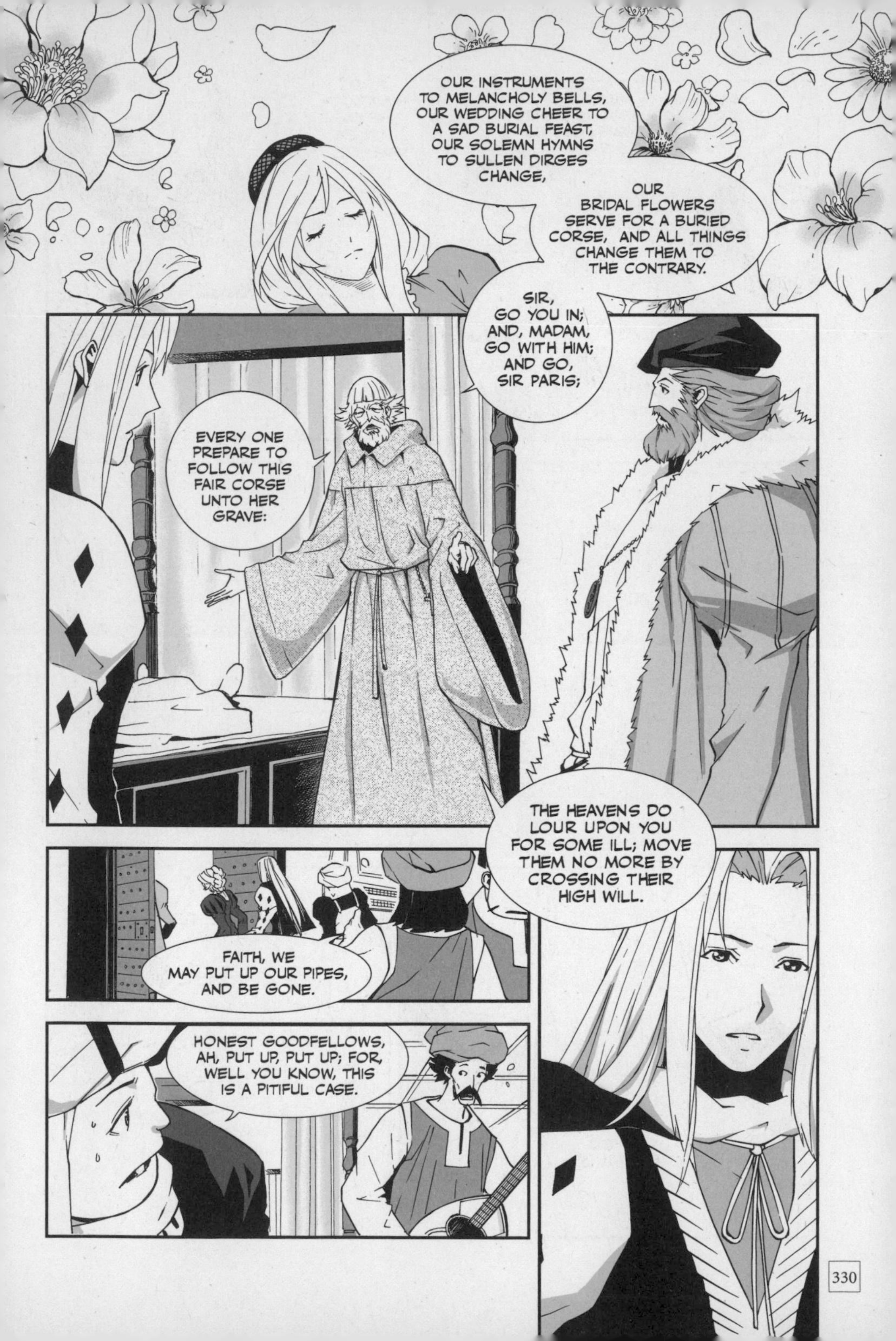
OUR INSTRUMENTS TO MELANCHOLY BELLS, OUR WEDDING CHEER TO A SAD BURIAL FEAST, OUR SOLEMN HYMNS TO SULLEN DIRGES CHANGE,
OUR BRIDAL FLOWERS SERVE FOR A BURIED CORSE, AND ALL THINGS CHANGE THEM TO THE CONTRARY.
SIR, GO YOU IN; AND, MADAM, GO WITH HIM; AND GO, SIR PARIS;
EVERY ONE PREPARE TO FOLLOW THIS FAIR CORSE UNTO HER GRAVE:
THE HEAVENS DO LOUR UPON YOU FOR SOME ILL; MOVE THEM NO MORE BY CROSSING THEIR HIGH WILL.
FAITH, WE MAY PUT UP OUR PIPES, AND BE GONE.
HONEST GOODFELLOWS, AH, PUT UP, PUT UP; FOR, WELL YOU KNOW, THIS IS A PITIFUL CASE.

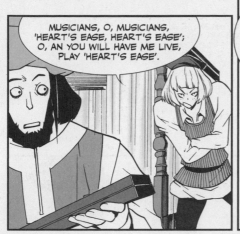

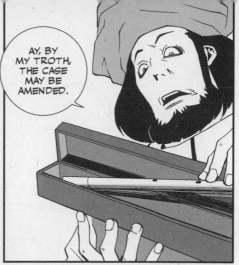

AY, BY MY TROTH, THE CASE MAY BE AMENDED.
MUSICIANS, O, MUSICIANS, 'HEART'S EASE, HEART'S EASE'; O, AN YOU WILL HAVE ME LIVE, PLAY 'HEART'S EASE'.
WHY 'HEART'S EASE'?
O, MUSICIANS, BECAUSE MY HEART ITSELF PLAYS 'MY HEART IS FULL OF WOE':
O, PLAY ME SOME MERRY DUMP, TO COMFORT ME.
NOT A DUMP WE; 'TIS NO TIME TO PLAY NOW.
HUFF
YOU WILL NOT, THEN?
NO.
I WILL THEN GIVE IT YOU SOUNDLY.

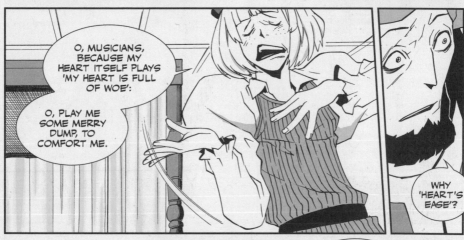

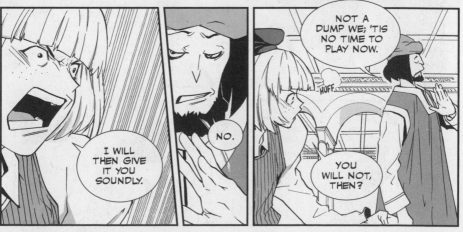

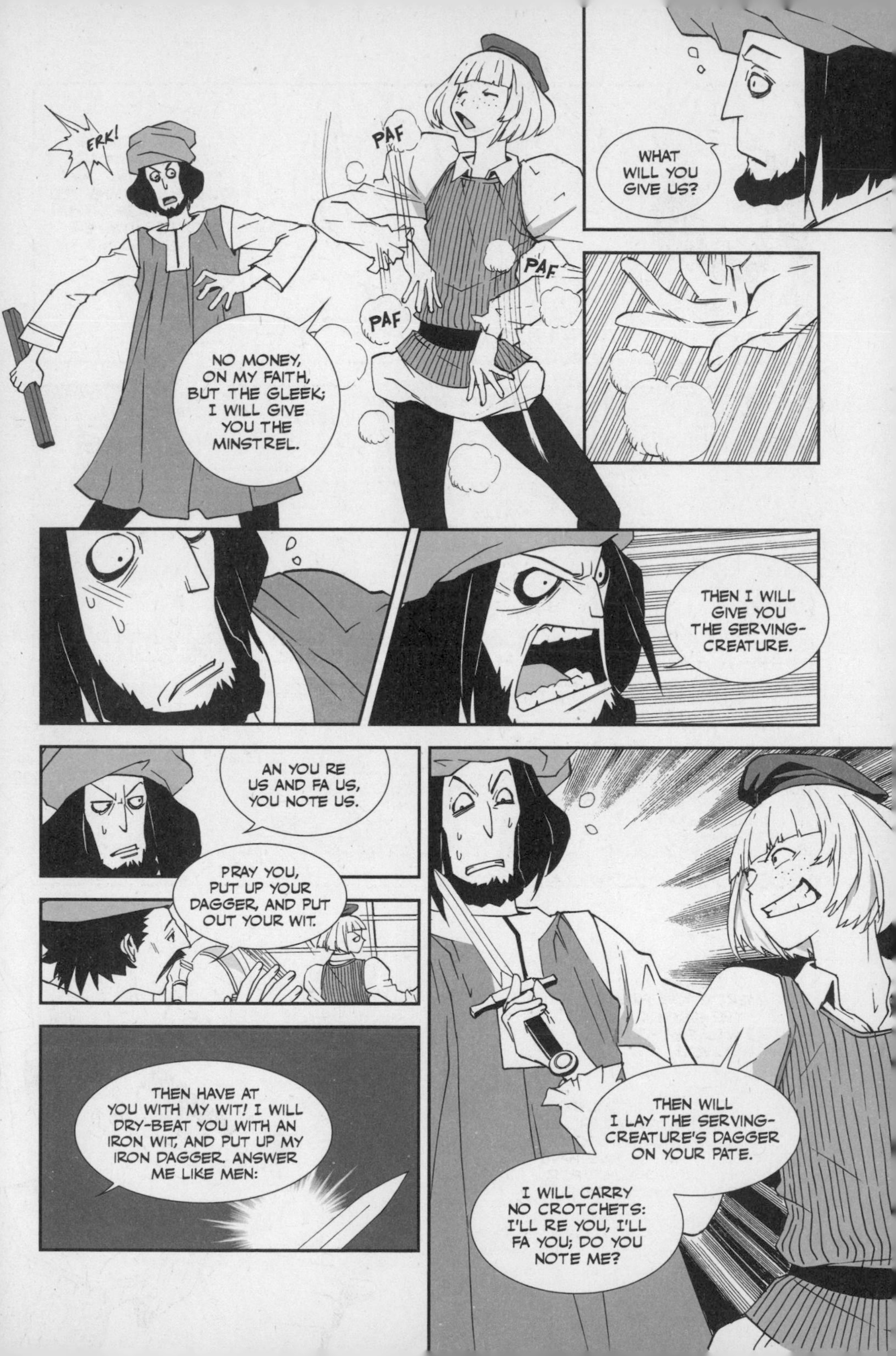
WHAT WILL YOU GIVE US?
PAF
ERK!
PAF
PAF
NO MONEY, ON MY FAITH, BUT THE GLEEK; I WILL GIVE YOU THE MINSTREL.
THEN I WILL GIVE YOU THE SERVING-CREATURE.
THEN WILL I LAY THE SERVING-CREATURE'S DAGGER ON YOUR PATE.
I WILL CARRY NO CROTCHETS: I'LL RE YOU, I'LL FA YOU; DO YOU NOTE ME?
AN YOU RE US AND FA US, YOU NOTE US.
PRAY YOU, PUT UP YOUR DAGGER, AND PUT OUT YOUR WIT.
THEN HAVE AT YOU WITH MY WIT! I WILL DRY-BEAT YOU WITH AN IRON WIT, AND PUT UP MY IRON DAGGER. ANSWER ME LIKE MEN:

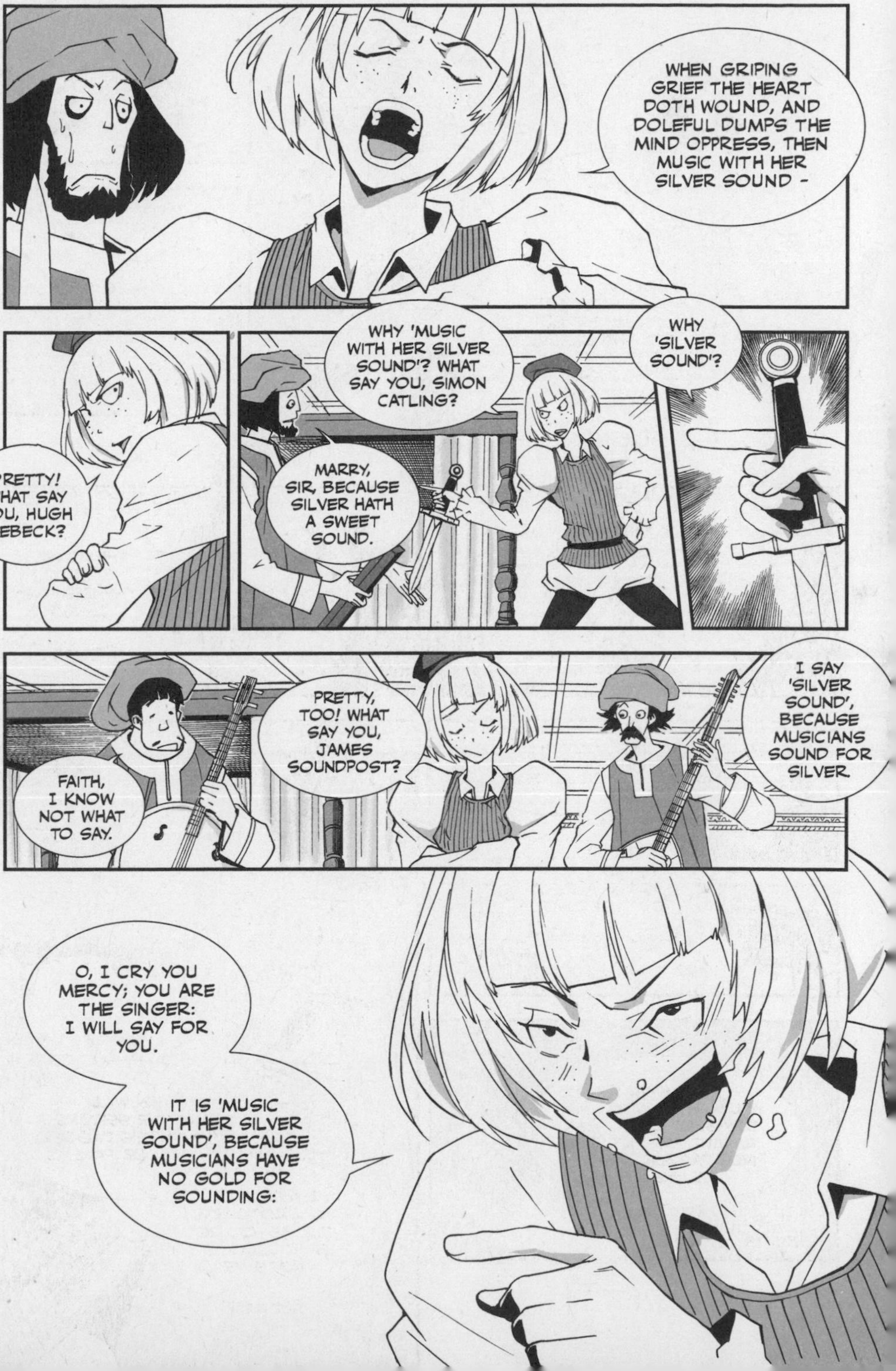
WHEN GRIPING GRIEF THE HEART DOTH WOUND, AND DOLEFUL DUMPS THE MIND OPPRESS, THEN MUSIC WITH HER SILVER SOUND -
WHY 'SILVER SOUND'?
WHY 'MUSIC WITH HER SILVER SOUND'? WHAT SAY YOU, SIMON CATLING?
MARRY, SIR, BECAUSE SILVER HATH A SWEET SOUND.
PRETTY! WHAT SAY YOU, HUGH REBECK?
I SAY 'SILVER SOUND', BECAUSE MUSICIANS SOUND FOR SILVER.
PRETTY, TOO! WHAT SAY YOU, JAMES SOUNDPOST?
FAITH, I KNOW NOT WHAT TO SAY.
O, I CRY YOU MERCY; YOU ARE THE SINGER: I WILL SAY FOR YOU.
IT IS 'MUSIC WITH HER SILVER SOUND', BECAUSE MUSICIANS HAVE NO GOLD FOR SOUNDING:

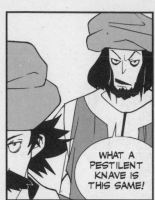

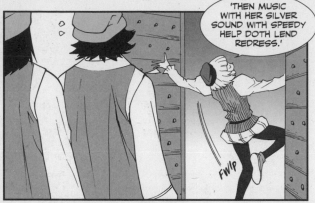

'THEN MUSIC WITH HER SILVER SOUND WITH SPEEDY HELP DOTH LEND REDRESS.'
FWIP
WHAT A PESTILENT KNAVE IS THIS SAME!
HANG HIM, JACK!
COME, WE'LL IN HERE; TARRY FOR THE MOURNERS, AND STAY DINNER.
ACT V
SCENE I
MANTUA

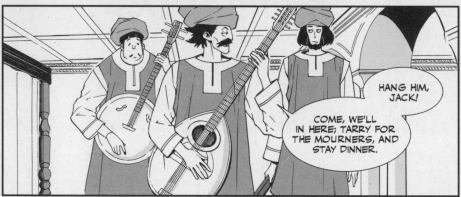

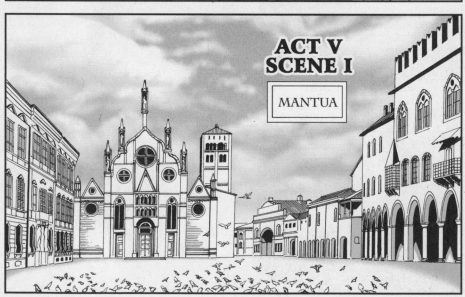

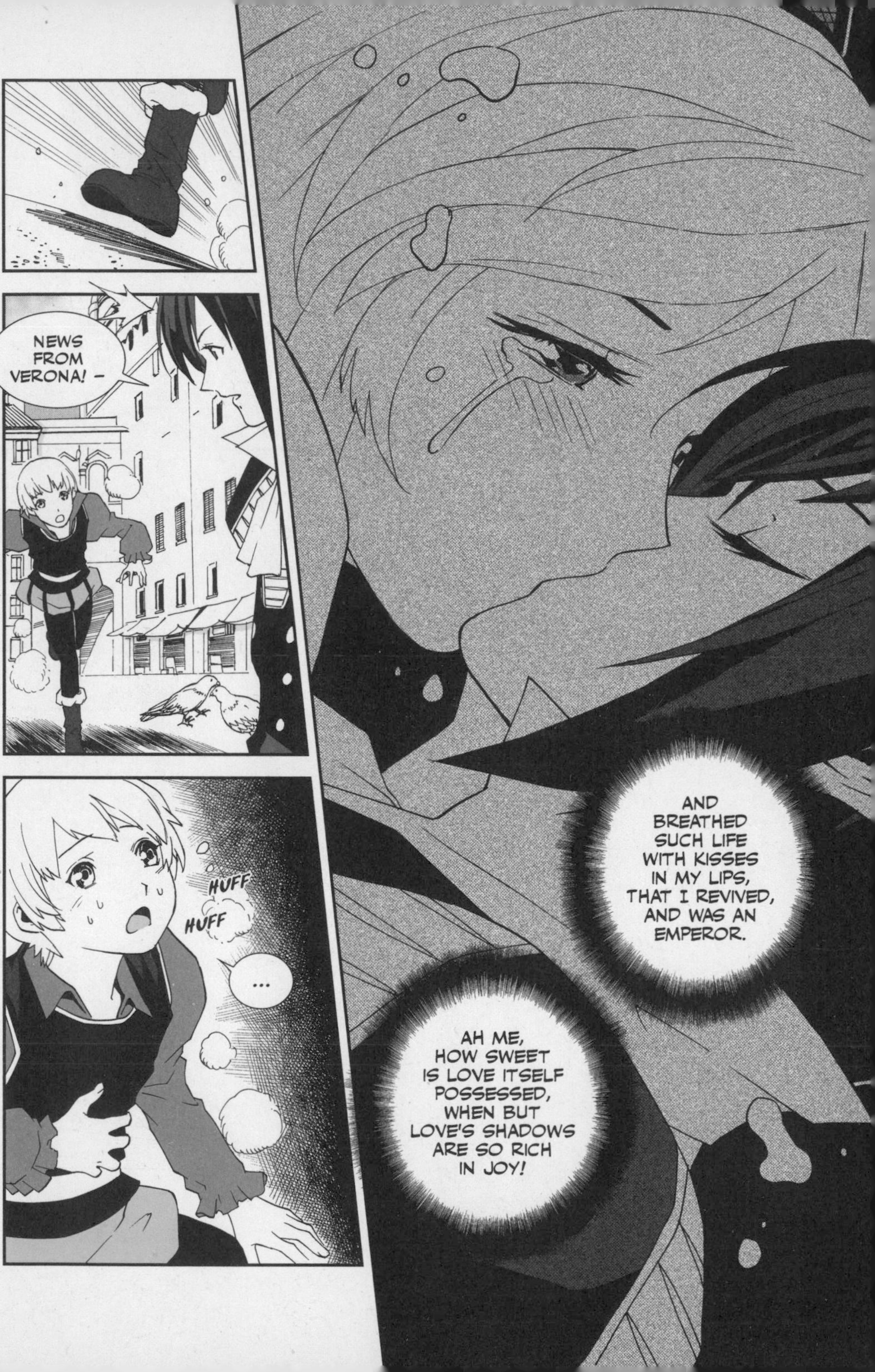
AND BREATHED SUCH LIFE WITH KISSES IN MY LIPS, THAT I REVIVED, AND WAS AN EMPEROR.
AH ME, HOW SWEET IS LOVE ITSELF POSSESSED, WHEN BUT LOVE'S SHADOWS ARE SO RICH IN JOY!
NEWS FROM VERONA! –
HUFF
HUFF
...

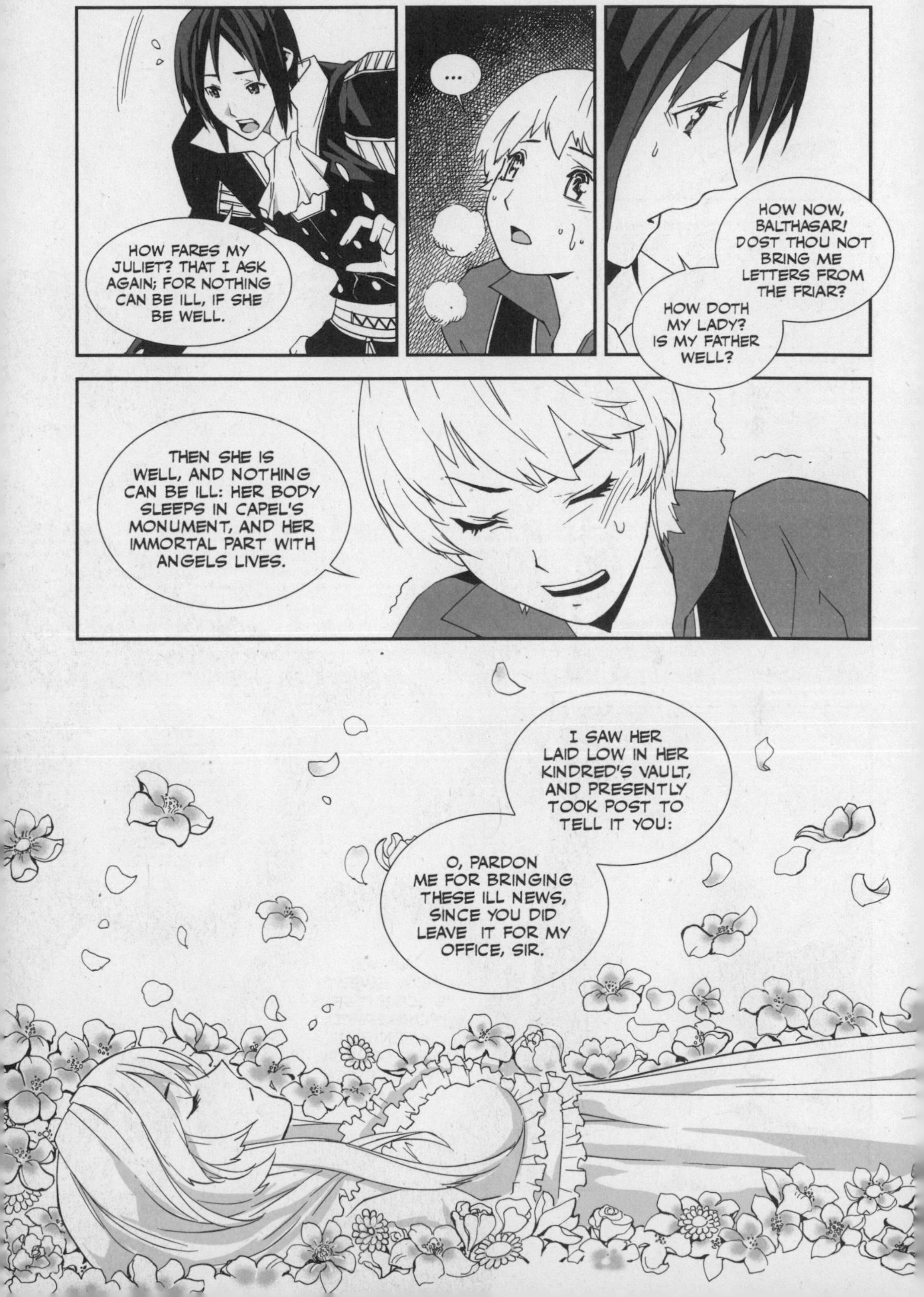
HOW NOW, BALTHASAR! DOST THOU NOT BRING ME LETTERS FROM THE FRIAR?
HOW DOTH MY LADY? IS MY FATHER WELL?
...
HOW FARES MY JULIET? THAT I ASK AGAIN; FOR NOTHING CAN BE ILL, IF SHE BE WELL.
THEN SHE IS WELL, AND NOTHING CAN BE ILL: HER BODY SLEEPS IN CAPEL'S MONUMENT, AND HER IMMORTAL PART WITH ANGELS LIVES.
I SAW HER LAID LOW IN HER KINDRED'S VAULT, AND PRESENTLY TOOK POST TO TELL IT YOU:
O, PARDON ME FOR BRINGING THESE ILL NEWS, SINCE YOU DID LEAVE IT FOR MY OFFICE, SIR.

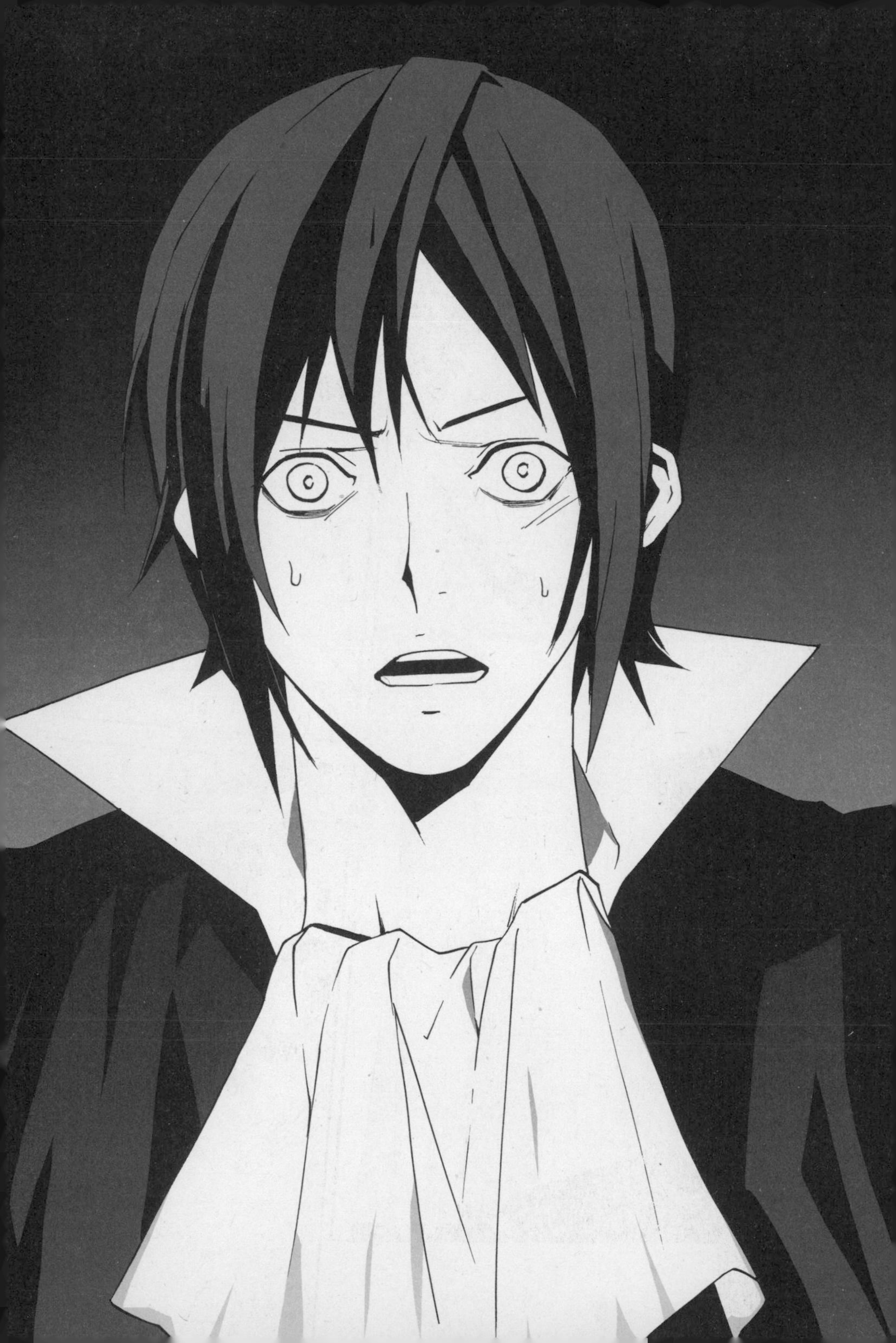

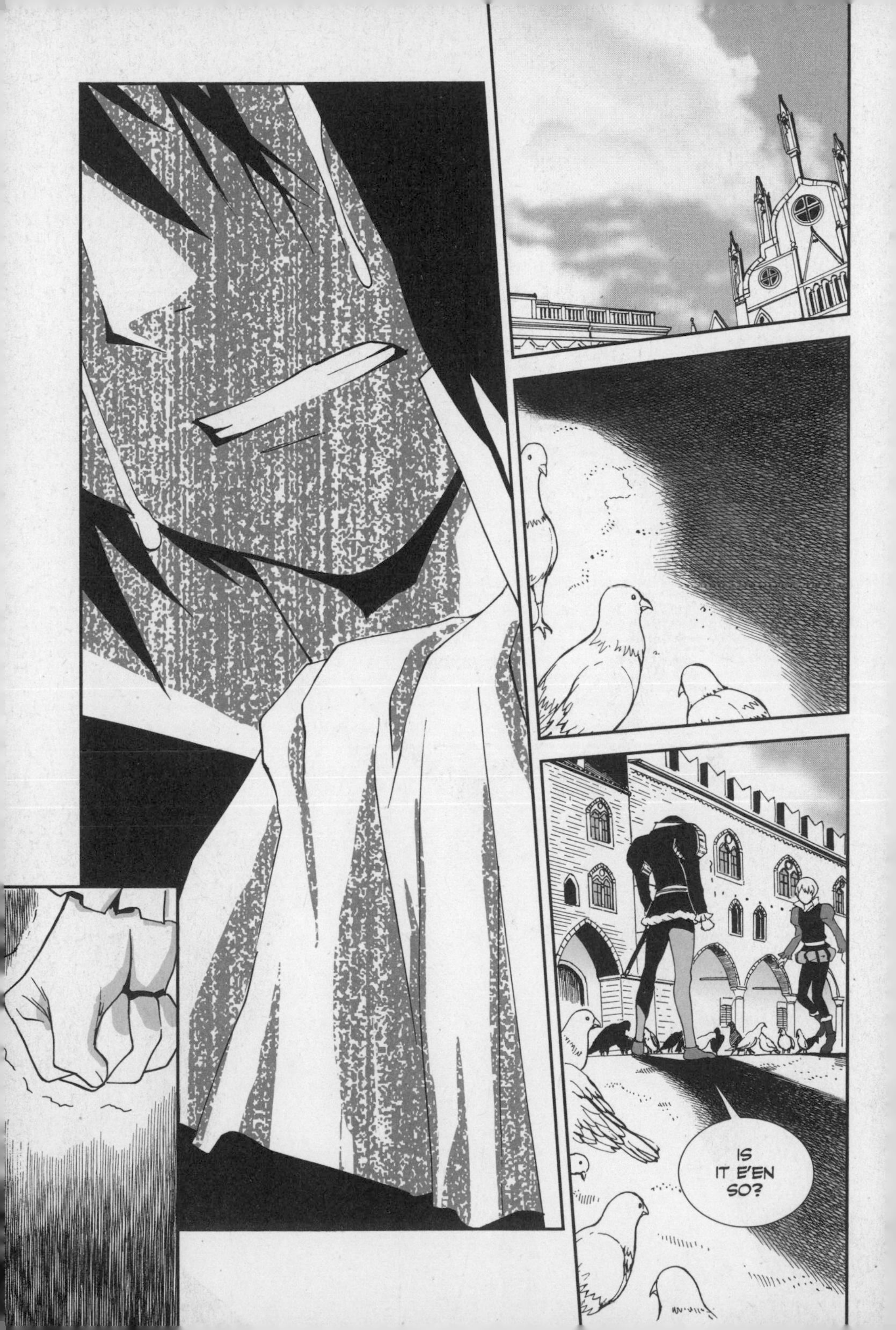
IS IT E'EN SO?

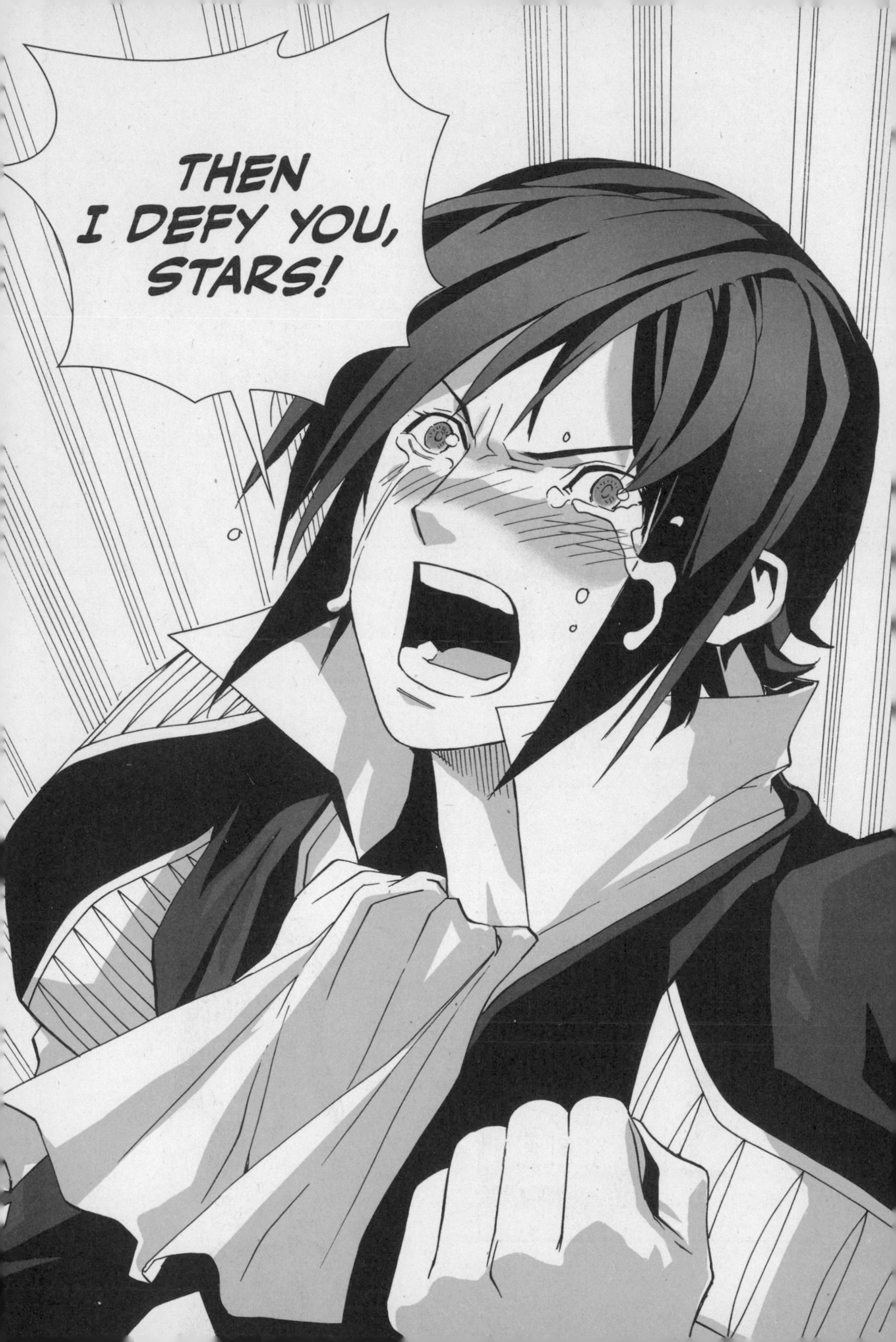
THEN I DEFY YOU, STARS!

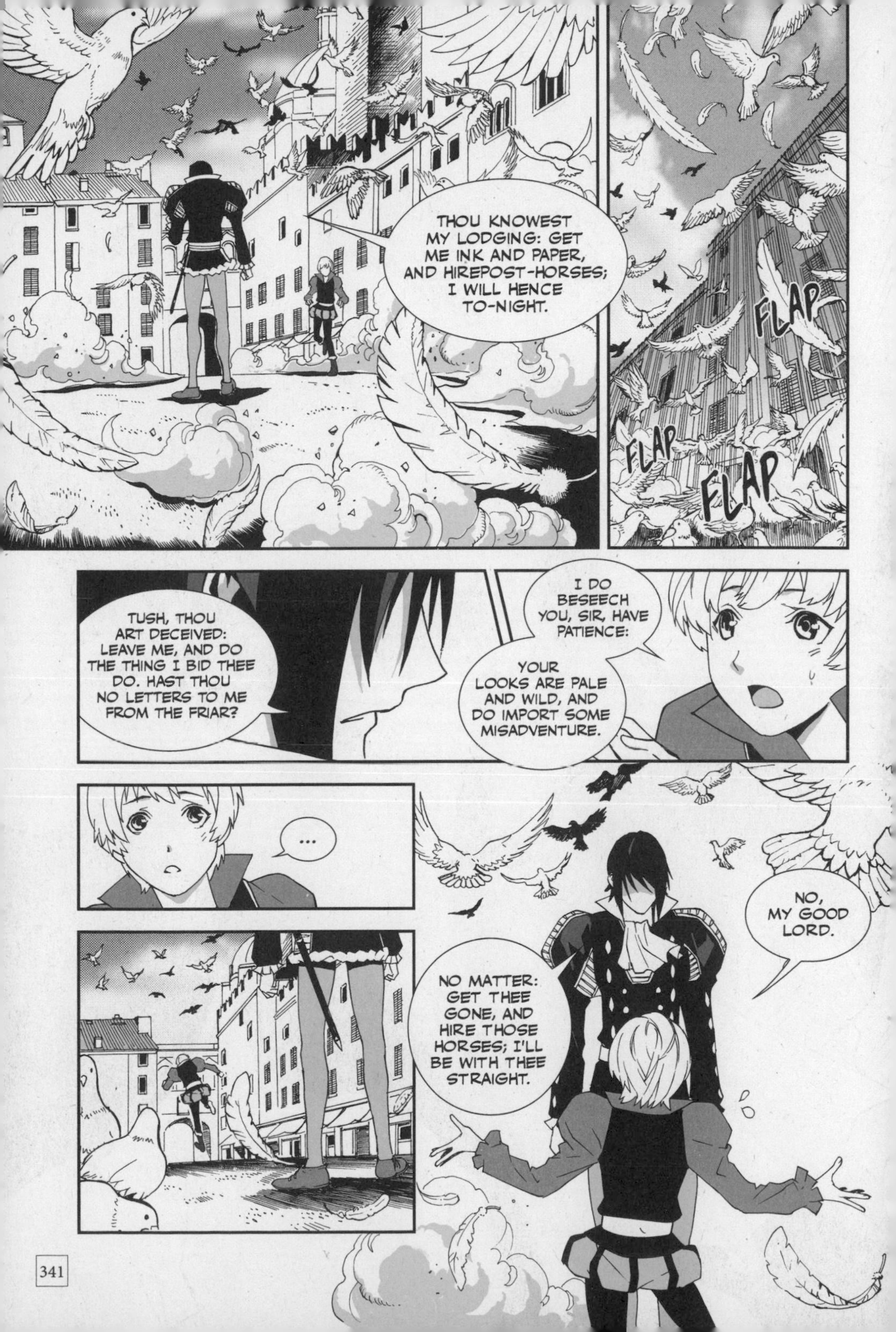
FLAP
FLAP
FLAP
THOU KNOWEST MY LODGING: GET ME INK AND PAPER, AND HIREPOST-HORSES; I WILL HENCE TO-NIGHT.
I DO BESEECH YOU, SIR, HAVE PATIENCE:
YOUR LOOKS ARE PALE AND WILD, AND DO IMPORT SOME MISADVENTURE.
TUSH, THOU ART DECEIVED: LEAVE ME, AND DO THE THING I BID THEE DO. HAST THOU NO LETTERS TO ME FROM THE FRIAR?
NO, MY GOOD LORD.
NO MATTER: GET THEE GONE, AND HIRE THOSE HORSES; I'LL BE WITH THEE STRAIGHT.
...

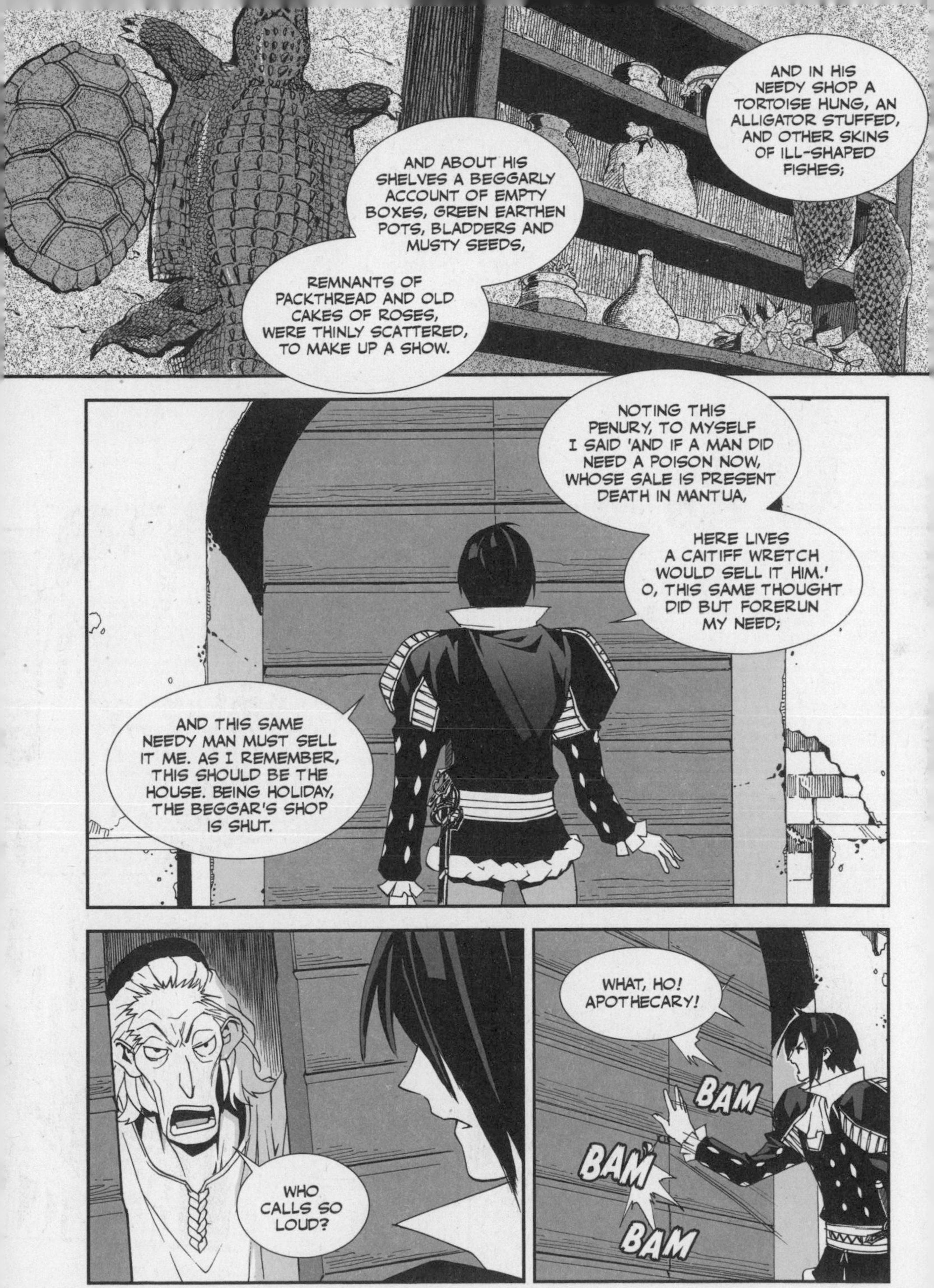
AND IN HIS NEEDY SHOP A TORTOISE HUNG, AN ALLIGATOR STUFFED, AND OTHER SKINS OF ILL-SHAPED FISHES;
AND ABOUT HIS SHELVES A BEGGARLY ACCOUNT OF EMPTY BOXES, GREEN EARTHEN POTS, BLADDERS AND MUSTY SEEDS,
REMNANTS OF PACKTHREAD AND OLD CAKES OF ROSES, WERE THINLY SCATTERED, TO MAKE UP A SHOW.
NOTING THIS PENURY, TO MYSELF I SAID 'AND IF A MAN DID NEED A POISON NOW, WHOSE SALE IS PRESENT DEATH IN MANTUA,
HERE LIVES A CAITIFF WRETCH WOULD SELL IT HIM.' O, THIS SAME THOUGHT DID BUT FORERUN MY NEED;
AND THIS SAME NEEDY MAN MUST SELL IT ME. AS I REMEMBER, THIS SHOULD BE THE HOUSE. BEING HOLIDAY, THE BEGGAR'S SHOP IS SHUT.
WHAT, HO! APOTHECARY!
BAM
BAM
BAM
WHO CALLS SO LOUD?

...

I SEE THAT THOU ART POOR: HOLD, THERE IS FORTY DUCATS:

LET ME HAVE A DRAM OF POISON, SUCH SOON-SPEEDING GEAR AS WILL DISPERSE ITSELF THROUGH ALL THE VEINS THAT THE LIFE-WEARY TAKER MAY FALL DEAD AND THAT THE TRUNK MAY BE DISCHARGED OF BREATH

AS VIOLENTLY AS HASTY POWDER FIRED DOTH HURRY FROM THE FATAL CANNON'S WOMB.

COME HITHER, MAN.

!

SUCH MORTAL DRUGS I HAVE; BUT MANTUA'S LAW IS DEATH TO ANY HE THAT UTTERS THEM.

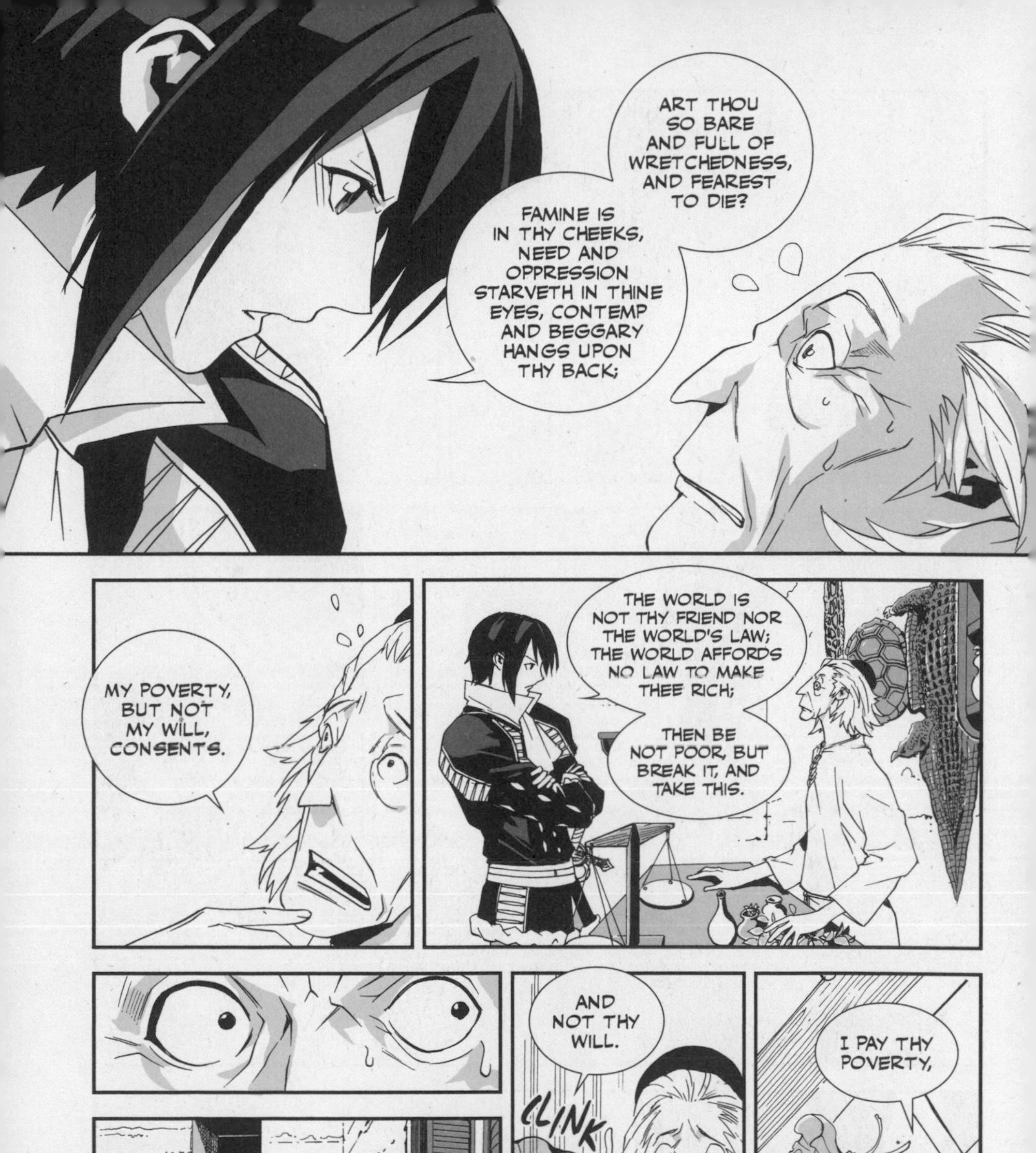
ART THOU SO BARE AND FULL OF WRETCHEDNESS, AND FEAREST TO DIE?
FAMINE IS IN THY CHEEKS, NEED AND OPPRESSION STARVETH IN THINE EYES, CONTEMP AND BEGGARY HANGS UPON THY BACK;
THE WORLD IS NOT THY FRIEND NOR THE WORLD'S LAW; THE WORLD AFFORDS NO LAW TO MAKE THEE RICH;
THEN BE NOT POOR, BUT BREAK IT, AND TAKE THIS.
MY POVERTY, BUT NOT MY WILL, CONSENTS.
I PAY THY POVERTY,
CLINK
AND NOT THY WILL.
CLINK
...

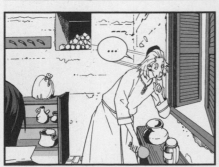

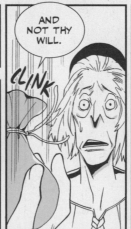

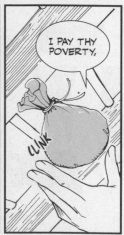

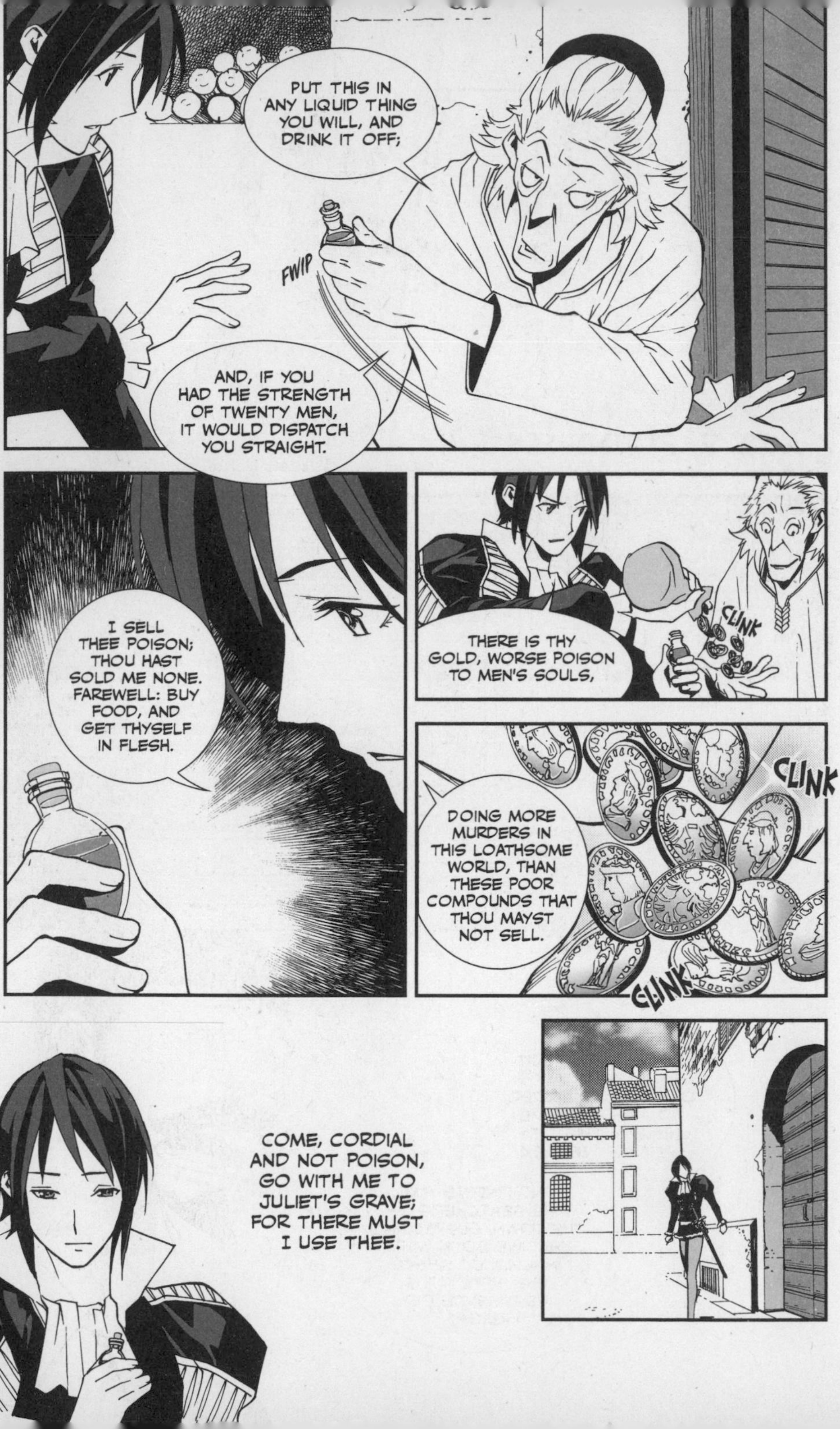
PUT THIS IN ANY LIQUID THING YOU WILL, AND DRINK IT OFF;
FWIP
AND, IF YOU HAD THE STRENGTH OF TWENTY MEN, IT WOULD DISPATCH YOU STRAIGHT.
CLINK
THERE IS THY GOLD, WORSE POISON TO MEN'S SOULS,
CLINK
DOING MORE MURDERS IN THIS LOATHSOME WORLD, THAN THESE POOR COMPOUNDS THAT THOU MAYST NOT SELL.
CLINK
I SELL THEE POISON; THOU HAST SOLD ME NONE. FAREWELL: BUY FOOD, AND GET THYSELF IN FLESH.
COME, CORDIAL AND NOT POISON, GO WITH ME TO JULIET'S GRAVE; FOR THERE MUST I USE THEE.

HOLY FRANCISCAN FRIAR! BROTHER, HO!

RATTLE RATTLE

ACT V SCENE II

WELCOME FROM MANTUA! WHAT SAYS ROMEO?

OR, IF HIS MIND BE WRIT, GIVE ME HIS LETTER.

THIS SAME SHOULD BE THE VOICE OF FRIAR JOHN.

FRIAR LAURENCE'S CELL

GOING TO FIND A BARE-FOOT BROTHER OUT, ONE OF OUR ORDER, TO ASSOCIATE ME, HERE IN THIS CITY VISITING THE SICK,

AND FINDING HIM, THE SEARCHERS OF THE TOWN, SUSPECTING THAT WE BOTH WERE IN A HOUSE WHERE THE INFECTIOUS PESTILENCE DID REIGN,

WHO BARE MY LETTER, THEN, TO ROMEO?

SEALED UP THE DOORS, AND WOULD NOT LET US FORTH; SO THAT MY SPEED TO MANTUA THERE WAS STAYED.

I COULD NOT SEND IT, – HERE IT IS AGAIN –

NOR GET A MESSENGER TO BRING IT THEE, SO FEARFUL WERE THEY OF INFECTION.

UNHAPPY FORTUNE! BY MY BROTHERHOOD, THE LETTER WAS NOT NICE BUT FULL OF CHARGE OF DEAR IMPORT, AND THE NEGLECTING IT MAY DO MUCH DANGER

NOW MUST I TO THE MONUMENT ALONE; WITHIN THREE HOURS WILL FAIR JULIET WAKE.

SHE WILL BESHREW ME MUCH THAT ROMEO HATH HAD NO NOTICE OF THESE ACCIDENTS; BUT I WILL WRITE AGAIN TO MANTUA, AND KEEP HER AT MY CELL TILL ROMEO COME – POOR LIVING CORSE, CLOSED IN A DEAD MAN'S TOMB!

FRIAR JOHN, GO HENCE; GET ME AN IRON CROW, AND BRING IT STRAIGHT UNTO MY CELL.

BROTHER, I'LL GO AND BRING IT THEE.

CLOP

CLOP CLOP

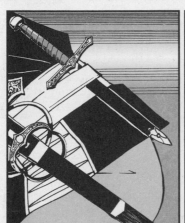

CLOP

CLOP

CLOP

ACT V SCENE III

CAPULET'S TOMB

YET PUT IT OUT, FOR I WOULD NOT BE SEEN.

GIVE ME THY TORCH, BOY. HENCE, AND STAND ALOOF.

WHISTLE THEN TO ME AS SIGNAL THAT THOU HEAREST SOMETHING APPROACH.

GIVE ME THOSE FLOWERS. DO AS I BID THEE, GO.

HOLDING THY EAR CLOSE TO THE HOLLOW GROUND,

SO SHALL NO FOOT UPON THE CHURCHYARD TREAD, BEING LOOSE, UNFIRM, WITH DIGGING UP OF GRAVES, BUT THOU SHALT HEAR IT.

UNDER YOND YEW TREES LAY THEE ALL ALONG,

I AM ALMOST AFRAID TO STAND ALONE HERE IN THE CHURCHYARD, YET I WILL ADVENTURE.

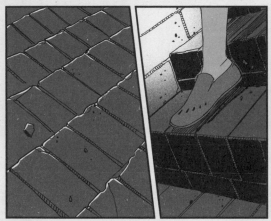

SWEET FLOWER, WITH FLOWERS THY BRIDAL BED I STREW –

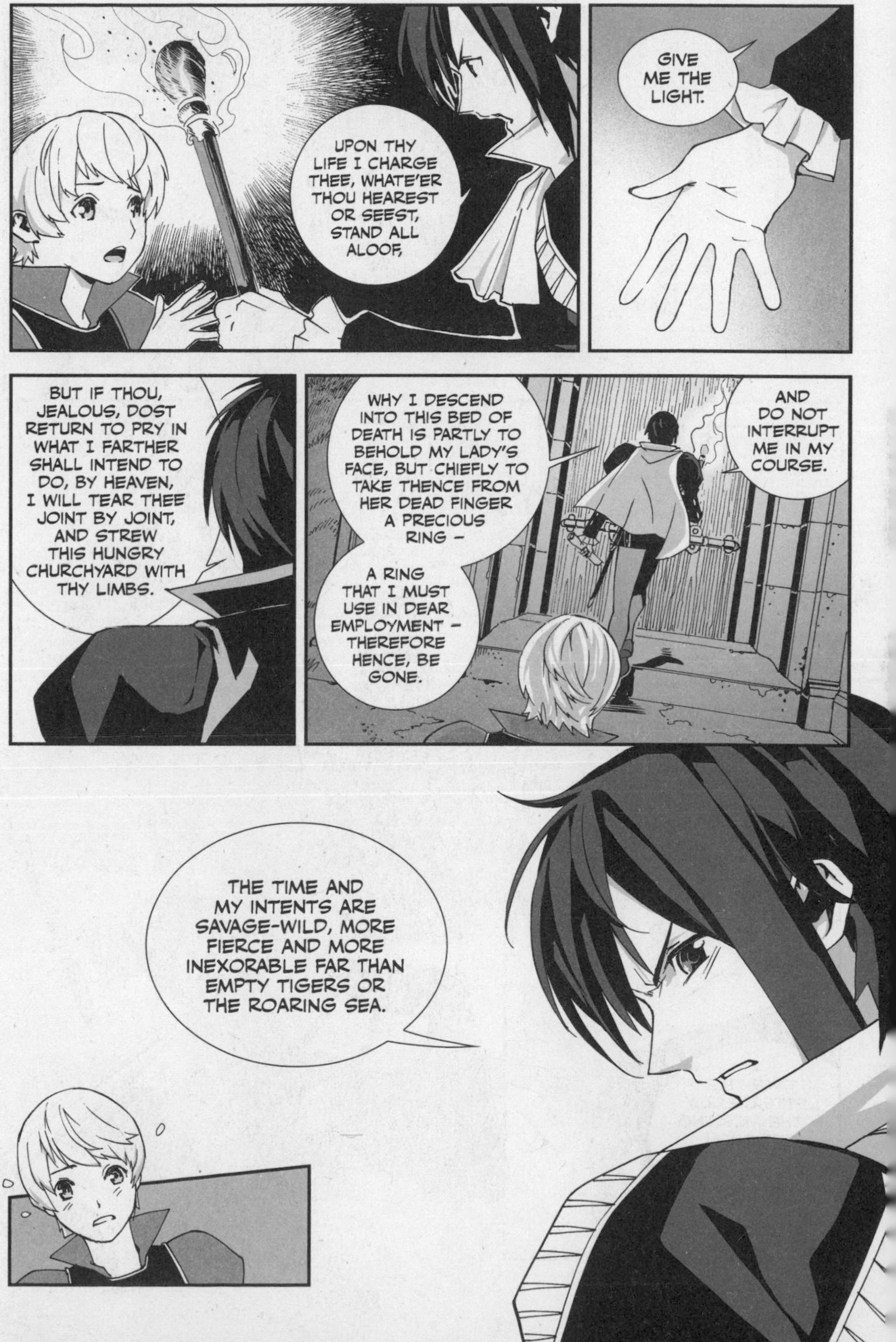
GIVE ME THE LIGHT.
UPON THY LIFE I CHARGE THEE, WHATE'ER THOU HEAREST OR SEEST, STAND ALL ALOOF,
AND DO NOT INTERRUPT ME IN MY COURSE.
WHY I DESCEND INTO THIS BED OF DEATH IS PARTLY TO BEHOLD MY LADY'S FACE, BUT CHIEFLY TO TAKE THENCE FROM HER DEAD FINGER A PRECIOUS RING –
A RING THAT I MUST USE IN DEAR EMPLOYMENT – THEREFORE HENCE, BE GONE.
BUT IF THOU, JEALOUS, DOST RETURN TO PRY IN WHAT I FARTHER SHALL INTEND TO DO, BY HEAVEN, I WILL TEAR THEE JOINT BY JOINT, AND STREW THIS HUNGRY CHURCHYARD WITH THY LIMBS.
THE TIME AND MY INTENTS ARE SAVAGE-WILD, MORE FIERCE AND MORE INEXORABLE FAR THAN EMPTY TIGERS OR THE ROARING SEA.

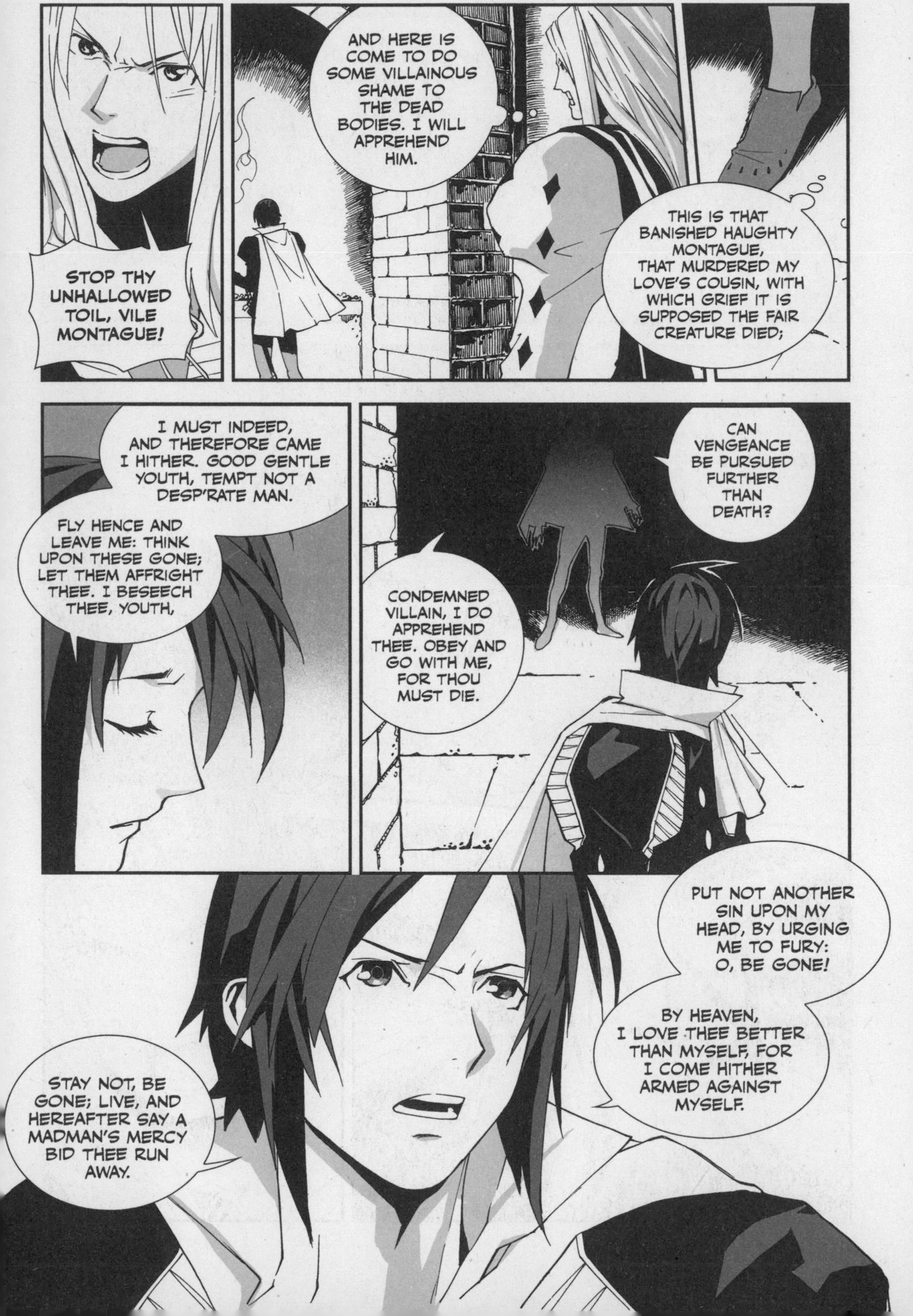
THIS IS THAT BANISHED HAUGHTY MONTAGUE, THAT MURDERED MY LOVE'S COUSIN, WITH WHICH GRIEF IT IS SUPPOSED THE FAIR CREATURE DIED;
AND HERE IS COME TO DO SOME VILLAINOUS SHAME TO THE DEAD BODIES. I WILL APPREHEND HIM.
STOP THY UNHALLOWED TOIL, VILE MONTAGUE!
CAN VENGEANCE BE PURSUED FURTHER THAN DEATH?
CONDEMNED VILLAIN, I DO APPREHEND THEE. OBEY AND GO WITH ME, FOR THOU MUST DIE.
I MUST INDEED, AND THEREFORE CAME I HITHER. GOOD GENTLE YOUTH, TEMPT NOT A DESP'RATE MAN.
FLY HENCE AND LEAVE ME: THINK UPON THESE GONE; LET THEM AFFRIGHT THEE. I BESEECH THEE, YOUTH,
PUT NOT ANOTHER SIN UPON MY HEAD, BY URGING ME TO FURY: O, BE GONE!
BY HEAVEN, I LOVE THEE BETTER THAN MYSELF, FOR I COME HITHER ARMED AGAINST MYSELF.
STAY NOT, BE GONE; LIVE, AND HEREAFTER SAY A MADMAN'S MERCY BID THEE RUN AWAY.

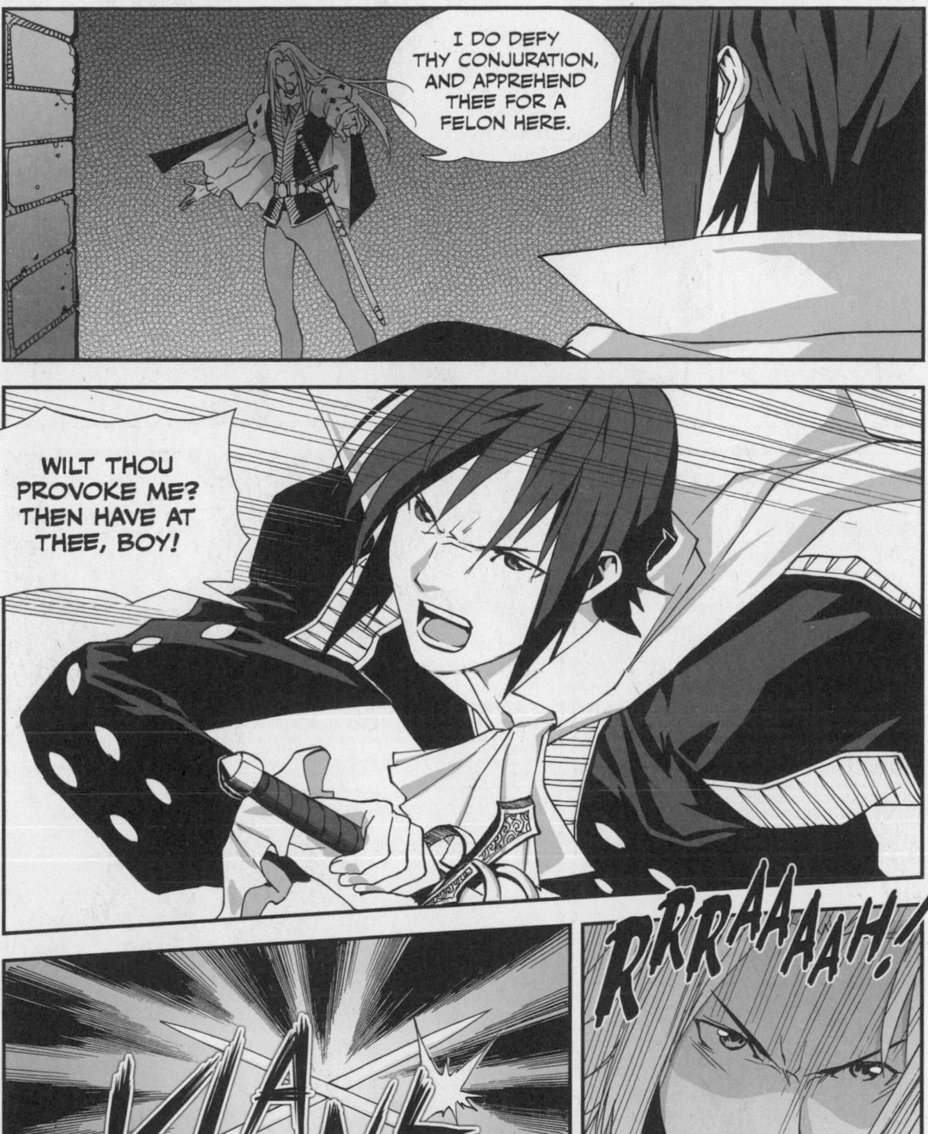
I DO DEFY THY CONJURATION, AND APPREHEND THEE FOR A FELON HERE.
WILT THOU PROVOKE ME? THEN HAVE AT THEE, BOY!
RRRAAAAH!
KLANK

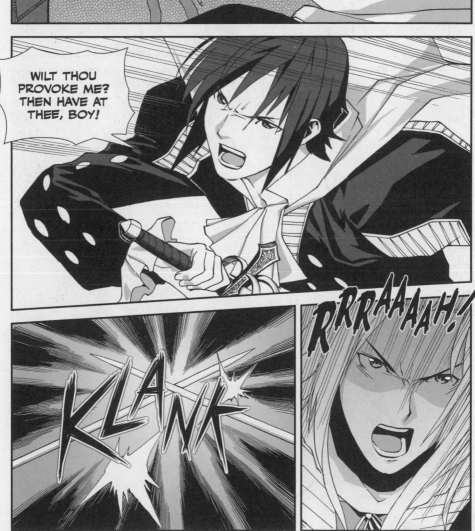

O LORD, THEY FIGHT! I WILL GO CALL THE WATCH.

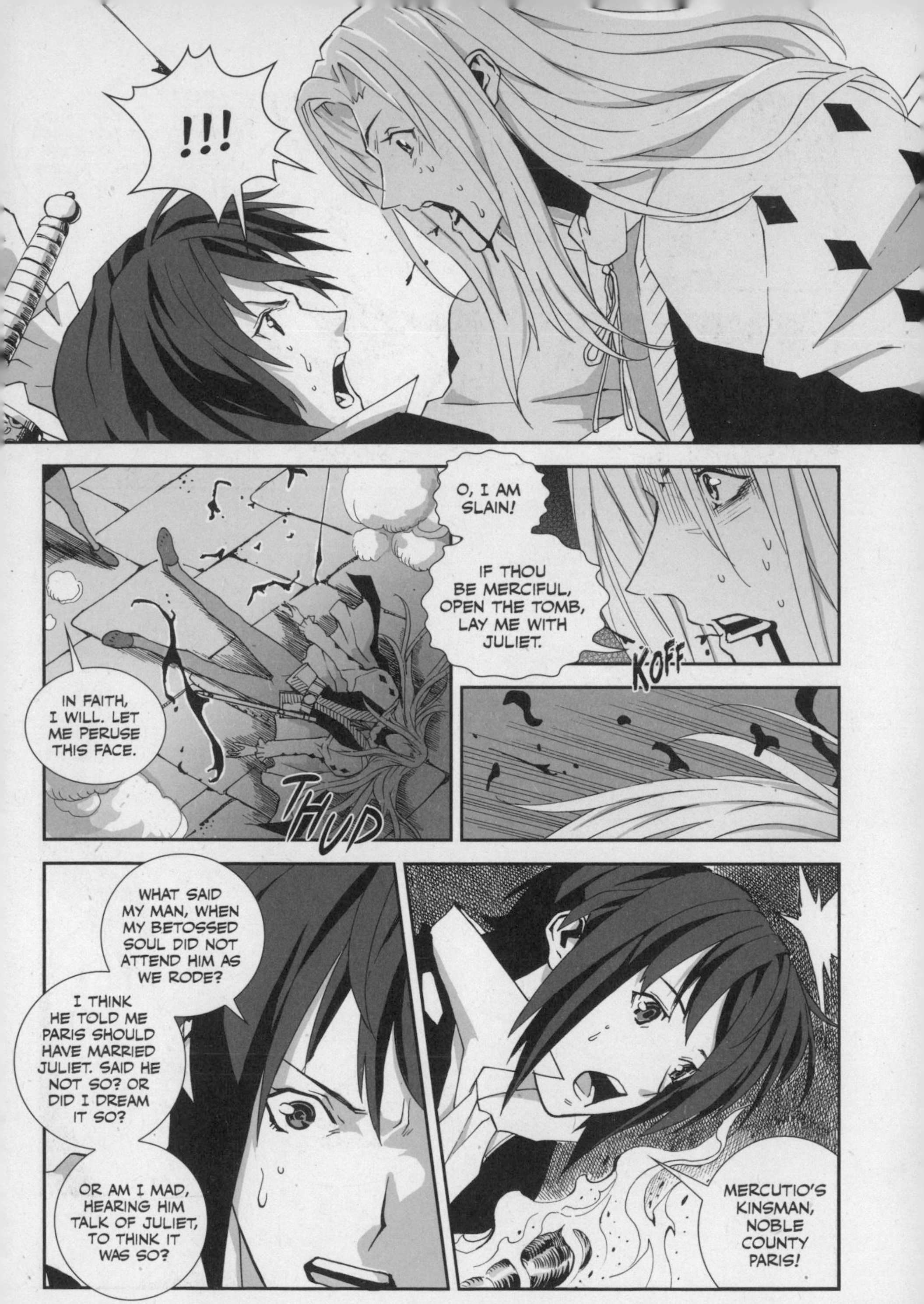

!!!
O, I AM SLAIN!
IF THOU BE MERCIFUL, OPEN THE TOMB, LAY ME WITH JULIET.
KOFF
IN FAITH, I WILL. LET ME PERUSE THIS FACE.
THUD
MERCUTIO'S KINSMAN, NOBLE COUNTY PARIS!
WHAT SAID MY MAN, WHEN MY BETOSSED SOUL DID NOT ATTEND HIM AS WE RODE?
I THINK HE TOLD ME PARIS SHOULD HAVE MARRIED JULIET. SAID HE NOT SO? OR DID I DREAM IT SO?
OR AM I MAD, HEARING HIM TALK OF JULIET, TO THINK IT WAS SO?

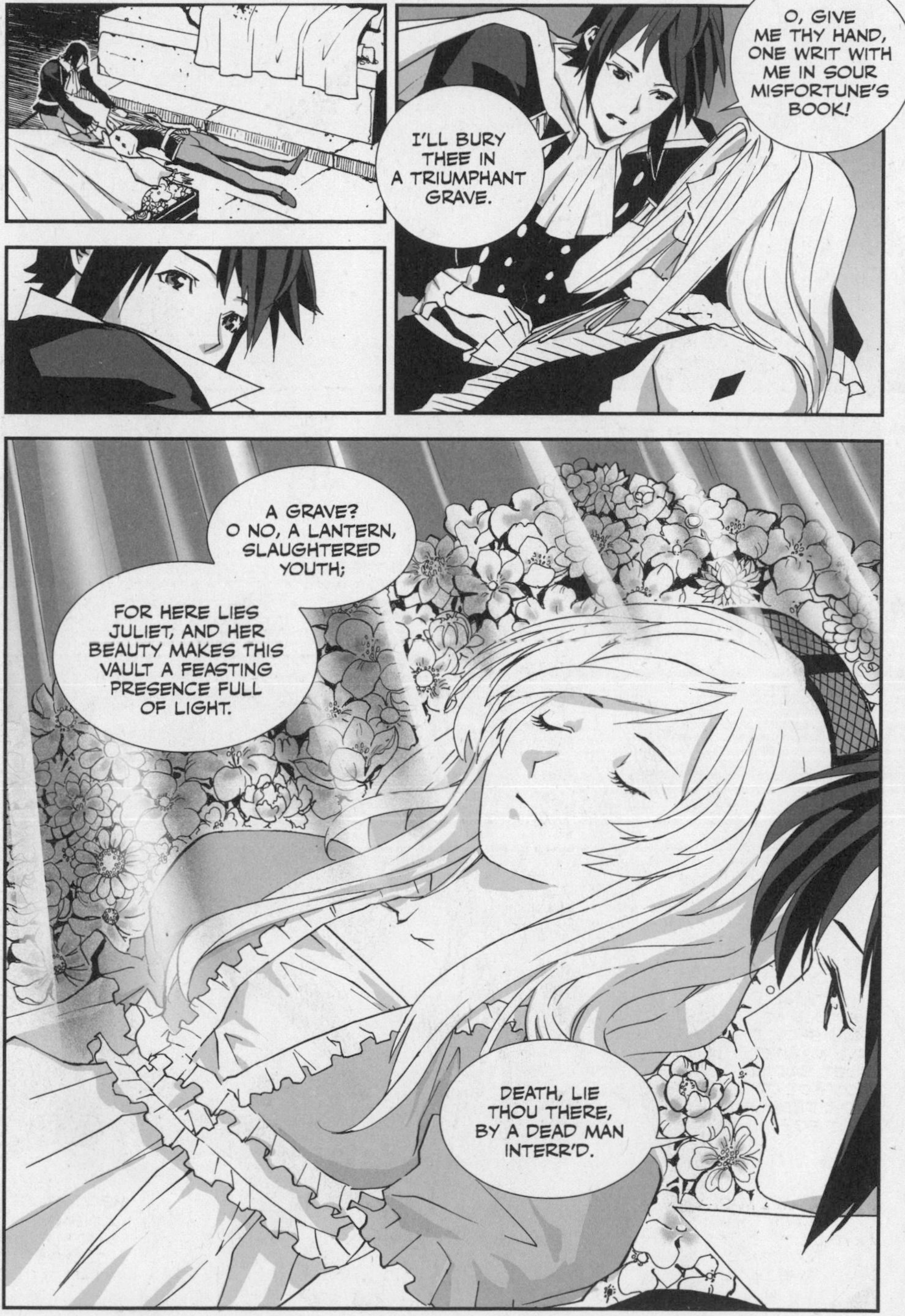
O, GIVE ME THY HAND, ONE WRIT WITH ME IN SOUR MISFORTUNE'S BOOK!
I'LL BURY THEE IN A TRIUMPHANT GRAVE.
A GRAVE? O NO, A LANTERN, SLAUGHTERED YOUTH;
FOR HERE LIES JULIET, AND HER BEAUTY MAKES THIS VAULT A FEASTING PRESENCE FULL OF LIGHT.
DEATH, LIE THOU THERE, BY A DEAD MAN INTERR'D.

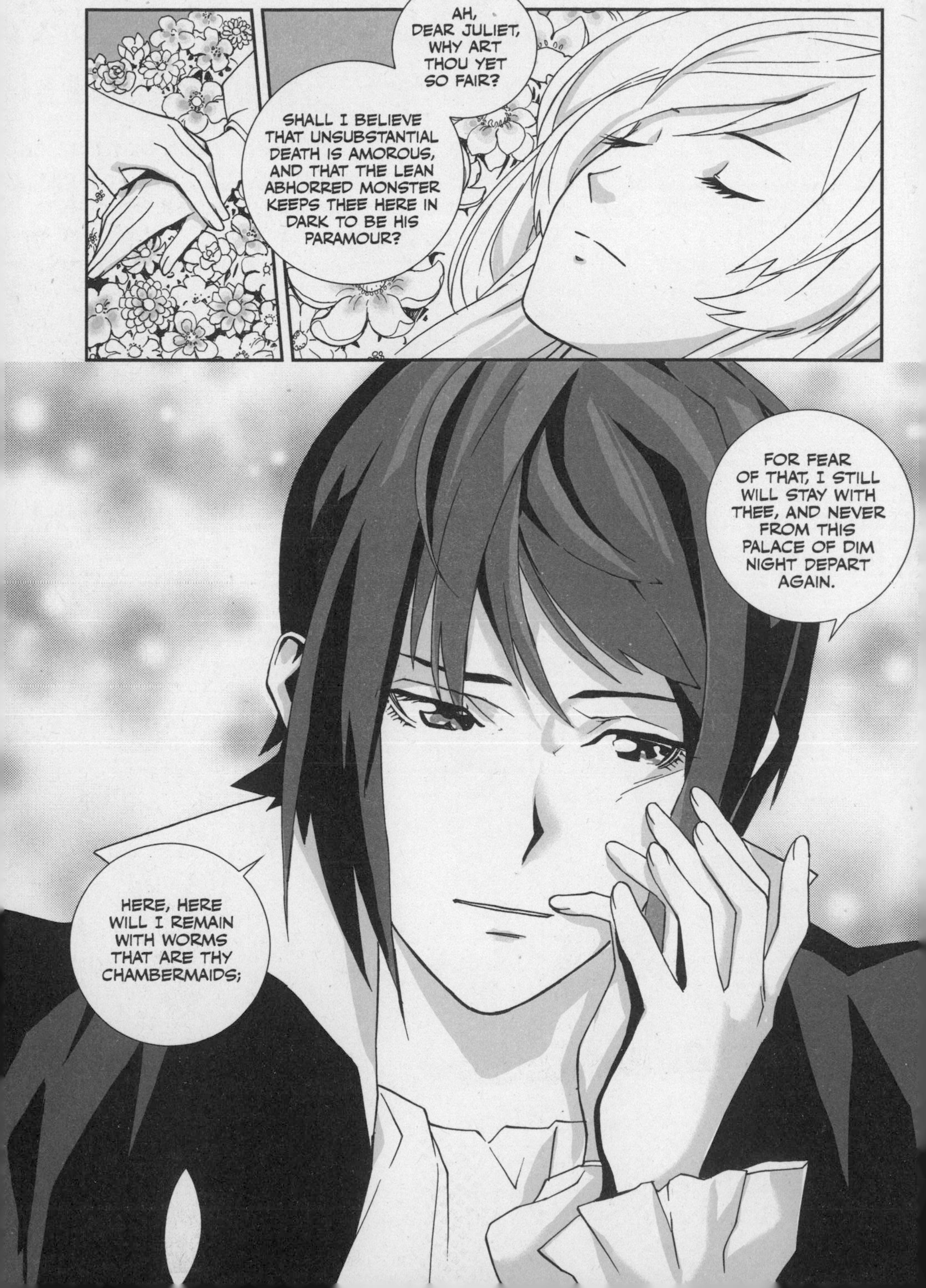
AH, DEAR JULIET, WHY ART THOU YET SO FAIR?
SHALL I BELIEVE THAT UNSUBSTANTIAL DEATH IS AMOROUS, AND THAT THE LEAN ABHORRED MONSTER KEEPS THEE HERE IN DARK TO BE HIS PARAMOUR?
FOR FEAR OF THAT, I STILL WILL STAY WITH THEE, AND NEVER FROM THIS PALACE OF DIM NIGHT DEPART AGAIN.
HERE, HERE WILL I REMAIN WITH WORMS THAT ARE THY CHAMBERMAIDS;

O, HERE WILL I SET UP MY EVERLASTING REST, AND SHAKE THE YOKE OF INAUSPICIOUS STARS FROM THIS WORLD-WEARIED FLESH.

EYES, LOOK YOUR LAST! ARMS, TAKE YOUR LAST EMBRACE! AND, LIPS, O YOU THE DOORS OF BREATH, SEAL WITH A RIGHTEOUS KISS A DATELESS BARGAIN TO ENGROSSING DEATH!

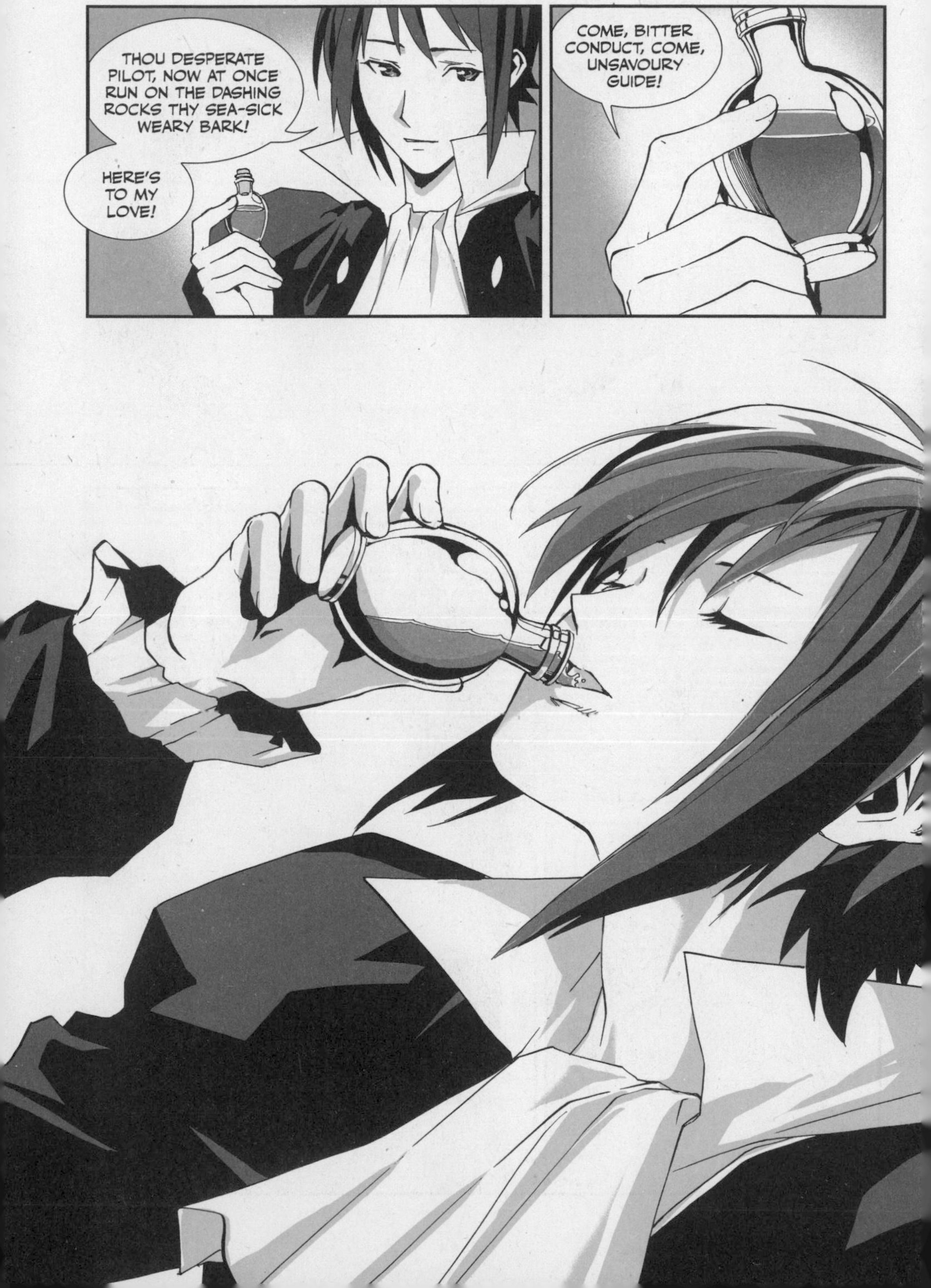
COME, BITTER CONDUCT, COME, UNSAVOURY GUIDE!
THOU DESPERATE PILOT, NOW AT ONCE RUN ON THE DASHING ROCKS THY SEA-SICK WEARY BARK!
HERE'S TO MY LOVE!

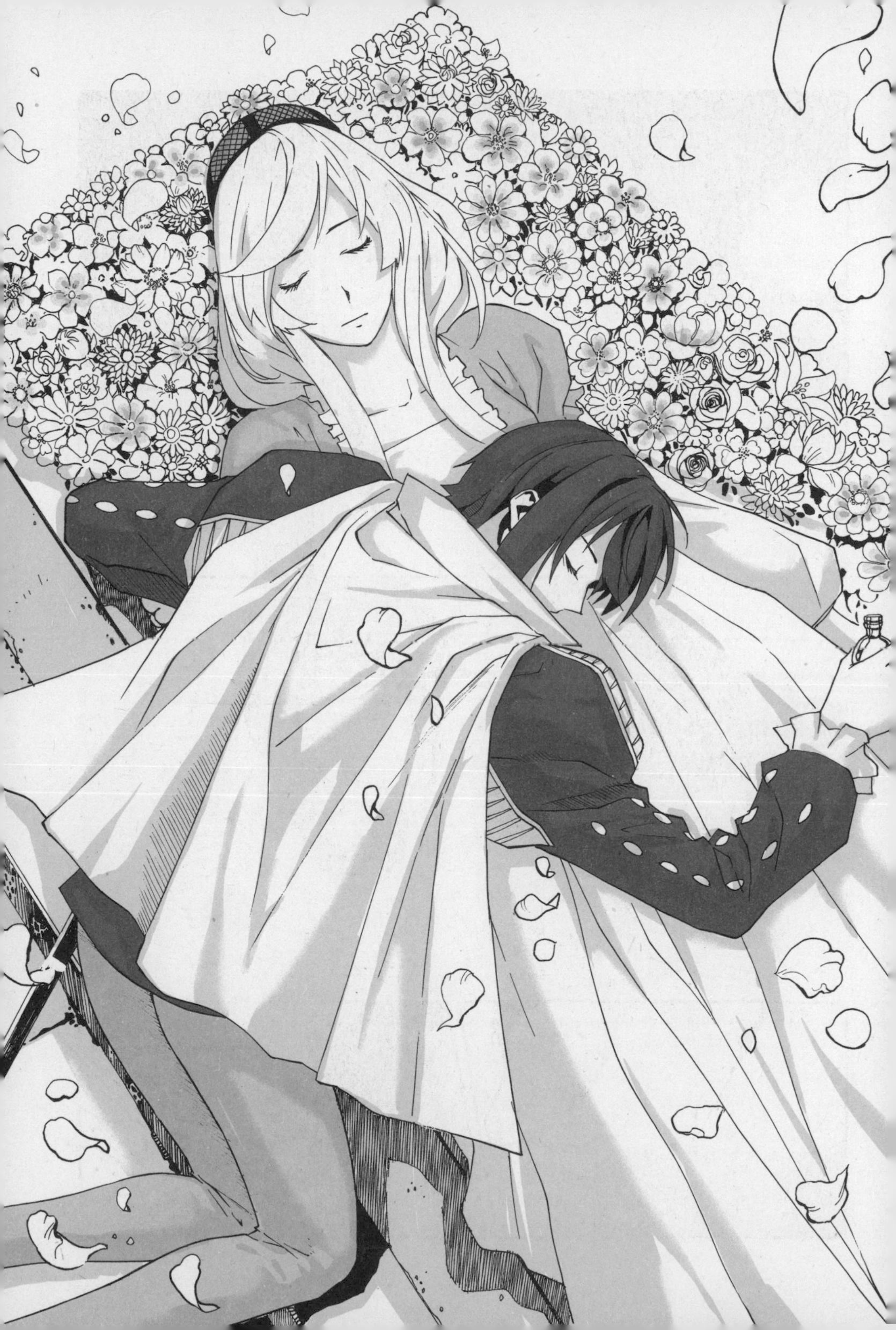

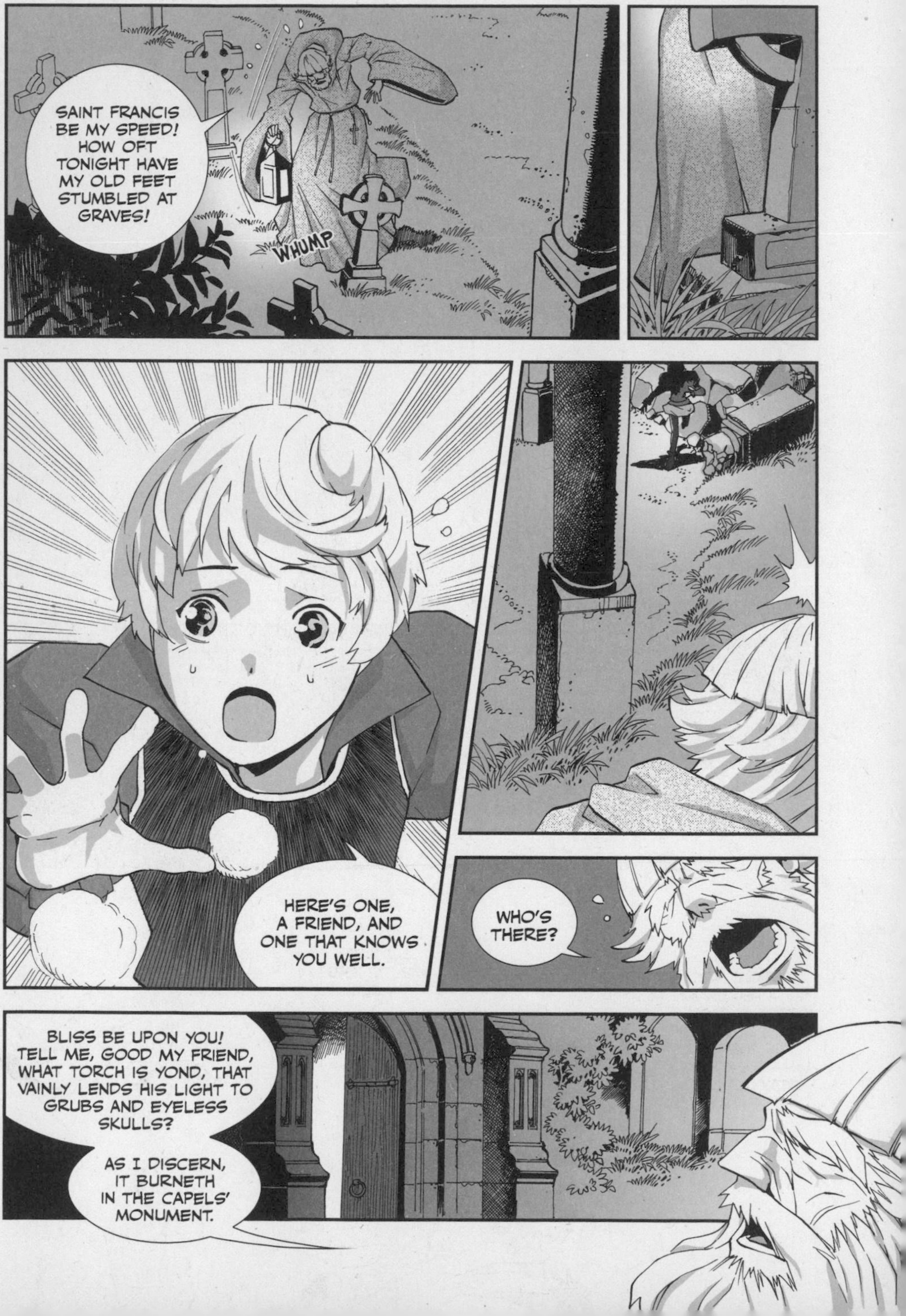
SAINT FRANCIS BE MY SPEED! HOW OFT TONIGHT HAVE MY OLD FEET STUMBLED AT GRAVES!
WHUMP
WHO'S THERE?
HERE'S ONE, A FRIEND, AND ONE THAT KNOWS YOU WELL.
BLISS BE UPON YOU! TELL ME, GOOD MY FRIEND, WHAT TORCH IS YOND, THAT VAINLY LENDS HIS LIGHT TO GRUBS AND EYELESS SKULLS?
AS I DISCERN, IT BURNETH IN THE CAPELS' MONUMENT.

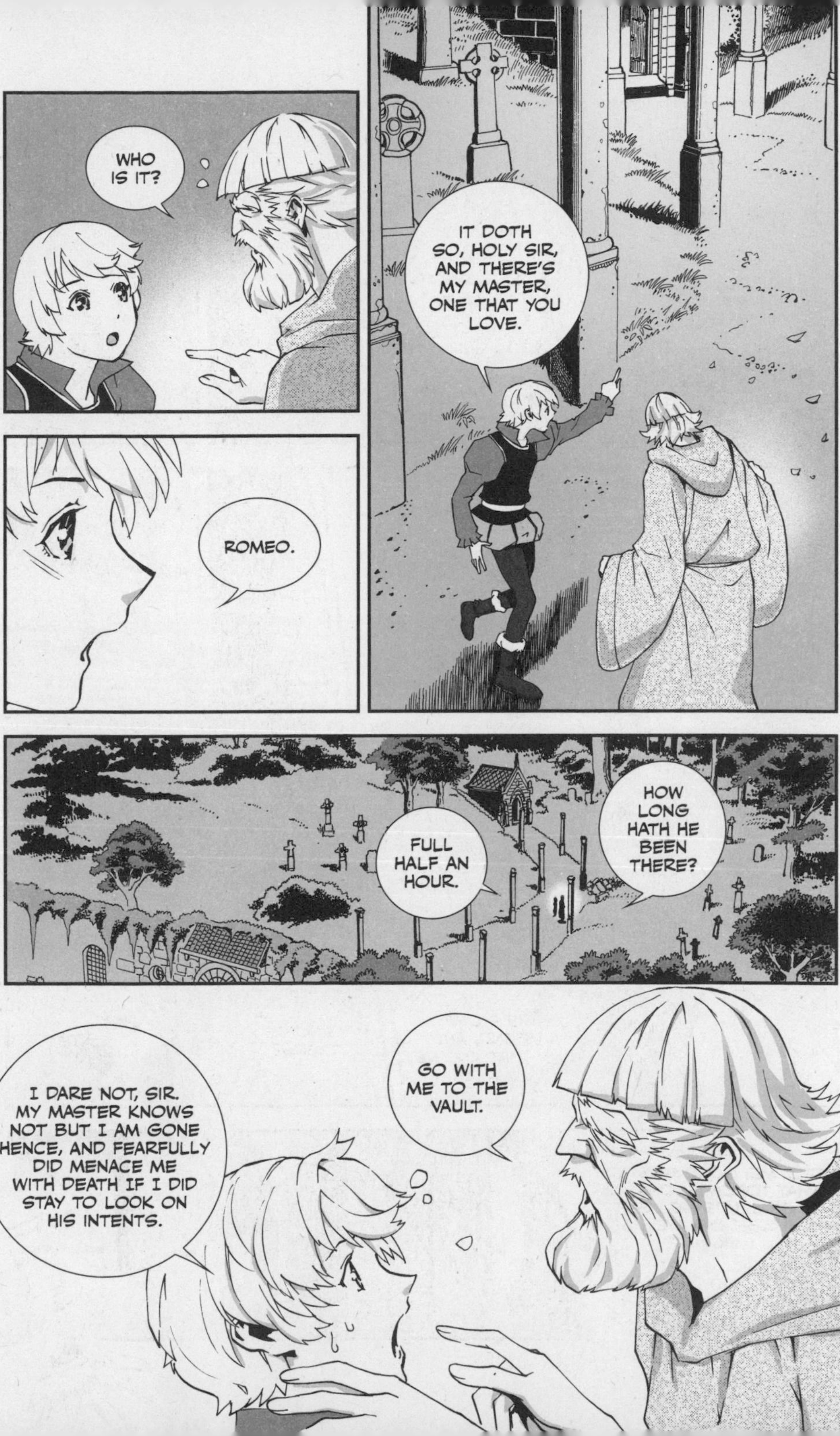
IT DOTH SO, HOLY SIR, AND THERE'S MY MASTER, ONE THAT YOU LOVE.
WHO IS IT?
ROMEO.
HOW LONG HATH HE BEEN THERE?
FULL HALF AN HOUR.
GO WITH ME TO THE VAULT.
I DARE NOT, SIR. MY MASTER KNOWS NOT BUT I AM GONE HENCE, AND FEARFULLY DID MENACE ME WITH DEATH IF I DID STAY TO LOOK ON HIS INTENTS.

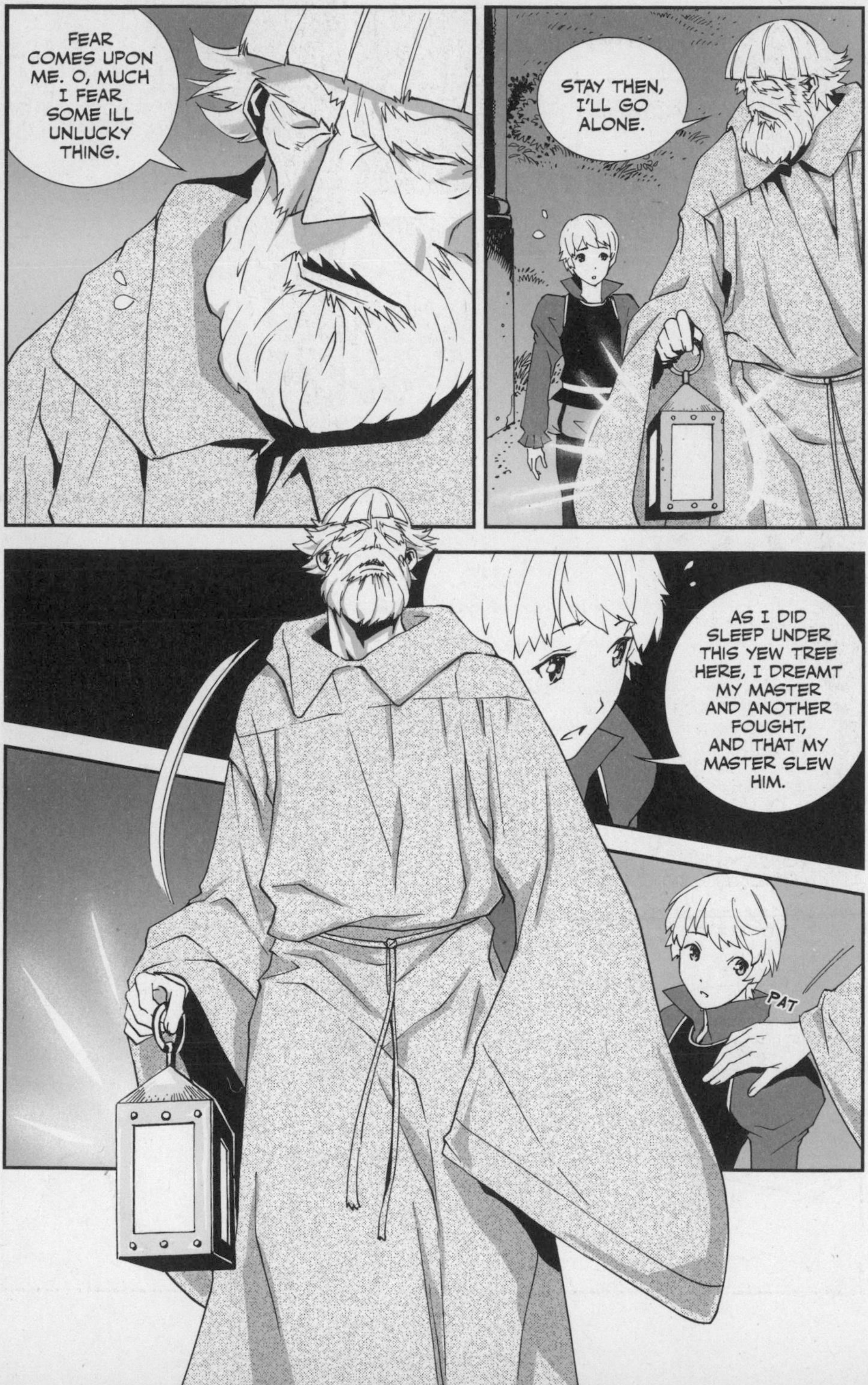
STAY THEN, I'LL GO ALONE.
FEAR COMES UPON ME. O, MUCH I FEAR SOME ILL UNLUCKY THING.
AS I DID SLEEP UNDER THIS YEW TREE HERE, I DREAMT MY MASTER AND ANOTHER FOUGHT, AND THAT MY MASTER SLEW HIM.
PAT

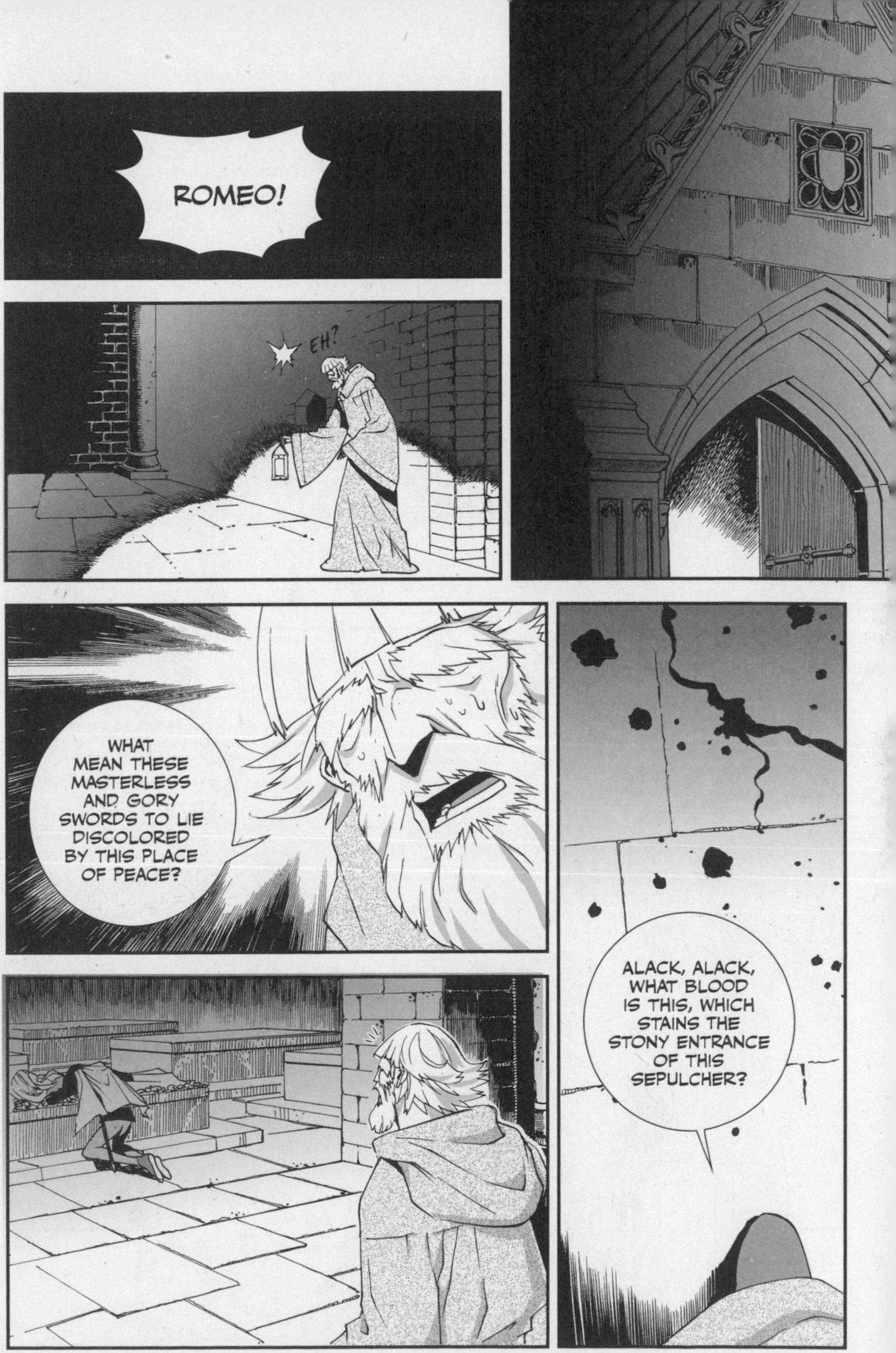
ROMEO!
EH?
ALACK, ALACK, WHAT BLOOD IS THIS, WHICH STAINS THE STONY ENTRANCE OF THIS SEPULCHER?
WHAT MEAN THESE MASTERLESS AND GORY SWORDS TO LIE DISCOLORED BY THIS PLACE OF PEACE?

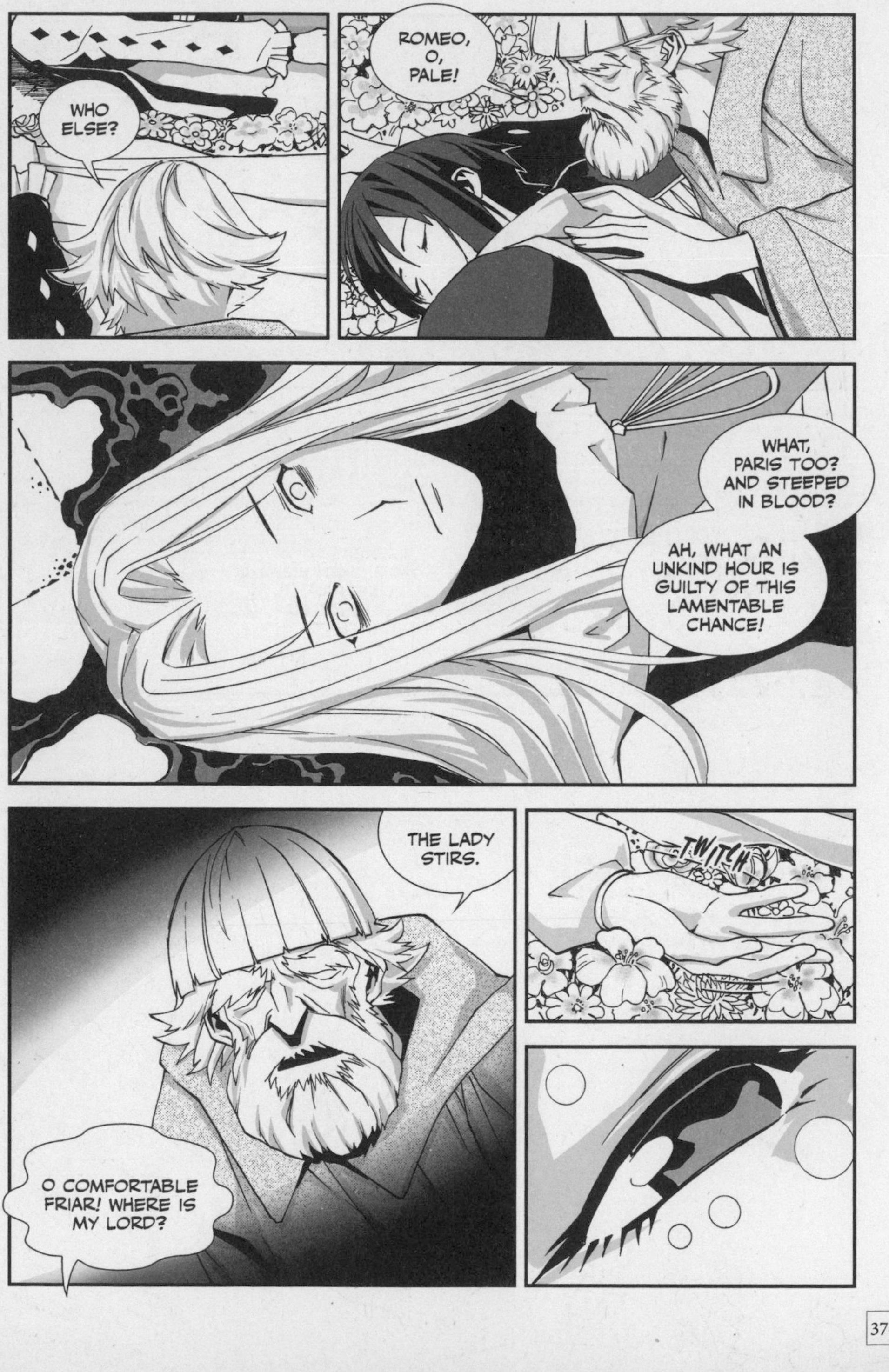
ROMEO, O, PALE!
WHO ELSE?
WHAT, PARIS TOO? AND STEEPED IN BLOOD?
AH, WHAT AN UNKIND HOUR IS GUILTY OF THIS LAMENTABLE CHANCE!
TWITCH
THE LADY STIRS.
O COMFORTABLE FRIAR! WHERE IS MY LORD?

BAM!

CLAT

CLAT

I DO REMEMBER WELL WHERE I SHOULD BE,

AND THERE I AM. WHERE IS MY ROMEO?

I HEAR SOME NOISE, LADY. COME FROM THAT NEST OF DEATH, CONTAGION, AND UNNATURAL SLEEP:

A GREATER POWER THAN WE CAN CONTRADICT HATH THWARTED OUR INTENTS.

COME, COME AWAY. THY HUSBAND IN THY BOSOM THERE LIES DEAD; AND PARIS TOO.

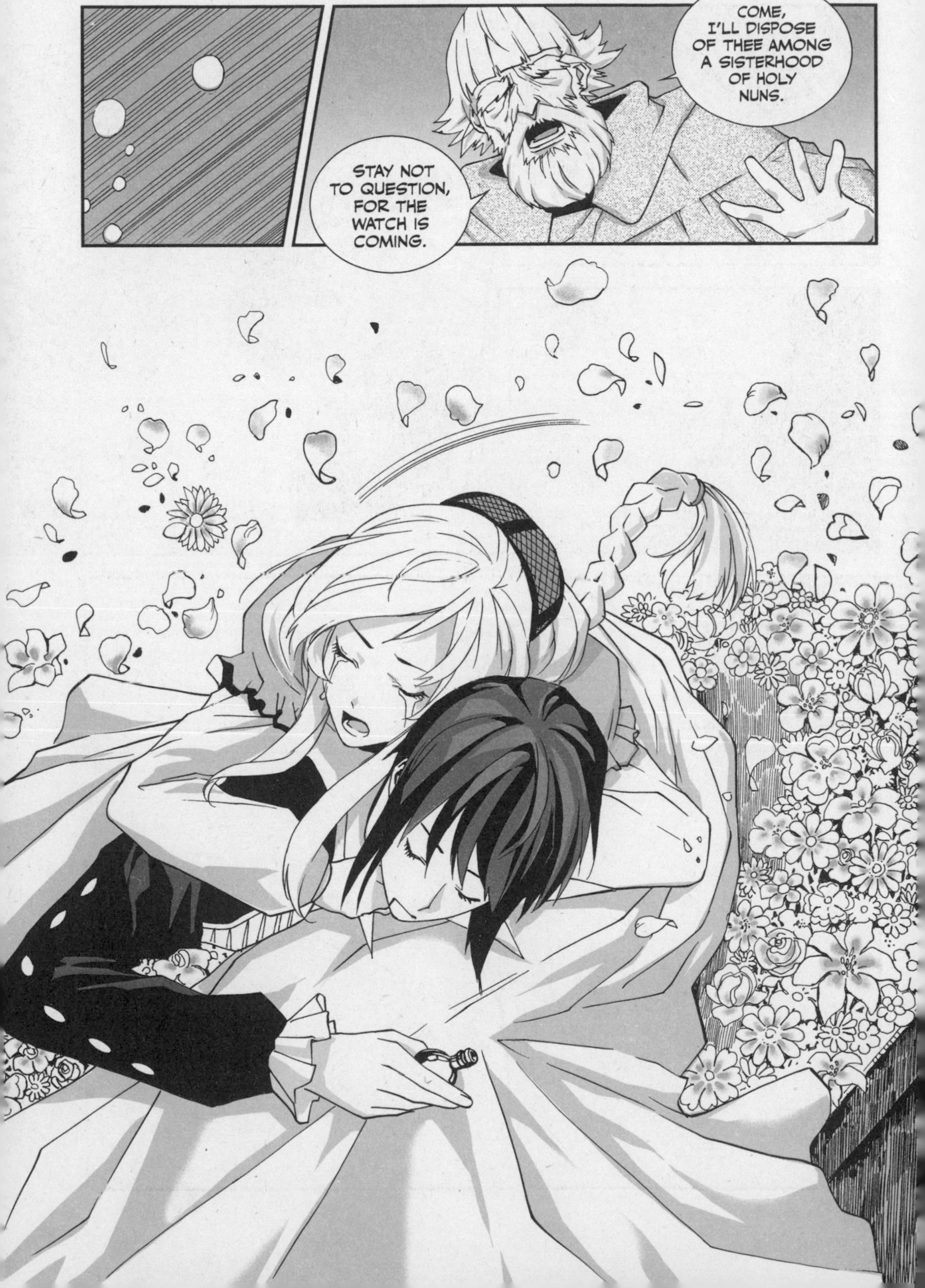
COME, I'LL DISPOSE OF THEE AMONG A SISTERHOOD OF HOLY NUNS.
STAY NOT TO QUESTION, FOR THE WATCH IS COMING.

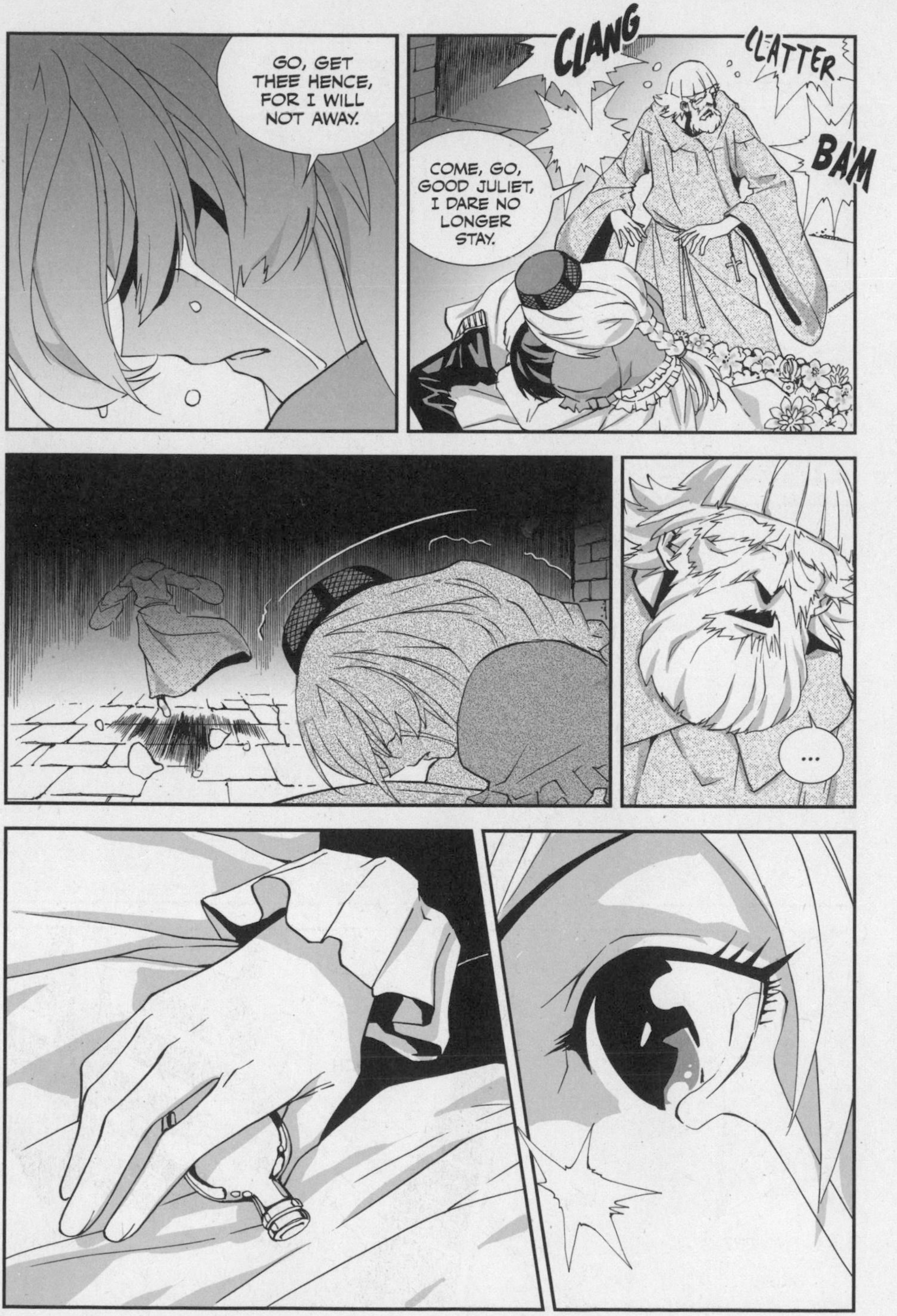

CLATTER
CLANG
BAM
COME, GO, GOOD JULIET, I DARE NO LONGER STAY.
GO, GET THEE HENCE, FOR I WILL NOT AWAY.
...

WHAT'S HERE? A CUP CLOSED IN MY TRUE LOVE'S HAND? POISON, I SEE, HATH BEEN HIS TIMELESS END.

O CHURL, DRUNK ALL, AND LEFT NO FRIENDLY DROP TO HELP ME AFTER?

I WILL KISS THY LIPS, HAPLY SOME POISON YET DOTH HANG ON THEM, TO MAKE ME DIE WITH A RESTORATIVE.

SHAKE

THY LIPS ARE WARM.

LEAD, BOY, WHICH WAY?

YEA, NOISE? THEN I'LL BE BRIEF.

STEP

STEP

379

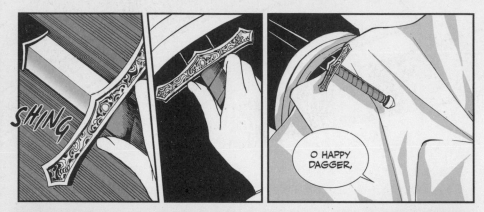

SHING

O HAPPY DAGGER,

THIS IS THY SHEATH;

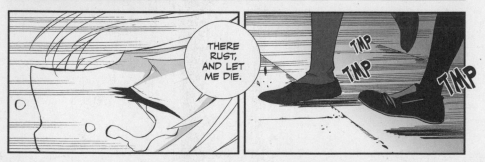

THERE RUST, AND LET ME DIE.

TMP
TMP
TMP

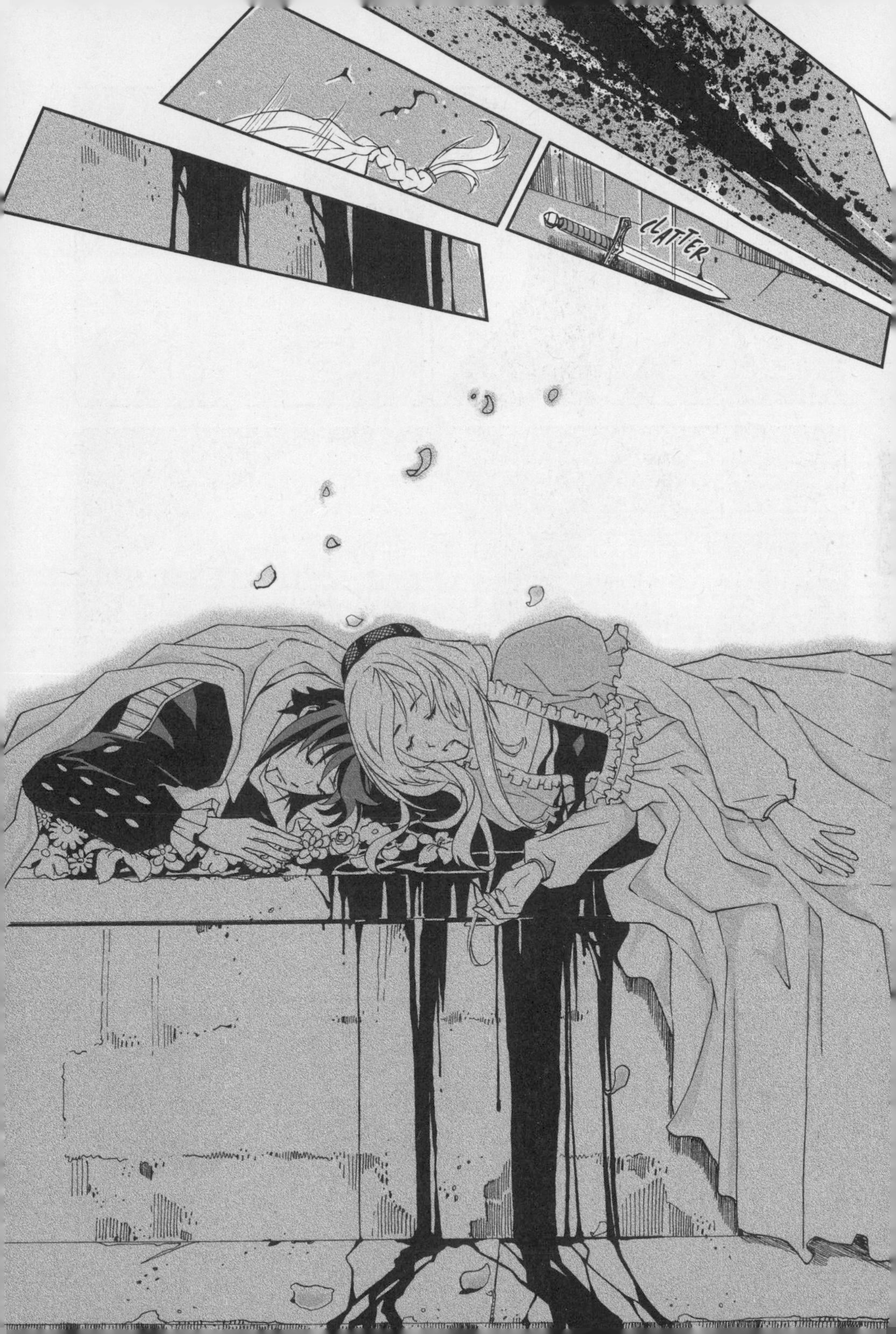
CLATTER

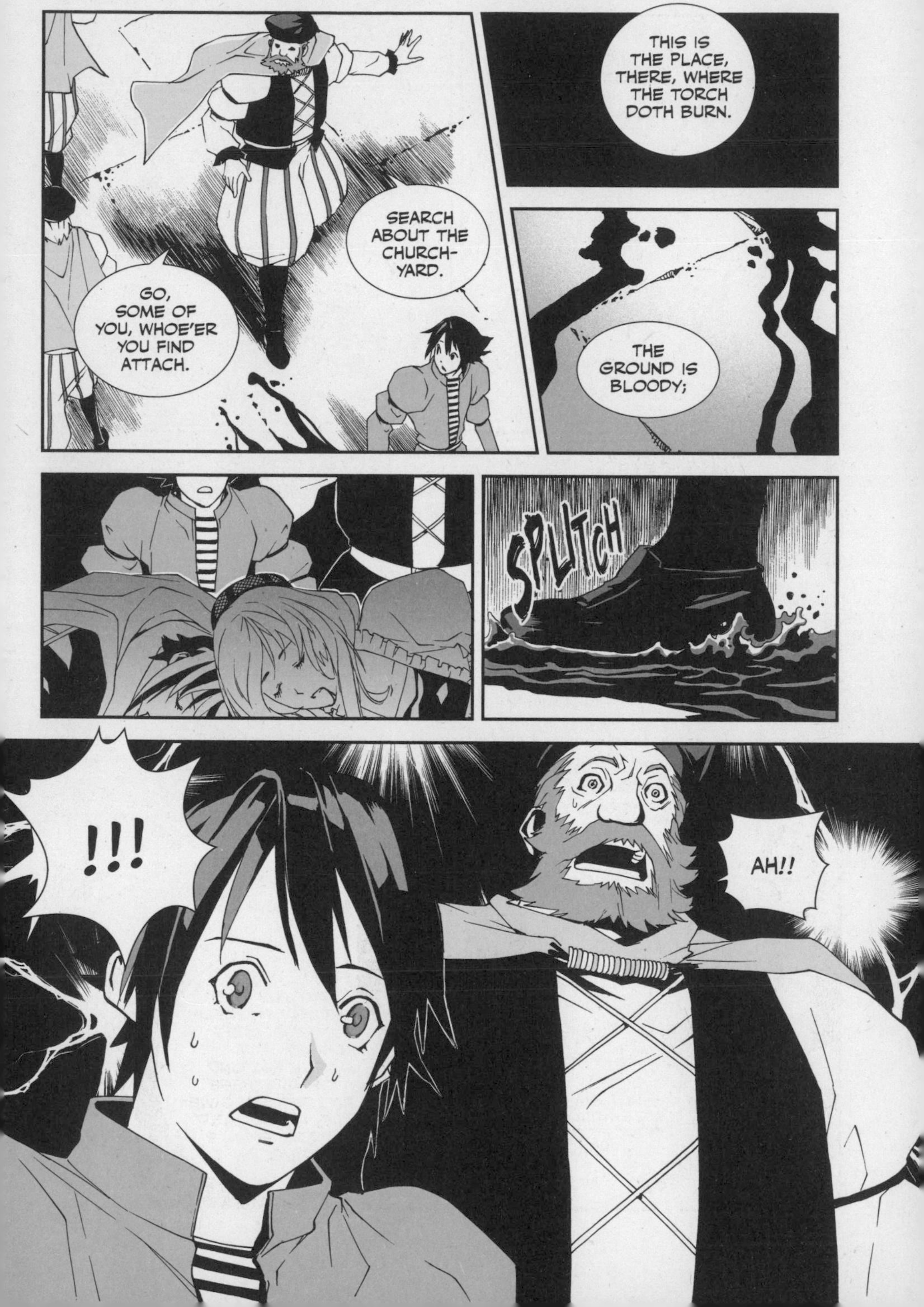
THIS IS THE PLACE, THERE, WHERE THE TORCH DOTH BURN.
THE GROUND IS BLOODY;
SEARCH ABOUT THE CHURCH-YARD.
GO, SOME OF YOU, WHOE'ER YOU FIND ATTACH.
SPLITCH
AH!!
!!!

PITIFUL SIGHT! HERE LIES THE COUNTY SLAIN,
AND JULIET BLEEDING, WARM, AND NEWLY DEAD, WHO HERE HATH LAIN THIS TWO DAYS BURIED.
GO, TELL THE PRINCE: RUN TO THE CAPULETS: RAISE UP THE MONTAGUES; SOME OTHERS SEARCH.
WE SEE THE GROUND WHEREON THESE WOES DO LIE, BUT THE TRUE GROUND OF ALL THESE PITEOUS WOES WE CANNOT WITHOUT CIRCUMSTANCE DESCRY.
HERE'S ROMEO'S MAN, WE FOUND HIM IN THE CHURCHYARD.
HOLD HIM IN SAFETY TILL THE PRINCE COME HITHER.

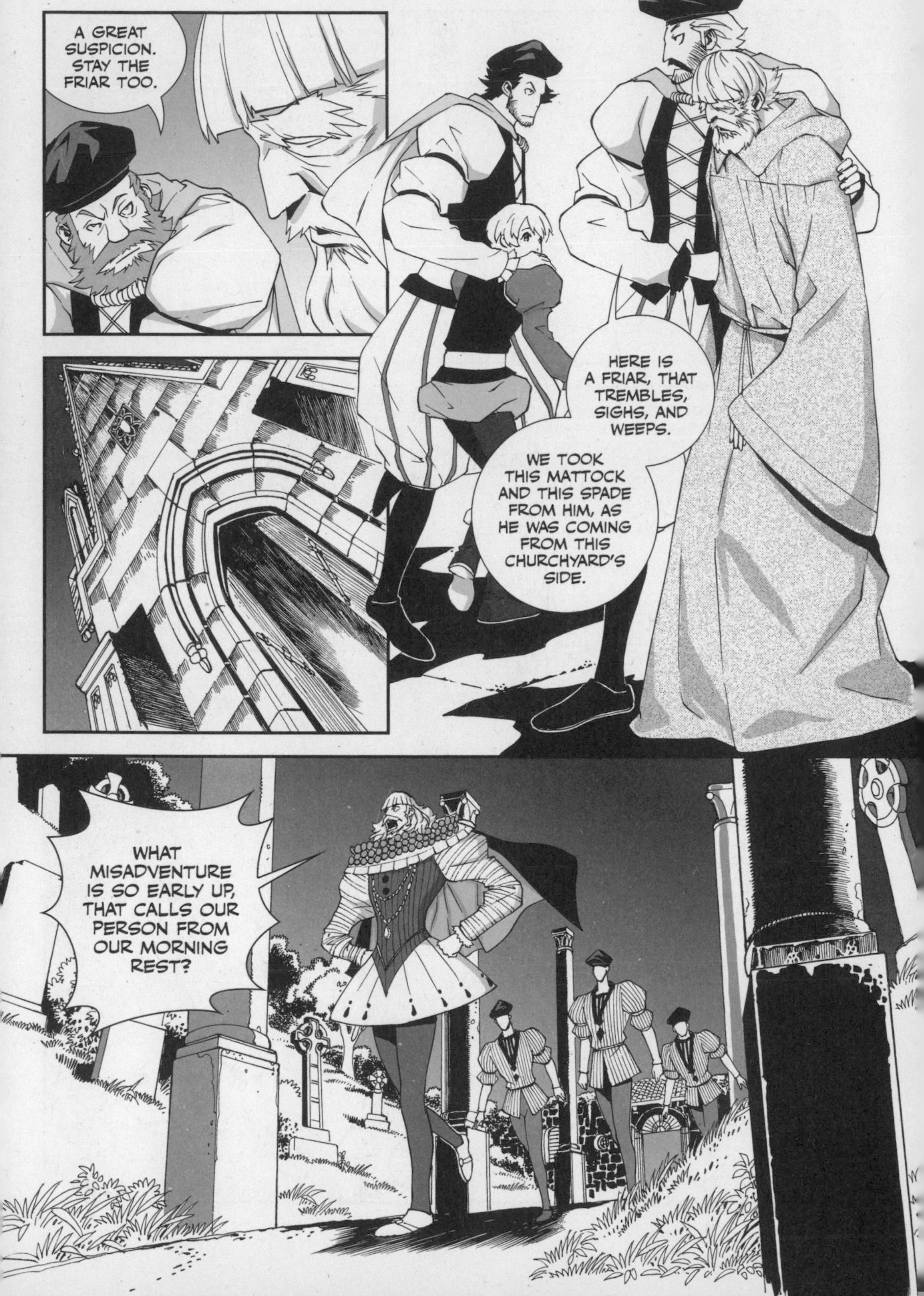
HERE IS A FRIAR, THAT TREMBLES, SIGHS, AND WEEPS.
WE TOOK THIS MATTOCK AND THIS SPADE FROM HIM, AS HE WAS COMING FROM THIS CHURCHYARD'S SIDE.
A GREAT SUSPICION. STAY THE FRIAR TOO.
WHAT MISADVENTURE IS SO EARLY UP, THAT CALLS OUR PERSON FROM OUR MORNING REST?

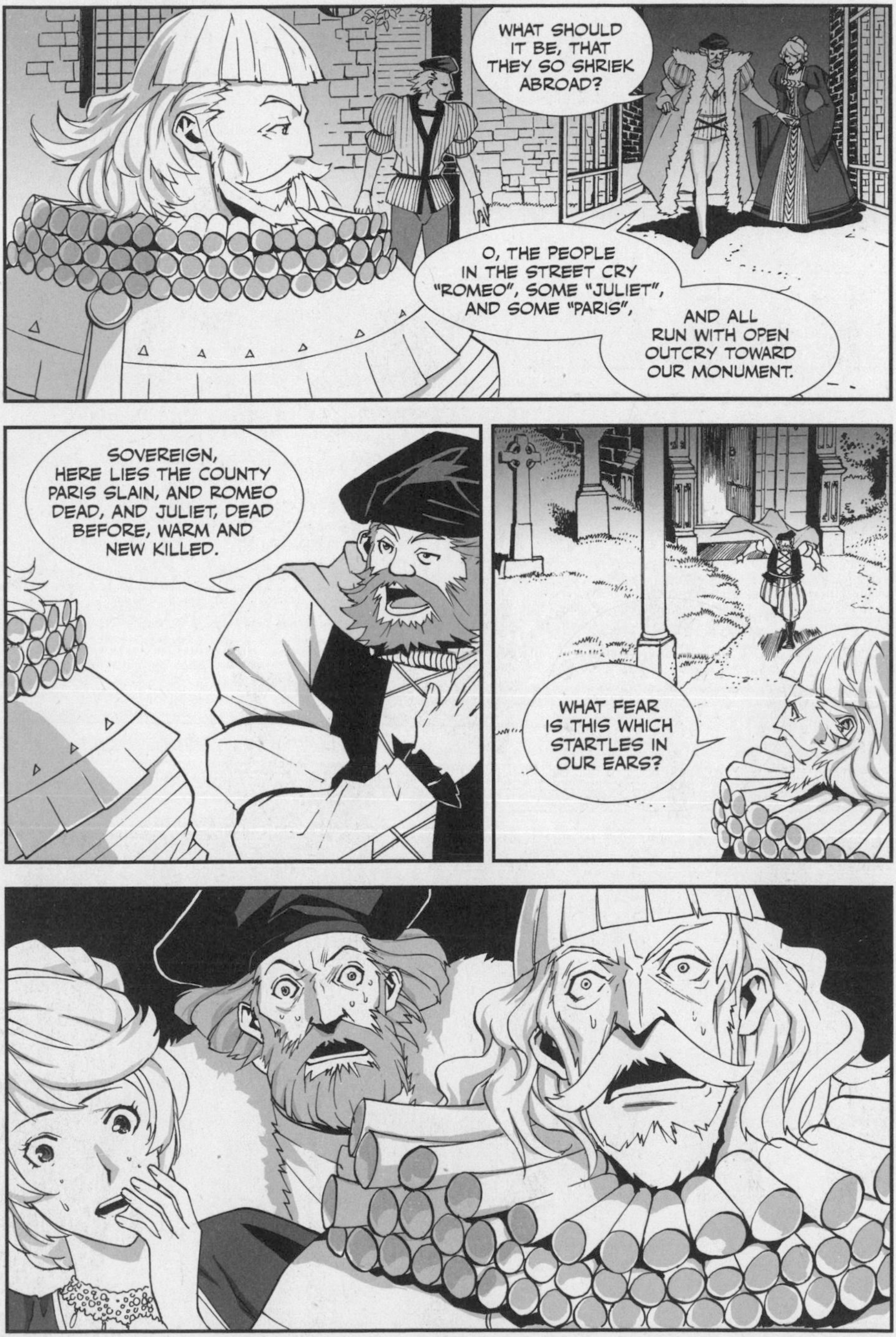
WHAT SHOULD IT BE, THAT THEY SO SHRIEK ABROAD?
O, THE PEOPLE IN THE STREET CRY "ROMEO", SOME "JULIET", AND SOME "PARIS",
AND ALL RUN WITH OPEN OUTCRY TOWARD OUR MONUMENT.
WHAT FEAR IS THIS WHICH STARTLES IN OUR EARS?
SOVEREIGN, HERE LIES THE COUNTY PARIS SLAIN, AND ROMEO DEAD, AND JULIET, DEAD BEFORE, WARM AND NEW KILLED.

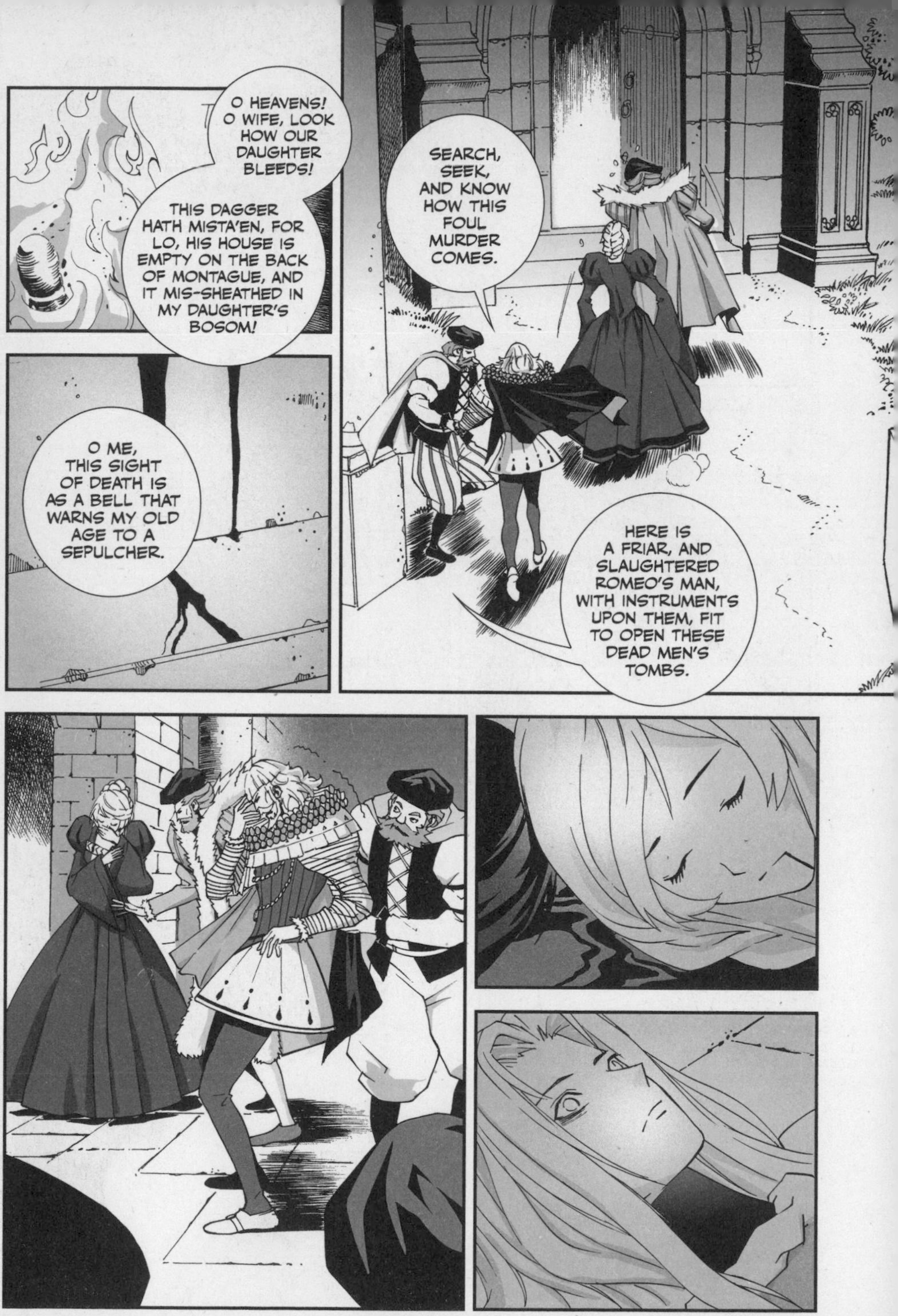
SEARCH, SEEK, AND KNOW HOW THIS FOUL MURDER COMES.
HERE IS A FRIAR, AND SLAUGHTERED ROMEO'S MAN, WITH INSTRUMENTS UPON THEM, FIT TO OPEN THESE DEAD MEN'S TOMBS.
O HEAVENS! O WIFE, LOOK HOW OUR DAUGHTER BLEEDS!
THIS DAGGER HATH MISTA'EN, FOR LO, HIS HOUSE IS EMPTY ON THE BACK OF MONTAGUE, AND IT MIS-SHEATHED IN MY DAUGHTER'S BOSOM!
O ME, THIS SIGHT OF DEATH IS AS A BELL THAT WARNS MY OLD AGE TO A SEPULCHER.

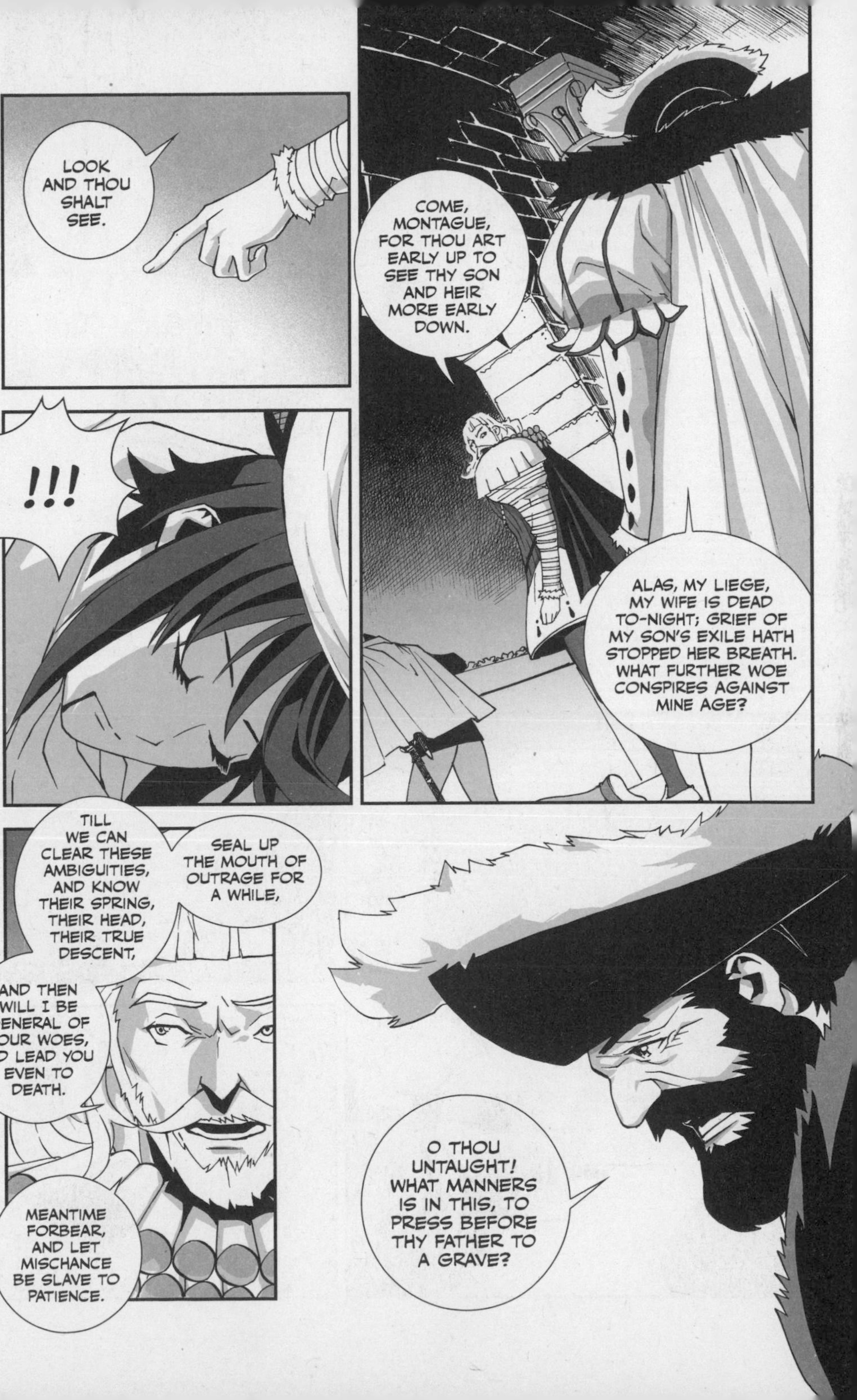
COME, MONTAGUE, FOR THOU ART EARLY UP TO SEE THY SON AND HEIR MORE EARLY DOWN.
ALAS, MY LIEGE, MY WIFE IS DEAD TO-NIGHT; GRIEF OF MY SON'S EXILE HATH STOPPED HER BREATH. WHAT FURTHER WOE CONSPIRES AGAINST MINE AGE?
LOOK AND THOU SHALT SEE.
!!!
O THOU UNTAUGHT! WHAT MANNERS IS IN THIS, TO PRESS BEFORE THY FATHER TO A GRAVE?
SEAL UP THE MOUTH OF OUTRAGE FOR A WHILE,
TILL WE CAN CLEAR THESE AMBIGUITIES, AND KNOW THEIR SPRING, THEIR HEAD, THEIR TRUE DESCENT,
AND THEN WILL I BE GENERAL OF YOUR WOES, AND LEAD YOU EVEN TO DEATH.
MEANTIME FORBEAR, AND LET MISCHANCE BE SLAVE TO PATIENCE.

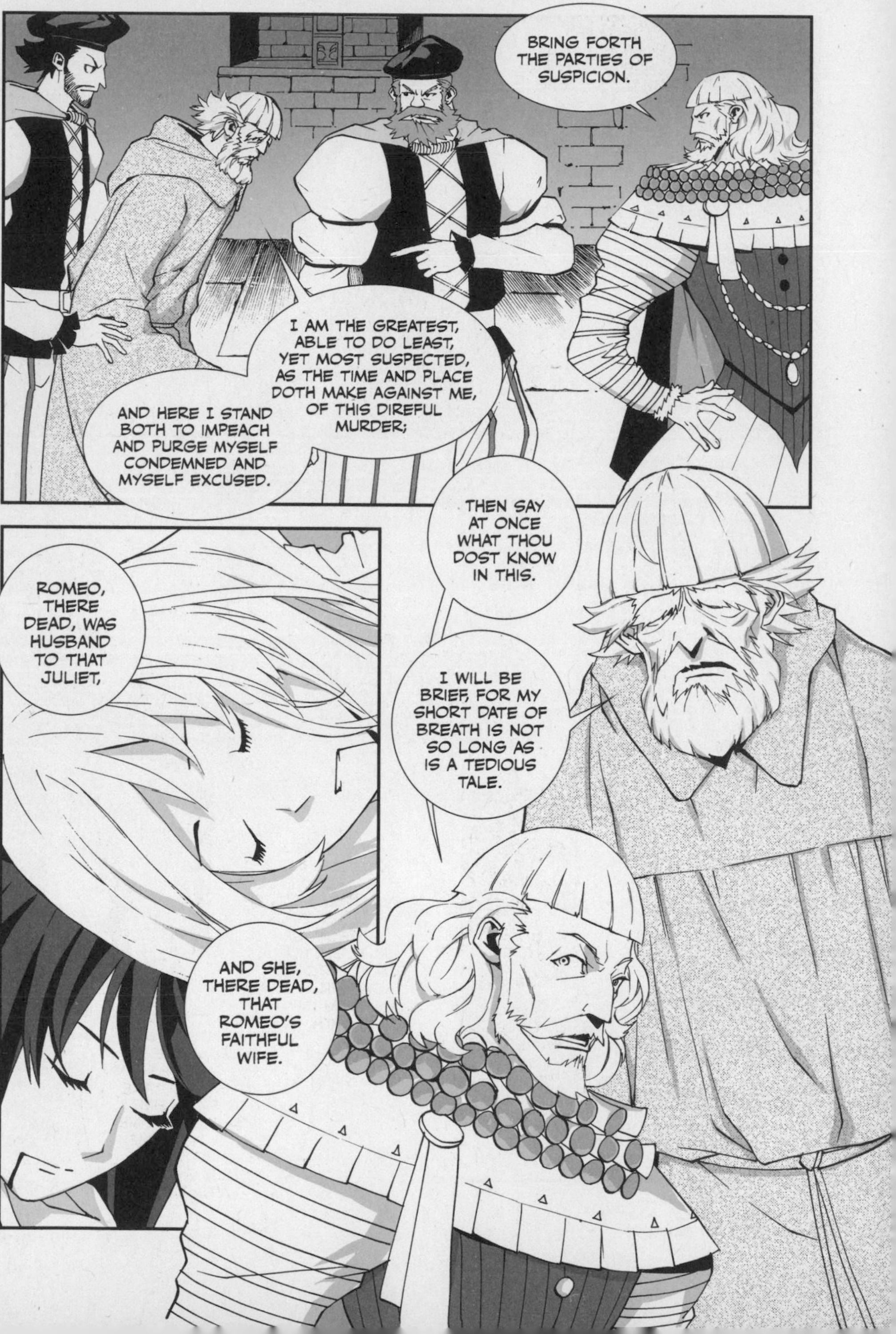
BRING FORTH THE PARTIES OF SUSPICION.
I AM THE GREATEST, ABLE TO DO LEAST, YET MOST SUSPECTED, AS THE TIME AND PLACE DOTH MAKE AGAINST ME, OF THIS DIREFUL MURDER;
AND HERE I STAND BOTH TO IMPEACH AND PURGE MYSELF CONDEMNED AND MYSELF EXCUSED.
THEN SAY AT ONCE WHAT THOU DOST KNOW IN THIS.
I WILL BE BRIEF, FOR MY SHORT DATE OF BREATH IS NOT SO LONG AS IS A TEDIOUS TALE.
ROMEO, THERE DEAD, WAS HUSBAND TO THAT JULIET,
AND SHE, THERE DEAD, THAT ROMEO'S FAITHFUL WIFE.

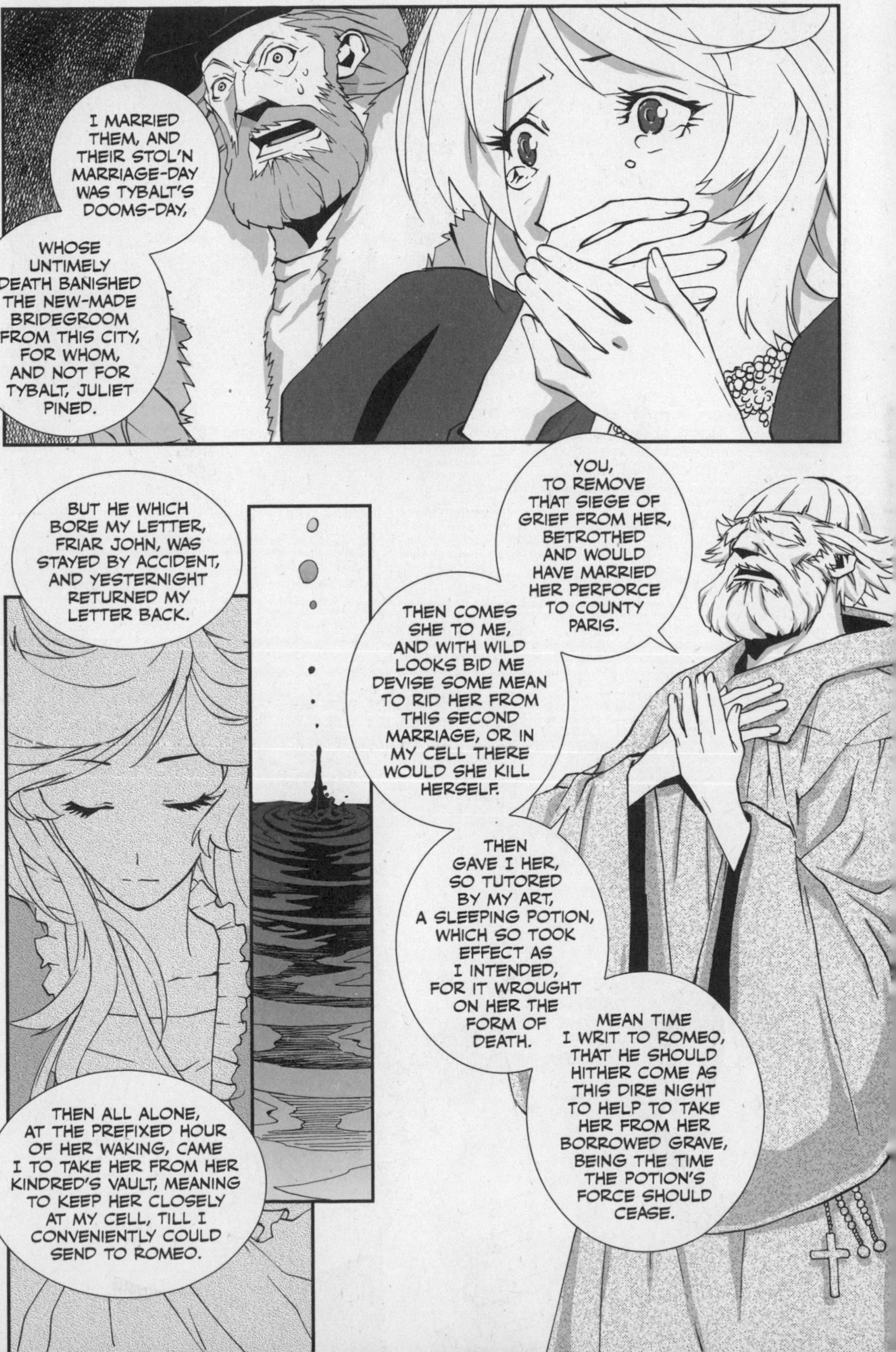

I MARRIED THEM, AND THEIR STOL'N MARRIAGE-DAY WAS TYBALT'S DOOMS-DAY,
WHOSE UNTIMELY DEATH BANISHED THE NEW-MADE BRIDEGROOM FROM THIS CITY, FOR WHOM, AND NOT FOR TYBALT, JULIET PINED.
YOU, TO REMOVE THAT SIEGE OF GRIEF FROM HER, BETROTHED AND WOULD HAVE MARRIED HER PERFORCE TO COUNTY PARIS.
THEN COMES SHE TO ME, AND WITH WILD LOOKS BID ME DEVISE SOME MEAN TO RID HER FROM THIS SECOND MARRIAGE, OR IN MY CELL THERE WOULD SHE KILL HERSELF.
THEN GAVE I HER, SO TUTORED BY MY ART, A SLEEPING POTION, WHICH SO TOOK EFFECT AS I INTENDED, FOR IT WROUGHT ON HER THE FORM OF DEATH.
MEAN TIME I WRIT TO ROMEO, THAT HE SHOULD HITHER COME AS THIS DIRE NIGHT TO HELP TO TAKE HER FROM HER BORROWED GRAVE, BEING THE TIME THE POTION'S FORCE SHOULD CEASE.
BUT HE WHICH BORE MY LETTER, FRIAR JOHN, WAS STAYED BY ACCIDENT, AND YESTERNIGHT RETURNED MY LETTER BACK.
THEN ALL ALONE, AT THE PREFIXED HOUR OF HER WAKING, CAME I TO TAKE HER FROM HER KINDRED'S VAULT, MEANING TO KEEP HER CLOSELY AT MY CELL, TILL I CONVENIENTLY COULD SEND TO ROMEO.

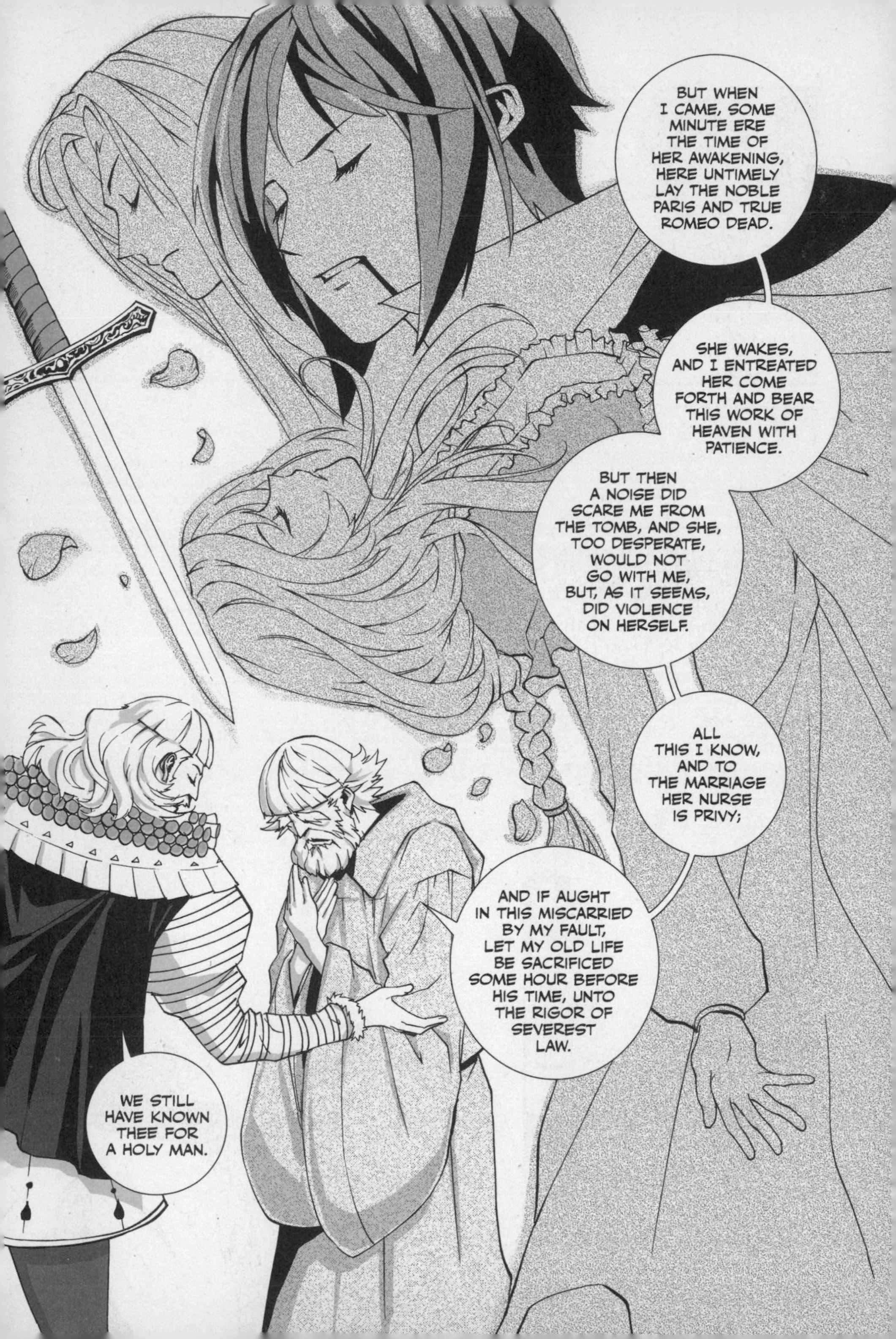
BUT WHEN I CAME, SOME MINUTE ERE THE TIME OF HER AWAKENING, HERE UNTIMELY LAY THE NOBLE PARIS AND TRUE ROMEO DEAD.
SHE WAKES, AND I ENTREATED HER COME FORTH AND BEAR THIS WORK OF HEAVEN WITH PATIENCE.
BUT THEN A NOISE DID SCARE ME FROM THE TOMB, AND SHE, TOO DESPERATE, WOULD NOT GO WITH ME, BUT, AS IT SEEMS, DID VIOLENCE ON HERSELF.
ALL THIS I KNOW, AND TO THE MARRIAGE HER NURSE IS PRIVY;
AND IF AUGHT IN THIS MISCARRIED BY MY FAULT, LET MY OLD LIFE BE SACRIFICED SOME HOUR BEFORE HIS TIME, UNTO THE RIGOR OF SEVEREST LAW.
WE STILL HAVE KNOWN THEE FOR A HOLY MAN.

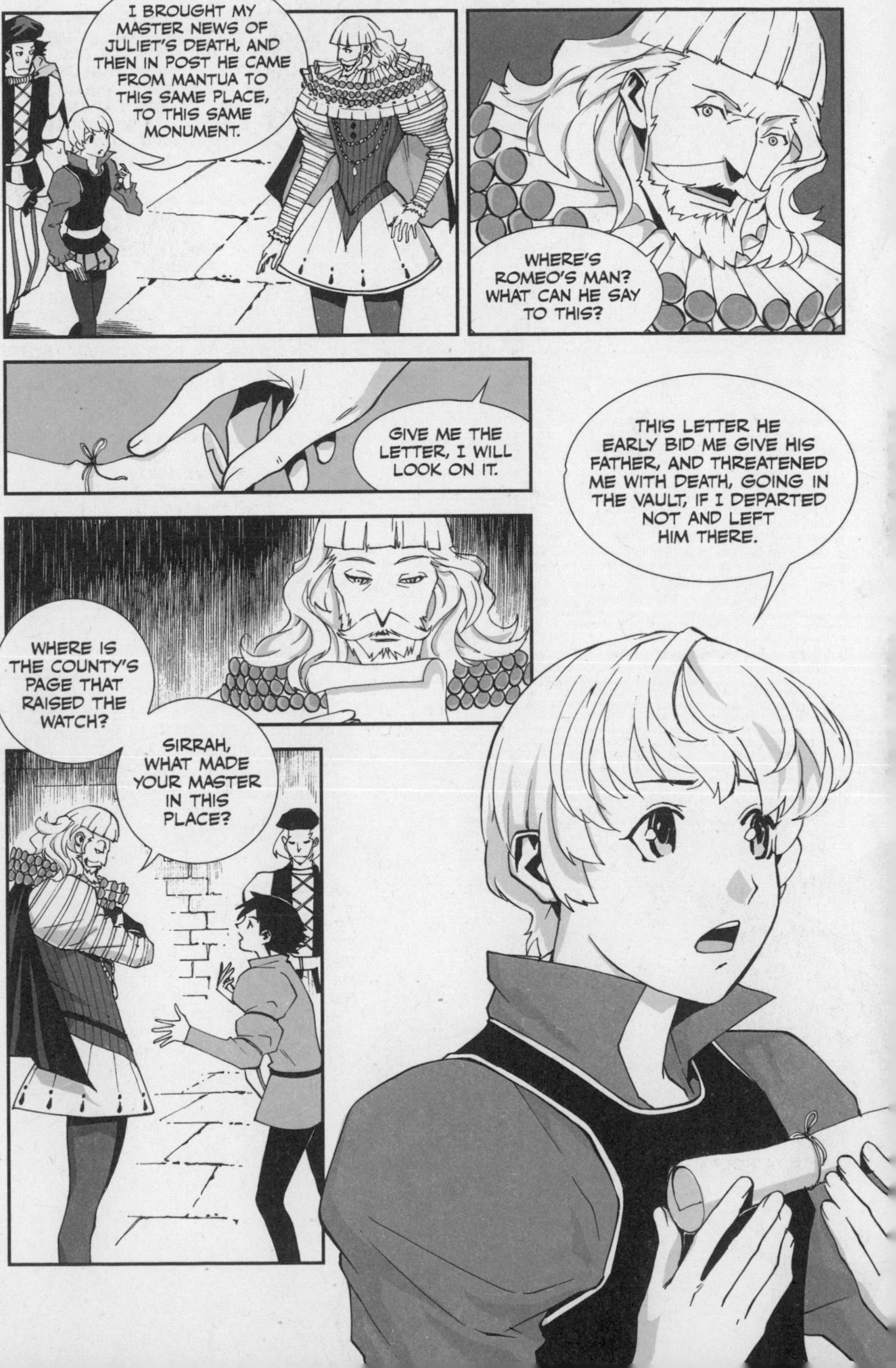
WHERE'S ROMEO'S MAN? WHAT CAN HE SAY TO THIS?
I BROUGHT MY MASTER NEWS OF JULIET'S DEATH, AND THEN IN POST HE CAME FROM MANTUA TO THIS SAME PLACE, TO THIS SAME MONUMENT.
THIS LETTER HE EARLY BID ME GIVE HIS FATHER, AND THREATENED ME WITH DEATH, GOING IN THE VAULT, IF I DEPARTED NOT AND LEFT HIM THERE.
GIVE ME THE LETTER, I WILL LOOK ON IT.
WHERE IS THE COUNTY'S PAGE THAT RAISED THE WATCH?
SIRRAH, WHAT MADE YOUR MASTER IN THIS PLACE?

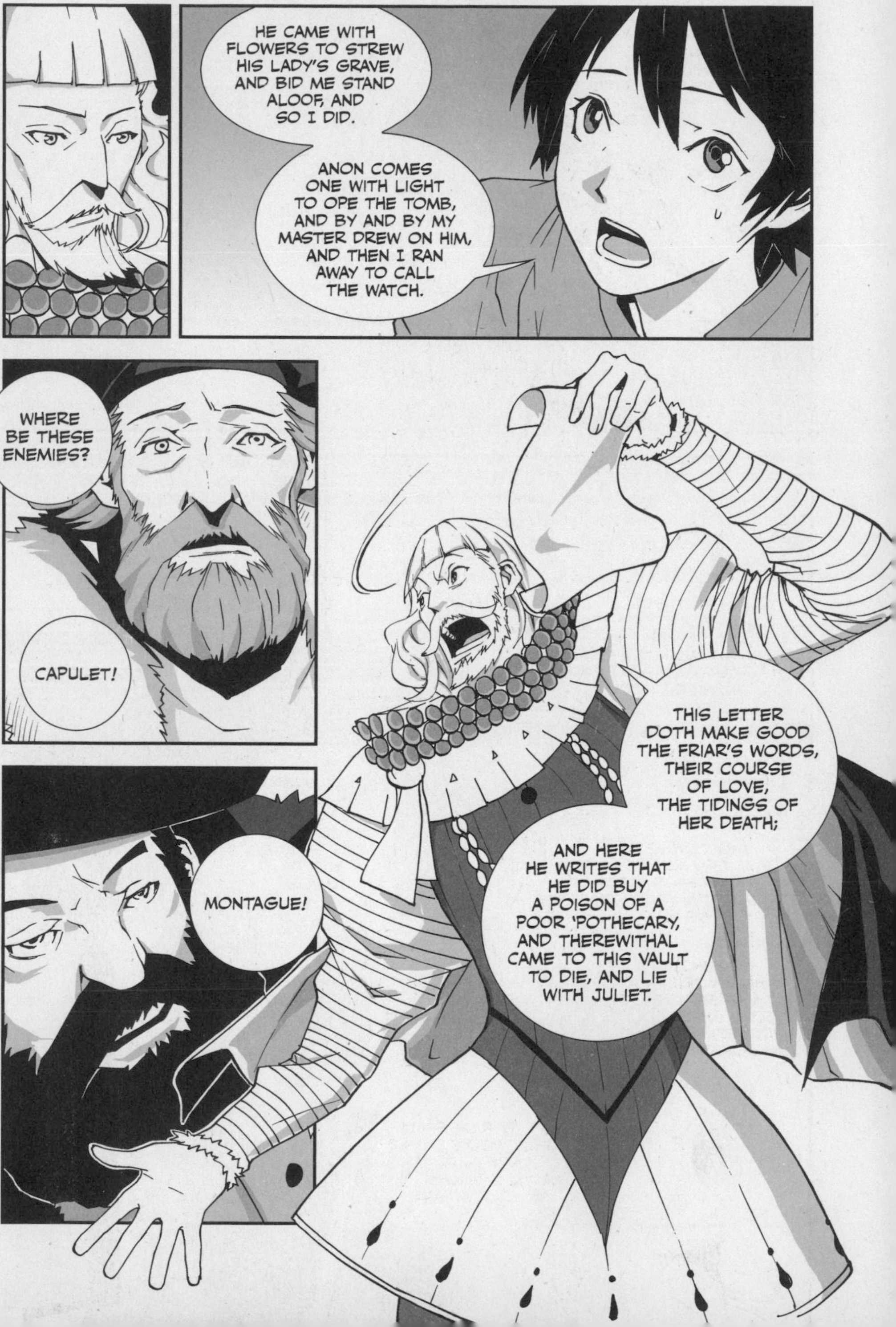
HE CAME WITH FLOWERS TO STREW HIS LADY'S GRAVE, AND BID ME STAND ALOOF, AND SO I DID.
ANON COMES ONE WITH LIGHT TO OPE THE TOMB, AND BY AND BY MY MASTER DREW ON HIM, AND THEN I RAN AWAY TO CALL THE WATCH.
THIS LETTER DOTH MAKE GOOD THE FRIAR'S WORDS, THEIR COURSE OF LOVE, THE TIDINGS OF HER DEATH;
AND HERE HE WRITES THAT HE DID BUY A POISON OF A POOR 'POTHECARY, AND THEREWITHAL CAME TO THIS VAULT TO DIE, AND LIE WITH JULIET.
WHERE BE THESE ENEMIES?
CAPULET!
MONTAGUE!

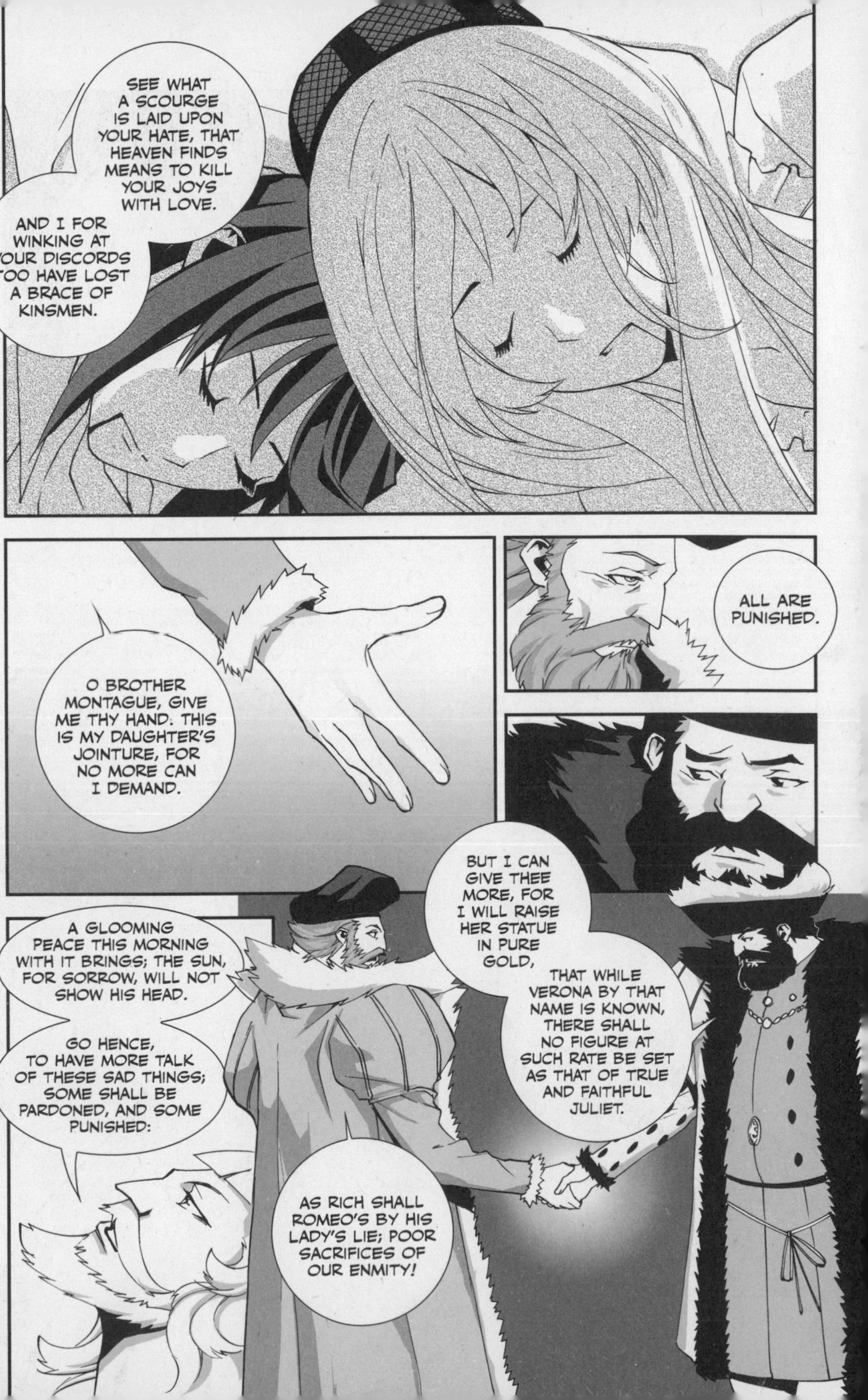
SEE WHAT A SCOURGE IS LAID UPON YOUR HATE, THAT HEAVEN FINDS MEANS TO KILL YOUR JOYS WITH LOVE.
AND I FOR WINKING AT YOUR DISCORDS TOO HAVE LOST A BRACE OF KINSMEN.
ALL ARE PUNISHED.
O BROTHER MONTAGUE, GIVE ME THY HAND. THIS IS MY DAUGHTER'S JOINTURE, FOR NO MORE CAN I DEMAND.
BUT I CAN GIVE THEE MORE, FOR I WILL RAISE HER STATUE IN PURE GOLD,
THAT WHILE VERONA BY THAT NAME IS KNOWN, THERE SHALL NO FIGURE AT SUCH RATE BE SET AS THAT OF TRUE AND FAITHFUL JULIET.
AS RICH SHALL ROMEO'S BY HIS LADY'S LIE; POOR SACRIFICES OF OUR ENMITY!
A GLOOMING PEACE THIS MORNING WITH IT BRINGS; THE SUN, FOR SORROW, WILL NOT SHOW HIS HEAD.
GO HENCE, TO HAVE MORE TALK OF THESE SAD THINGS; SOME SHALL BE PARDONED, AND SOME PUNISHED:

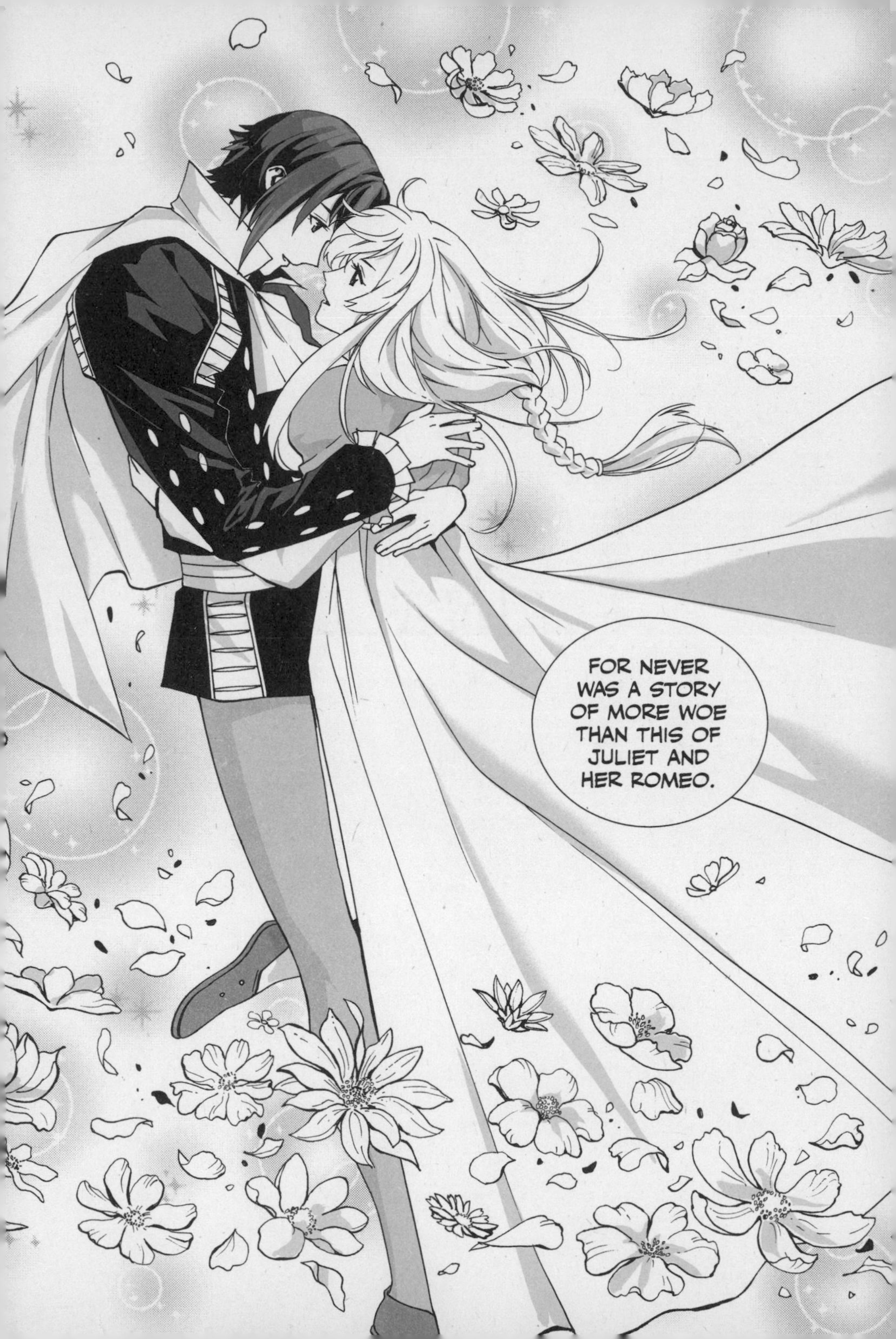
FOR NEVER WAS A STORY OF MORE WOE THAN THIS OF JULIET AND HER ROMEO.

~ *FINALE* ~

Romeo. Juliet is complaining that her nurse was no longer young and could not possibly hurry fast enough to suit her, so Juliet vents her anxiety by flicking little pebbles around. These little pebbles are also "*as swift in motion as a ball*", connecting the dialogue and the visual together.

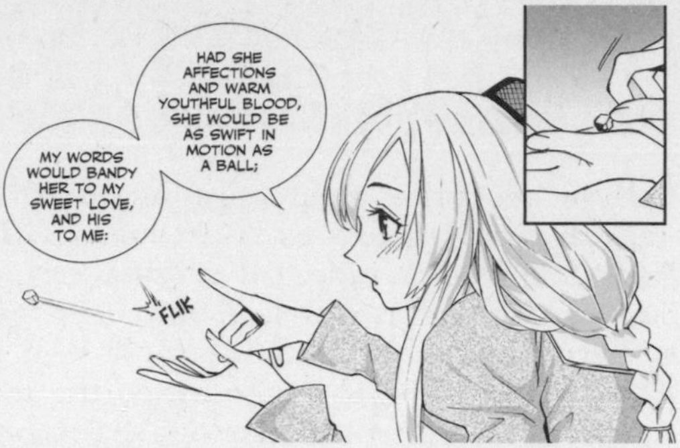
HAD SHE AFFECTIONS AND WARM YOUTHFUL BLOOD, SHE WOULD BE AS SWIFT IN MOTION AS A BALL;
MY WORDS WOULD BANDY HER TO MY SWEET LOVE, AND HIS TO ME:
FLIK

PROVIDING SPECIAL HINTS BASED ON THE PLOT:

In the original manuscript, not only dialogue but basic stage directions are provided to the actors. However, the size of a stage is limited, and in the manga world we can have a way broader environment for our characters to play out the story! Therefore, my adaptation work also includes expanding the locations and planning ahead on their actions to give the artist enough information to work with. For example: in ***Act 5, Scene 3***, Romeo meets Paris in the Capulet's tomb, argues with him, and eventually duels him. After the duel, however, Romeo is shocked: "*Let me peruse this face. Mercutio's kinsman, noble County Paris*!" Romeo did not recognize Paris until that very moment, when it was too late. I pointed this out in my script and suggested that the artist design the lighting and panel layout to make it clear that Romeo never sees Paris' face until the end - this allowed the artist to make informed decisions when storyboarding the manga. Thus, the readers won't find it strange that Romeo could not recognize Paris straight away, since they couldn't see his face either.

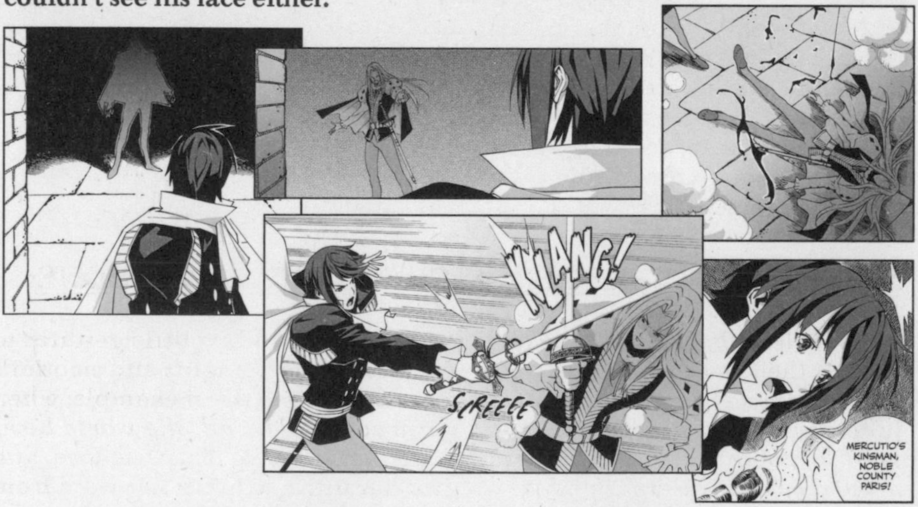
MERCUTIO'S KINSMAN, NOBLE COUNTY PARIS!
KLANG!
SCREEEE

Continues on Page 3...

CRYSTAL S. CHAN:
ADAPTING ROMEO & JULIET

I believe everyone must have heard of ***ROMEO AND JULIET***, the great stage play which exists in many different mediums. Our ***MANGA CLASSICS*** version takes the original script of the play and make sure that it is a word by word translation onto the pages. So you might ask, then, what am I here to talk about "adaptation"? Well, after all, stage plays and manga are two very different mediums, so the means of presenting the story is different as well. I would like to take this opportunity to tell you how much efforts our team has put in to bring this legendary masterpiece to life, using the characteristics of manga!

VISUALS ARE GREAT AIDS TO EXPRESSING METAPHORS:

Shakespeare's work is full of metaphor. When the show is staged with actors - as a stage play, a movie, a television show, or similar - it is only through the acting and the suggestion in dialogue that the metaphors can be presented to the audience. Manga has a lesser restriction on the visuals, so these metaphors can be drawn and presented more directly to the reader. For example: in ***Act 3, Scene 2***, when Juliet says, "***Hood my unmanned blood, bating in my cheeks, with thy black mantle; till strange love, grown bold, think true love acted simple modesty,***" she is shy and blushing because she is looking forward to meeting her new husband on their wedding night. She imagines herself as a tamed eagle, with its head covered by a hood; she would need to be hooded so that no one could see her blushing. Therefore, I included a panel of the image in Juliet's imagination - did you notice that?

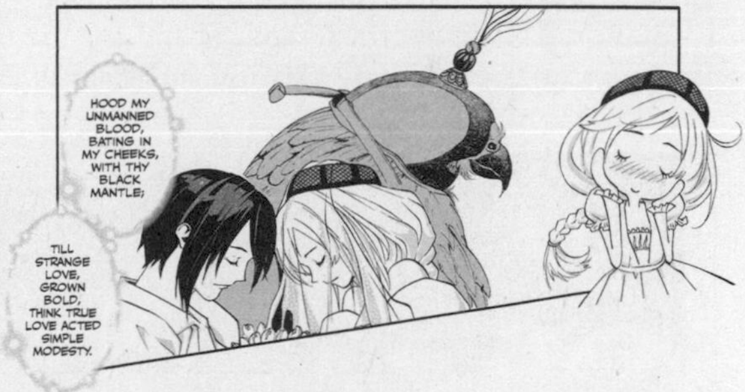
HOOD MY UNMANNED BLOOD, BATING IN MY CHEEKS, WITH THY BLACK MANTLE;
TILL STRANGE LOVE, GROWN BOLD, THINK TRUE LOVE ACTED SIMPLE MODESTY.

ADDING GESTURES TO MATCH WITH THE DIALOGUE:

I also believe that some of the dialogue calls for including little gestures to express their implications, as well as expressing the thoughts and emotions of the characters in the moment. Take ***Act 2, Scene 5***, as an example: when Juliet says, "***Had she affections and warm youthful blood, she would be as swift in motion as a ball; my words would bandy her to my sweet love, and his to me,***" she was waiting anxiously for her nurse to bring her word from

VISITING THE LOCATION:

As the original manuscript clearly mentions that the story takes place in Verona, Italy, I decided to visit the place in person, much like I did when I was working on ***The Count Of Monte Cristo.*** Not only was I doing research, I was getting a feel for the atmosphere of the city - it was important to me to experience the same environment as the characters. Many literary analysts point out that Shakespeare may never have gone to Verona in person; however, since he chose this beautiful city as the stage for his story, I wanted to try my best to present the story to the readers as something that specifically happened in Verona.

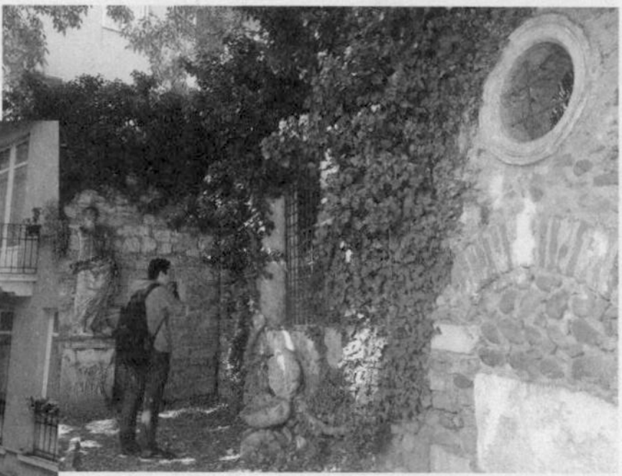

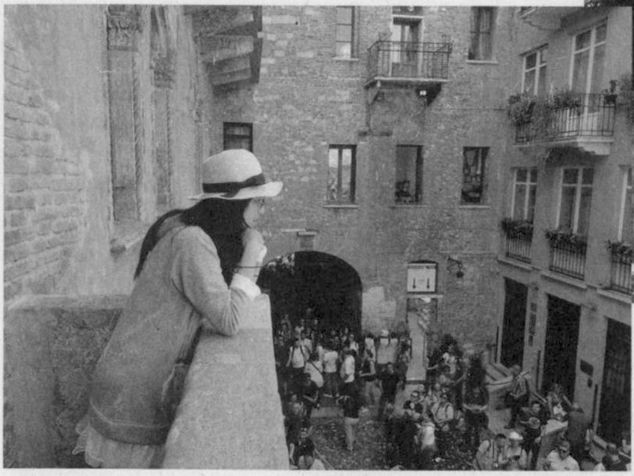

Juliet's house is a must-see for tourists, and I also went to the less-visited site of Juliet's tomb. The pillars in the photos were slightly redesigned and then used in the drawings of ***Act 5, Scene 3.***

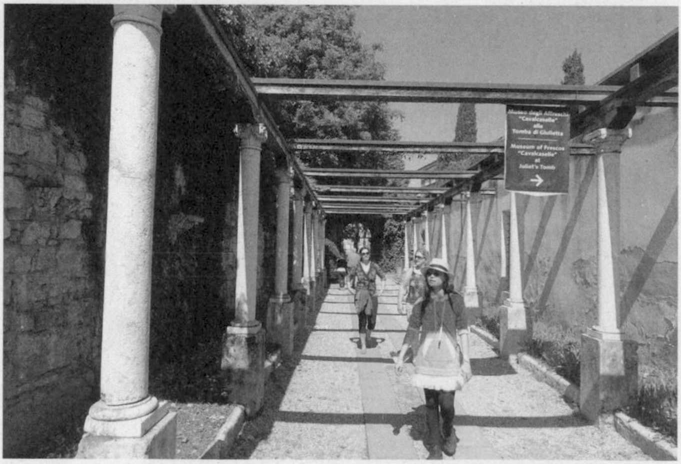
"Cavalcaselle"
alla
Tomba di Giulietta
Museum of Frescos
"Cavalcaselle"
at
Juliet's Tomb

Continues on Page 5...

...continued from Page 2

Another important thing is the interchange between scenes. If it is not well done in the layouts, the readers can be confused. In a traditional play, change of scene is signified by the change of background panels and props; in the manga, such changes are signified through the language of the camera. In *Act 5, Scene 3*, everything takes place in various places outside the Capulet's tomb. The original manuscript only mentions when characters enter or exit the scene. That isn't enough for a manga artist to go on, so I divided the scene into six different 'areas' and drafted a floor plan for reference. This allows him to make informed decisions about where to set up the point of view for the readers, so that he can clearly present how the characters move among the different locations.

D
Stairs
Juliet's Tomb
Capulet's family graves
E
F
Romeo & Paris fight here
Tybalt's Tomb

CAPULET'S TOMB
C
B
A
Romeo and Balthasar get off horse here
Columns
Verona Graveyard Wall

Ⓓ Stairs
Ⓕ Juliet
Ⓔ Romeo vs Paris
Columns
(Blue colour mark)

(Stone)
Slabs

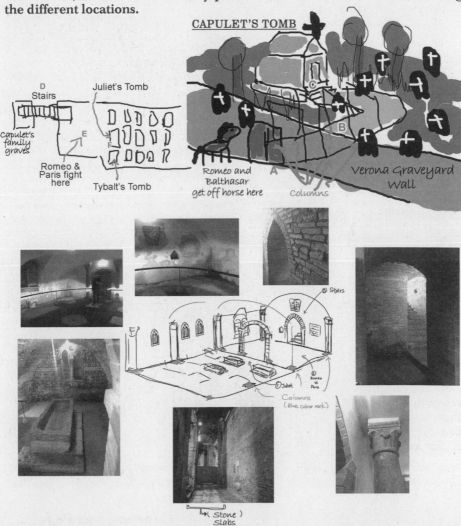

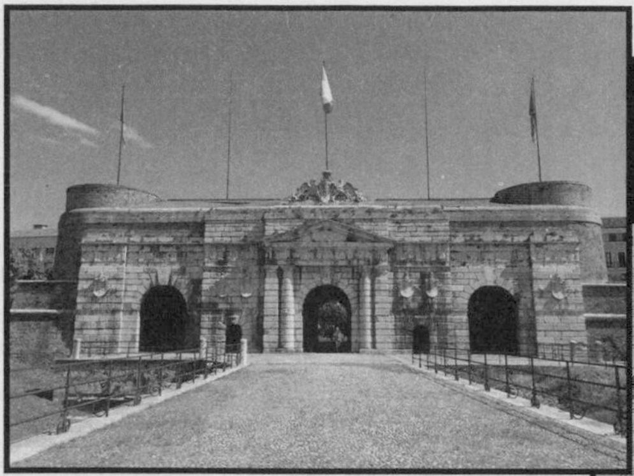

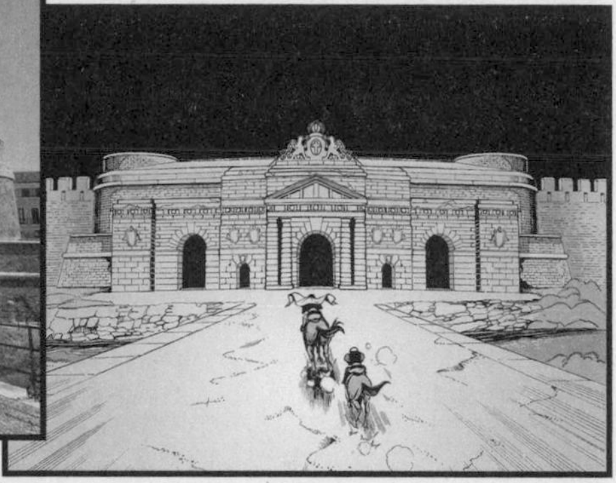

The above is *Porta Nuova*. It's not only some of the most famous architecture in the city, it was also built before ***Romeo and Juliet*** takes place - therefore, it's well suited to use in the manga, to strengthen the feeling of the characters being in Verona. I arranged for Romeo to pass by this building when he rushes back to Verona before ***Act 5***. The photo here is not exactly the same as the drawing of the building in the manga; when I researched the city I discovered that *Porta Nuova* had been part of the city wall at the time of ***Romeo and Juliet***. I suggested that the artist add the wall when drawing the background, to match the historical detail.

DESIGNING THE COVER:

Finally, I want to share a little secret with you: the cover layout was designed by me. When I read the phrase "*star-cross'd lovers*", I had this vision of ***Romeo and Juliet*** wanting to be together and being prevented by fate. After some thoughts I added other elements to represent this pair of tragic lovers that were not accepted by their world. As you can see, ***Romeo and Juliet*** are reaching towards each other, but the sword between them represents the fate which keeps them apart and prevents them from ever touching. I discussed this with the artist after finishing the draft, and he thought that it was well suited to the main theme. After he polished it up, the cover became the one you hold in your hands now.

I hope that my extensive adaptation work shows through the beautiful illustrations and smooth storyboards done by the artist. I truly believe this adaptation will help the readers achieve a better understanding of the story, expressing the thoughts and emotions of the original work in a way better suited for the manga medium. This is the goal I wanted to achieve through my hard work.

Crystal (Silvermoon) Chan

...continued from Page 4

This is one of the architectural landmarks of the city: the *Palazzo del Comune*. Today there is no cover over the stairs; however, inside the building (in the *Galleria d'Arte Moderna Achille Forte*) there is an old painting that shows the *Palazzo del Comune* complete with covered stairs. Therefore, I suggested that we add that cover to the manga version, to correspond with the classic appearance of the building.

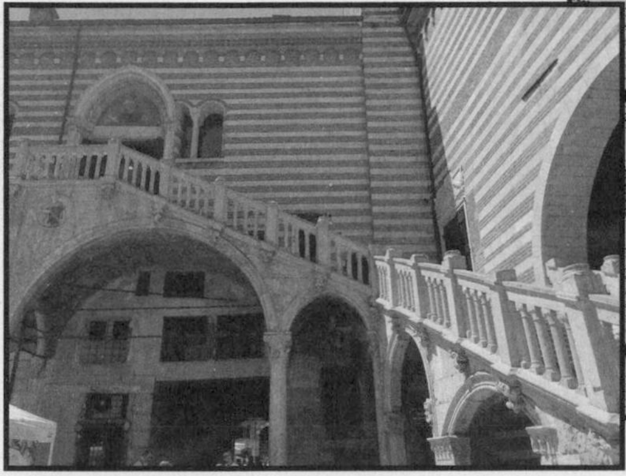

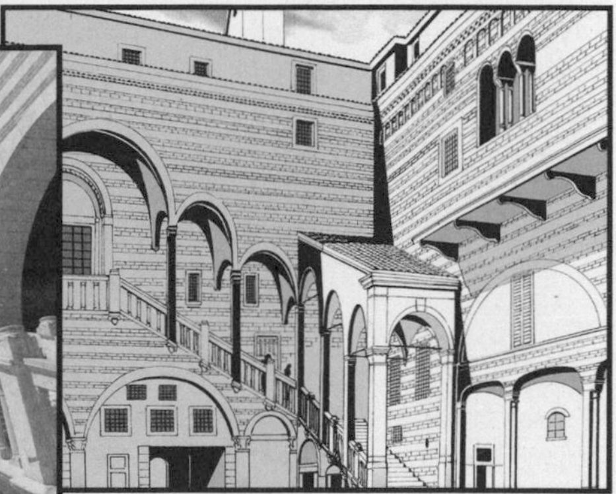

When I found suitable scenery during my visit to the city, I used it as the background to give the city atmosphere. Did you notice that there's a building similar to the Colosseum in one of the scenes in *Act 3*? This is actually another landmark of Verona: the *Arena di Verona*, which was built around the same time. Since it is a building associated with combat and competition, I suggested that we use it as part of that scene, to fit with Tybalt's killing of Mercutio and his own subsequent death at Romeo's hands.

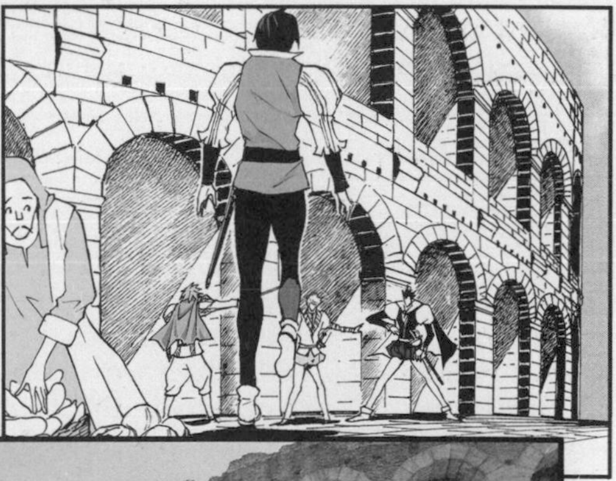

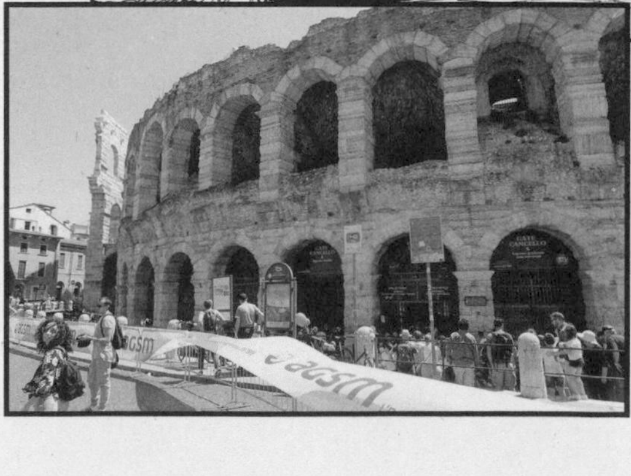

Shakespeare is one of the world's pre-eminent writers, and his works are the world's heritage.

It was really exciting for me to draw his work as a manga, but it also made me nervous. Especially since it was **ROMEO AND JULIET**, the classic story that is so well known. Ever since I was small, I have read and watched many versions of the story.

I am over the moon to have been the artist of this book. I feel so fortunate – this is the most overwhelming experience I have ever had in my years in the comic industry.

Thank you, **MANGA CLASSICS**, for publishing graphic novels based on classic literature, and for establishing such great creative opportunities. The production principle is to present a touching story as faithful as possible to the original work, and I unleashed all my creativity according to this principle. Therefore, no matter whether it was adaptation or illustration, I had to try my very best to master the actual era of the story.

Every stage of the manga production is carefully done; everyone was meticulous, from the producer to the scriptwriter to the artist and the assistants. We did not take it lightly – we did endless research to present a comprehensive version of the story. I have never before in my career felt so nervous about a title. Fortunately, I had a lot of help from the producer, Mr. Tai, and the scriptwriter, Crystal, who always fixed the mistakes I made; whenever I put dialogue in the wrong panel or duplicated dialogue by mistake or drew the wrong costume detail, they would make sure it was corrected. I will never forget these tidbits.

The whole team poured our hearts in every single panel of this classic piece. We all worked together to amend every panel over and over in order to take care of readers of all levels; we strived to do our best to bring our readers a masterpiece that would provide enjoyment and pleasure.

I hope this book will bring you satisfaction. We are all very proud of it!

Thank you for supporting us!

Julien Choy

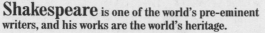

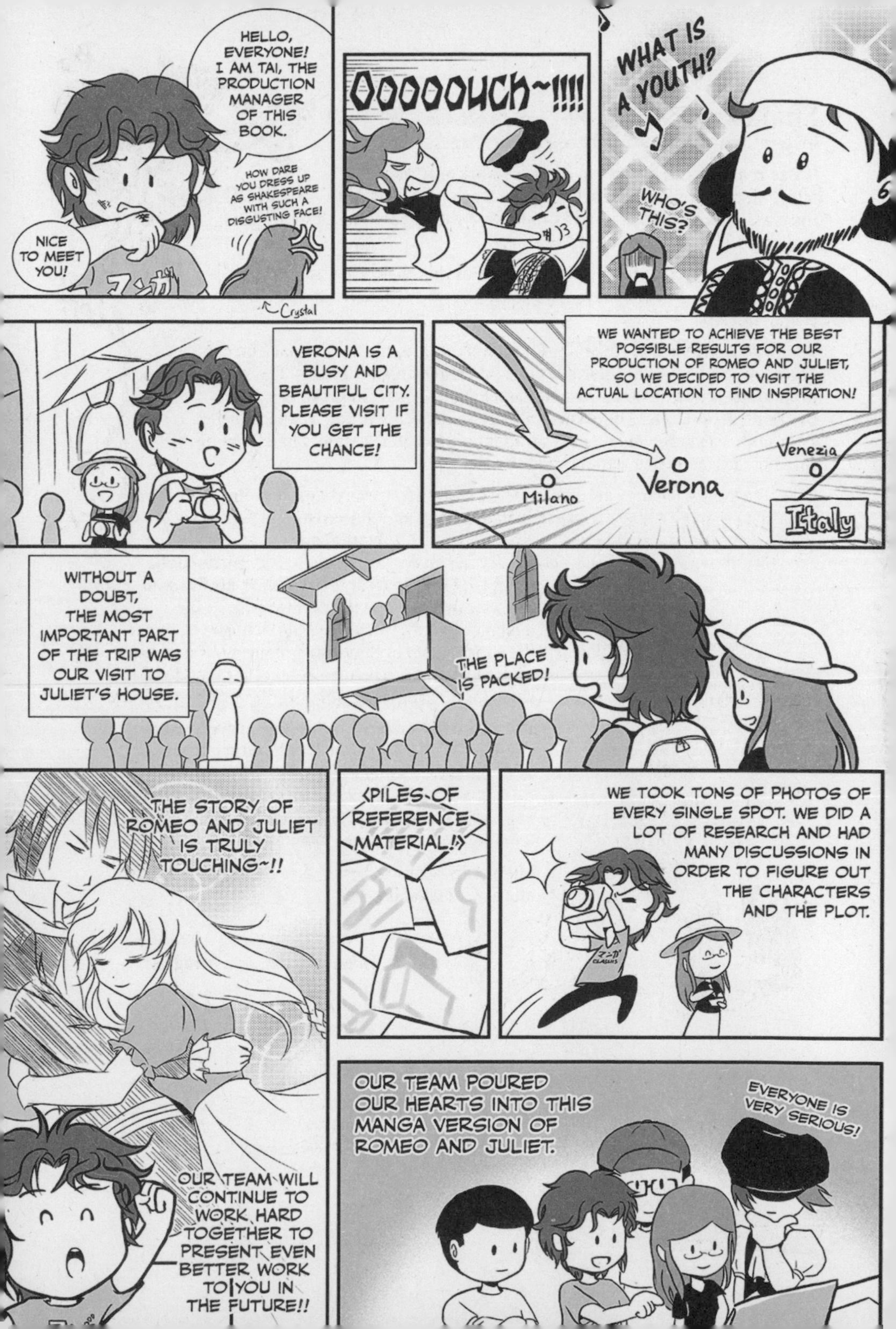
WHAT IS A YOUTH?
WHO'S THIS?
OOOOOUCH~!!!!
HELLO, EVERYONE! I AM TAI, THE PRODUCTION MANAGER OF THIS BOOK.
HOW DARE YOU DRESS UP AS SHAKESPEARE WITH SUCH A DISGUSTING FACE!
NICE TO MEET YOU!
Crystal
WE WANTED TO ACHIEVE THE BEST POSSIBLE RESULTS FOR OUR PRODUCTION OF ROMEO AND JULIET, SO WE DECIDED TO VISIT THE ACTUAL LOCATION TO FIND INSPIRATION!
Venezia
Verona
Milano
Italy
VERONA IS A BUSY AND BEAUTIFUL CITY. PLEASE VISIT IF YOU GET THE CHANCE!
WITHOUT A DOUBT, THE MOST IMPORTANT PART OF THE TRIP WAS OUR VISIT TO JULIET'S HOUSE.
THE PLACE IS PACKED!
WE TOOK TONS OF PHOTOS OF EVERY SINGLE SPOT. WE DID A LOT OF RESEARCH AND HAD MANY DISCUSSIONS IN ORDER TO FIGURE OUT THE CHARACTERS AND THE PLOT.
⟨PILES OF REFERENCE MATERIAL!⟩
OUR TEAM POURED OUR HEARTS INTO THIS MANGA VERSION OF ROMEO AND JULIET.
EVERYONE IS VERY SERIOUS!
THE STORY OF ROMEO AND JULIET IS TRULY TOUCHING~!!
OUR TEAM WILL CONTINUE TO WORK HARD TOGETHER TO PRESENT EVEN BETTER WORK TO YOU IN THE FUTURE!!

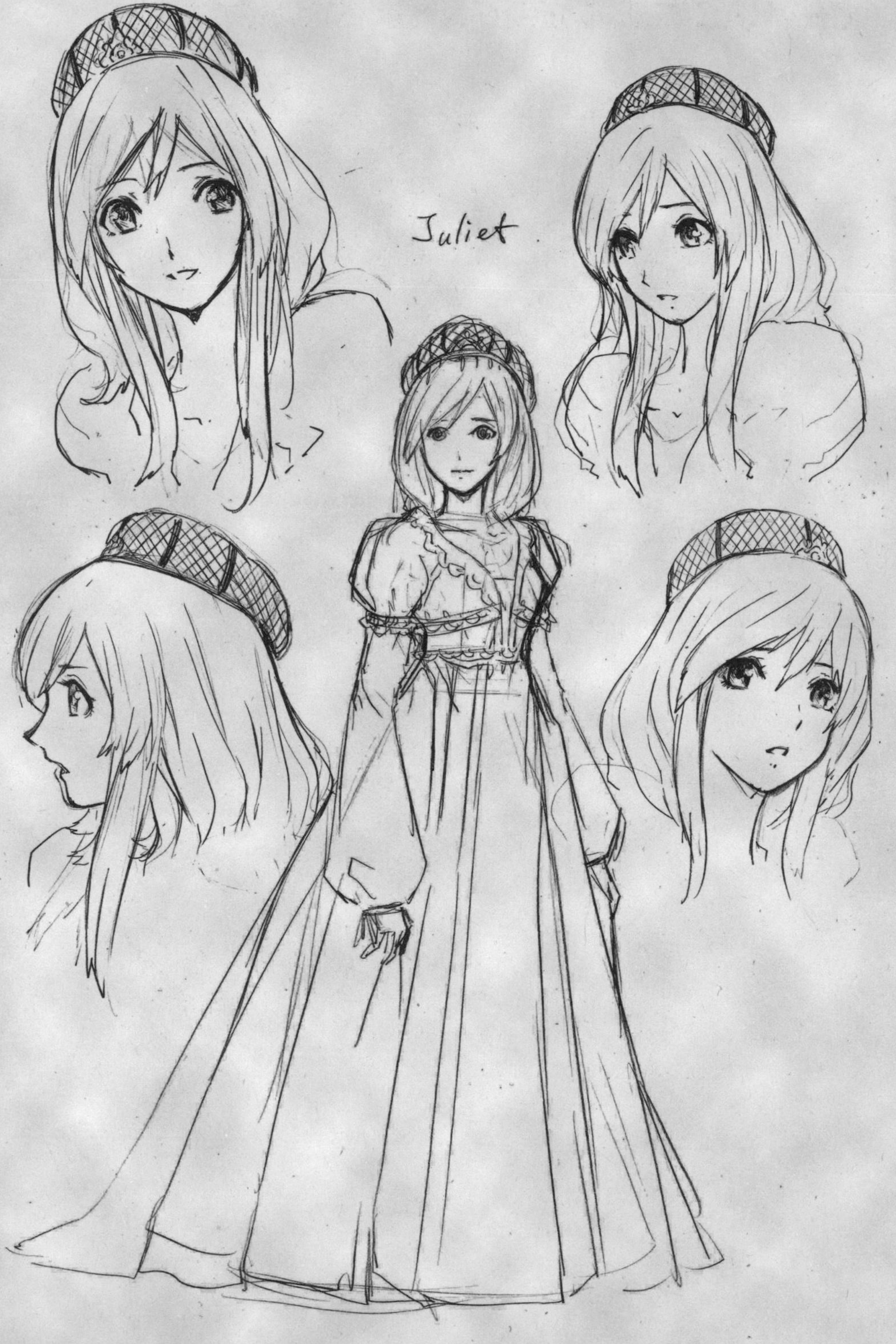
Juliet

CHARACTER DESIGN SKETCHBOOK

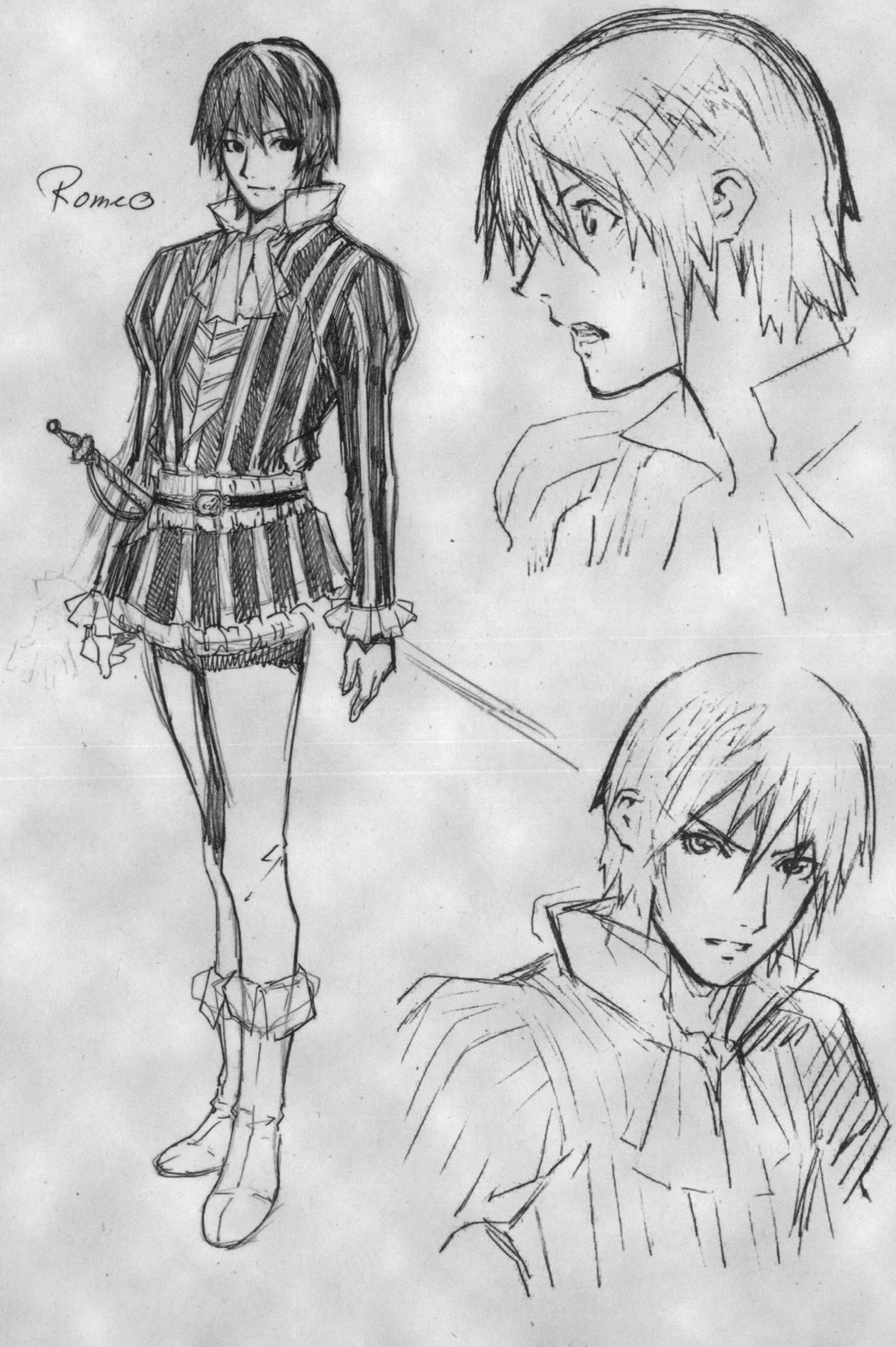
Romeo

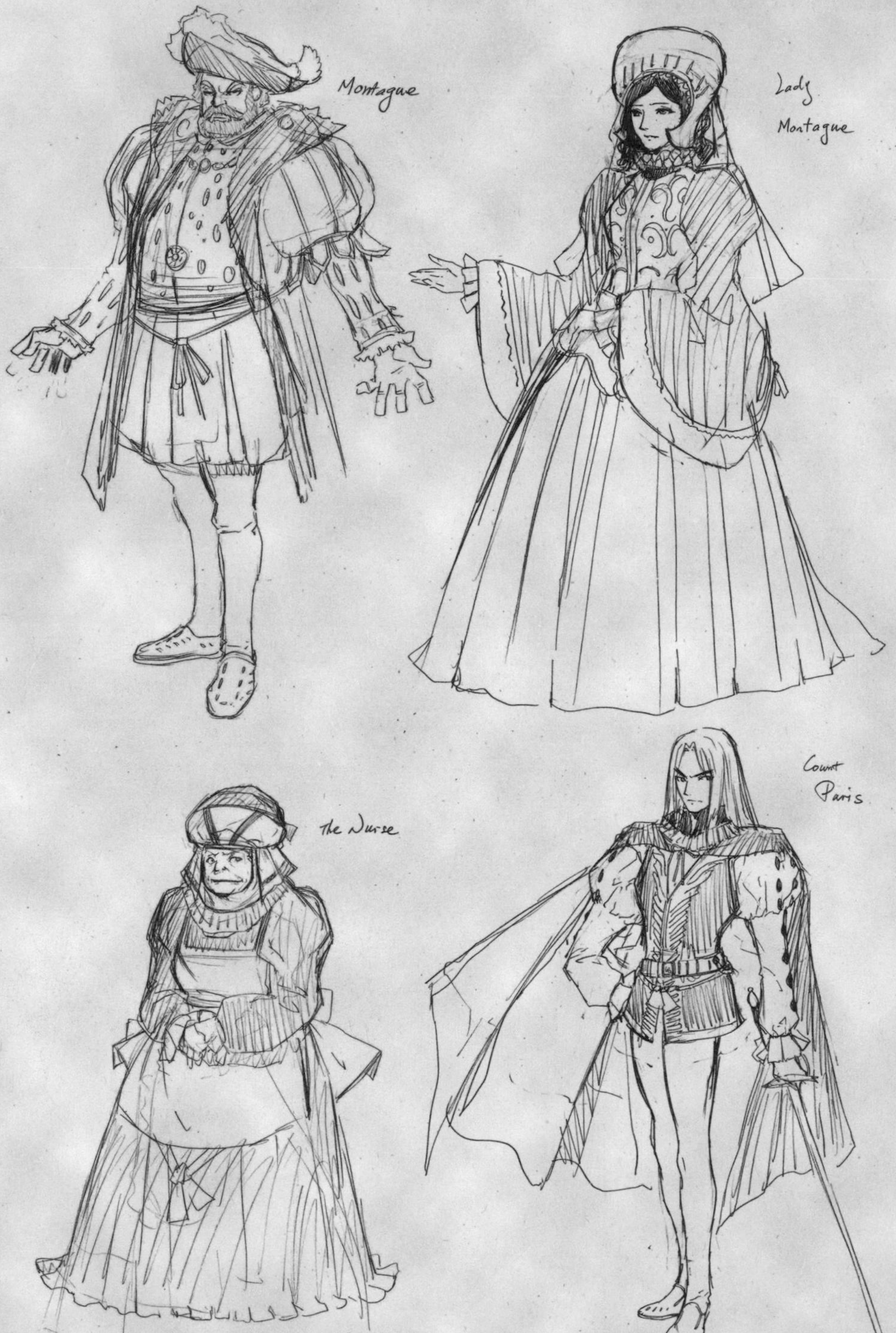
Montague
Lady Montague
The Nurse
Count Paris

CHARACTER DESIGN SKETCHBOOK

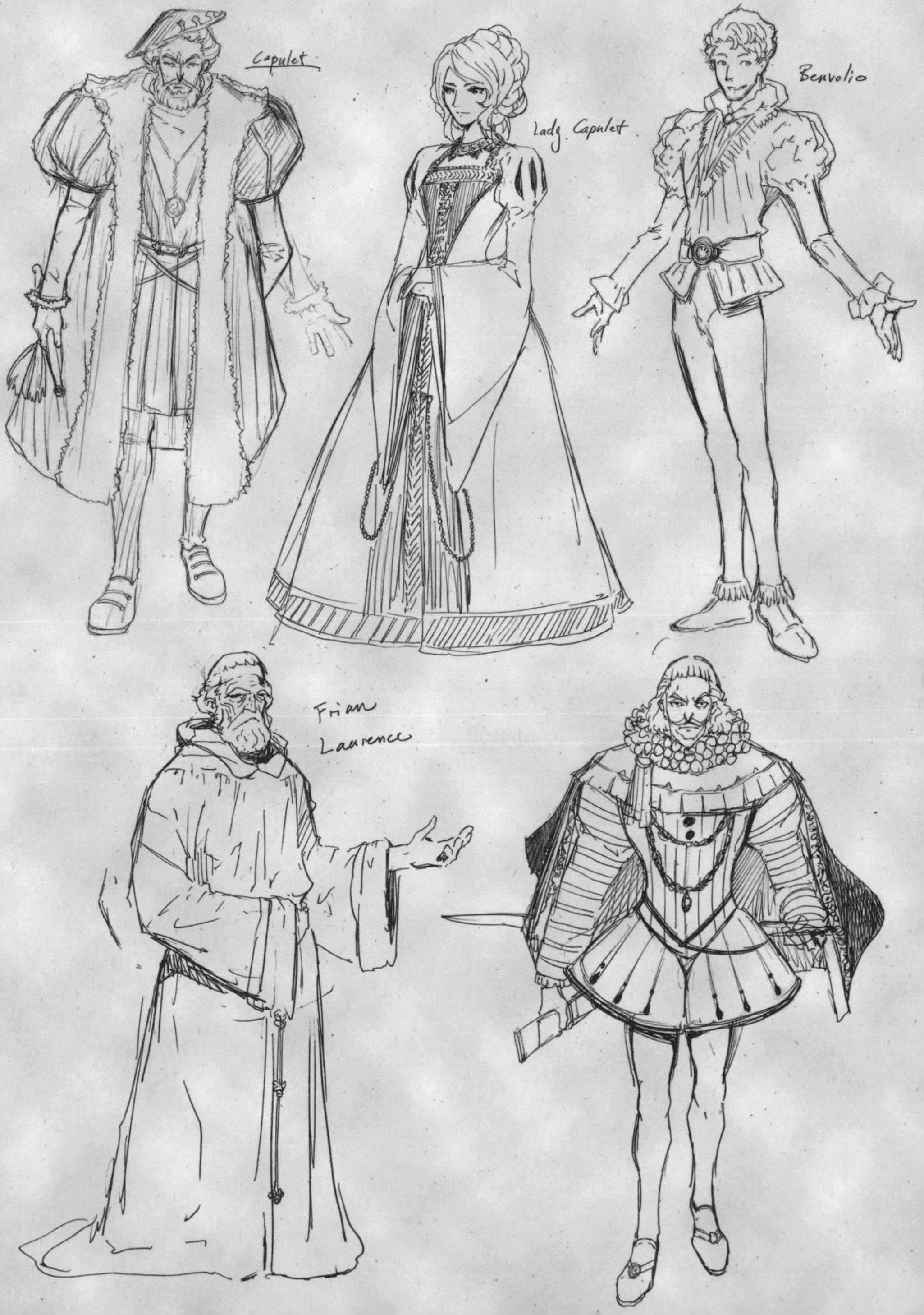
Capulet
Lady Capulet
Benvolio
Friar Laurence

Swordfights play a key role throughout **Romeo and Juliet**. From Sampson, Gregory, Abram, and Benvolio introducing the conflict between the two families at the beginning, to the unfortunate deaths of Mercutio and Tybalt, to the inevitable duel between Romeo and Paris near the end, the characters clash again and again - and all of them wield their own personalized weapons in battle.

Since the props in a play are very important elements, we paid a lot of attention to the characters' weapons when we were designing them. We decided that, since all these men are wealthy or work for wealthy families, they would all have had their swords customized to their liking. Thus, we made sure that everyone's blade was different.

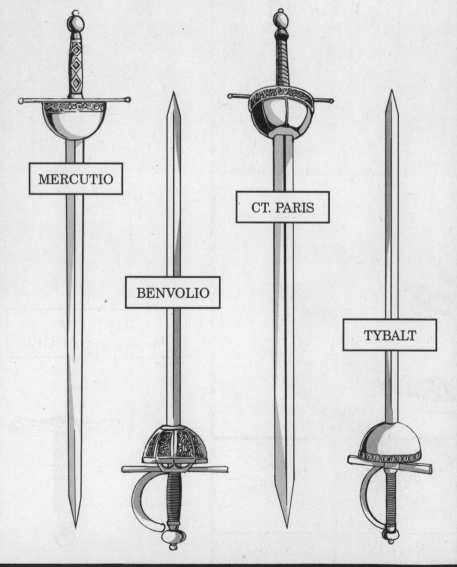

MERCUTIO

CT. PARIS

BENVOLIO

TYBALT

THE SWORDS IN ROMEO AND JULIET

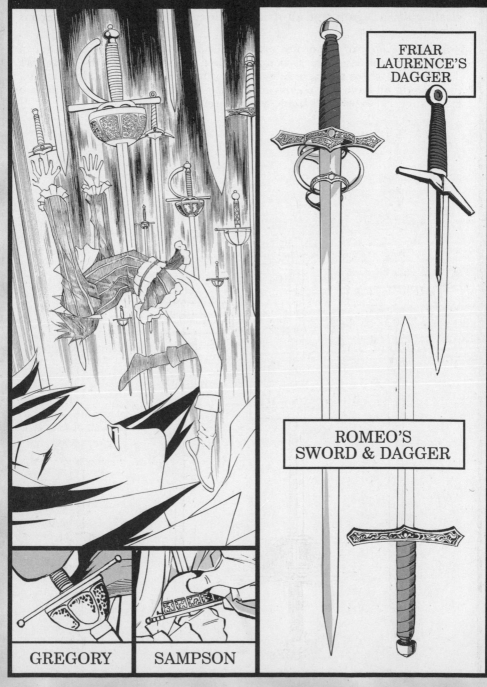

FRIAR LAURENCE'S DAGGER

ROMEO'S SWORD & DAGGER

GREGORY

SAMPSON